FOUNDATIONS OF MUSIC AND MUSICIANSHIP

FOUNDATIONS OF MUSIC AND MUSICIANSHIP

David Damschroder
The University of Minnesota

Schirmer Books
A Division of Macmillan, Inc.
New York
Maxwell Macmillan Canada
Toronto
Maxwell Macmillan International
New York Oxford Singapore Sydney

Schirmer Books
A Division of Macmillan, Inc.
866 Third Avenue
New York, NY 10022

Maxwell Macmillan Canada, Inc.
1200 Eglinton Avenue East, Suite 200
Don Mills, Ontario M3C 3N1

Macmillan, Inc., is part of the Maxwell
Communication Group of Companies

Library of Congress Catalog Card Number: 91-15056

Printed in the United States of America

printing number
1 2 3 4 5 6 7 8 9 10

Library of Congress Cataloging-in-Publication Data

Damschroder, David
Foundations of music and musicianship / David Damschroder.
p. cm.
includes index.
ISBN 0-02-870661-7
1. Music—Theory. I. Title.
MT6.D17F7 1992
781.2—dc20

91-15056
CIP
MN

The paper used in this publication meets the minimum requirements of American National Standard for Information Sciences—Permanence of Paper for Printed Library Materials. ANSI Z39.48-1984.∞™

Contents

Preface

Foundations of Music and Musicianship is a textbook for the beginning student who wants to develop a facility in music and who seeks a thorough yet efficient presentation of its fundamental principles and conventions. The spectrum of topics and activities found within the text parallels the training that first-term music majors receive, but with a pace and emphasis on detail that are geared to the needs of students who have no prior experience in reading music notation or performing. Instructors will find a wealth of resources for shaping a beginners' course that emphasizes not only the basic concepts of pitch and rhythm, but also step-by-step training in keyboard skills, singing, and discriminative listening. Students should benefit from the integration of concepts and interactive experiences that this text affords.

Each chapter contains three instructional segments—Pitch, Rhythm, and Laboratory—followed by homework Exercises in each of these areas and a Mastery Test. The Pitch segments emphasize intervals, chords, and scales, culminating in a clear and detailed account of harmonization using the tonic, subdominant, and dominant chords. The Rhythm segments cover the standard meters, all common note and rest values, and special topics such as triplets, syncopation, and hemiola. The Laboratory segments offer performance opportunities—keyboard, vocal, and rhythmic—as well as a graduated program of ear-training. The abundant Exercises are designed to offer instructors and students a variety of options, from basic drills to thought-provoking challenges. The Mastery Tests give students an opportunity to evaluate the level of their accomplishment and identify areas that may require further study. A Glossary of all terms highlighted in the individual chapters appears at the end of the text.

Supplementing the text are two ninety-minute cassette tapes (the Audio Exercises) for students; an Instructor's Manual that includes solutions to all Pitch, Rhythm, and Audio Exercises and the Mastery Tests; and a computerized Test Bank for generating course quizzes and tests. This text package supplies all necessary course materials for both instructors and students.

The text is suitable for either quarter or semester courses. The first nine or ten chapters might be covered within a quarter, while the remaining chapters contain materials suitable for the additional weeks that a semester offers. Of course, instructors may choose to omit some materials (for example, the later Laboratory or Rhythm segments) in order to concentrate more fully on fewer topics. An instructor who elects to cover all of the text's contents and assign most of the exercises will require about sixty classroom hours during the term, with the average student spending about one hundred twenty hours studying, practicing the Laboratory drills, and working through the Exercises. Because they are often very challenging for beginning students, the various singing, clapping, and listening drills of the Laboratory segments should occupy at least one-third of all class time if they are assigned and contribute to a student's course grade. If the keyboard drills are assigned, each student should be able to spend, on average, about one hour per week at a keyboard.

The topics traditionally found in an introductory music fundamentals text are all present in this volume, but in an arrangement that contrasts that of many other textbooks. For example, the treble and bass clefs are taught at different points, so that students can devote about a month to attaining fluency in each, rather than confronting them both simultaneously. Likewise, the three forms of the minor scale are divided between two non-adjacent chapters, so that the natural minor scale is thoroughly mastered before the special treatment of the sixth and seventh scale degrees is examined.

The first draft of this text was completed in India during 1989. I wish to extend my thanks to the people of Delhi and Pune for their warm hospitality and for the often bewildering, always fascinating non-Western environment that so pleasantly juxtaposed this thoroughly Western undertaking. Back in Minnesota, numerous classes of students and several of my teaching assistants tolerated the shortcomings of the early drafts and helped me discover how best to express what I envisioned. Especially to those students who asked questions whose answers were not to be found in those early drafts, I offer my thanks for such care and thoughtfulness.

FOUNDATIONS OF MUSIC AND MUSICIANSHIP

1

Intervals

Terms and Concepts

pitch	*fifth*	*third*
score notation	*sixth*	*fifth*
staff	*seventh*	*rhythm*
notehead	*octave*	*pulses*
lines	*acoustics*	*beats*
spaces	*fundamental*	*measure*
ledger line	*overtones*	*meter*
note	*interval quality*	*bar line*
interval	*half step*	*quarter note*
interval size	*major*	*stem*
unison	*minor*	*time signature*
second	*perfect*	*double bar*
third	*major triad*	*common time*
fourth	*root*	*middle C*

PITCH

Pitch and Its Notation

Music is the organized arrangement of sounds in time. It can express the most profound and appealing emotions of the human spirit. Most sounds used in music have a distinct ***pitch***, a specific position within the range of sounds from low to high. Pitches are created by vibrations. Pianists and violinists cause strings to vibrate by striking the keys of the piano or drawing the bow across the violin. Singers cause their vocal cords to vibrate by controlling how the breath exits the lungs. Scientists can measure the number of vibrations emitted each second by any pitch. For example, the 88 pitches of the piano emit from 26 vibrations per second (the lowest pitch) to over 4,000 vibrations per second (the highest pitch). The shorter, thinner strings toward the right side of the piano vibrate more quickly than do the longer, thicker strings toward the left side. Absolute frequencies of vibration are of little practical importance, except to the artisans who build and maintain instruments. Musicians instead pay attention to how low or high each pitch sounds *in relation to* the other pitches of a composition.

pitch

Score notation—the visual representation of music—is how composers preserve their ideas and communicate them to performers. Its standard format is a set of five evenly spaced horizontal lines called a ***staff.*** Elliptical ***noteheads*** placed

score notation

staff

notehead

through or between these lines correspond to individual pitches. The higher the pitch, the closer to the top of the staff its notehead appears. The staff in Example 1-1 contains three noteheads. The notehead on the left represents the lowest of these pitches, while the one on the right represents the highest.

Example 1-1

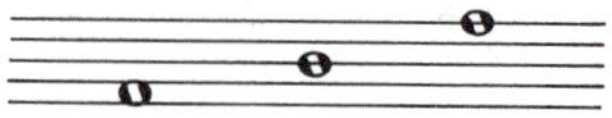

lines
spaces

The positions on the staff are called ***lines*** and ***spaces***. Example 1-1 shows how a notehead may either intersect a line or fill a space. By convention, the five lines and four spaces are numbered in ascending order from the bottom upward. The example shows first-space, third-line, and fifth-line noteheads.

ledger line

Often a melody cannot be confined by the boundaries of the first and fifth lines. In such cases, temporary extensions of the staff called ***ledger lines*** are used. The distance between adjacent ledger lines is the same as that between adjacent lines of the staff. Example 1-2 shows how ledger lines are used to notate several high and several low noteheads. Observe that a notehead that fills a space has a ledger line on its interior side only.

Example 1-2

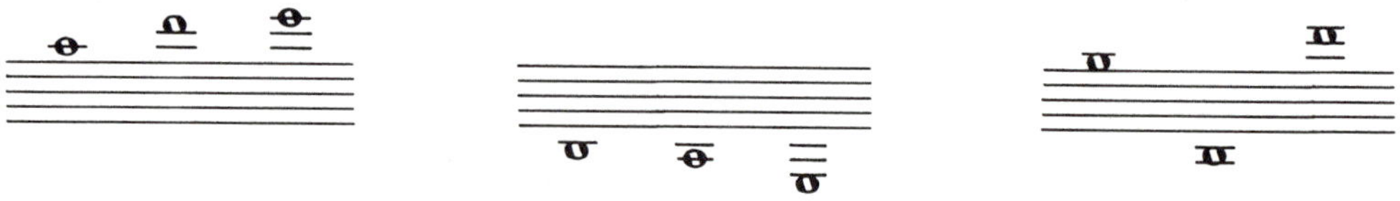

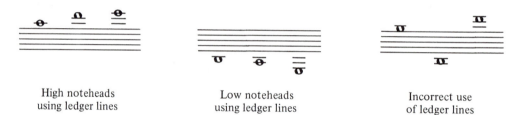

High noteheads using ledger lines — Low noteheads using ledger lines — Incorrect use of ledger lines

Intervals

note
interval

The staff carries a large amount of information in addition to noteheads (or ***notes***), as we shall see. We can begin to explore how two pitches relate by comparing the positions of the noteheads used to represent them on the staff.

An ***interval*** is a relationship between any two pitches. If the pitches that form an interval sound successively, the two noteheads that represent them are separated horizontally and are read from left to right. If the pitches sound simultaneously, the two noteheads are placed either in vertical alignment on the staff or, if the notes share the same or adjacent positions on the staff, as close together as is possible. Several examples of intervals are shown in Example 1-3.

Example 1-3

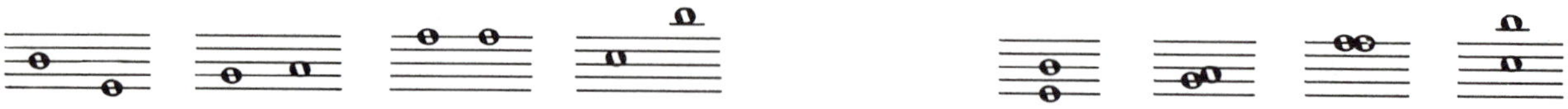

SUCCESSIVE — SIMULTANEOUS

interval size

Interval size is a measure of how close or far apart an interval's two pitches are from one another. To find the interval size, count the number of lines and spaces enclosed by the two noteheads that represent the interval on the staff. It is important to include the line or space on which each of the two noteheads is positioned, as well as all the lines and spaces in between, as shown in Example 1-4.

Example 1-4

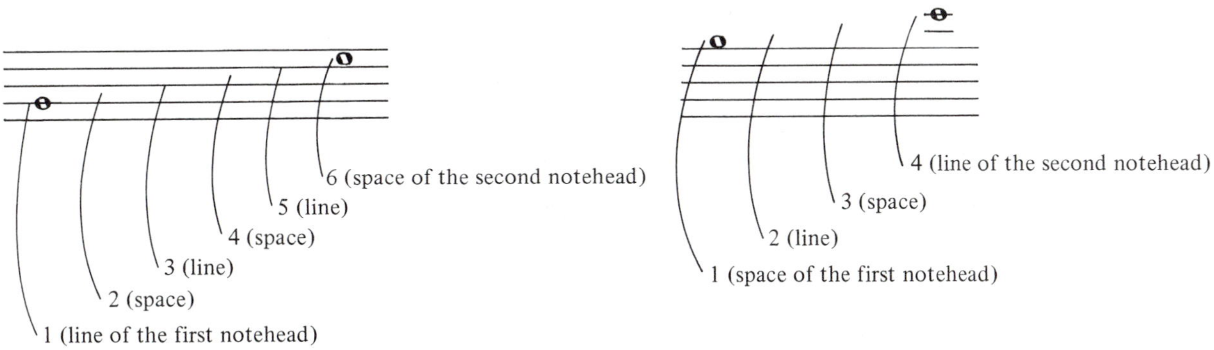

unison

The interval of size one, called the ***unison,*** is notated using two noteheads on the same line or space. A unison occurs when a pitch is struck twice in succession or when two voices or instruments sound the same pitch simultaneously. When a simultaneous unison is notated on a single staff, the two noteheads touch one another, as in Example 1-5.

Example 1-5

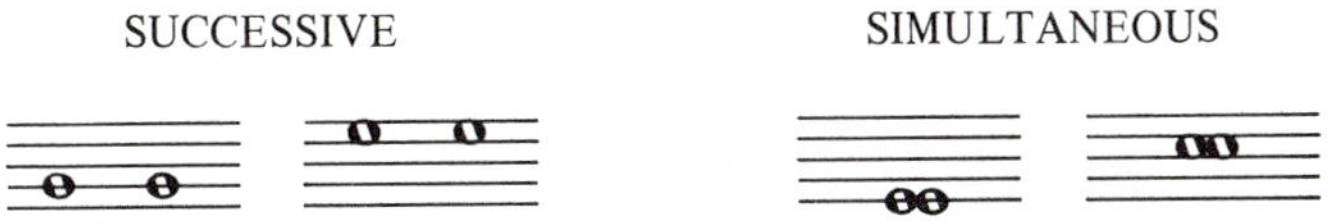

second

The interval of size two, the ***second,*** is notated using noteheads on an adjacent line and space. When a simultaneous second is notated on a single staff, the two noteheads touch one another and the lower notehead appears to the left of the upper notehead, as in Example 1-6.

Example 1-6

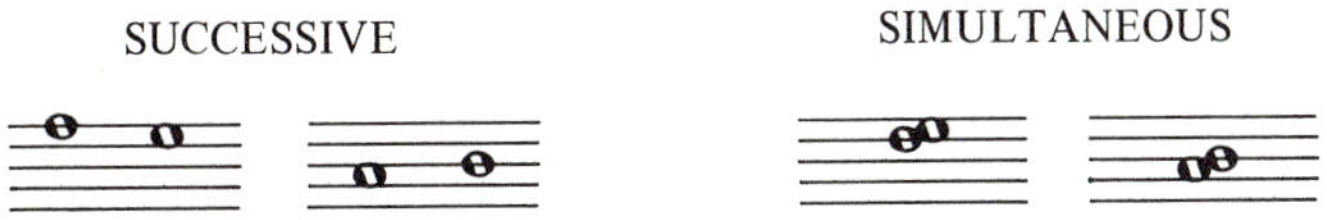

third

The interval of size three, the ***third,*** is notated using noteheads on adjacent lines or adjacent spaces (Ex. 1-7).

Example 1-7

fourth
fifth
sixth
seventh
octave

Examples of the ***fourth, fifth, sixth, seventh,*** and ***octave,*** the term used for an interval of size eight, are shown in Example 1-8.

Example 1-8

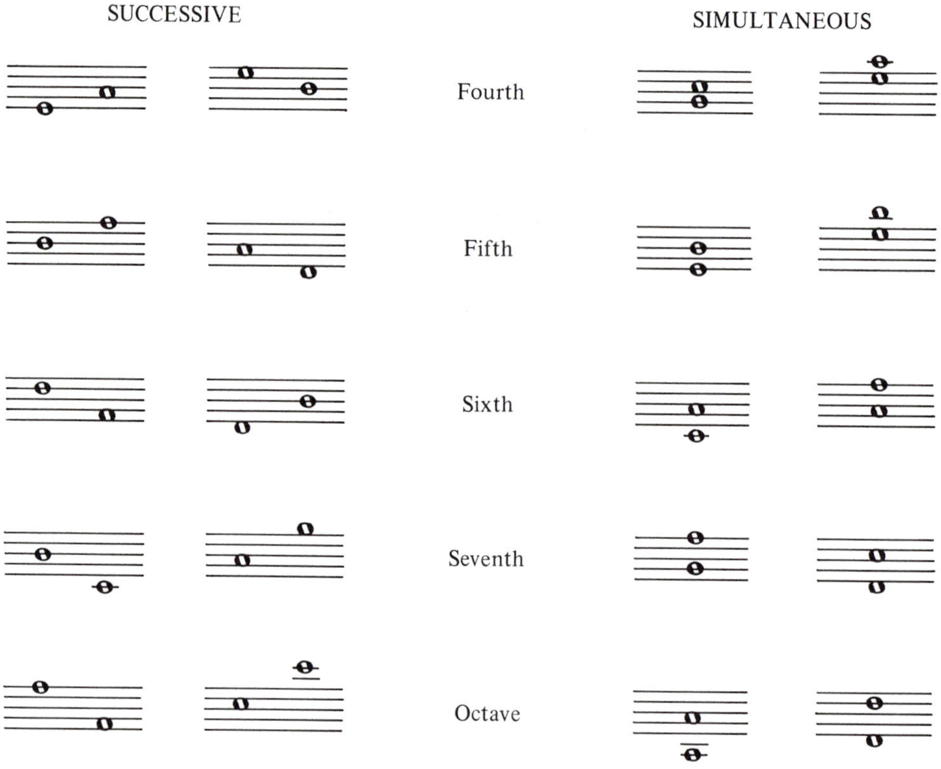

The sounds of the two pitches that form an octave blend together more fully than do those of any other interval besides the unison, even though they are farther apart. This special property of the octave affects many aspects of music, including the way pitches are named and the rules composers have followed when composing. Whenever men and women sing a melody together, they take advantage of this property as well: men will generally sing a melody an octave lower than women will.

As we have seen, the line or space on which each notehead is placed must be counted when computing the interval size. Observe that the combination of two intervals yields an interval whose size is smaller than the sum of the interval sizes of its components. For example, if we sing an ascending third and, from that point, another ascending third, the interval between the first and last pitches is a fifth, not a sixth (Ex. 1-9).

Example 1-9

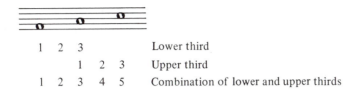

1	2	3			Lower third
		1	2	3	Upper third
1	2	3	4	5	Combination of lower and upper thirds

Acoustical Foundations of Music

Why composers make use of the pitches that are currently available on the piano and other instruments, rather than some other collection of pitches, is a question whose answer resides in the domain of ***acoustics,*** the science of the physical properties of sound. Though the conventions of composers and performers preceded acoustical explanation by centuries, instrument builders and tuners of the past had a good understanding of how pitches interact. What scientists can now tell us by analyzing sounds in a laboratory, earlier musicians understood through experimentation.

For example, a stretched string, such as a violin or guitar string, emits a sound with a distinct pitch when plucked. If we press firmly at its midpoint, so that only one-half the string length vibrates when plucked, the pitch that results is an octave higher than the initial pitch. That this simple ratio of string lengths—the entire string versus one-half the string—produces such a pleasing and stable interval was appreciated by the ancient Greeks. Continuing with one-third, one-fourth, one-fifth, and one-sixth of the string, pitches that occupy the positions shown on the keyboard diagram in Example 1-10 are produced. (In this experiment, the string is tuned so that the pitch named *C* sounds when the entire string vibrates.)

Example 1-10

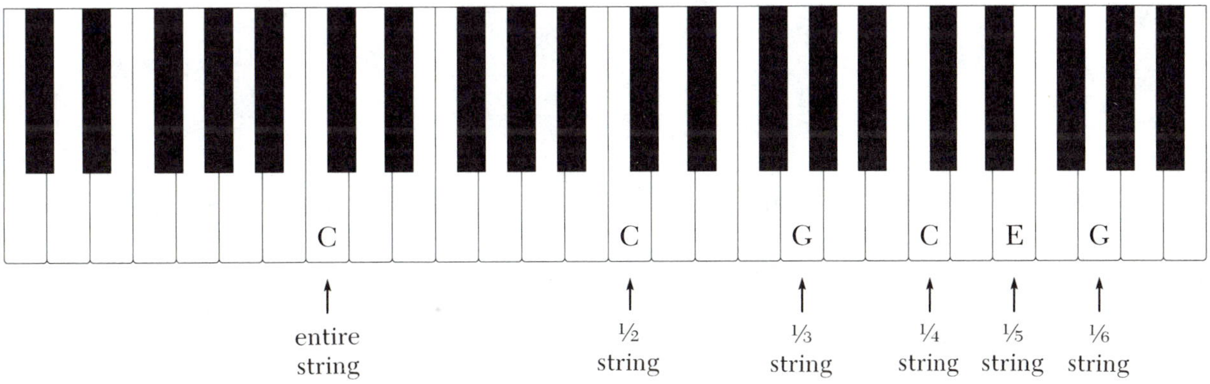

The letters *C, E,* and *G* are used to name the pitches produced by these segments of the string. For centuries justification for using these pitches was based upon the simplicity of the string divisions that form them. Yet no one could explain *why* these subdivisions of the string produce pitches that sound so agreeable when played together. (Play these six pitches at a piano to confirm that this is true!) Around 1700 scientists made a startling discovery: every pitch is actually a combination of many component sounds—a ***fundamental*** pitch and numerous ***overtones,*** higher pitches that support and enrich the fundamental. If a fundamental pitch vibrates 100 times per second, its overtones will vibrate 200, 300, 400, 500, 600, etc., times per second. The first five overtones are the same pitches that are produced by dividing a string into one-half, one-third, one-fourth, one-fifth, and one-sixth. Early musicians chanced upon the series of overtone pitches because string length and frequency of vibration are inversely proportional: one-half of the string vibrates twice as fast as the entire string, one-third of the string vibrates three times as fast as the entire string, and so on.

fundamental

overtone

The keyboard diagram in Example 1-11 illustrates keys that correspond to overtones of the pitch C. The interval size between any pair of these pitches reflects the distance between their positions on the keyboard. As with counting lines and spaces on a staff, count the two keys that activate the interval's pitches plus all of the *white* keys in between when computing the interval size. (The procedure for measuring interval size will be refined in Chapter 2. The method presented here is valid when the pitches of an interval are spelled using simple letter names such as *C, E,* and *G.*) Some of these intervals are shown in Example 1-11.

Example 1-11

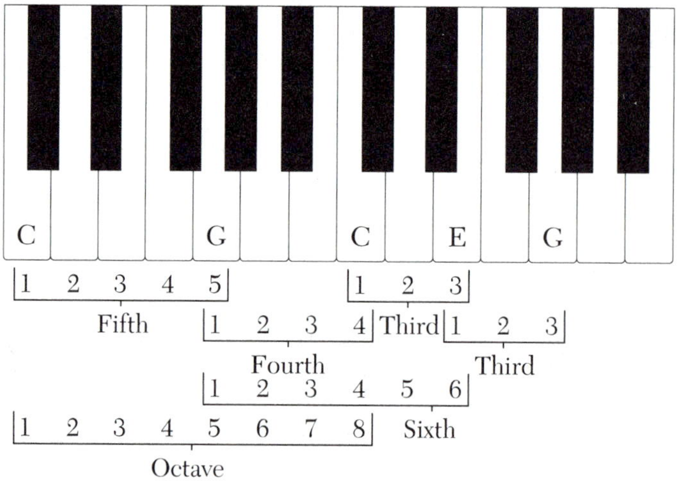

In the keyboard diagrams shown in Examples 1-10 and 1-11, all pitches an octave apart share the same letter name. Observe that each C shares the same relationship with the pattern of white and black keys in its vicinity, as does each G. Following this principle, a few more of the keys on the piano can be named, as shown in Example 1-12. C and E always appear to the left and right of clusters of *two* black keys, while G always appears between the left and middle keys of clusters of *three* black keys.

Example 1-12

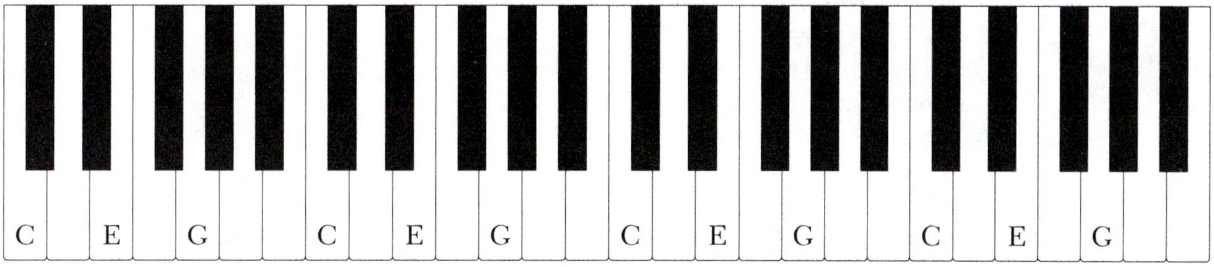

The Major Triad

The precise measure of the distance between two pitches depends upon more than interval size alone. ***Interval quality,*** a qualifier such as "major," "minor," or "perfect," distinguishes among various intervals that, though of the same interval size, are not identical. For example, the intervals C–E and E–G are of the same size: they are both thirds. By counting how many white *and black* keys separate C from E and E from G, we observe that the interval C–E is larger than the interval E–G. Though they are both thirds, they are not of the same quality.

interval quality

To measure an interval with such precision, we use as our unit the ***half step,*** the distance between adjacent keys, considering both white and black keys. Every half step on the modern keyboard is equivalent, regardless of whether it appears between a white and a black key or between two adjacent white keys. By convention, we label a third like C–E a ***major*** third and a third like E–G a ***minor*** third. The major third contains four half steps, while the minor third contains three half steps. In Example 1-13, the numbers below the keys show that the interval size depends upon how many white keys are enclosed by the two pitches, while the arcs above the keys show that the interval quality depends upon how many half steps separate the two pitches.

half step

major

minor

Example 1-13

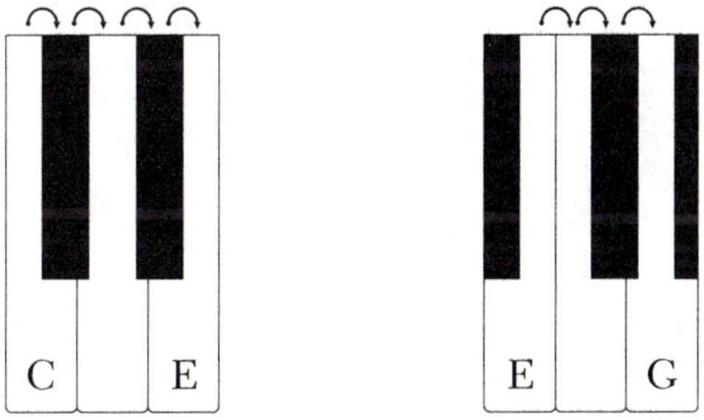

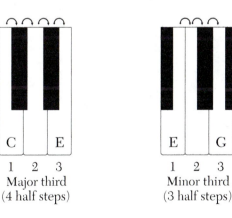

1 2 3
Major third
(4 half steps)

1 2 3
Minor third
(3 half steps)

perfect

The qualities "major" and "minor" apply to seconds, sixths, and sevenths as well as to thirds, as we shall see in Chapter 3. The quality ***perfect*** is reserved for those intervals created by the fundamental and its first three overtones: the unison (the fundamental with itself), the octave (the fundamental and the first overtone), the fifth (the first and second overtones), and the fourth (the second and third overtones) (Ex. 1-14).

Example 1-14

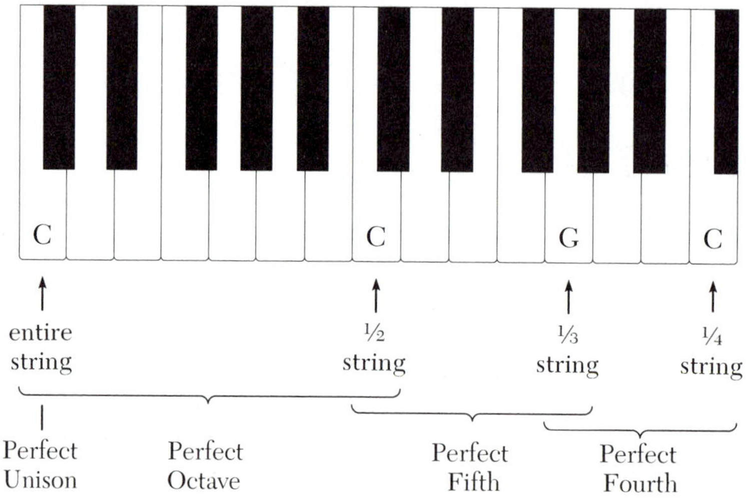

The perfect fifth is as large as a major third and a minor third combined. It contains seven half steps (Ex. 1-15).

Example 1-15

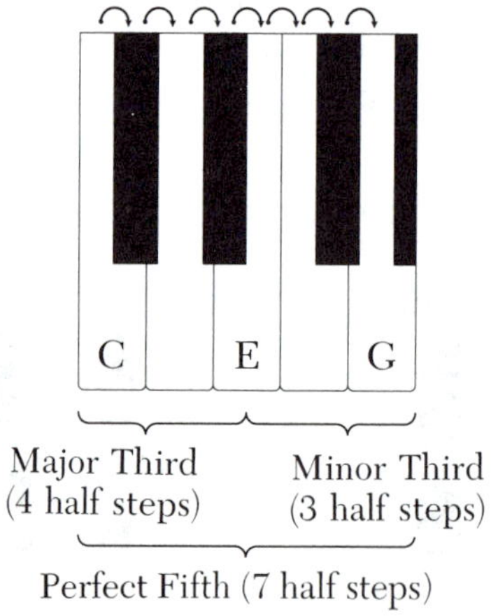

major triad
root
third
fifth

The pitches C, E, and G can be combined to form a ***major triad.*** All major triads contain three pitches. The lowest and middle pitches form a major third, the lowest and highest pitches form a perfect fifth, and the middle and highest pitches form a minor third. The lowest pitch is called the ***root*** of the triad, while the middle and highest pitches are called the ***third*** and the ***fifth,*** respectively. Example 1-16 shows how major triads can be created using both white and black keys on the keyboard. In each case, four half steps separate the root and third of the triad, while three half steps separate the third and fifth of the triad.

Example 1-16

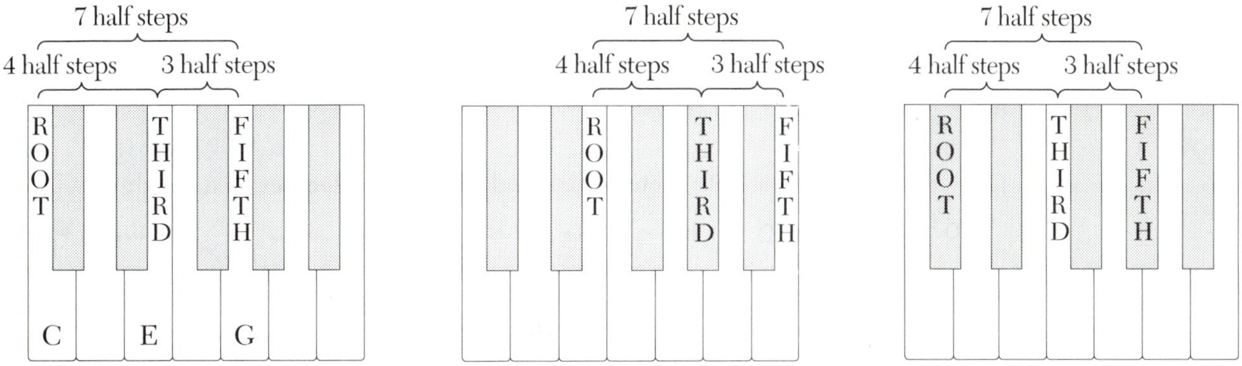

Pitch exercises for Chapter 1 are on pages 17–25.

RHYTHM

Rhythm

rhythm

To study ***rhythm*** is to explore how musical sounds unfold over time. The symbols on the staff reveal both what pitches to perform and when to perform them. Without notation for the relative durations of musical sounds, composers could not convey their intentions. Performance by an ensemble of musicians would be next to impossible. Though rhythmic notation need not be obeyed slavishly—a conductor may "bend" the rhythm for interpretive reasons, for example—the arithmetical integrity of the system ensures that each performer understands the symbols in the same way.

Meter

pulses
beats

Rhythmic notation depends upon a continuous flow of ***pulses*** or ***beats.*** Such pulses follow one another at a uniform rate, resembling the ticking of a clock, the dripping of water, or the beating of the heart. Heartbeats recur from about forty times per minute to about two hundred times per minute. So also do the beats of music. The bass drum is used in marching bands to reinforce the beats, so that everyone marches at the same pace and performs the music at the same speed.

measure

Music's pulses are generally segmented into ***measures,*** groupings of two, three, or four beats. Some of the beats within a measure are emphasized ("strong beats"), while others are not ("weak beats"). In the pattern of four beats per measure, for example, the first beat is the strongest and the third is the next strongest, while the second and fourth beats are weak. By segmenting uniform pulses into measures and by organizing the pulses within each measure into strong and weak beats, we create ***meter*** (Ex. 1-17).

meter

Example 1-17

Uniform pulses without meter

o o o o   o o o o   o o o o   o o o o   o o o o

Uniform pulses with meter (O, o, **and** ∘ **represent degrees of strength**)

| O ∘ o ∘ | O ∘ o ∘ | O ∘ o ∘ | O ∘ o ∘ | O ∘ o ∘ |

To get a sense of what meter is, that is to say, how beats are grouped into measures and how some beats are perceived as strong or accented while others are perceived as weak or unaccented, recite the two lines in Example 1-18 at the rate of one number per second. Use greater emphasis the bolder the number appears.

Example 1-18

Without meter: 1 1 1 1 1 1 1 1 1 1 1 1 1 1 1 1 1 1 1 1

With meter: 1 2 3 4 1 2 3 4 1 2 3 4 1 2 3 4 1 2 3 4

Four Quarter Notes per Measure: The $\frac{4}{4}$ Meter

bar line

quarter note

Vertical lines called ***bar lines*** extend from the first to the fifth line of the staff to show the boundaries between measures, as in Example 1-19. The symbol used to represent one beat is called a ***quarter note.*** As this name suggests, the rhythmic values of music obey the rules of arithmetic.

stem

The quarter note is formed by filling in the interior of a notehead and adding a vertical line called a ***stem*** to one side—up from the right side if the notehead is placed below the center line on the staff; down from the left side if the notehead is placed on or above the center line on the staff. The melody shown in Example 1-19 contains sixteen quarter notes, which fill four measures.

Example 1-19

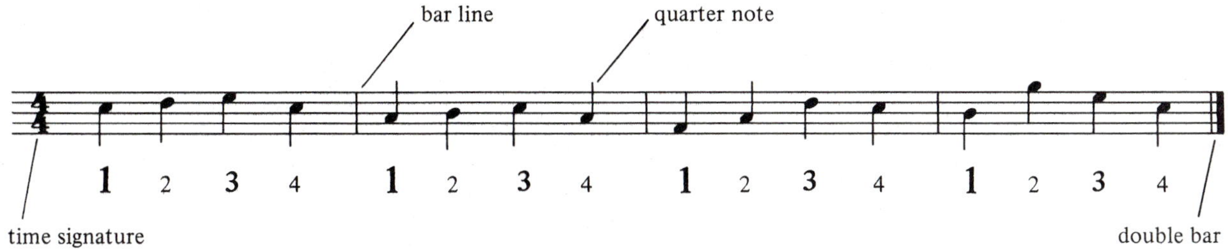

The symbol $\frac{4}{4}$, which appears at the left edge of the staff (Ex. 1-19), is a ***time signature.*** It designates which of the many possible meters applies to the music notated on that staff. The term "meter signature" would be more accurate, but musicians typically say "time signature" instead. The lower 4 of the time signature indicates that the quarter note serves as the standard unit for the notation. The upper 4 indicates that four such units fill a measure. Observe that the time signature appears *instead of* a bar line at the beginning of a melody, and that a ***double bar*** (two vertical lines, the second of which is thicker than the first) appears instead of a single bar line at the end of a melody.

time signature

double bar

The $\frac{4}{4}$ meter occurs so frequently that it is often called ***common time.*** Sometimes the symbol C substitutes for the time signature $\frac{4}{4}$, as in Example 1-20.

common time

Example 1-20

Rhythm exercises for Chapter 1 are on page 26.

LABORATORY

middle C

L1-1. Sit down at a keyboard and observe how the keys are arranged. The pattern of white and black keys repeats itself several times from one end of the keyboard to the other. Every eighth white key appears in the same relationship with the other white keys and the black keys. If you are facing the center of the keyboard, you should find the key labeled "C" in the diagram below in vertical alignment with your left eye. This pitch is called ***middle C.*** By striking various keys individually, confirm that those to the right of middle C correspond to higher pitches, while those to the left of middle C correspond to lower pitches.

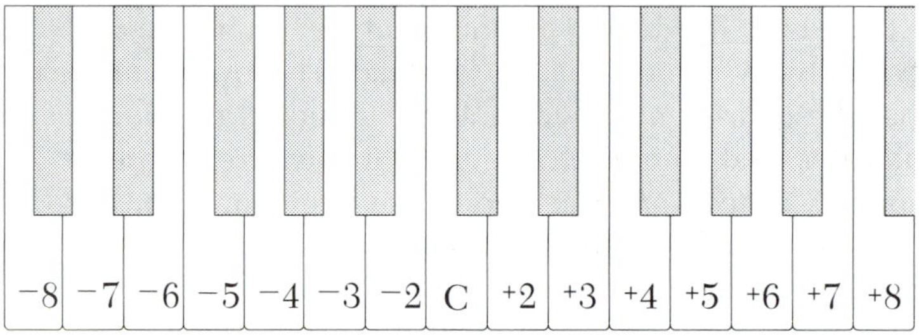

Ascending and Descending Intervals from Middle C

a. Form the ascending intervals of a second through an octave from middle C. Remember to *count only the white keys*. The numbers on the diagram above will help you locate the keys that correspond to pitches used for these intervals. An ascending third is formed by the key labeled "C" and the white key to the right of "C" labeled "+3," for example. The unison, which neither ascends nor descends, is formed by striking the C key twice in succession.

b. Now form the descending intervals of a second through an octave from middle C. The numbers to the left of C on the diagram will help you.

c. Choose any pitch other than middle C on the keyboard and form ascending and descending intervals with it, counting the appropriate number of keys. For example, the key labeled "+7" to the right of middle C forms an ascending third with the key labeled "+5," while the key labeled "+2" forms a descending fourth with the key labeled "+5."

d. Melodies are formed from successions of intervals. The melodies below will come to life if you perform the requested successions of ascending and descending intervals. Each melody begins with middle C. Ascending intervals are indicated with a plus sign (+) preceding the number for the interval size, while descending intervals are indicated with a minus sign (−) preceding the number. In these melodies, use only the white keys. Each new interval should be counted *from the key just sounded* (not from middle C). Because the unison neither ascends nor descends, the symbol "=1" will appear when a pitch is to be repeated.

Attempt to strike successive keys at the rate of about one key per second. When you see the word "HOLD," hang on to the preceding key for an extra second. Strike each key gently with the index finger of your right hand unless you have had experience playing the piano. Hold the key down until it is time to strike the next key.

1. Middle C +2 +2 −3 =1 +2 +2 −3 +3 +2 +2 HOLD −3 +2 +2 HOLD

2. Middle C HOLD +3 +3 +2 −4 +4 HOLD +3 HOLD +2 −5 +4 HOLD

3. Middle C =1 +5 =1 +2 =1 −2 HOLD −2 =1 −2 =1 −2 =1 −2 HOLD

4. Middle C =1 +2 +2 −3 +3 −2 −5 +4 =1 +2 +2 −3 HOLD −2 −3 +4 =1 +2 +2 +2 −2 −2 −2 −2 −3 +2 +2 +2 HOLD =1 HOLD

L1-2. In the preceding exercise, you formed intervals of specific sizes using only the white keys. In this exercise both size and quality must be considered in forming intervals. Both white and black keys will be used. The goal is to form a major triad for any selected root. To do this, find the keys that correspond to pitches a major third and a perfect fifth above the root.

Since the major third contains four half steps and the perfect fifth contains seven half steps, the appropriate keys are found by counting four adjacent keys to the right from the selected root, and then three more adjacent keys to the right. The root and the two derived pitches will form a major triad. Study the following examples and then form major triads using various white and black keys near the middle of the keyboard as roots.

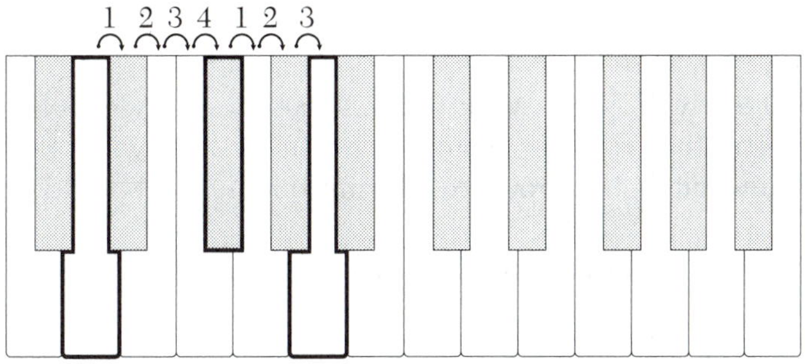

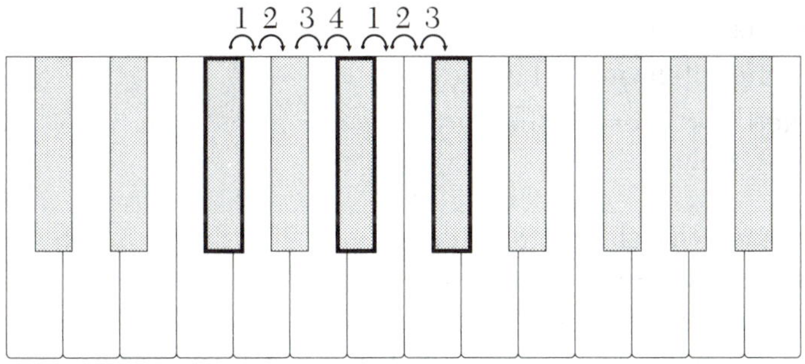

L1-3. At the keyboard, strike middle C and attempt to sing it. For most men, this will be one of the highest pitches you can sing—higher than your speaking voice. For most women, this will be one of the lowest pitches you can sing—lower than your speaking voice. Now explore your own vocal range. Go to both the right and the left of middle C on the keyboard, striking each white key in turn and attempting to sing it. Put an *X* inside the key in the diagram below if you can sing the pitch that it represents.

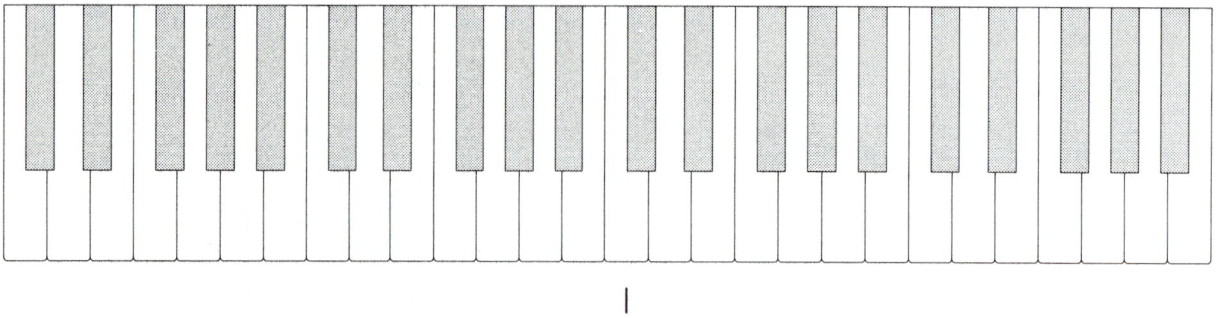

Middle C

If there are eight or more *X*'s on your chart, you can sing the interval of an octave. Put a circle around each *X* near the left side of your chart for which there is an *X* an octave higher. Put a square around each *X* near the right side of your chart for which there is an *X* an octave lower.

a. Practice the following exercise over a period of days or weeks until you have mastered it perfectly.

- Strike one of the circle-*X* keys near the left side of your chart.
- Sing that pitch.
- Sing the pitch one octave higher.
- Strike the corresponding key to confirm that you have sung the correct pitch.

At some point early in your work on this exercise, have a classmate or your instructor confirm that you are "matching pitches"—that when you think you are singing the same pitch that you are playing on the keyboard, you actually are singing it.

b. Once you are doing well in singing ascending octaves, practice the following exercise.

- Strike one of the square-*X* keys near the right side of your chart.
- Sing that pitch.
- Sing the pitch one octave lower.
- Strike the corresponding key to confirm that you have sung the correct pitch.

L1-4. Divide the class into three groups. The first group begins by clapping at the rate of one clap per second. Once this pulse is established, the second group begins to clap along once every two seconds. Finally, the third group joins in, reinforcing every fourth clap of the first group and every second clap of the second group. The following chart shows the pattern of claps that should result. Be careful not to speed up as the exercise progresses.

Group 1:	x	x	x	x	x	x	x	x
Group 2:	x		x		x		x	
Group 3:	x				x			

L1-5. Find a clock or watch that displays seconds. Clap the following patterns, counting the syllables for the beats ("1 2 3 4 1 2 3 4 . . .") out loud at the same rate as your claps.

a. One clap and syllable per second
b. One clap and syllable every two seconds
c. Two claps and syllables per second

L1-6. This exercise requires that a student or the instructor serve as the performer at a keyboard.

a. The performer places three fingers on any three keys of the keyboard and strikes each key once, in any order. Indicate whether the highest pitch was struck first, second, or third. Alternatively, indicate whether the lowest pitch was struck first, second, or third. Do likewise with the middle pitch.

b. Again, the performer strikes three pitches. Indicate the comparative position of each of the three pitches. The following arrangements are possible.

High, Middle, Low
High, Low, Middle
Middle, High, Low
Middle, Low, High
Low, High, Middle
Low, Middle, High

c. The performer plays two pitches in either ascending or descending order, and then plays them together. Indicate whether the interval performed is or is not an octave.

Audio exercises for Chapter 1 are on pages 26–27.

Name: ______________________
Instructor: ______________________
Date: ______________________

EXERCISES

Pitch Exercises

P1-1. For each interval shown below, put a circle around the staff if the score notation indicates that the two notes are to be performed successively. Put a square around the staff if the notation indicates that the two notes are to be performed simultaneously. Below the staff, indicate the size of the interval.

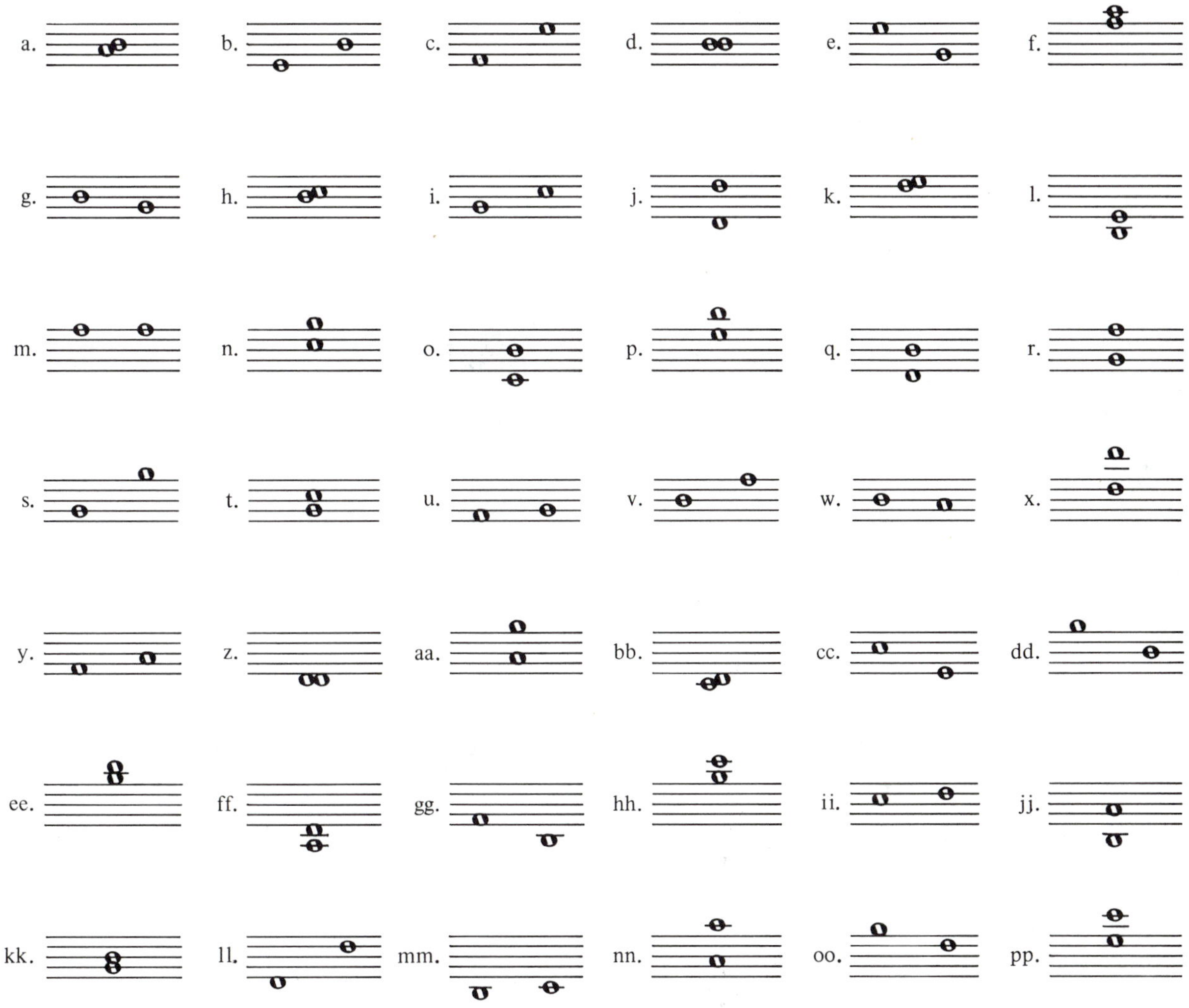

P1-2. On the right half of each staff, supply the notehead that forms the requested intervalic relationship with the given notehead. You may wish to confirm your answers by numbering the lines and spaces enclosed by the two noteheads.

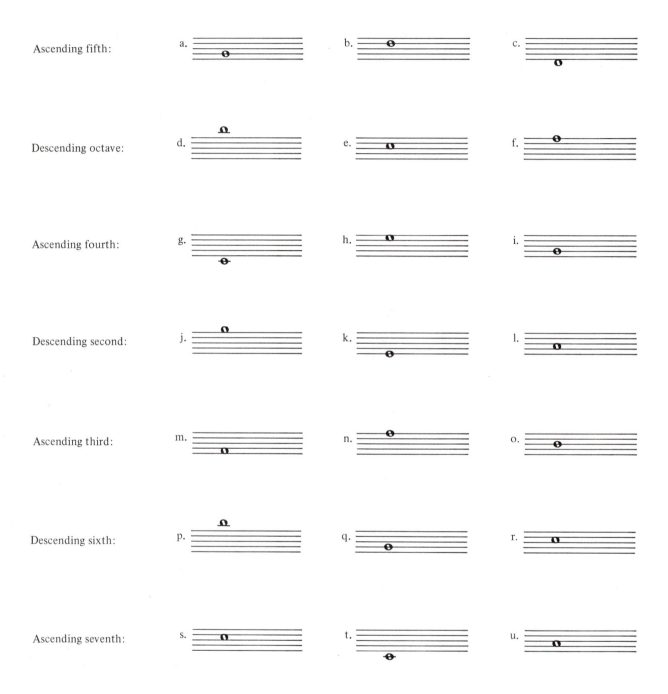

Ascending fifth:

a. 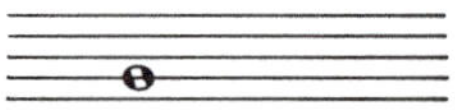

b. 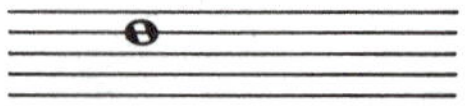

c. 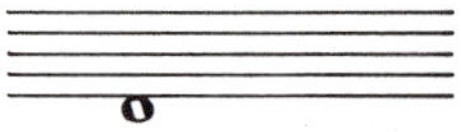

Descending octave:

d. 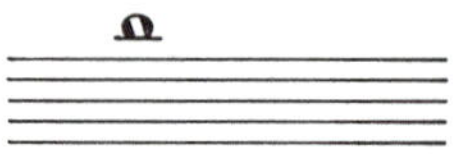

e. 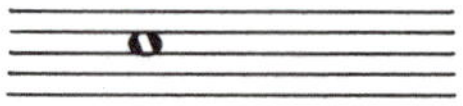

f. 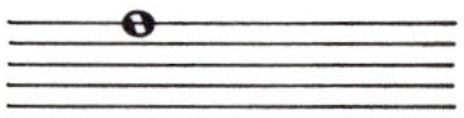

Ascending fourth:

g. 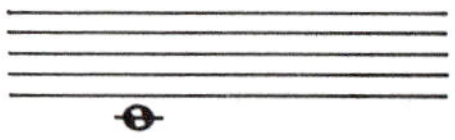

h. 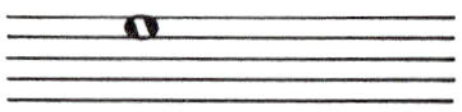

i. 

Descending second:

j. 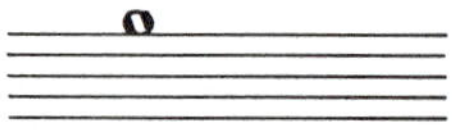

k. 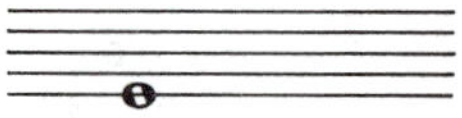

l. 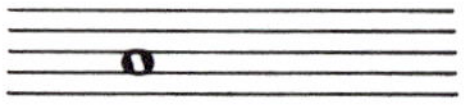

Ascending third:

m. 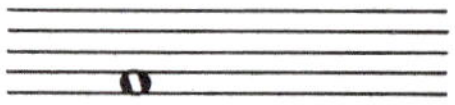

n. 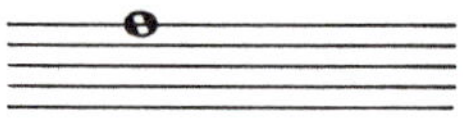

o. 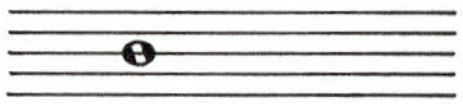

Descending sixth:

p. 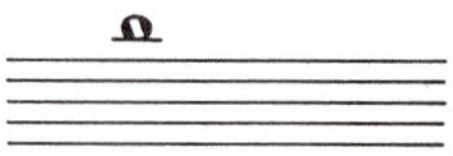

q. 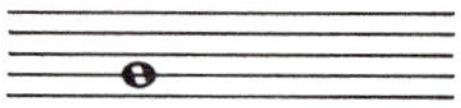

r. 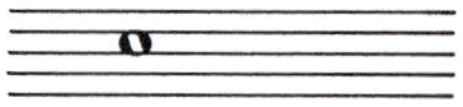

Ascending seventh:

s. 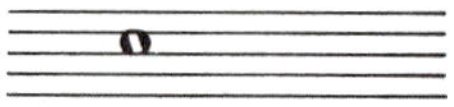

t. 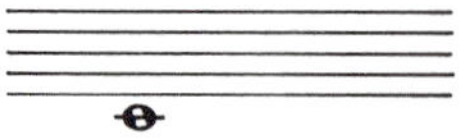

u. 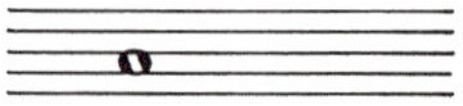

Name: ______________________
Instructor: ___________________
Date: _______________________

P1-3. In the Work Area provided, select any convenient notehead and form the two intervals requested. Then measure the interval between the first and third noteheads.

SAMPLE: An ascending third followed by an ascending sixth
SOLUTION: Ascending octave

a. A descending second followed by a descending second
Solution:

b. An ascending fourth followed by an ascending fifth
Solution:

c. A descending fifth followed by a descending second
Solution:

d. A descending seventh followed by a descending second
Solution:

e. An ascending third followed by a descending second
Solution:

f. A descending fourth followed by an ascending fifth
Solution:

g. An ascending second followed by a descending fifth
Solution:

h. A descending octave followed by an ascending fourth
Solution:

Work Area:

P1-4. For every key outlined in bold, mark with an *X* the key that would sound the pitch a major third higher. Mark with a check the key that would sound the pitch a major third lower.

a.
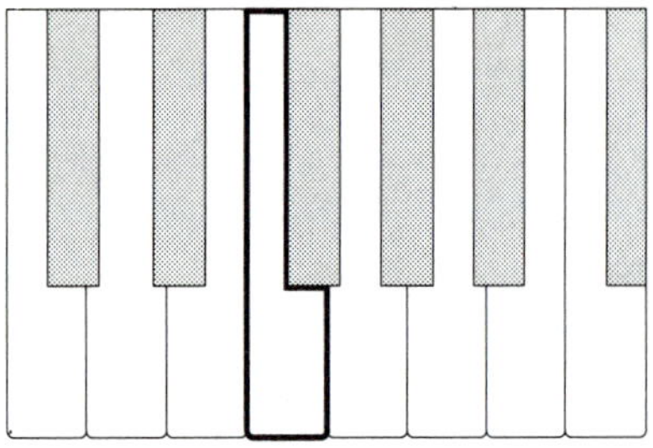
b.
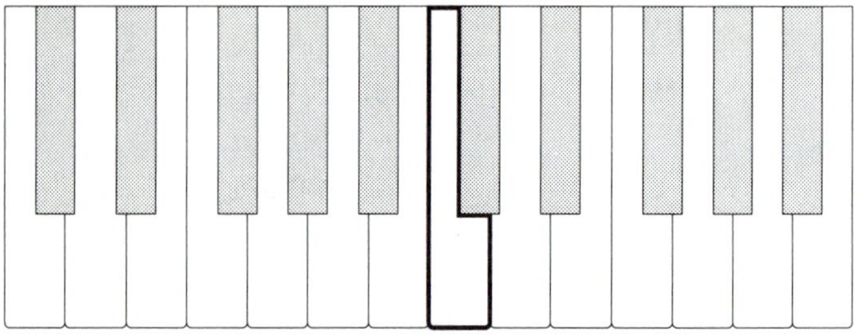
c.
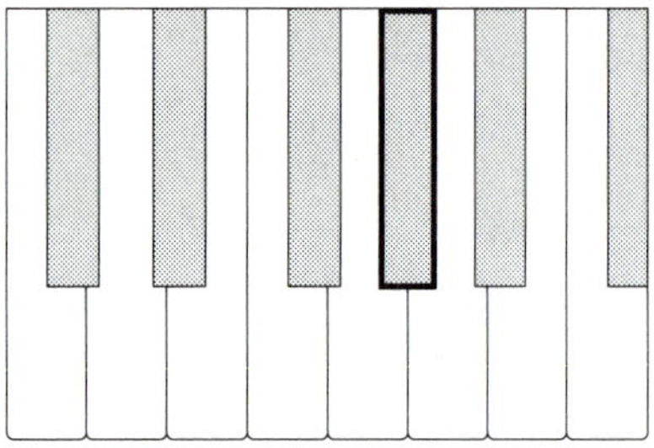
d.
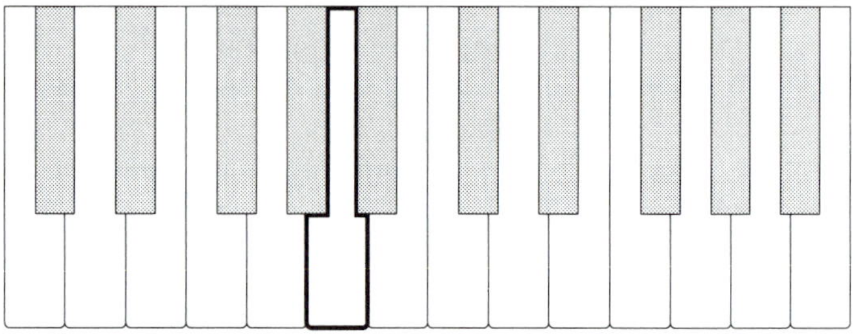

P1-5. For every key outlined in bold, mark with an *X* the key that would sound the pitch a minor third higher. Mark with a check the key that would sound the pitch a minor third lower.

a.
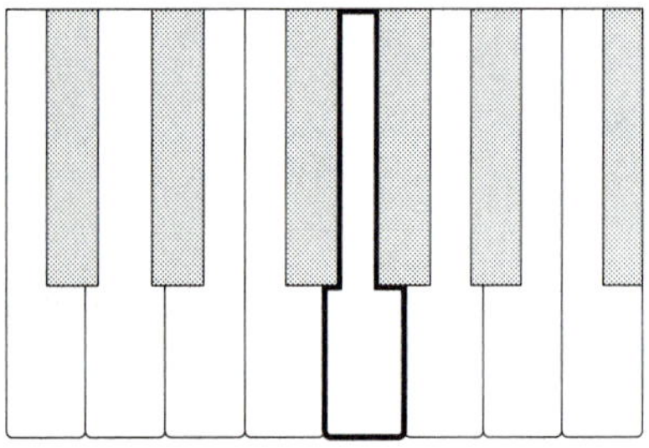
b.
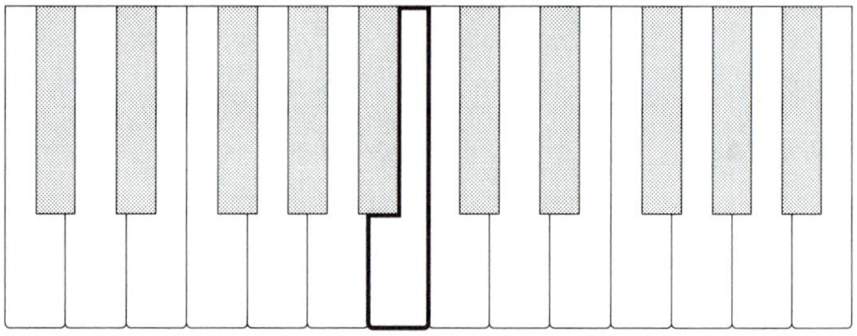
c.
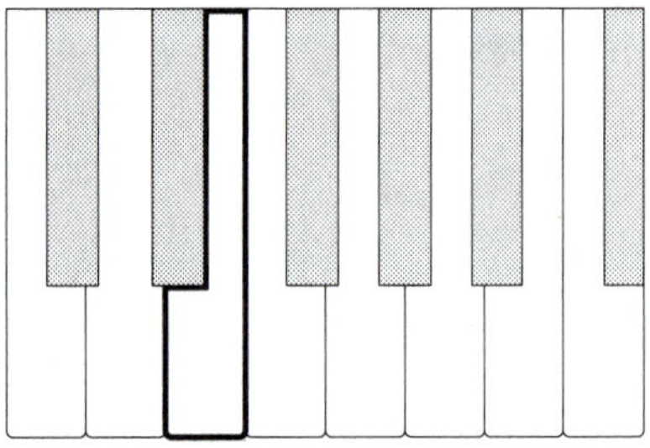
d.
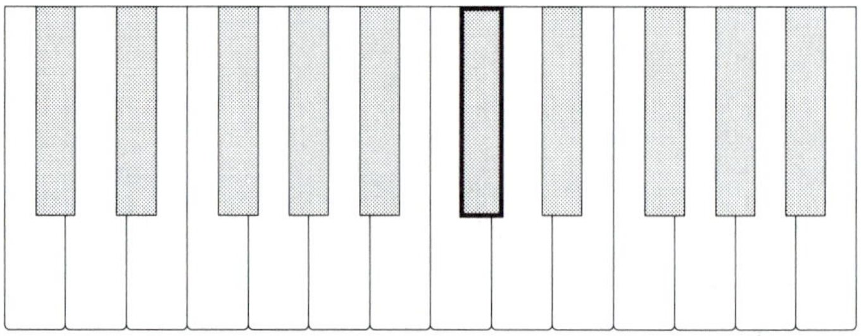

Name: ______________________________

Instructor: __________________________

Date: _______________________________

P1-6. For every key outlined in bold, mark with an *X* the key that would sound the pitch a perfect fifth higher. Mark with a check the key that would sound the pitch a perfect fifth lower.

a.

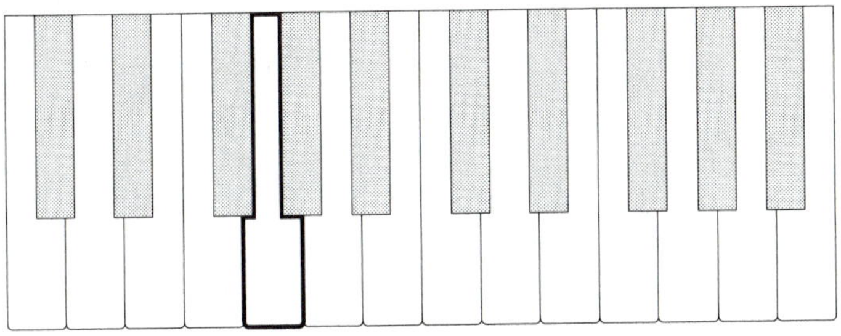

b.

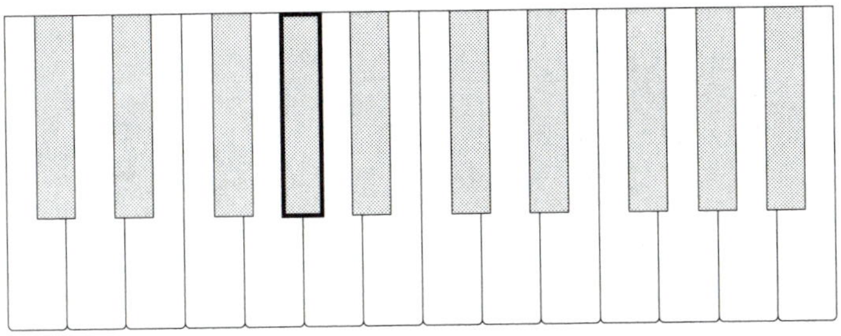

c.

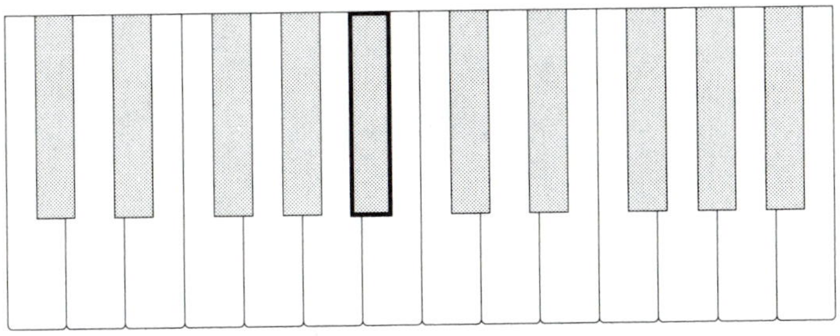

d.

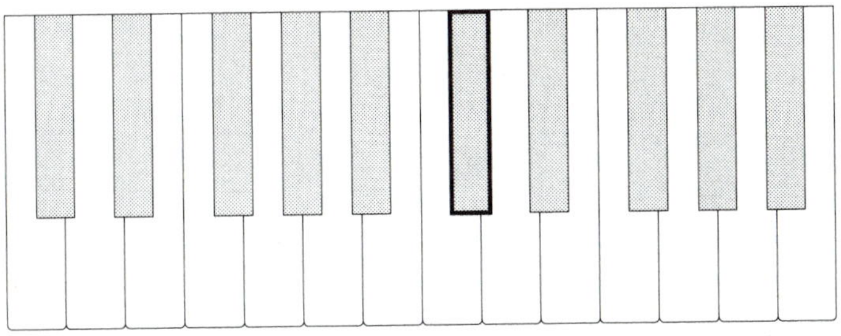

e.

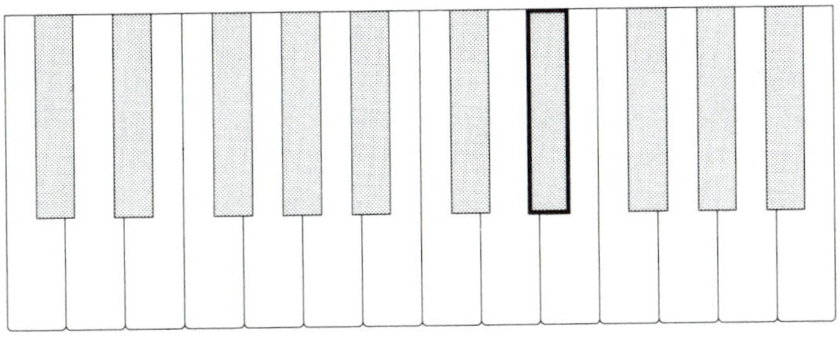

P1-7. Select the two keys that should be struck with the given root to form a major triad. Notate them "THIRD" and "FIFTH."

a.

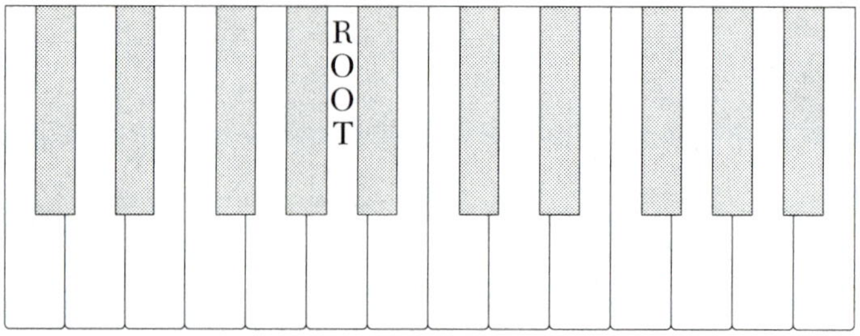

b.

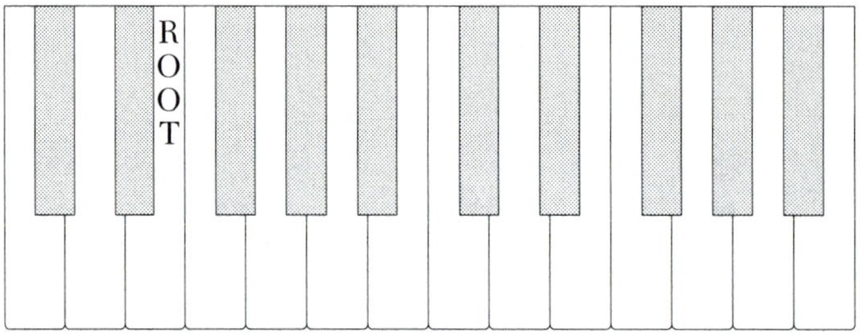

c.

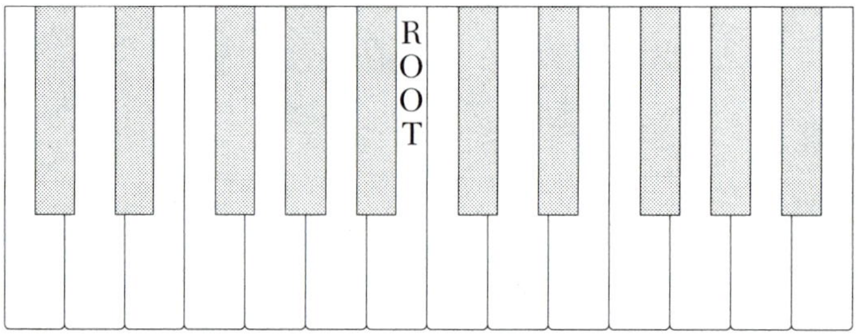

d.

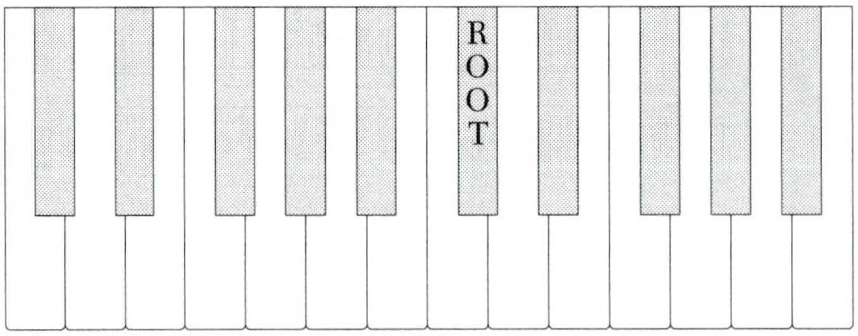

Name: ______________________

Instructor: ______________________

Date: ______________________

P1-8. Select the two keys that should be struck with the given third to form a major triad. Notate them "ROOT" and "FIFTH."

a.

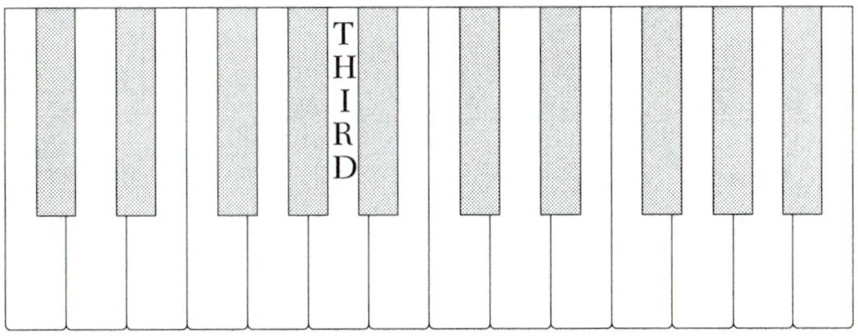

b.

c.

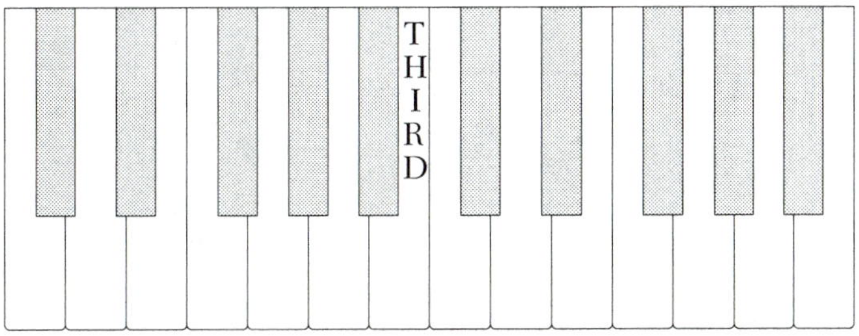

d.

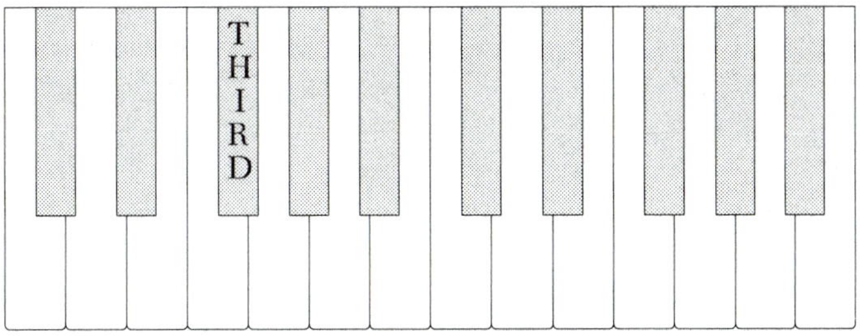

P1-9. Select the two keys that should be struck with the given fifth to form a major triad. Notate them "ROOT" and "THIRD."

a.

b.

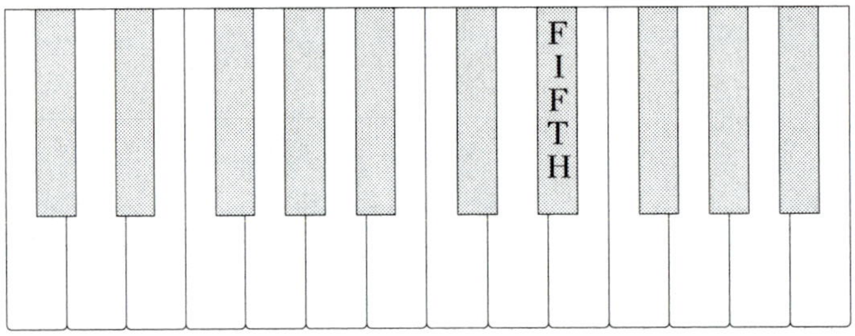

c.

d.

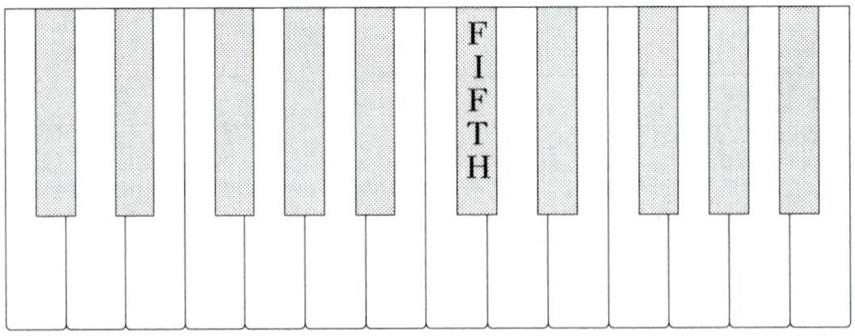

Name: ______________________

Instructor: ______________________

Date: ______________________

P1-10. The positions of the pitch C and of its first five overtones are shown on the keyboard diagram below. On the remaining diagrams provided, place the numbers 1 through 5 inside the keys that correspond to the first five overtones of the pitches E and G.

Hint: How many half steps separate C from its first overtone? Its first overtone from its second overtone? The same number of half steps should apply also when E or G serves as the fundamental.

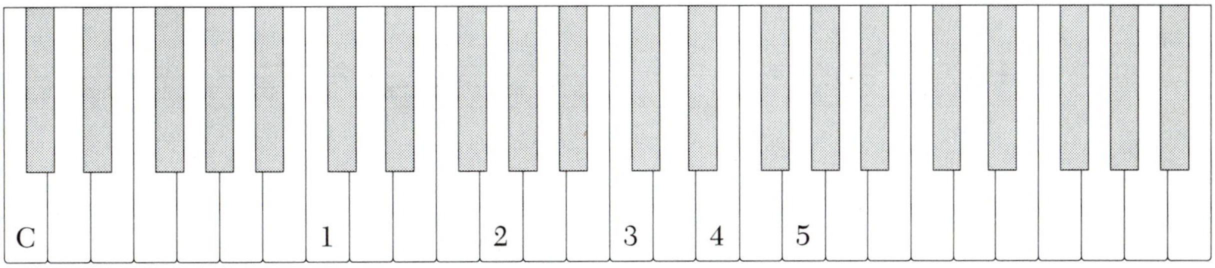

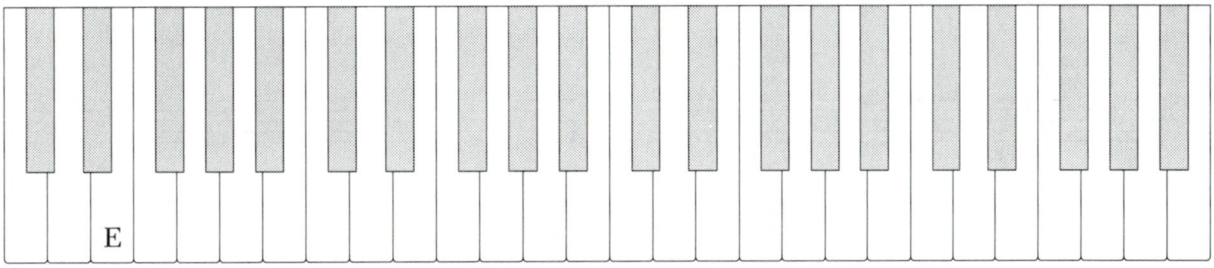

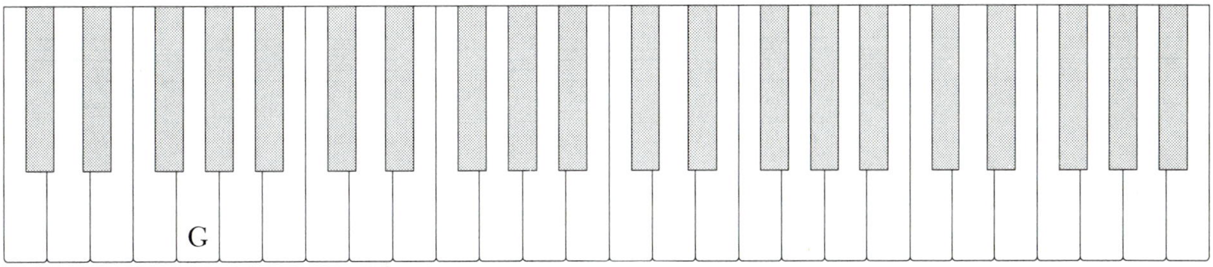

Rhythm Exercises

R1-1. Convert each notehead below into a quarter note, making all necessary changes. Be careful to use the correct stem direction. Assuming that the melody begins on the first beat of a measure, add bar lines and a double bar at appropriate spots.

a.

b.

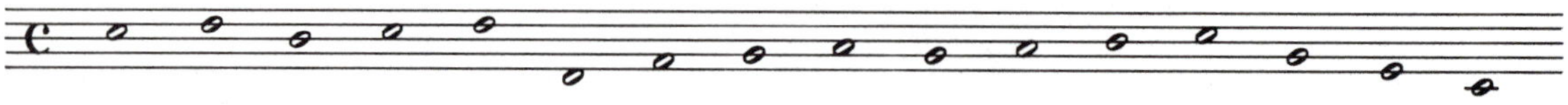

R1-2. Form a melody using the fragments provided. Only one ordering of these fragments results in measures that contain the correct number of beats.

a.

b.

Audio Exercises

A1-1. Three pitches will be performed.

a. Indicate which of the three pitches is the *highest*.

1. First Second Third
2. First Second Third
3. First Second Third
4. First Second Third
5. First Second Third

Name: ______________________

Instructor: ______________________

Date: ______________________

b. Indicate which of the three pitches is the *lowest*.

1.	First	Second	Third
2.	First	Second	Third
3.	First	Second	Third
4.	First	Second	Third
5.	First	Second	Third

c. Indicate which of the three pitches is in the *middle*.

1.	First	Second	Third
2.	First	Second	Third
3.	First	Second	Third
4.	First	Second	Third
5.	First	Second	Third

A1-2. Two pitches will be performed in either ascending or descending order and then together. Circle "Yes" if the pitches form an octave, "No" if they do not.

a.	Yes	No	f.	Yes	No
b.	Yes	No	g.	Yes	No
c.	Yes	No	h.	Yes	No
d.	Yes	No	i.	Yes	No
e.	Yes	No	j.	Yes	No

A1-3. You will hear several attempts at clapping the following rhythmic pattern. Decide whether the pattern is performed correctly or is subject to one of the following errors: speeding up, slowing down, or irregular beats (some of greater duration than others). Circle the correct response.

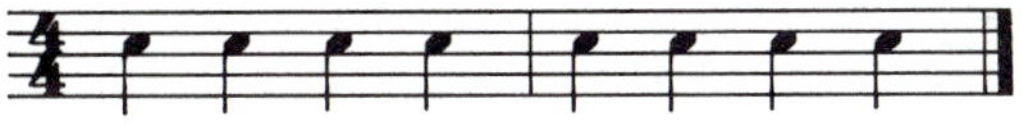

a.	Correct	Speeding up	Slowing down	Irregular beats
b.	Correct	Speeding up	Slowing down	Irregular beats
c.	Correct	Speeding up	Slowing down	Irregular beats
d.	Correct	Speeding up	Slowing down	Irregular beats
e.	Correct	Speeding up	Slowing down	Irregular beats

Name: ______________________

Instructor: ______________________

Date: ______________________

Mastery Test, Chapter 1

________ 1. Which one of the notes on the right is a sixth above the first note?

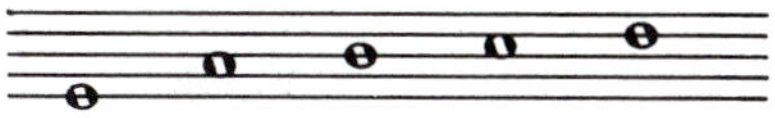

W. X. Y. Z.

________ 2. Which one of the notes on the right is a seventh below the first note?

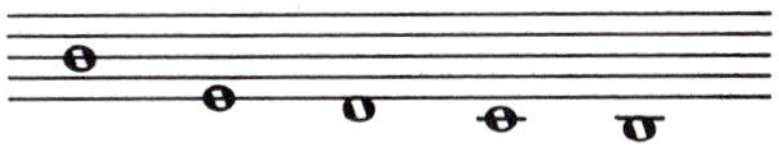

W. X. Y. Z.

________ 3. Which interval is shown?

W. Fourth X. Fifth Y. Sixth Z. Seventh

________ 4. Which interval is shown?

W. Fifth X. Sixth Y. Seventh Z. Octave

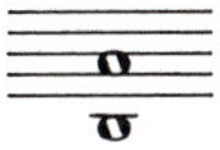

________ 5. What is the interval between the first and last notes of the following three-note melody: An ascending third followed by a descending sixth?

W. Descending second X. Descending third
Y. Descending fourth Z. Descending fifth

________ 6. What is the interval between the first and last notes of the following three-note melody: An ascending octave followed by a descending fourth?

W. Ascending fourth X. Ascending fifth
Y. Ascending sixth Z. Ascending seventh

Diagram for Questions 7–9:

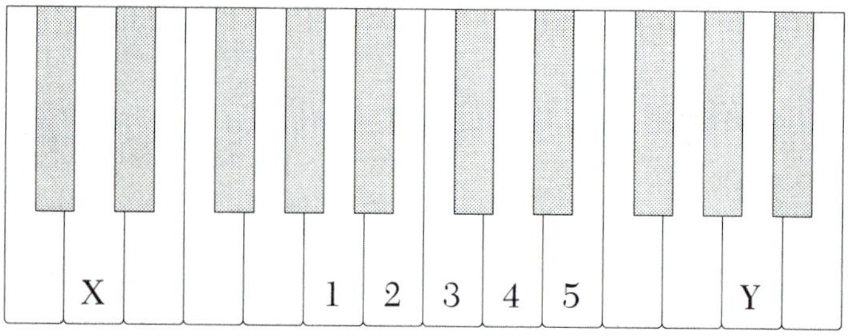

________ 7. Which one of the five numbered keys corresponds to the pitch E?

________ 8. Which one of the five numbered keys is an octave above the key labeled *X*?

________ 9. Which one of the five numbered keys is a perfect fifth below the key labeled *Y*?

________ 10. If you build a major triad using the key marked *X* for the root, which other keys are required?
W. 1 and 3 X. 1 and 4 Y. 2 and 3
Z. 2 and 4

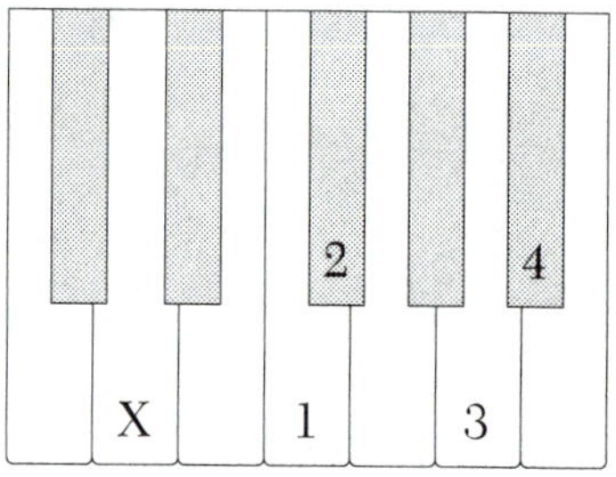

________ 11. If you build a major triad using the key marked *X* for the third, which other keys are required?
W. 1 and 3 X. 1 and 4 Y. 2 and 3
Z. 2 and 4

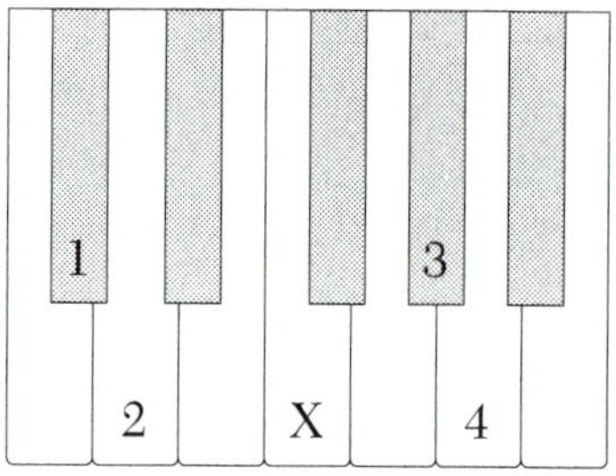

________ 12. If you build a major triad using the key marked *X* for the fifth, which other keys are required?
W. 1 and 3 X. 1 and 4
Y. 2 and 3 Z. 2 and 4

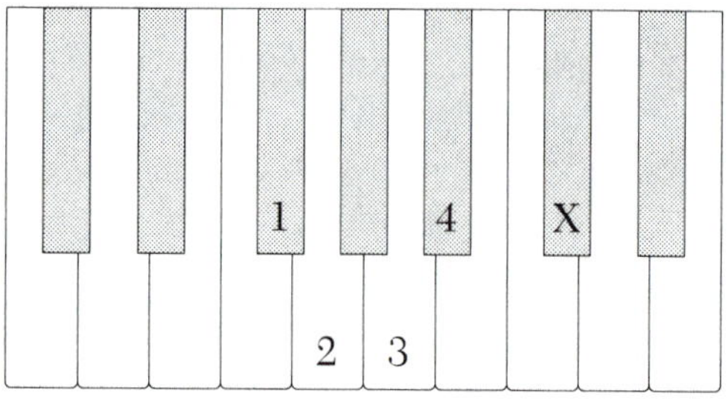

Name: ______________________

Instructor: ______________________

Date: ______________________

_________ 13. Which one of the four symbols on the staff is a correctly notated quarter note?

Diagram for Questions 14 and 15:

_________ 14. Which arrow points to what is called a measure?

_________ 15. Which arrow points to what is called a time signature?

_________ 16. Three pitches will be performed. Which of them is the highest?

X. The first   Y. The second   Z. The third

_________ 17. Three pitches will be performed. Which of them is the lowest?

X. The first   Y. The second   Z. The third

_________ 18. Three pitches will be performed. Which of them is in the middle?

X. The first   Y. The second   Z. The third

_________ 19. Is the interval performed an octave?

Y. Yes   Z. No

_________ 20. You will hear an attempt at clapping the rhythmic pattern displayed. Decide whether the pattern is correctly performed, or whether it is subject to one of the following errors: speeding up, slowing down, or irregular beats.

W. Correct
X. Speeding up
Y. Slowing down
Z. Irregular beats

2

Treble Clef and Accidentals

Terms and Concepts

clef	*flat*	*whole note*
treble clef	*enharmonic equivalent*	*augmentation dot*
pitch class	*natural*	*tempo*
accidental	*half note*	*metronome*
sharp	*dotted half note*	*tie*

PITCH

Treble Clef

The lines and spaces of the staff and the white keys of the keyboard correlate closely. For example, an octave is drawn using two noteheads that are eight positions apart on the staff (Ex. 2-1).

Example 2-1

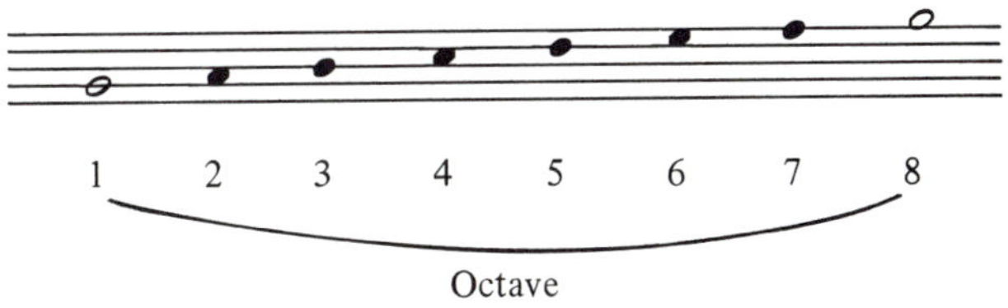

Similarly, every eighth white key on the keyboard is octave related (Ex. 2-2).

Example 2-2

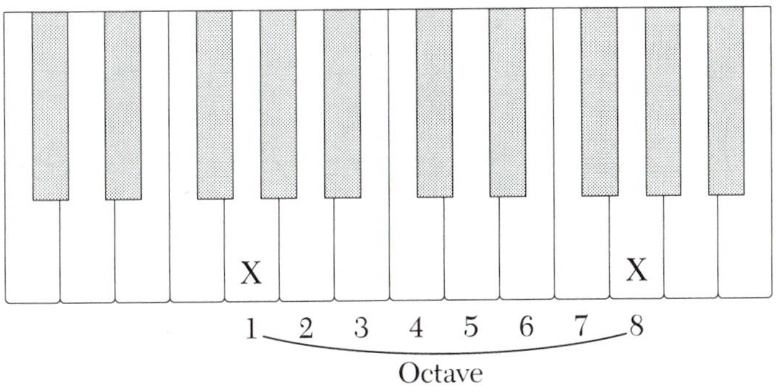

clef

treble clef

Yet in order to be useful to musicians, the staff must correlate even more closely with musical pitches. Only if specific noteheads correspond to specific keys on the keyboard—only if each notehead represents a unique pitch—can staff notation accurately represent the composer's ideas. To achieve this correlation we use a ***clef,*** a symbol placed at the left edge of the staff to define which pitches are represented by the noteheads drawn on that staff.

In most music, pitches in the middle to high range are notated using the ***treble clef.*** (The clef used for pitches in the low to middle range will be introduced in Chapter 5.) The treble clef shows which line on the staff corresponds to the pitch G above middle C. Once that pitch is fixed, notes on all other lines and spaces—and, by extension, notes written above or below the staff using ledger lines—fall into place as well.

The bottom part of the treble clef symbol circles the second line of the staff, marking the position of the pitch G above middle C, illustrated in Example 2-3a. The symbols in Example 2-3b tell us only that two pitches form the interval of an ascending octave. The symbols in Example 2-3c tell us exactly which pitches are to be performed. A musician would play G above middle C and then its upper octave.

Example 2-3

Pitches named using the letters C, E, and G (introduced in Chapter 1) are notated on the staff in Example 2-4. The C at the left edge of the accompanying keyboard diagram represents middle C, the C located just left of center on the keyboard.

Example 2-4

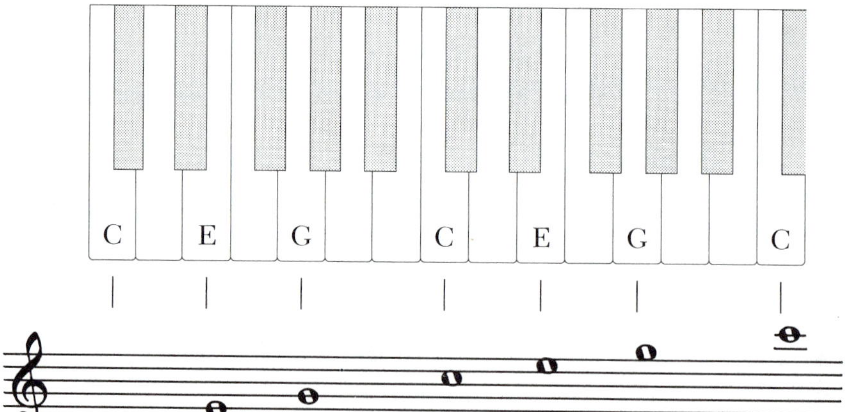

The pitches that correspond to the remaining white keys are named using the letters A, B, D, and F. Their positions on the keyboard and on the staff are shown in Example 2-5.

Example 2-5

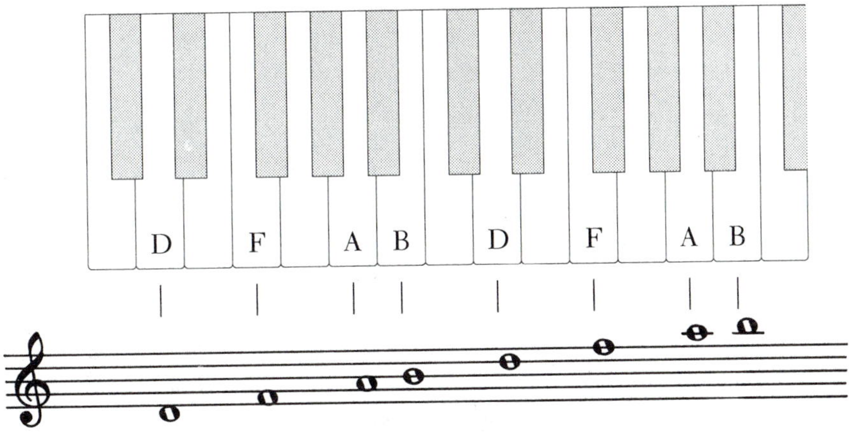

You might wish to learn the notes in the two groupings displayed or in terms of notes that fall on lines (E G B D F) and in spaces (F A C E). Remember that additional notes can be drawn using ledger lines above and below the staff. For example, consider the notehead shown in Example 2-6. Since the notehead on the first ledger line below the staff is middle C, and since five positions (that is, line-space-line-space-line) separate the notehead shown from middle C, the pitch represented by this notehead is F, a fifth below middle C.

Example 2-6

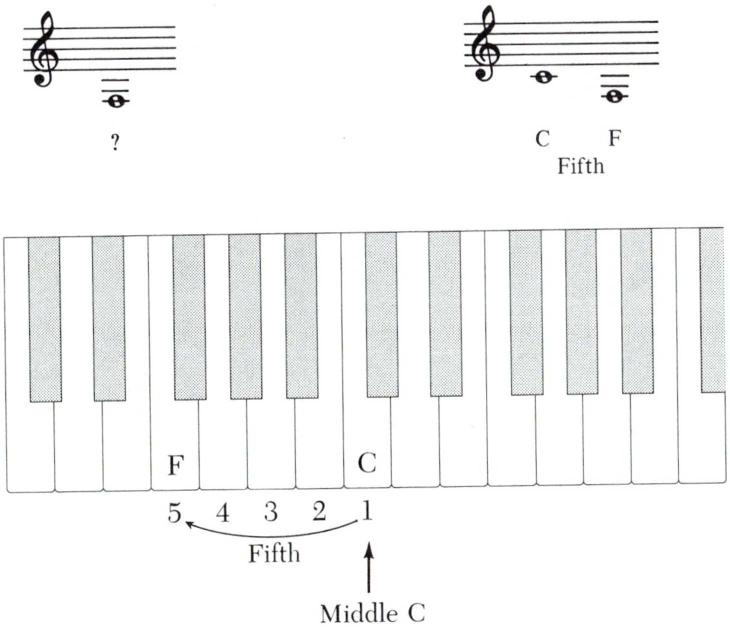

Accidentals

pitch class

The letters A, B, C, D, E, F, and G represent seven of the twelve ***pitch classes*** used in music. A pitch class is a collection of all pitches that can be spelled using the same name, without reference to their highness or lowness. For example, two pitches that form an octave may both be named "A." Though they are not the same pitch, they are members of the same pitch class. Eight different keys on the piano sound pitches that would be labeled "A." Some are high; others are low. They are all members of the same pitch class: pitch class A.

accidental

sharp

flat

The five remaining pitch classes correspond to the black keys on the keyboard. Observe that there are five black keys within the span of any octave. Each represents a different pitch class. How shall we name and notate them? Consecutive letters are used for the pitches that correspond to adjacent white keys, which in turn correspond to all of the available positions on the staff. For this reason, the pitches that correspond to black keys must always be named and notated using special symbols called ***accidentals.*** Every black-key pitch has two alternative names and notations derived from the names and notations of the adjacent white-key pitches. The ***sharp*** (♯) is an accidental that instructs the performer to *raise* the pitch of the notehead or pitch name to which it is applied by one half step. The ***flat*** (♭) is an accidental that instructs the performer to *lower* the pitch of the notehead or pitch name to which it is applied by one half step. Their use in naming and notating the black-key pitches is shown in Example 2-7.

Example 2-7

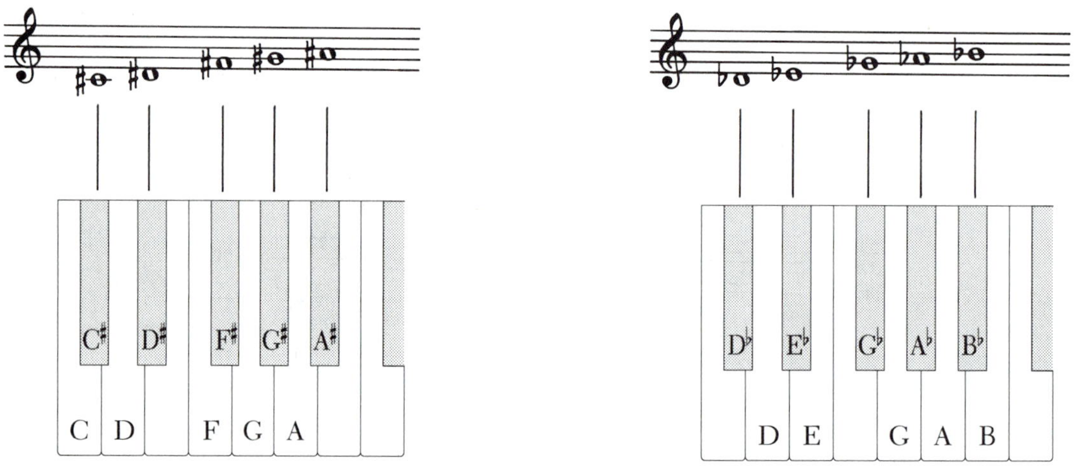

enharmonic equivalent

Observe that the pitch class between C and D can be notated either as C♯ (read "C-sharp") or as D♭ (read "D-flat"). The different names that may be applied to the same pitch class are called ***enharmonic equivalents.*** The other enharmonic equivalents shown above are D♯ and E♭, F♯ and G♭, G♯ and A♭, and A♯ and B♭.

In score notation sharps and flats are placed to the left of noteheads (Ex. 2-8a), but when modifying letter names in verbal text they are placed to the right (Ex. 2-8b).

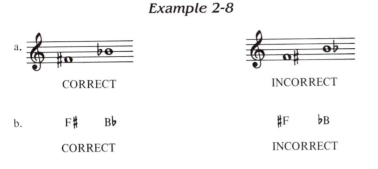

Example 2-8

a.

CORRECT

INCORRECT

b. F♯ B♭

CORRECT

♯F ♭B

INCORRECT

Even though pitches named using enharmonic equivalents might sound the same on the modern piano, composers have reasons for choosing one spelling over another. In English, the letters *f* and *ph* represent the same sound, yet we always spell *fate* using *f* and *phase* using *ph*. You would be confused if, when reading, you saw the words *phate* and *fase*. Likewise, musicians expect correct spellings in music notation and would be confused if the wrong spelling of a pitch appeared. Examples 2-9 through 2-16 show some of the reasons why one spelling of a pitch would be correct while its enharmonic equivalent would be incorrect.

Suppose a composer wants to build a major triad whose root is A. By definition, the major triad contains a major third and a perfect fifth above its root. These positions are shown on the keyboard diagram in Example 2-9.

Example 2-9

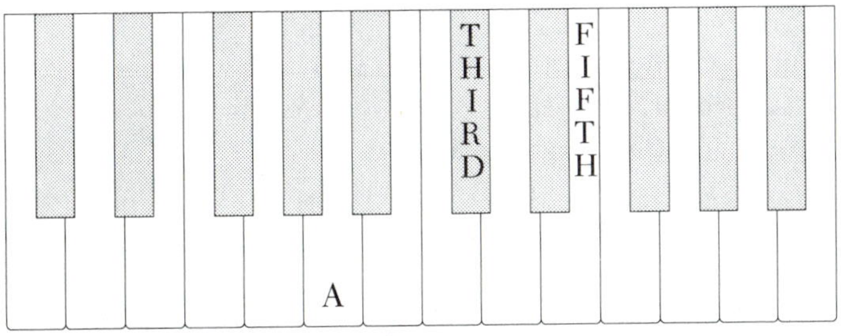

The correct spellings for the third and fifth of this triad are C♯ and E. The third may not be spelled as D♭, because the interval from A up to D♭ is a fourth (A through both B and C to D♭). An accidental will never change the numerical *size* of an interval. It affects only the interval's *quality*. Correct and incorrect spellings of the triad are shown in Example 2-10.

Example 2-10

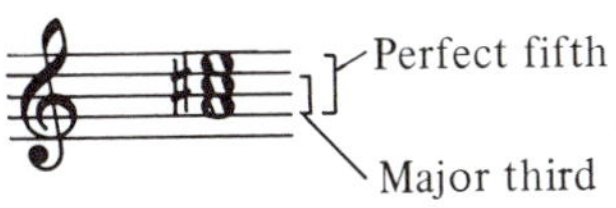

CORRECT

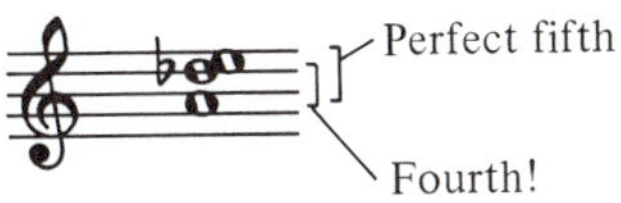

INCORRECT

Suppose a composer wants to build a major triad whose third is F. By definition, the major triad contains a major third between its root and third and a minor third between its third and fifth. These positions are shown on the keyboard diagram in Example 2-11.

Example 2-11

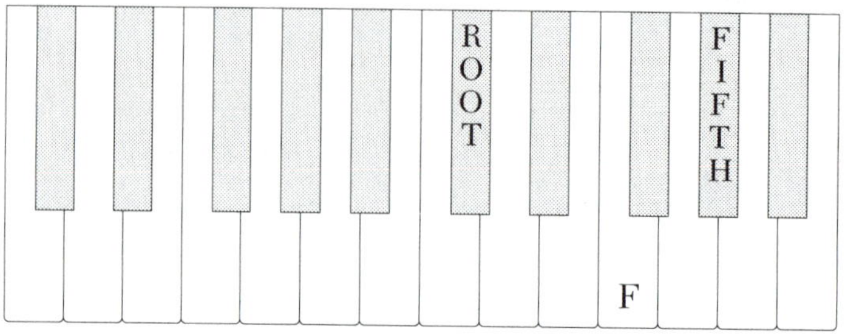

The correct spellings for the root and fifth of this triad are D♭ and A♭. The root may not be spelled as C♯, because the interval from C♯ up to F is a fourth. The fifth may not be spelled as G♯, because the interval from F up to G♯ is a second. Correct and incorrect spellings of the triad are shown in Example 2-12.

Example 2-12

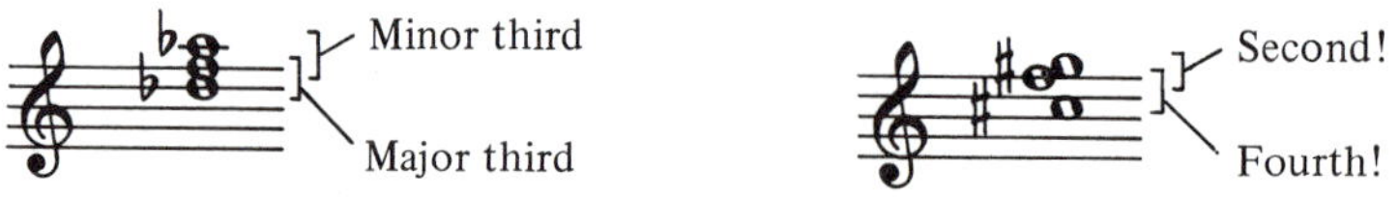

CORRECT INCORRECT

These examples demonstrate that the choice of whether to name a black-key pitch using a sharp or a flat depends upon its context. In one example, C♯ was required. In the other, D♭ was required.

Even white keys are sometimes named using an enharmonic equivalent. A composer might build a major triad whose root is spelled as G♯, for example. On the keyboard diagram in Example 2-13, the choice for the third of this triad appears to be C. But the interval between a pitch spelled G♯ and a pitch spelled C is a fourth, not a third.

Example 2-13

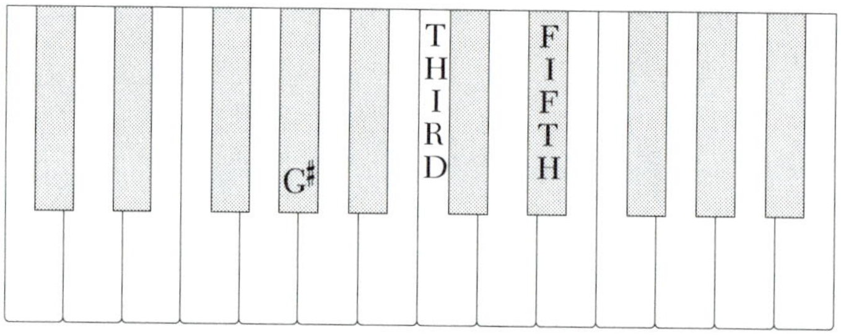

The third of a major triad whose root is G♯ must be spelled B♯, the enharmonic equivalent of C. The meaning of the sharp does not change: it raises the pitch of B by one half step. What is different in this case is that a white key, rather than a black key, is one half step to the right of B. Correct and incorrect spellings of the triad are shown in Example 2-14.

Example 2-14

CORRECT INCORRECT

A composer might also build a major triad whose third is spelled as E♭. On the keyboard diagram in Example 2-15 the choice for the root of this triad appears to be B. But the interval between a pitch spelled B and a pitch spelled E♭ is a fourth, not a third. Likewise the fifth of the triad, if spelled as F♯, would form a second rather than a third with E♭.

Example 2-15

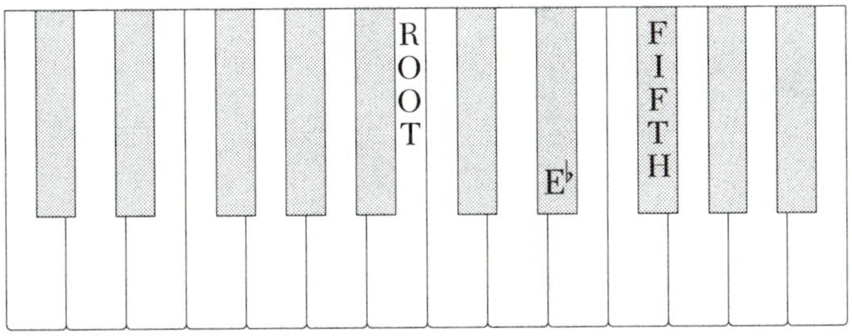

The root of a major triad whose third is E♭ must be spelled C♭, the enharmonic equivalent of B. The meaning of the flat does not change: it lowers the pitch of C by one half step. What is different in this case is that a white key, rather than a black key, is one half step to the left of C. The fifth must be spelled as G♭, since it must form the intervals of a fifth and third with the other components of the triad. Correct and incorrect spellings of the triad are shown in Example 2-16.

Example 2-16

CORRECT INCORRECT

natural

An accidental, when used in actual music, alters the meaning of a line or space not only for the notehead that it precedes but also for all other noteheads written on that line or space *until the next bar line.* To cancel the effect of such an accidental before the bar line, the ***natural*** (♮) must be used. In Example 2-17a the pitch A♭ appears on all four beats of the measure; in Example 2-17b the third and fourth beats have A♮ (read "A-natural") instead.

Example 2-17

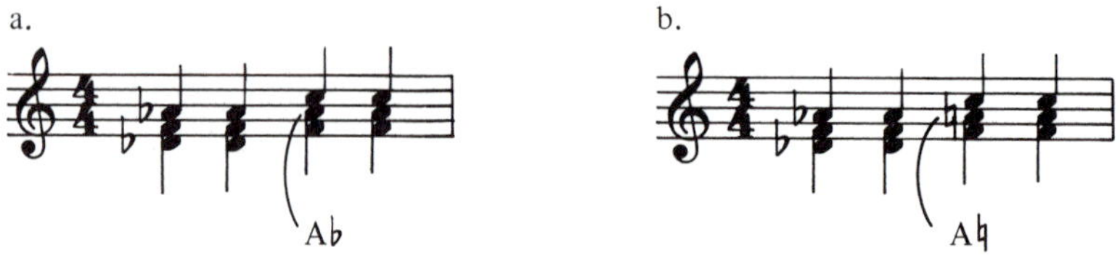

The accidentals that apply to the noteheads of a triad are always arranged in the same manner. When only one accidental is used, it is placed directly to the left of the notehead. When two accidentals are used, that which modifies the lower of the two noteheads is placed further to the left. When all three noteheads of a triad require accidentals, that which modifies the fifth of the triad is placed directly to the left of the notehead, that which modifies the root is placed further to the left, and that which modifies the third is placed to the left of both of the other accidentals (Ex. 2-18).

Example 2-18

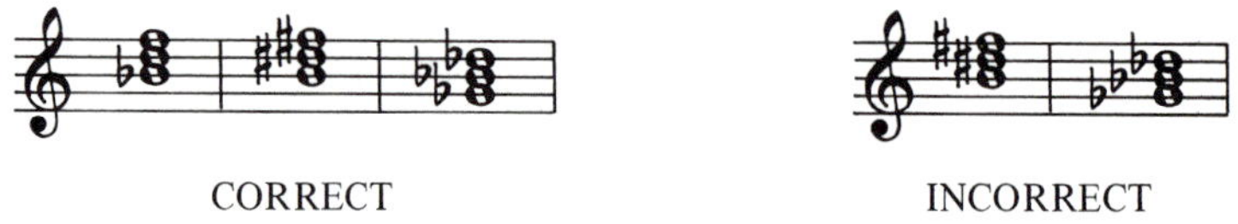

The keyboard diagram shown in Example 2-19 displays all of the pitch names that use the letters A through G, the sharp, and the flat.

Example 2-19

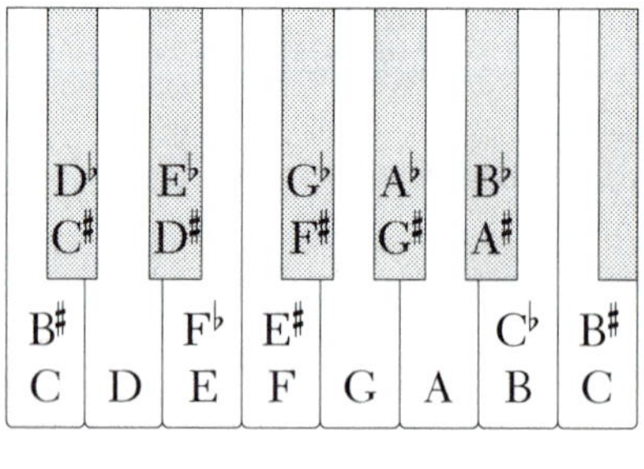

Pitch exercises for Chapter 2 are on pages 51–57.

RHYTHM

Combinations of Quarter-Note Beats

If composers employed only quarter notes, their works would not sustain our interest for long. The fascination of music is heightened when several rhythmic values interact. Just as the spoken language contains syllables of longer and shorter durations, so also does music. Some notes span several beats, while other notes result from the subdivision of a beat. Almost any combination of durations can coexist between two adjacent bar lines, so long as the sum of the rhythmic values equals that defined by the meter.

half note

dotted half note

whole note

The ***half note, dotted half note,*** and ***whole note*** fill two, three, and four beats, respectively, in $\frac{4}{4}$ meter. Their notational symbols are shown in Example 2-20.

Example 2-20

Symbol	*Name*	*Equivalent in Quarter Notes*	
𝅗𝅥	Half note	♩ + ♩	(2 beats)
𝅗𝅥.	Dotted half note	♩ + ♩ + ♩	(3 beats)
𝅝	Whole note	♩ + ♩ + ♩ + ♩	(4 beats)

As with the stems of quarter notes, those of half and dotted half notes extend upward or downward depending upon the placement of the notehead on the staff. Example 2-21 demonstrates their use.

Example 2-21

augmentation dot

The dotted half note is one of several symbols that employ an ***augmentation dot.*** A single dot will always increase the time value of a note by one-half. In this case the time value of the half note is two beats (2), to which half of two (1) is added, resulting in a total value of three beats (3). When the notehead is on a line or ledger line, the dot is placed in the middle of the space above the line rather than on the line itself, as shown in Example 2-22.

Example 2-22

CORRECT INCORRECT

Counting the Beats

In the preceding melodies (Ex. 2-21), counting numbers for the beats are shown below each staff. These numbers must flow evenly and without interruption. There should be no extra time before a bar line, for example. You should count these numbers out loud when practicing. If you are performing at a keyboard, your fingers must keep up with the even flow of pulses, rather than the pulses slowing down to accommodate your fingers. When singing you should continue to maintain a regular pulse even though you cannot count the numbers out loud. You might practice a melody that you intend to sing by first clapping its rhythm while counting out loud.

tempo

The ***tempo*** is the speed at which beats follow one another. A suitable tempo for your practice might be about one beat per second. If you cannot maintain that tempo, choose a slower tempo and eventually work up to one beat per second. *Choose a tempo that you can maintain even in difficult passages. Do not slow down during performance.*

In some published music, a suggested tempo is indicated numerically. A moderate tempo, such as one beat per second, would be notated as ♩ = 60 (60 quarter notes per minute). A fast tempo might be notated as ♩ = 120 (120 quarter notes per minute). A slow tempo might be notated as ♩ = 40 (40 quarter notes per minute). A mechanical device called a ***metronome***, which can be adjusted to tick from 40 to over 200 times per minute, is a common tool in the performer's practice room. Even without a metronome to reinforce your counting, you should make a special effort to maintain whatever tempo you establish at the beginning of an exercise.

metronome

$\frac{2}{4}$ *and* $\frac{3}{4}$ *Meters*

The $\frac{2}{4}$ and $\frac{3}{4}$ meters share with $\frac{4}{4}$ the basic unit of the quarter note but are restricted to two and three beats per measure, respectively. As in $\frac{4}{4}$, the first beats of $\frac{2}{4}$ or $\frac{3}{4}$ measures are the strongest. The second beat in $\frac{2}{4}$ and the second and third beats in $\frac{3}{4}$ are weak. Because they occupy more beats than the measure contains, dotted half and whole notes do not appear in $\frac{2}{4}$ meter, while whole notes do not appear in $\frac{3}{4}$ meter. The melodies in Example 2-23 demonstrate these meters.

Example 2-23

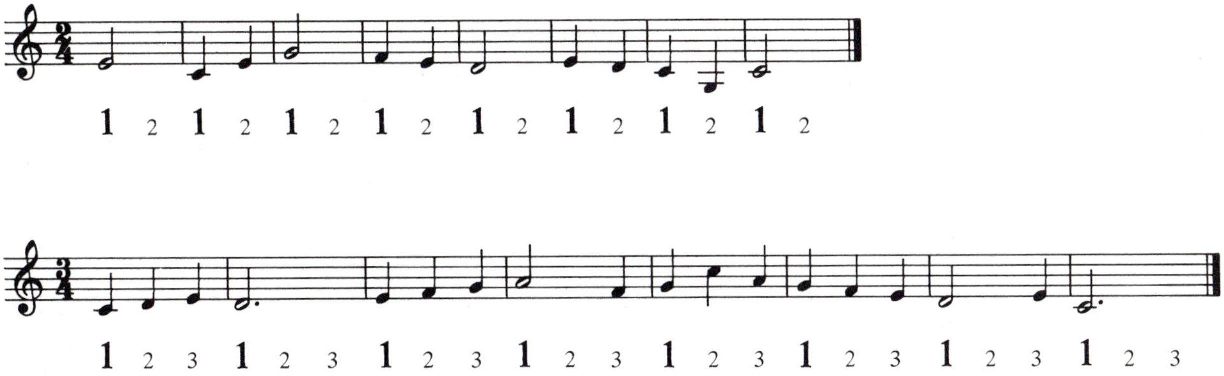

The Tie

A pitch may sound for more beats than can fit within one measure. In such cases, two noteheads are drawn in adjacent measures on the staff and are connected with a curved line called a ***tie***, which instructs the performer to continue the sound of the first notehead without striking or singing it again when the second notehead appears. The two noteheads must represent the same pitch. The last pitch in the melody in Example 2-24 should be held for two measures rather than one measure. If you are playing this melody on a piano, you would strike the pitch C at the beginning of the next-to-last measure and hold your finger down for six beats. It would be incorrect to hit the key again after three beats. Observe that the tie is placed on the side of the noteheads opposite the stems.

tie

Example 2-24

Rhythm exercises for Chapter 2 are on pages 58–60.

LABORATORY

L2-1. Each of the twelve pitch classes (C, C♯/D♭, D, etc.) can serve as the root, third, or fifth of a major triad. Select twelve adjacent white and black keys on the keyboard, perhaps from middle C up to B. For each key, form the three major triads that include that key. For example, middle C is the root of the triad C, E, G, the third of the triad A♭, C, E♭, and the fifth of the triad F, A, C. Proceed similarly for the eleven remaining pitch classes.

L2-2.a. Perform each of the following triads at the keyboard using your right hand.

1.

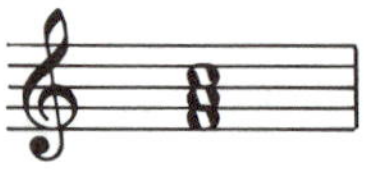

2.

3.

4.

5.

6.

7.

8.

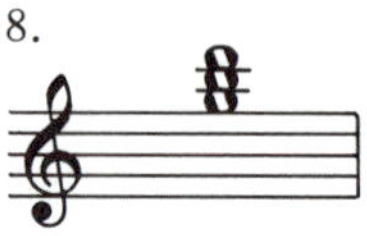

9.

10.

b. Perform each of the following melodies at the keyboard using your right hand. Recommended fingerings are included. Your thumb is labeled "1," while the remaining fingers are labeled "2," "3," "4," and "5." The fingers should be somewhat rounded so that the tips of the fingers touch the keys. (Correct hand position and long fingernails are incompatible!)

1. Westminster Chimes

2. Schumann: Humming Song

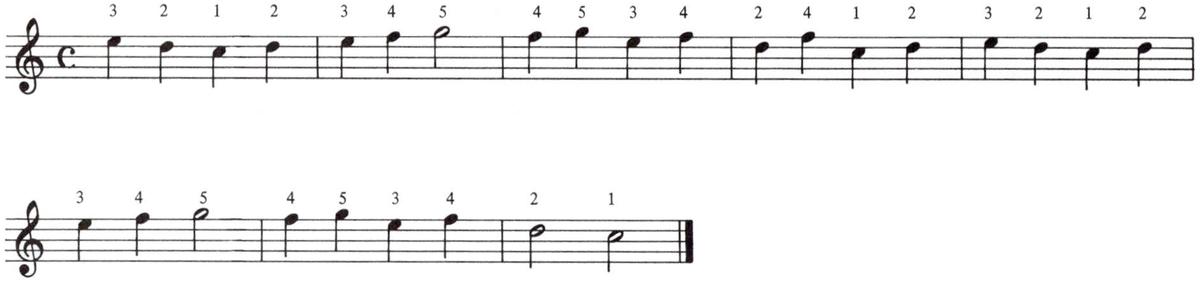

3. Where Did You Get That Hat?

L2-3. Put an *X* inside all white and black keys that fall within your vocal range in the diagram below. Put a circle around each *X* near the left side of your chart for which there is an *X* a perfect fifth higher.

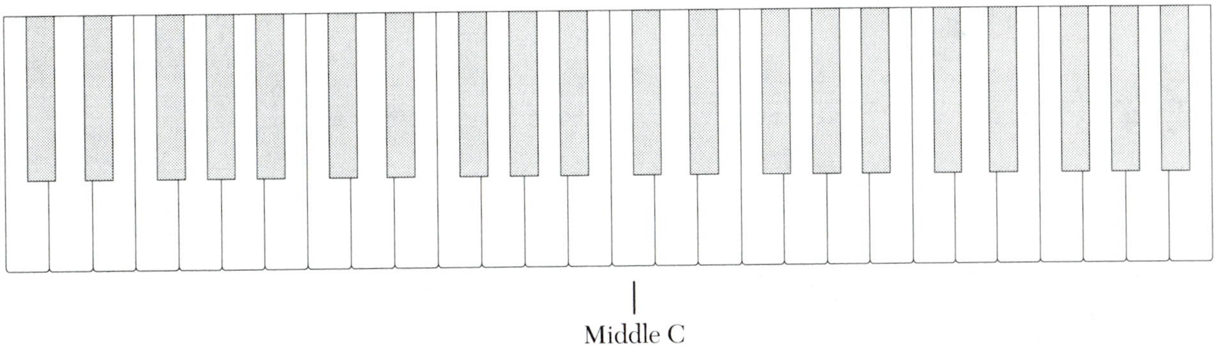

a. Practice the following exercise over a period of days or weeks until you have mastered it perfectly.

- Build a major triad using one of the circle-*X* keys as the root and perform the triad.
- Strike the root alone.
- Sing the root and then the third.
- Strike the third to confirm that you have sung the correct pitch.
- Strike the root again.
- Sing the root and then the fifth.
- Strike the fifth to confirm that you have sung the correct pitch.

b. Once the above exercise is going well, add the following steps.

- Perform the triad again.
- Strike the third alone.
- Sing the third and then the root.
- Strike the root to confirm that you have sung the correct pitch.
- Strike the third again.
- Sing the third and then the fifth.
- Strike the fifth to confirm that you have sung the correct pitch.
- Perform the triad again.
- Strike the fifth alone.
- Sing the fifth and then the root.
- Strike the root to confirm that you have sung the correct pitch.
- Strike the fifth again.
- Sing the fifth and then the third.
- Strike the third to confirm that you have sung the correct pitch.

L2-4. Practice the following melodies at the keyboard, simultaneously singing and playing each pitch. Sing the letter names that correspond to the pitches. Men should perform these melodies an octave lower than they are written. To do so, treat the C to the left of middle C on the keyboard as if it were middle C and perform the melodies in that region.

a.

b.

c.

d.

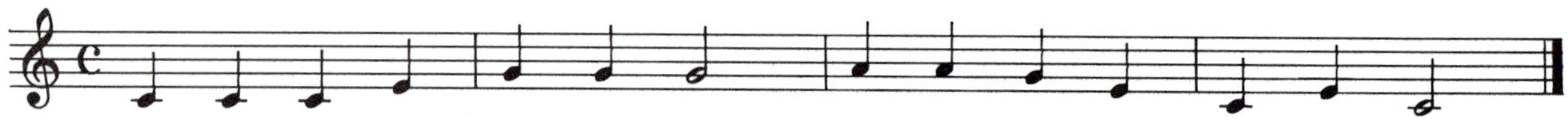

e.

L2-5. The following compositions are *duets*, two melodies intended to be sung by two performers at the same time. These duets could be sung by two women or groups of women, two men or groups of men, or a woman or group of women performing Voice 1 and a man or group of men performing Voice 2. Sing the letter names that correspond to the pitches. A student or the instructor may play both parts at the keyboard. Men should perform these melodies an octave lower than they are written. To do so, treat the C to the left of middle C on the keyboard as if it were middle C and perform the melodies in that region.

a.

b.

L2-6. Write in the beat numbers (that is, "1 2 1 2 . . ." or "1 2 3 1 2 3 . . ." or "1 2 3 4 1 2 3 4 . . .") below the notated rhythms. Then perform each by clapping the rhythm or playing the pitch F at the keyboard while pronouncing the syllables for the beats aloud. Practice until you can perform each exercise at a tempo of about ♩ = 60.

Sample

a.

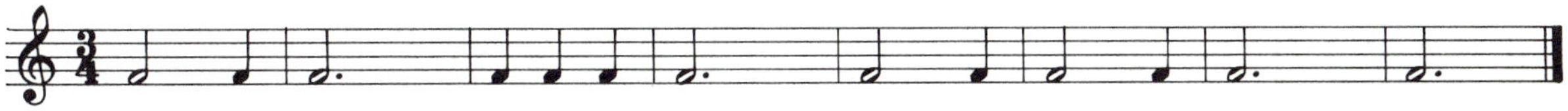

b.

c.

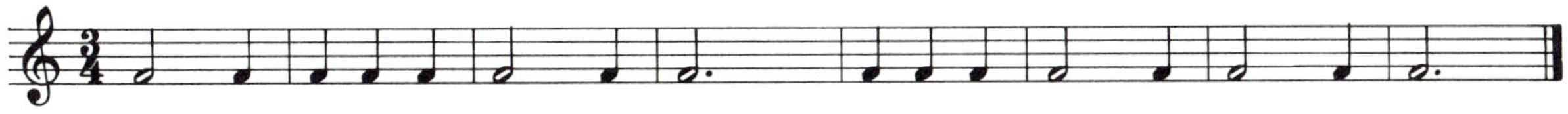

d.

L2-7. Write in the beat numbers below the notated rhythms. Then perform them by dividing the class into two groups, with each group clapping one part while pronouncing the syllables for the beats aloud. Alternatively, individual students may perform both parts simultaneously at the keyboard, pronouncing the syllables for the beats aloud while the index finger of the right hand strikes C and the index finger of the left hand strikes F, as notated. Observe that when two parts share the same staff, the stems of the upper part always point upward while the stems of the lower part always point downward.

SAMPLE

a. 

b. 

c. 

d. 

L2-8. This exercise requires that a student or the instructor serve as the performer at a keyboard.

a. The performer places three fingers above keys that sound a major triad and then performs one of the following:

1. A major triad
2. A triad with the root and fifth of a major triad, but sounding the pitch a half step lower than the third.
3. A triad with the root and third of a major triad, but sounding the pitch a half step higher than the fifth.

Indicate whether the triad performed is or is not a major triad.

b. The performer places three fingers above keys that sound a major triad and performs them in ascending order. Then the performer plays one of the following:

Root–Third
Root–Fifth
Third–Fifth

Indicate which of the three choices is performed.

Audio exercises for Chapter 2 are on pages 60–61.

Name: ______________________
Instructor: ______________________
Date: ______________________

EXERCISES

Pitch Exercises

P2-1. Cut this page along the dotted lines. Form these slips into a pile and examine them one by one, identifying each note as you view it. (The answer is on the reverse.) Reshuffle the slips frequently. Practice until you can go through the pile with no errors in 30 seconds or less.

Hint: In the beginning, you may want to include only a few of the slips, for example, those slips that contain C, E, or G. Eventually add to your pile until it contains all of the slips.

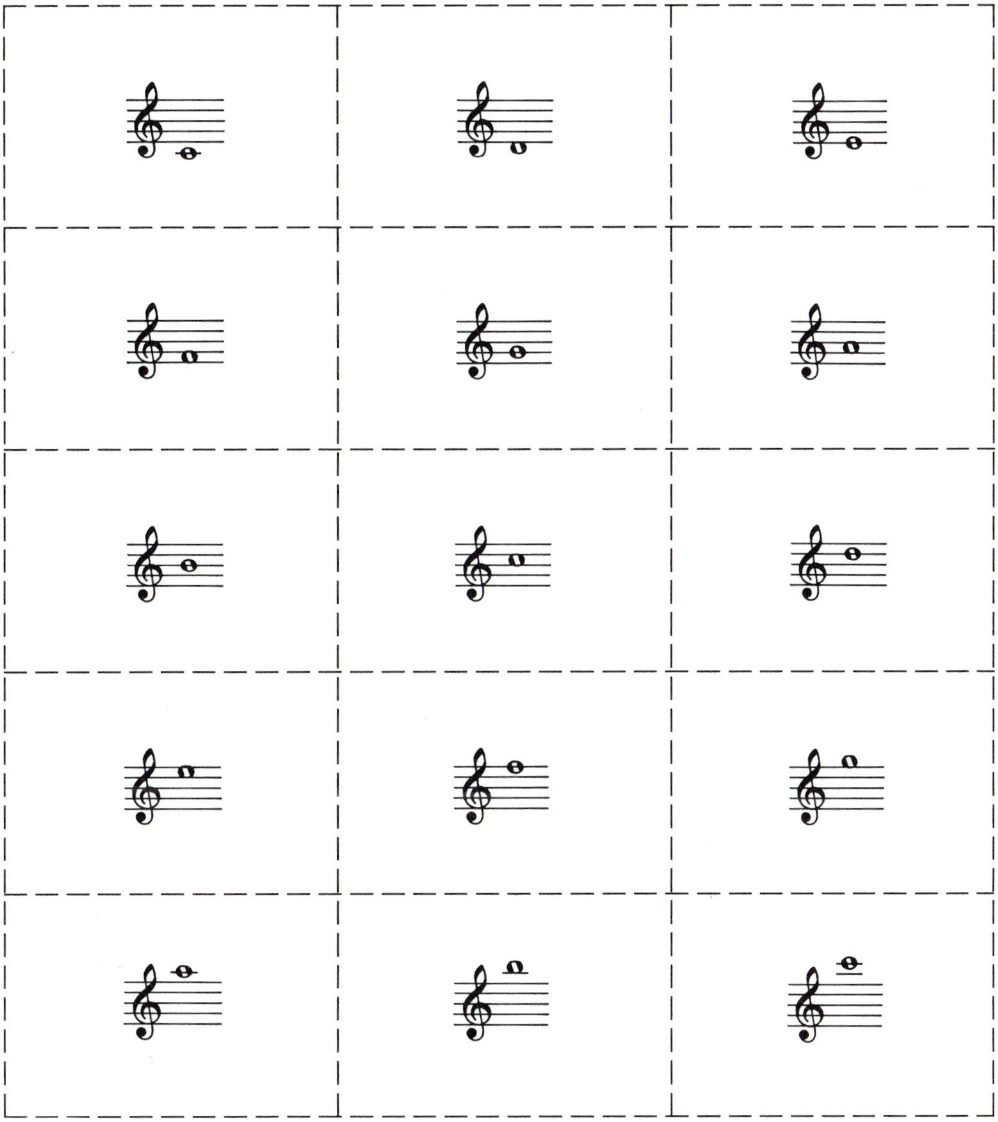

E	D	C
A	G	F
D	C	B
G	F	E
C	B	A

Name: ____________________
Instructor: ____________________
Date: ____________________

P2-2. To the right of each notehead, supply the notehead that forms the interval requested. Use the keyboard diagram as an aid in counting the appropriate number of half steps: four for the major third, three for the minor third, and seven for the perfect fifth. Underneath the noteheads, indicate their names (A♯, D♭, etc.).

Hint: If the given notehead is on a line, the notehead you add will be also. If it is in a space, the notehead you add will be also.

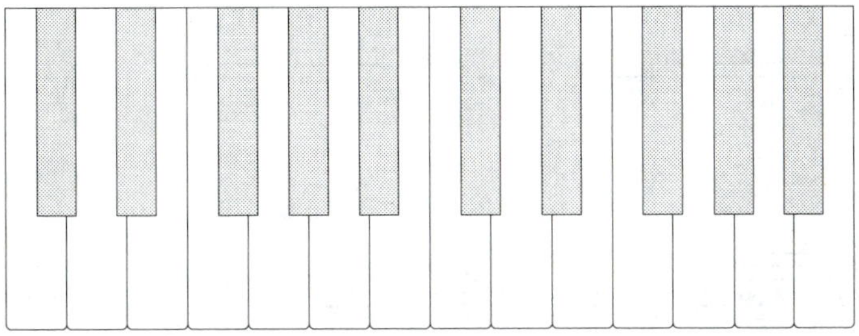

a. ASCENDING MAJOR THIRDS

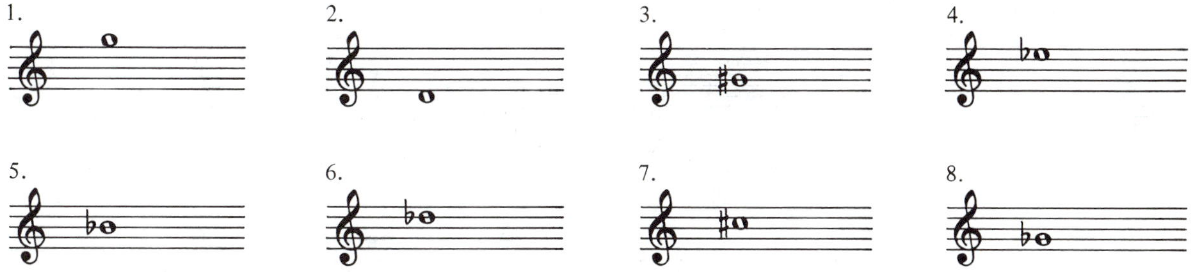

b. DESCENDING MAJOR THIRDS

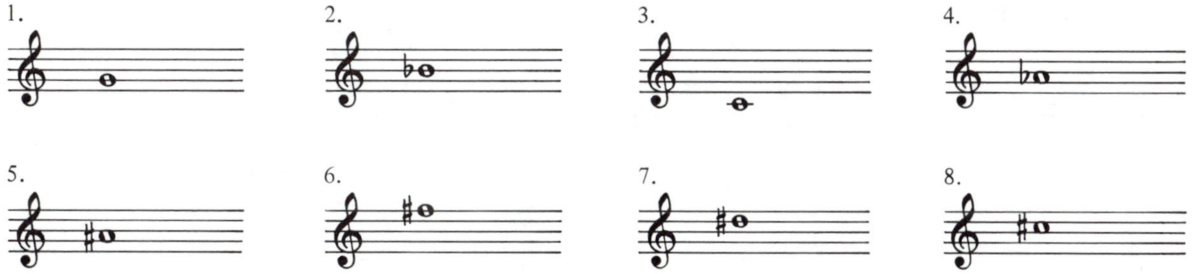

c. ASCENDING MINOR THIRDS

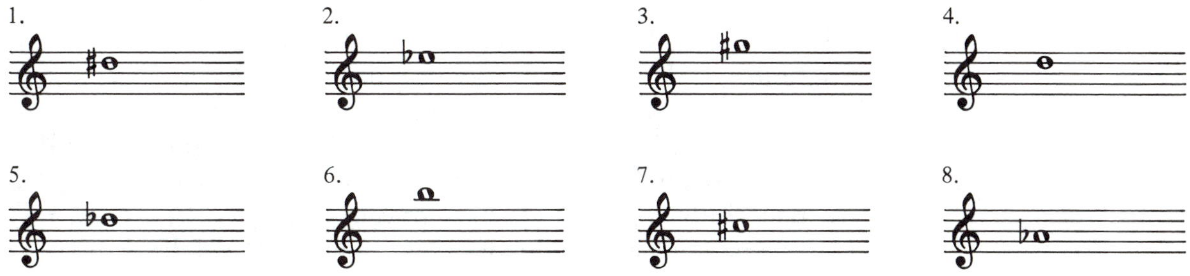

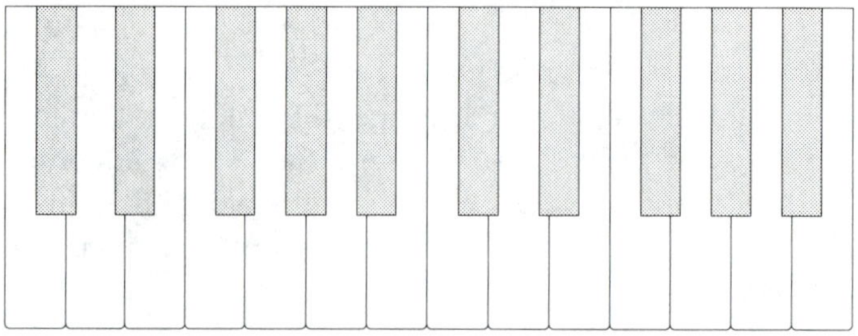

d. DESCENDING MINOR THIRDS

1. 2. 3. 4.

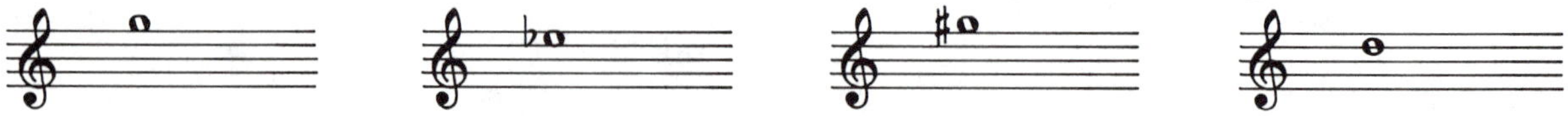

5. 6. 7. 8.

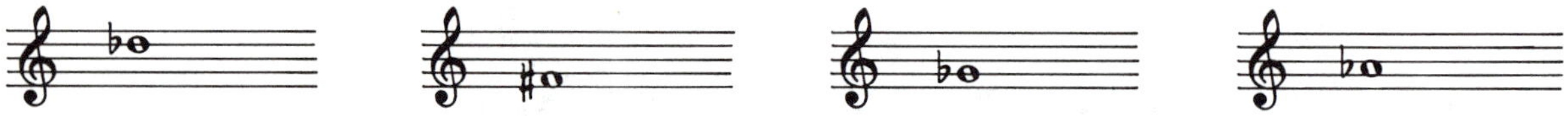

e. ASCENDING PERFECT FIFTHS

1. 2. 3. 4.

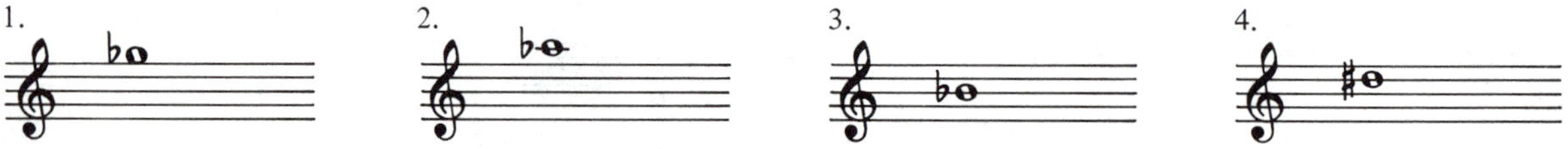

5. 6. 7. 8.

f. DESCENDING PERFECT FIFTHS

1. 2. 3. 4.

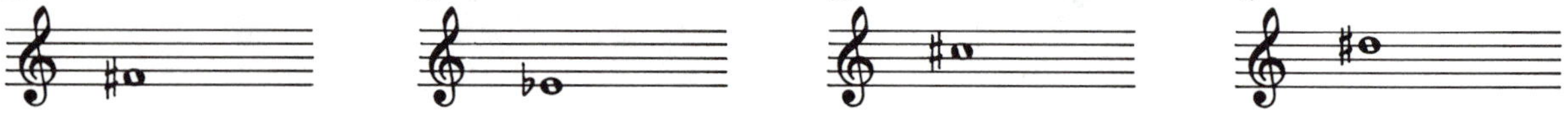

5. 6. 7. 8.

P2-3. Build major triads using the given pitches in the triadic positions specified. First mark *X*'s on the keyboard diagram, then use staff notation, being sure to draw a treble clef on each staff. Regard the C at the left edge of each keyboard diagram as middle C. In several cases you must decide whether to build the triad on the left side or the right side of the keyboard diagram. Either is correct, though you should make sure that your notation on the staff agrees with that on the keyboard diagram.

Name: ______________________
Instructor: ____________________
Date: ______________________

Sample. F♯, third

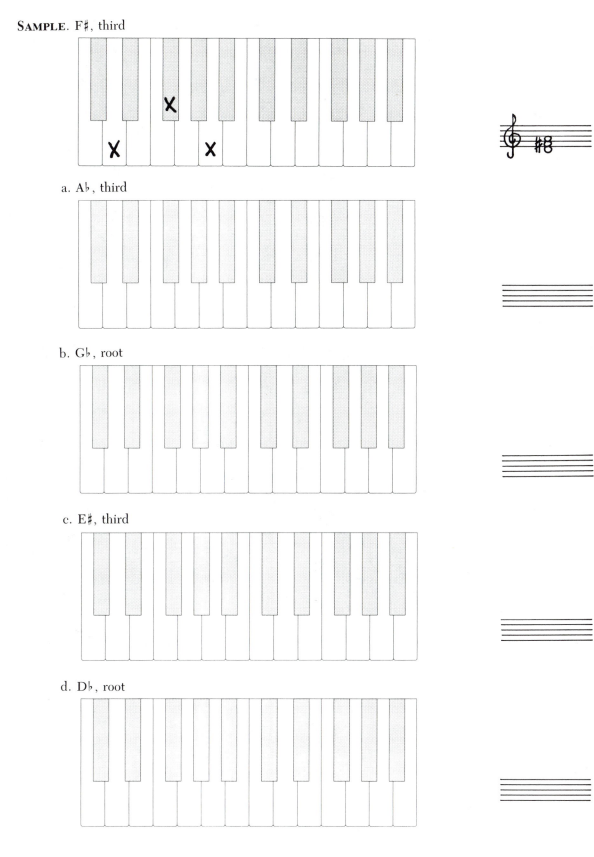

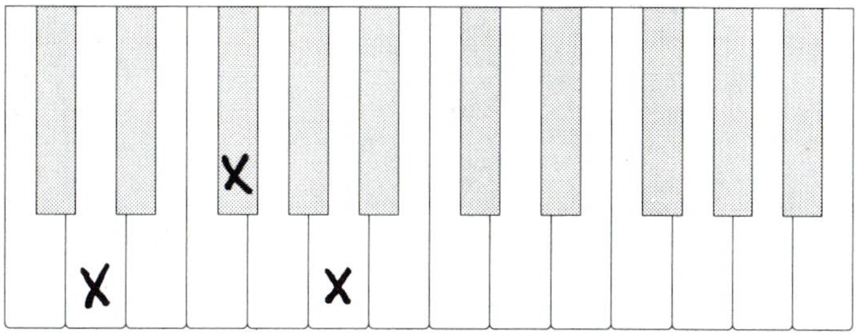

a. A♭, third

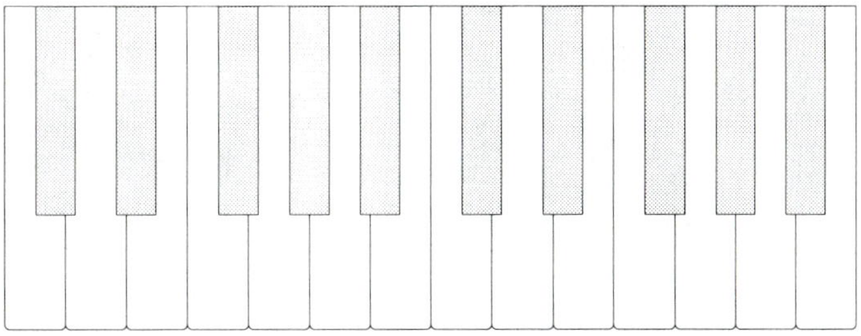

b. G♭, root

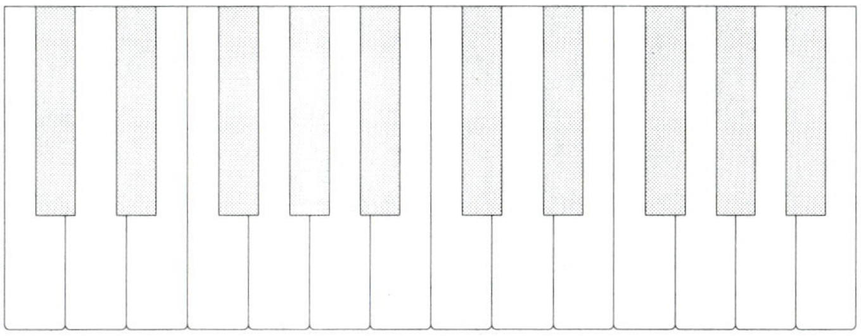

c. E♯, third

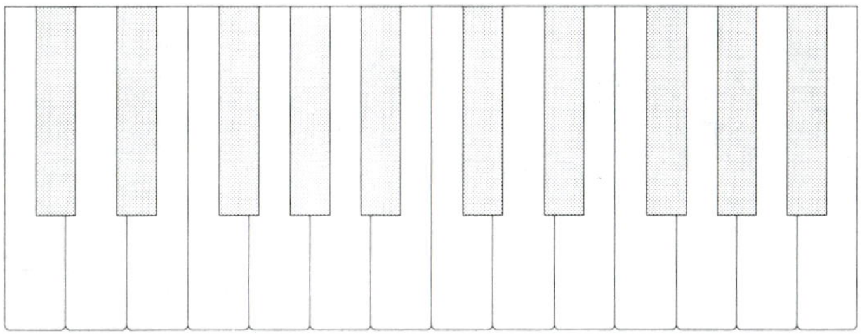

d. D♭, root

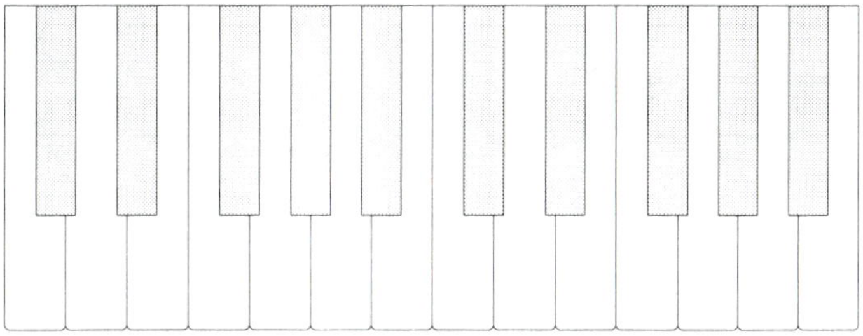

e. D♯, fifth

f. A♯, third

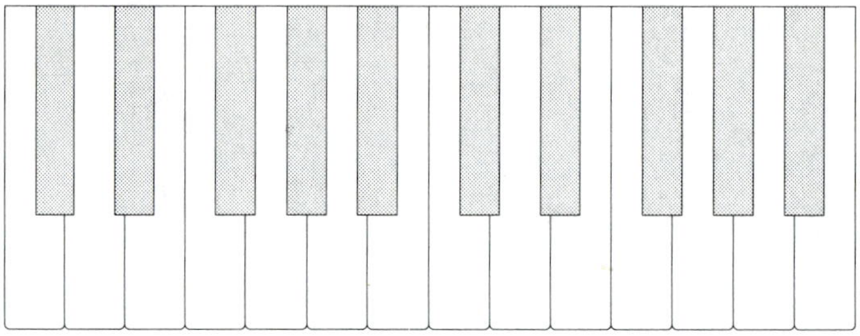

g. C, third

h. E♭, root

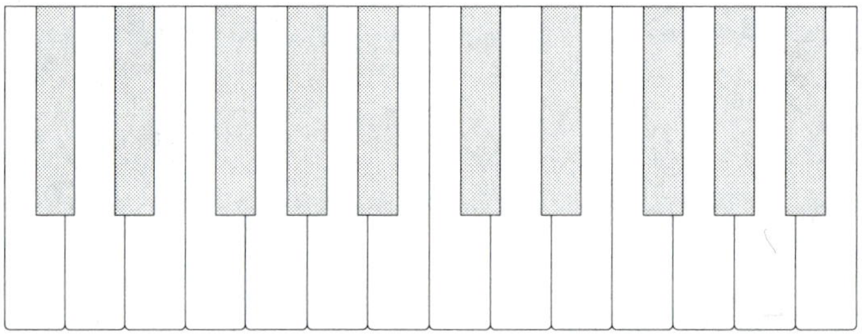

i. F♯, fifth

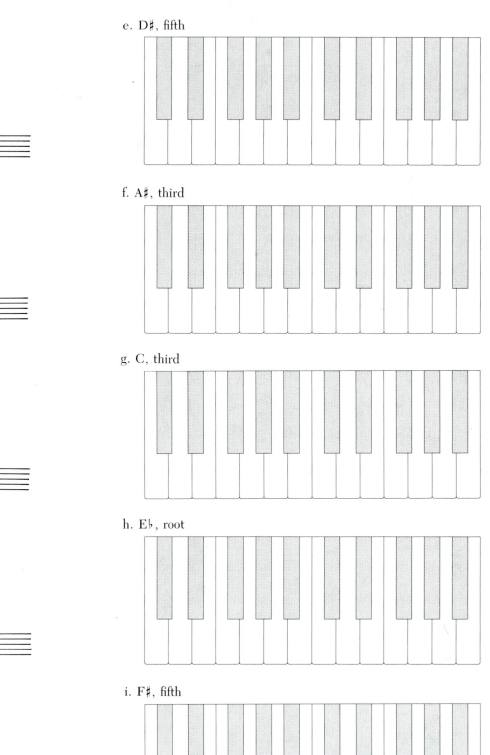

Name: ____________________

Instructor: ____________________

Date: ____________________

P2-4. Spell major triads using letter names, filling in the blank slots in the following chart. Use the keyboard diagram as an aid in counting the appropriate number of half steps.

	Root	*Third*	*Fifth*
a.	___	G♯	___
b.	E♭	___	___
c.	___	___	G♯
d.	___	B♭	___
e.	A	___	___
f.	___	___	A♭
g.	___	___	F♯
h.	___	E	___
i.	___	B	___
j.	G♯	___	___
k.	A♭	___	___
l.	___	___	F
m.	___	C♯	___
n.	B	___	___
o.	___	___	C
p.	F♯	___	___
q.	___	___	A

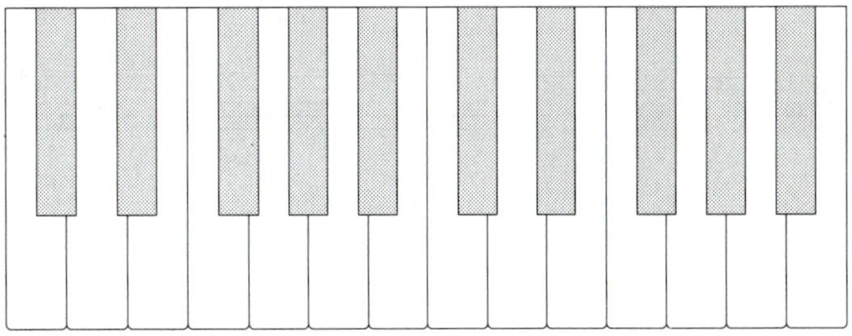

Rhythm Exercises

R2-1. Convert each notehead on staff (a) below into a half note, and each notehead on staff (b) into a dotted half note. Make all necessary changes. Be careful to use the correct stem direction. Assuming that each melody begins on the first beat of a measure, add bar lines and a double bar at appropriate spots.

a.

b.

R2-2. Use the model rhythm of the first two measures to form identical patterns in measures 3–4, 5–6, and 7–8 of the following melodies. Make all necessary changes. Add bar lines at appropriate spots.

a.

b.

c.

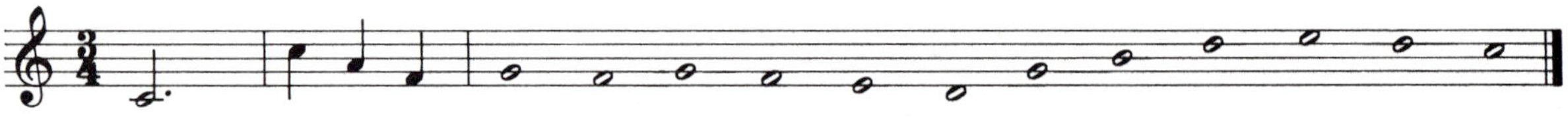

d.

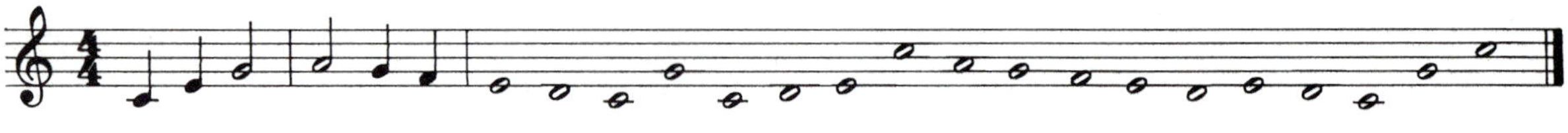

Name: ______________________

Instructor: ______________________

Date: ______________________

R2-3. Modify the noteheads indicated by arrows to form measures containing the appropriate number of beats.

a.

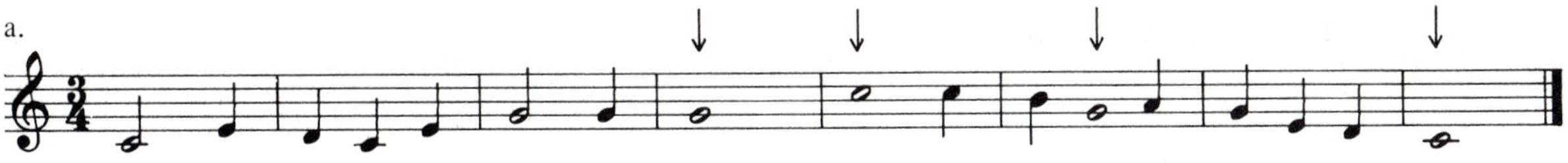

b.

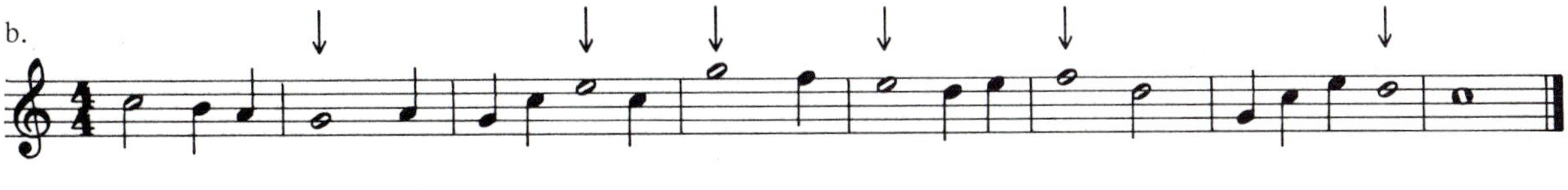

c.

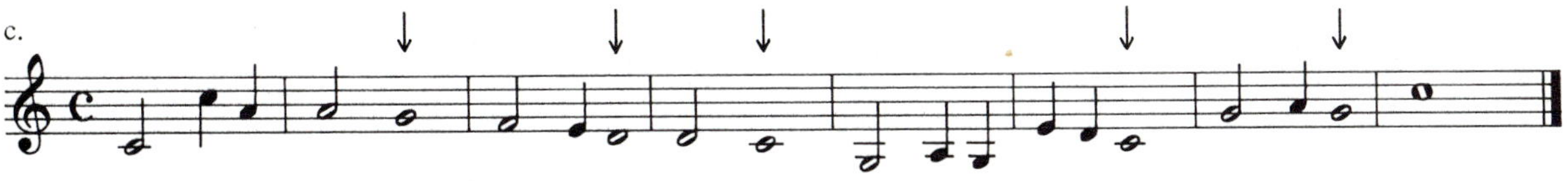

d.

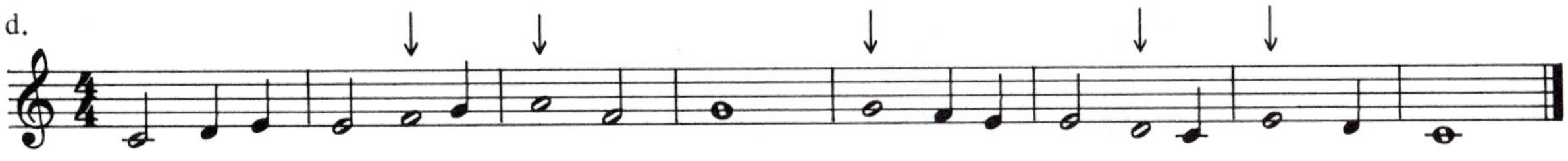

R2-4. Form a melody using the fragments provided. Only one ordering of these fragments results in measures that contain the correct number of beats.

a.

b.

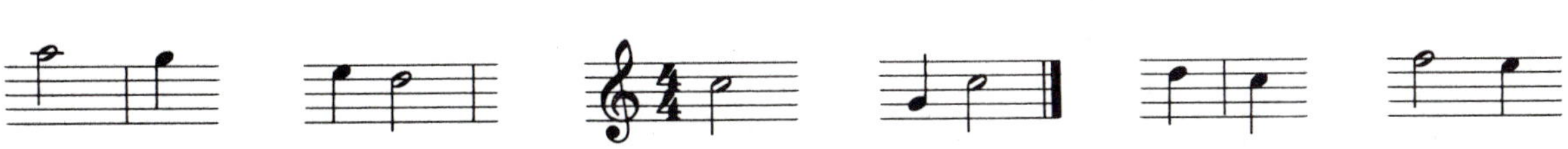

R2-5. Notate the melodies indicated by the positioning of the pitch names in relation to the counting syllables. Use only seconds, thirds, and fourths as melodic intervals. Ties may be required.

a.

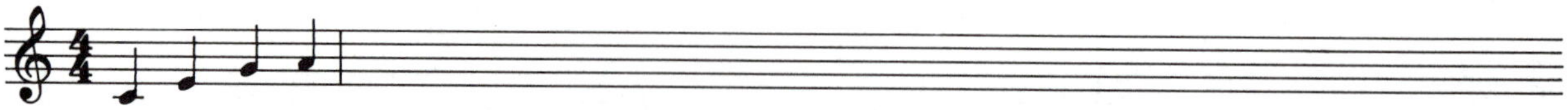

C E G A G F E D E D C D B C

1 2 3 4 1 2 3 4 1 2 3 4 1 2 3 4 1 2 3 4 1 2 3 4

b.

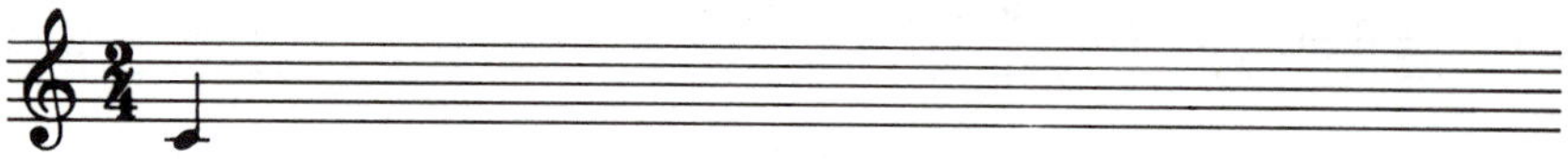

C D E G A G F E D C

1 2 1 2 1 2 1 2 1 2 1 2 1 2 1 2

c.

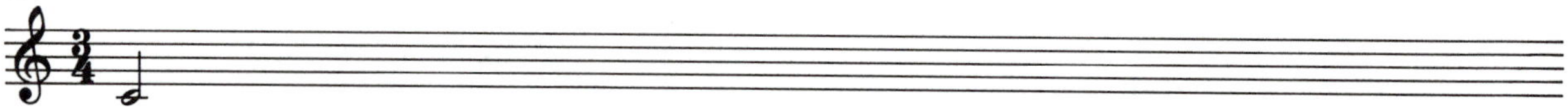

C D F E G A G F E D E C

1 2 3 1 2 3 1 2 3 1 2 3 1 2 3 1 2 3 1 2 3 1 2 3

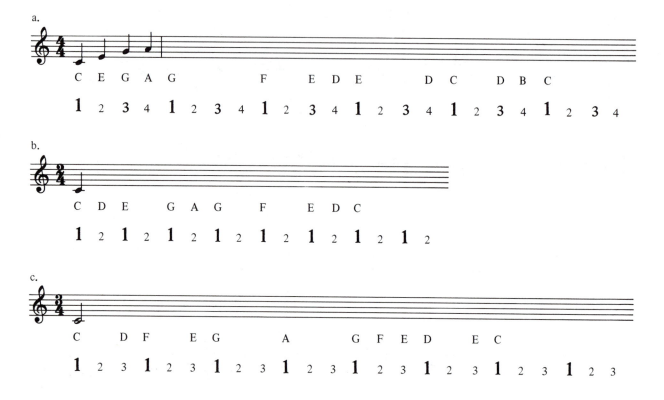

Audio Exercises

A2-1. Three pitches will be performed simultaneously. Circle "Yes" if the pitches form a major triad, "No" if they do not.

a. Yes No
b. Yes No
c. Yes No
d. Yes No
e. Yes No
f. Yes No
g. Yes No
h. Yes No
i. Yes No
j. Yes No

Name: ______________________
Instructor: ______________________
Date: ______________________

A2-2. The three pitches of a major triad will be performed in ascending order. Two of the three pitches will be performed a second time. Indicate which two.

a. Root–Third Root–Fifth Third–Fifth
b. Root–Third Root–Fifth Third–Fifth
c. Root–Third Root–Fifth Third–Fifth
d. Root–Third Root–Fifth Third–Fifth
e. Root–Third Root–Fifth Third–Fifth
f. Root–Third Root–Fifth Third–Fifth
g. Root–Third Root–Fifth Third–Fifth
h. Root–Third Root–Fifth Third–Fifth
i. Root–Third Root–Fifth Third–Fifth
j. Root–Third Root–Fifth Third–Fifth

A2-3. Four rhythms will be performed. In each case circle the score that shows the correct notation.

a.

b.

c.

d.

Name: ______________________
Instructor: ______________________
Date: ______________________

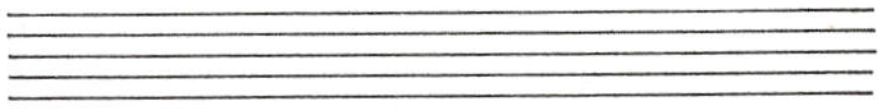

Mastery Test, Chapter 2

______ 1. Which one of the major triads shown includes the pitch F♯?

X. Y. Z.

______ 2. Which one of the major triads shown includes the pitch A♭?

X. Y. Z.

______ 3. Which one of the triads shown is a major triad?

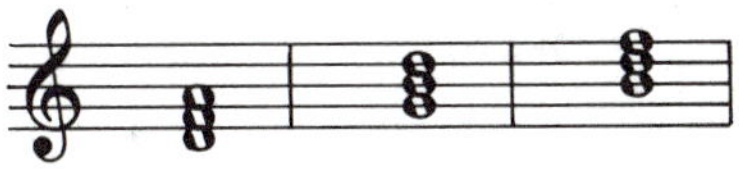

X. Y. Z.

______ 4. Which one of the triads shown is a major triad?

X. Y. Z.

______ 5. Which notehead is a major third above G♯?

X. Y. Z.

______ 6. Which notehead is a minor third below F♯?

X. Y. Z.

______ 7. Which notehead is a perfect fifth below B♭?

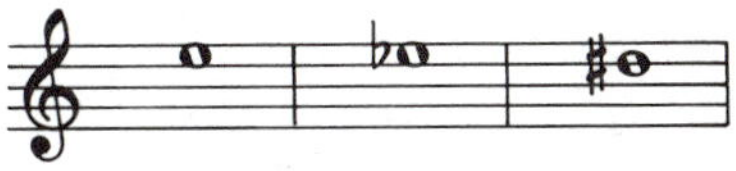

X. Y. Z.

______ 8. Which pitch should be added above the root and third shown to serve as the fifth of a major triad?

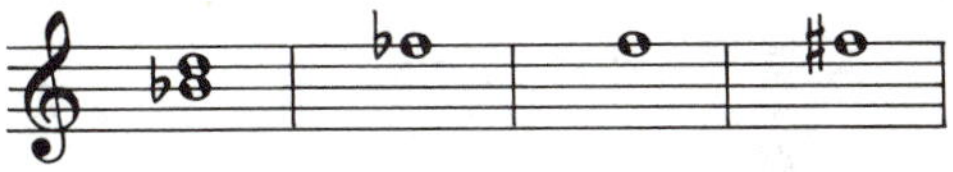

X. Y. Z.

_________ 9. Which pitch should be added between the root and fifth shown to serve as the third of a major triad?

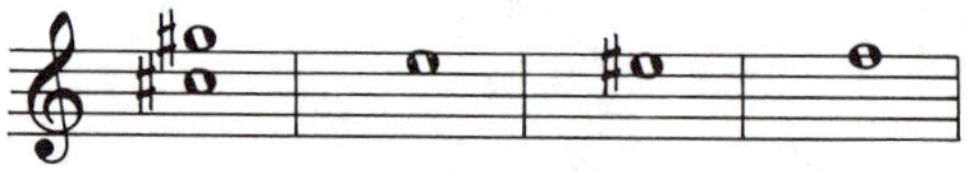

X. Y. Z.

_________ 10. Which pitch should be added below the third and fifth shown to serve as the root of a major triad?

X. Y. Z.

_________ 11. Which pitch is an enharmonic equivalent of the pitch F?

X. E Y. E♯ Z. G♭

_________ 12. Which pitch is an enharmonic equivalent of the pitch B♭?

X. A♯ Y. C♭ Z. B

_________ 13. In $\frac{4}{4}$ meter, how many beats does the following symbol fill?

X. 2 Y. 2½ Z. 3

_________ 14. What kind of note should be inserted at the arrow to complete the measure?

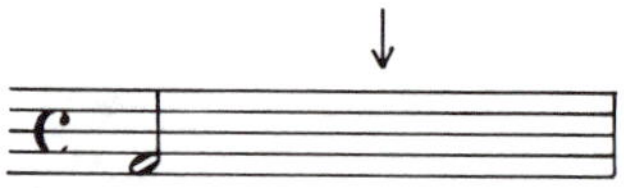

X. Quarter note Y. Half note Z. Dotted half note

_________ 15. What kind of note should be inserted at the arrow to complete the measure?

X. Quarter note Y. Half note Z. Dotted half note

Three pitches will be performed simultaneously. Do they form a major triad?

_________ 16. Y. Yes Z. No

_________ 17. Y. Yes Z. No

Name: ____________________

Instructor: ____________________

Date: ____________________

The three pitches of a major triad will be performed in ascending order. Two of the three pitches will be performed a second time. Indicate which two.

________ 18. X. Root and Third Y. Root and Fifth Z. Third and Fifth

________ 19. X. Root and Third Y. Root and Fifth Z. Third and Fifth

________ 20. Which score shows the correct notation for the rhythm performed?

X. 

Y. 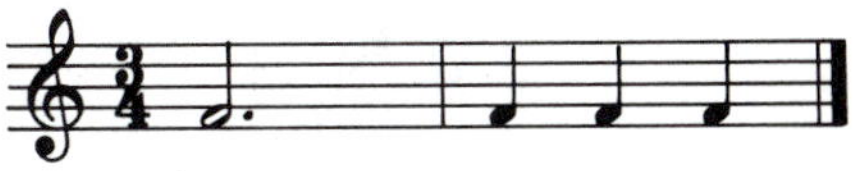

Z. 

3

The Major Mode

TERMS AND CONCEPTS

tonal music	*subdominant*	*dissonant*
tonal center	*scale*	*inversion*
tonic	*scale degree*	*rest*
key	*diatonic*	*whole rest*
modes	*chromatic*	*half rest*
dominant	*whole step*	*quarter rest*
	consonant	

PITCH

Tonal Center, Key, and Mode

Now that we have learned how the twelve pitch classes are named and drawn on the staff, we can begin to explore how they are used in musical contexts. In this chapter we examine three essential facts that will guide our study: (1) only seven of the twelve pitch classes play a central role at any time; (2) six of these seven pitch classes are subordinate to the one called the *tonal center*, or *tonic*, as defined below; and (3) any of the twelve pitch classes may serve as the tonal center and may do so in either of two modes. This chapter demonstrates how C may function as tonic in the major mode. We will apply what we learn in this context to each of the other pitch classes in Chapter 4.

Though our study focuses on the foundations of most classical and popular music, we should remember that in recent decades the principles described in this book have been rejected by some composers. ***Tonal music***—that in which a specific pitch class serves as tonal center—is to some a dead end, a method exhausted through centuries of use. Various alternative ways of organizing musical ideas have been advanced, sometimes in reaction to the principles of tonal music. Nonetheless, tonal music continues to play a significant role in the activities of most musicians, and gaining an understanding of its principles remains an essential part of musical training. tonal music

To say that C serves as the ***tonal center***, or ***tonic***, implies that of all the pitch classes that sound in a composition, C is the most stable, restful, or final-sounding. When C is tonic the composer would likely include several prominent ascents or descents to pitch class C within the melody. If the composition is in C *major* (as defined below), the melody is likely to emphasize the other pitch classes of the major triad rooted on C as well. C, E, and G are the only pitch classes appropriate at the end of a melody in C major. Though the composer may neglect the pitch classes of the major triad rooted on tonic during portions of a melody and may even tonal center tonic move temporarily to another tonal center, the original tonal center will always return. The melody in Example 3-1 demonstrates these procedures.

Example 3-1

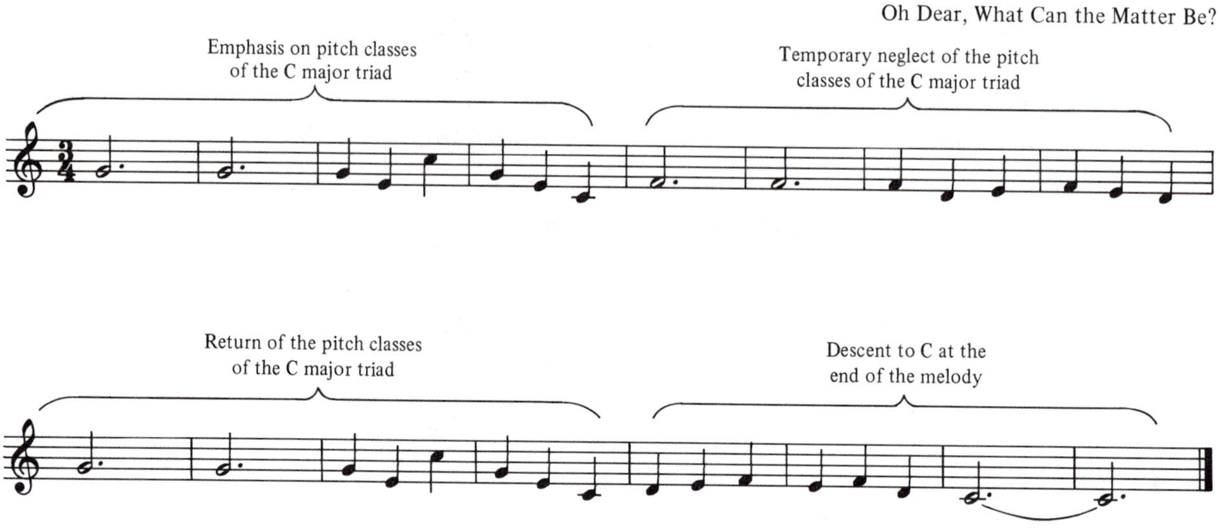

key

A ***key*** is a label applied to a musical composition. It indicates which pitch class serves as the tonic and which six subordinate pitch classes reinforce the tonic through their relationships with one another and with the tonic. When we say that a symphony by Beethoven is in "the key of C major," we imply two things: (1) that pitch class C serves as the tonic; and (2) that six subordinate pitch classes—namely, D, E, F, G, A, and B—reinforce C as tonic.

modes

In tonal music, two different collections of six subordinate pitch classes can be used to reinforce C as tonic. Thus there are two ***modes,*** or manners, in which C may serve as tonic—major and minor. In Chapters 6 and 10 we will examine the minor mode. In the *major* mode, the tonic and the six subordinate pitch classes form major triads rooted not only on the tonic but on two other important pitch classes as well: the ***dominant,*** a perfect fifth above the tonic (in this case, G); and the ***subdominant,*** a perfect fifth below the tonic (in this case, F). Example 3-2 shows that in building major triads on C, G, and F, seven different pitch classes are required.

dominant

subdominant

Example 3-2

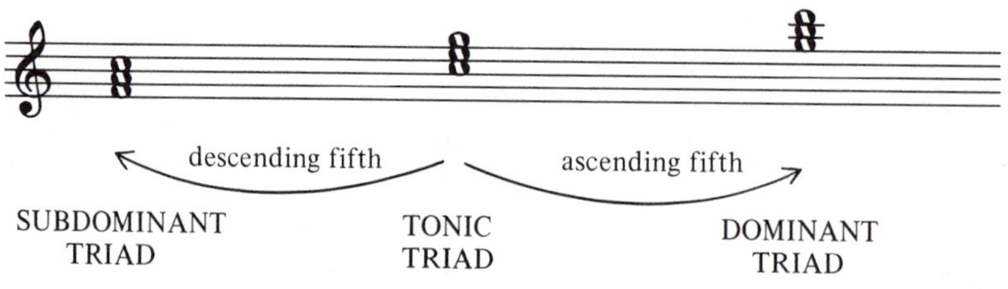

The Major Scale

The seven pitch classes of a key can be arranged in a linear succession called a ***scale***, with the tonic appearing at both its beginning and end. Ascending and descending scales in the key of C major are shown in Example 3-3.

scale

Example 3-3

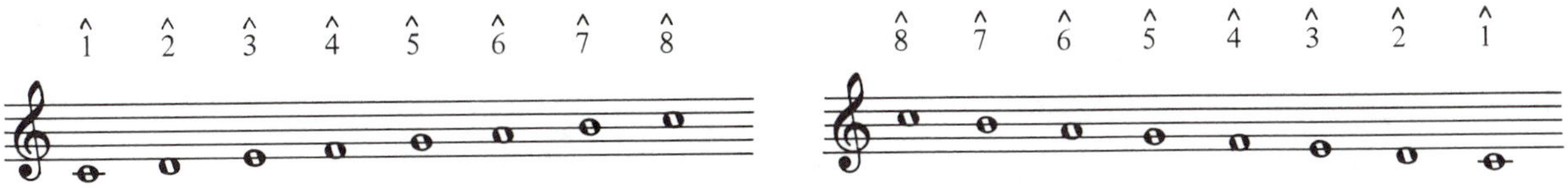

Observe that the position of each pitch within the scale is labeled using an Arabic number topped by a circumflex (ˆ). This number is called the ***scale degree.*** Since $\hat{8}$ is the same pitch class as $\hat{1}$, we confirm that the key of C major employs seven of the twelve pitch classes. We have introduced special names for three of these pitch classes: $\hat{1}$ is the tonic, $\hat{4}$ is the subdominant, and $\hat{5}$ is the dominant.

scale degree

The seven pitch classes that form the scale of a key are classified as ***diatonic.*** The remaining five pitch classes are called ***chromatic.*** In C major, the diatonic pitch classes correspond to the white keys on the keyboard, while the chromatic pitch classes correspond to the black keys. In most musical contexts, the chromatic pitches embellish the diatonic pitches. The chromatic pitches in the melody in the key of C major shown in Example 3-4 are marked with asterisks.

diatonic

chromatic

Example 3-4

While Strolling Through the Park One Day

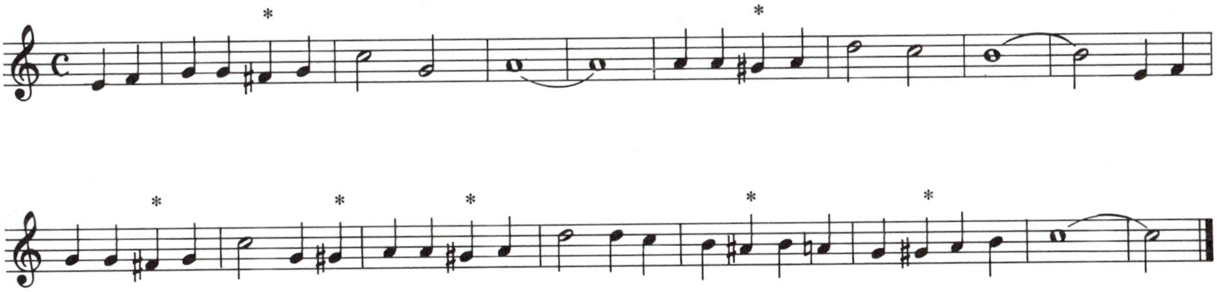

Though it may appear in Example 3-3 that the eight scale degrees are a uniform distance from one another, observe on the keyboard diagram shown in Example 3-5 that this is not the case. Some of the adjacent scale degrees are separated by a half step, while others are separated by *two* half steps. The combination of two half steps is called a ***whole step.***

whole step

Example 3-5

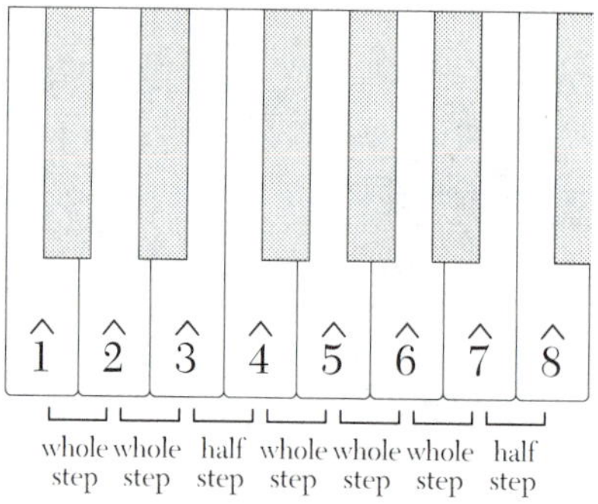

The relationships among the scale degrees give the major mode its distinctive character. Between most adjacent scale degrees, there is a whole step. But between $\hat{3}$ and $\hat{4}$ and between $\hat{7}$ and $\hat{8}$, there is only a half step. Any change in this set of interrelationships would contradict the mode.

Intervals of the Major Scale

Each scale degree forms intervalic relationships not only with the adjacent scale degrees but with all other scale degrees as well. One set of relationships, the intervals created between $\hat{1}$ and the remaining seven scale degrees, is displayed in Example 3-6.

Example 3-6

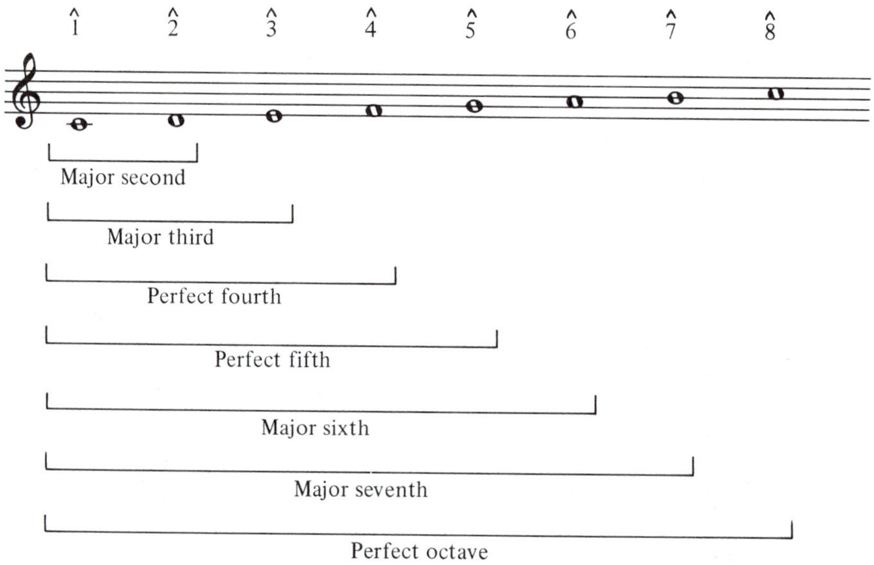

In addition to the major third and perfect fifth—components of the major triad rooted on tonic—there are intervals of size two, six, and seven with major quality, and intervals of size four and eight with perfect quality.

The chart in Example 3-7 shows the number of half steps that separate the two pitches of each of these intervals. Yet it is perhaps more appropriate to consider each interval in terms of its position within the major scale. In Chapter 1 it was convenient to define the perfect fifth as an interval whose two pitches are separated by seven half steps. Now that we know a perfect fifth is formed by $\hat{1}$ and $\hat{5}$ in the major scale, we can ascend the major scale to $\hat{5}$ to find the pitch that forms a perfect fifth above $\hat{1}$. We can think, "Whole step, whole step, half step, whole step," rather than, "Half step, half step, half step, half step, half step, half step, half step," because three whole steps and a half step come between $\hat{1}$ and $\hat{5}$ in the major scale. The rating of each interval as *consonant* or *dissonant*, also included on the chart, will be discussed below.

Example 3-7

Scale Degrees	*Interval Name*	*Size in Half Steps*	*Consonant/ Dissonant*
$\hat{1}$ $\hat{1}$	Perfect unison	0	Consonant
$\hat{1}$ $\hat{2}$	Major second	2	Dissonant
$\hat{1}$ $\hat{3}$	Major third	4	Consonant
$\hat{1}$ $\hat{4}$	Perfect fourth	5	Dissonant
$\hat{1}$ $\hat{5}$	Perfect fifth	7	Consonant
$\hat{1}$ $\hat{6}$	Major sixth	9	Consonant
$\hat{1}$ $\hat{7}$	Major seventh	11	Dissonant
$\hat{1}$ $\hat{8}$	Perfect octave	12	Consonant

Consonance and Dissonance

consonant
dissonant

Two pitches played together are ***consonant*** if they sound stable or restful and ***dissonant*** if they sound unstable or restless, evoking a sense of pressing forward. The major third, perfect fifth, major sixth, and perfect octave are consonant, while the major second, perfect fourth, and major seventh are dissonant. The perfect unison is, of course, a consonant interval as well.

When the two pitches of an interval are played or sung successively rather than simultaneously, the effect of dissonance is lessened considerably. When one singer ascends a major second melodically, the effect is relatively stable. But when two singers perform the two pitches of a major second at the same time, the effect is unstable.

The most surprising of the classifications listed in Example 3-7 for intervals created between $\hat{1}$ and the other scale degrees is that the perfect fourth functions as a dissonance. There seems to be a contradiction between the label "perfect," which describes very stable intervals such as the unison and the octave, and the label "dissonant," which implies instability. To understand why composers have treated the fourth as a dissonance, examine the first five overtones of C, shown in Example 3-8a. Observe that both E and G are prominent overtones of C. When F—a half step above E and a whole step below G—appears above C, it clashes against these overtones. As an experiment, play the pitches in Example 3-8b, substituting F for E. You should sense an instability that is resolved only when E is restored.

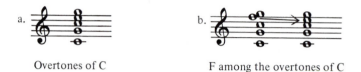

Example 3-8

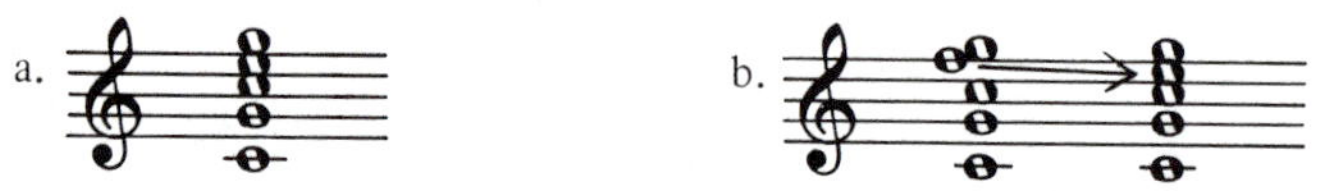

Overtones of C   F among the overtones of C

In later chapters, when we explore combinations of three or more notes in detail, we shall see how a fourth may function as a consonance in some contexts. Even among the overtones shown in Example 3-8a, there is a consonant fourth (from G up to C). This fourth is a by-product of the fifth C to G and the octave C to C, shown in Example 3-9a. As long as C—*not* G—is the lowest pitch, there is no tendency for the C of this fourth to move to B or to D. But if G were the lowest pitch, the overtones of G, which include B and D (but not C) would come into play. In that context the C would function as a dissonant fourth and resolve, most likely, to B, as shown in Example 3-9b.

Example 3-9

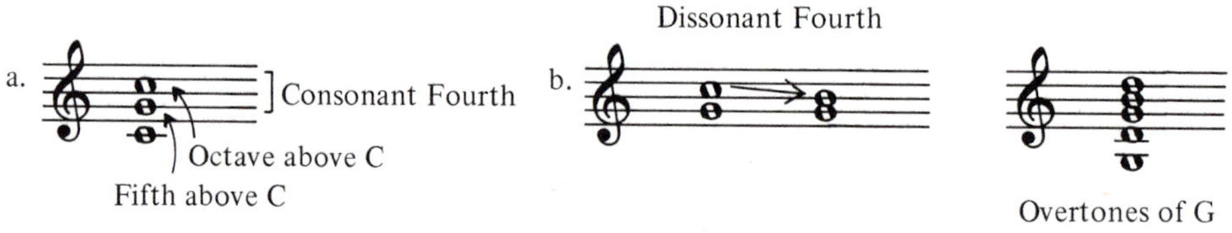

Composers use dissonant intervals in many contexts, but when they do so they pay attention to the tendencies for motion or resolution that are implied. Play the interval progressions in Example 3-10 at the keyboard. Observe the difference between consonance and dissonance and how the dissonant intervals may be said to "resolve" to consonances. The dissonances are marked with asterisks. (Observe that measure 2 of Example 3-10a contains the interval of a second resolving to a third. The downward stem touches only the C. The D that sounds against C is a whole note and should continue to sound against the B in the second half of the measure.)

Example 3-10

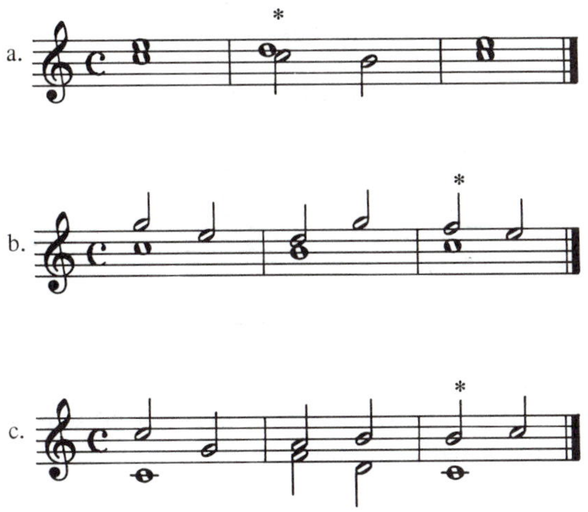

Interval Inversion

Just as intervals can be formed between $\hat{1}$ and each of the other scale degrees, other intervals can be formed between each scale degree and $\hat{8}$. Instead of learning these intervals independently, we can explore their relationships with the intervals already introduced. For example, compare $\hat{1}$–$\hat{2}$ and $\hat{2}$–$\hat{8}$, as shown in Example 3-11.

Example 3-11

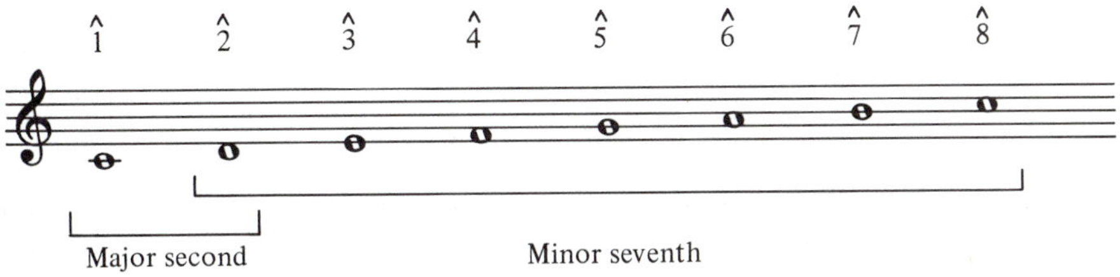

$\hat{1}$–$\hat{2}$ and $\hat{2}$–$\hat{8}$ combine to form an octave. $\hat{1}$–$\hat{2}$ (two half steps) forms a major second, while $\hat{2}$–$\hat{8}$ (ten half steps—one half step smaller than the major seventh) forms a *minor* seventh. (All intervals of minor quality are one half step smaller than major intervals of the same size.) Because an octave contains twelve half steps and the major second contains two half steps, it was not necessary to count the number of half steps in the minor seventh. It is twelve minus two, or ten. Half steps, unlike interval sizes, may be added or subtracted.

inversion

Any two intervals that combine to form an octave are called ***inversions*** of one another. The sum of their interval sizes is always nine, one larger than the size of the octave. (Similarly, as we have seen, combining two thirds yields a fifth even though the sum of their interval sizes is one larger, six.) The inversion of an interval of major quality is always minor; the inversion of an interval of minor quality is always major.

Now compare $\hat{1}$–$\hat{5}$ and $\hat{5}$–$\hat{8}$, shown in Example 3-12. $\hat{1}$–$\hat{5}$ and $\hat{5}$–$\hat{8}$ combine to form an octave. They are inversions of one another. $\hat{1}$–$\hat{5}$ (seven half steps) forms a perfect fifth, while $\hat{5}$–$\hat{8}$ (five half steps) forms a perfect fourth. We observe that the inversion of an interval of perfect quality is also perfect. As is always the case with inversions, the sum of their interval sizes is nine.

Example 3-12

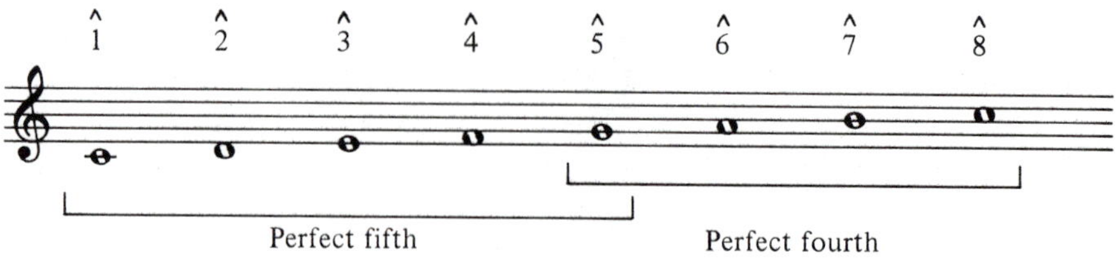

The chart in Example 3-13 shows all intervals that can be formed using $\hat{1}$ or $\hat{8}$. Each interval is paired with its inversion.

Example 3-13

Scale Degrees	*Interval Name*	*Size in Half Steps*	*Consonant/ Dissonant*
$\hat{1}$ $\hat{1}$	Perfect unison	0	Consonant
$\hat{1}$ $\hat{8}$	Perfect octave	12	Consonant
$\hat{1}$ $\hat{2}$	Major second	2	Dissonant
$\hat{2}$ $\hat{8}$	Minor seventh	10	Dissonant
$\hat{1}$ $\hat{3}$	Major third	4	Consonant
$\hat{3}$ $\hat{8}$	Minor sixth	8	Consonant
$\hat{1}$ $\hat{4}$	Perfect fourth	5	Dissonant
$\hat{4}$ $\hat{8}$	Perfect fifth	7	Consonant
$\hat{1}$ $\hat{5}$	Perfect fifth	7	Consonant
$\hat{5}$ $\hat{8}$	Perfect fourth	5	Dissonant
$\hat{1}$ $\hat{6}$	Major sixth	9	Consonant
$\hat{6}$ $\hat{8}$	Minor third	3	Consonant
$\hat{1}$ $\hat{7}$	Major seventh	11	Dissonant
$\hat{7}$ $\hat{8}$	Minor second	1	Dissonant
$\hat{1}$ $\hat{8}$	Perfect octave	12	Consonant
$\hat{8}$ $\hat{8}$	Perfect unison	0	Consonant

Pitch exercises for Chapter 3 are on pages 85–90.

RHYTHM

Rests

Rhythmic notation reflects the precision of arithmetic. The time values of the symbols placed within a measure always add up to what the time signature specifies. For this reason, those moments when a performer is silent are notated with the same care that is devoted to the notation of pitches. Some of the symbols, called ***rests***, that designate periods of silence are shown in Example 3-14.

rest

Example 3-14

Rest Symbol	*Rest Name*	*Number of Beats* (𝄽 = 1 beat)
𝄻	***Whole rest***	An entire measure
𝄼	***Half rest***	2 beats
𝄽	***Quarter rest***	1 beat

whole rest

half rest

quarter rest

Only the whole rest is centered horizontally within a measure. All other rests appear in the segment of the measure that corresponds to the appropriate beat or beats. In Example 3-15, observe that the whole rest hangs from the fourth line, the half rest sits on the third line, and the quarter rest extends vertically through most of the staff.

Example 3-15

Conventions of Rest Notation

Several conventions regarding rest notation deserve special mention. First, the whole rest is used for an entire measure of silence, even when the meter is $\frac{2}{4}$, $\frac{3}{4}$, or almost any of the other meters we shall study later (Ex. 3-16).

Example 3-16

CORRECT:

INCORRECT:

Second, a half rest will never span beats 2 and 3 of a measure in $\frac{4}{4}$ meter, nor will it ever appear in $\frac{3}{4}$ meter. This rule promotes accuracy in reading rhythmic notation by allowing the strong third beat in $\frac{4}{4}$ meter and each of the three beats in $\frac{3}{4}$ meter to be notated with a rest regardless of the rhythmic context (Ex. 3-17). (A half note, in contrast, may span across the midpoint of a $\frac{4}{4}$ measure or two beats of a $\frac{3}{4}$ measure.)

Example 3-17

CORRECT:

INCORRECT:

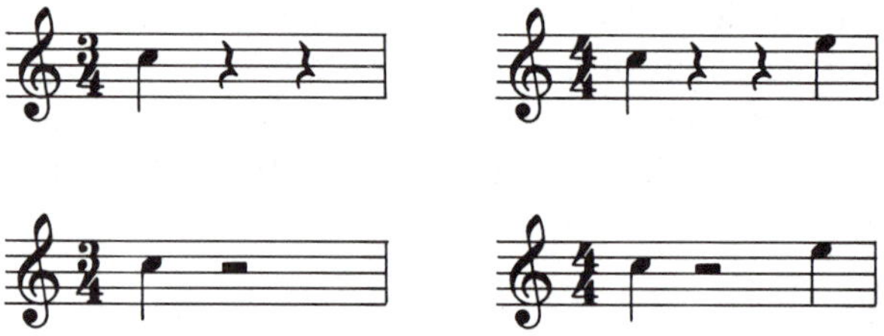

Third, a dotted half rest is not used in either $\frac{3}{4}$ or $\frac{4}{4}$ meter. In $\frac{3}{4}$ meter, the whole rest would be used instead, because silence fills the entire measure. In $\frac{4}{4}$ meter, a quarter and half rest are employed, in the order that allows the half rest to correspond to the first or second half of the measure (Ex. 3-18).

Example 3-18

CORRECT:

INCORRECT:

Rhythm exercises for Chapter 3 are on pages 91–93.

LABORATORY

L3-1.a. Perform each of the following triads at the keyboard using your right hand.

1.

2.

3.

4.

5.

b. Perform each of the following melodies at the keyboard using your right hand. Recommended fingerings are included.

Long, Long Ago

1.

Oh Dear, What Can the Matter Be?

2.

Twinkle, Twinkle Little Star

3.
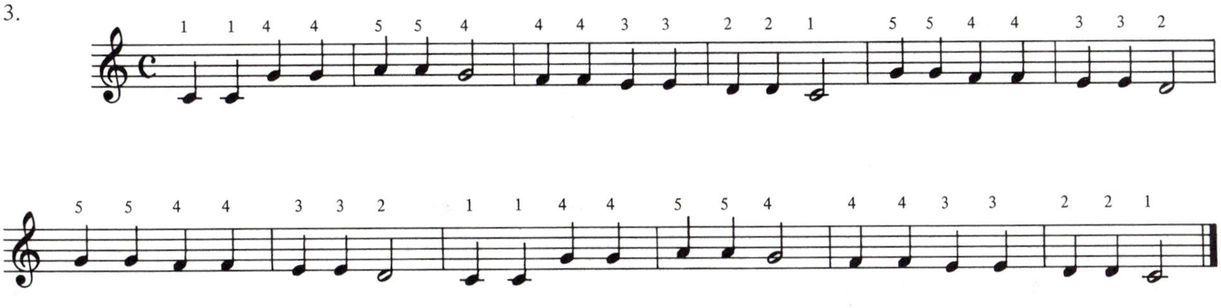

c. Perform each of the following compositions at the keyboard using your right hand. Recommended fingerings are included. Pay particular attention to the dissonances, which are marked with asterisks.

1.

2.

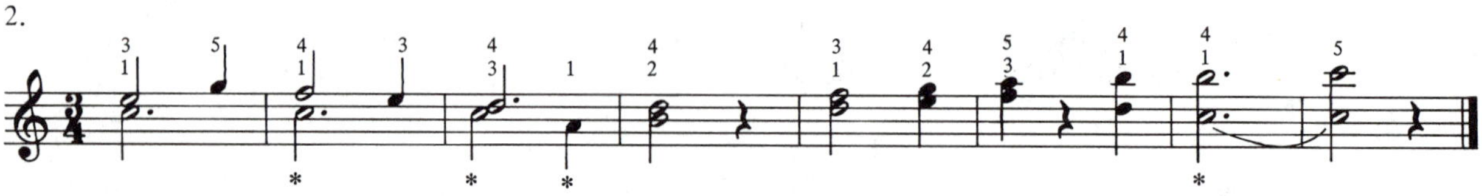

L3-2. Mark the lowest and highest notes you can sing on the diagram below. Do not let your fingers extend beyond these boundaries.

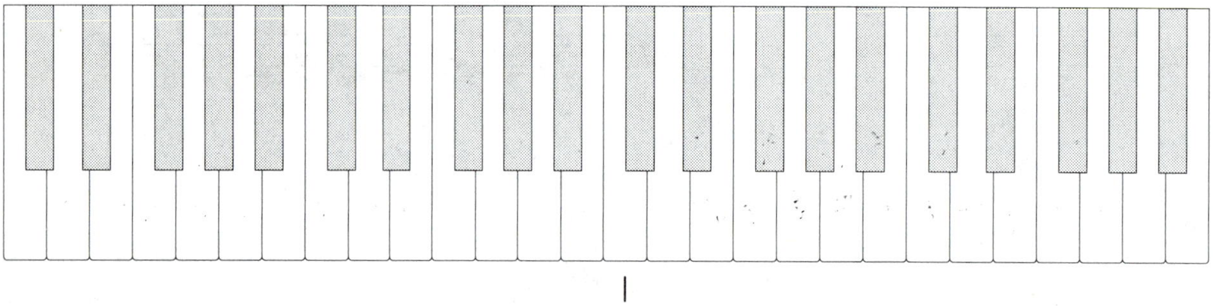

a. Practice the following exercise until you have mastered it.

- Position two fingers on top of keys that are a perfect fifth apart, but do not strike them.
- Strike the lower key.
- Sing that pitch.
- Sing the pitch a perfect fifth higher.
- Strike the higher key and confirm that it is what you have sung.

b. Once the above exercise is going well, add the following steps.

- Position two fingers on top of keys that are a perfect fifth apart, but do not strike them.
- Strike the upper key.
- Sing that pitch.
- Sing the pitch a perfect fifth lower.
- Strike the lower key and confirm that it is what you have sung.

L3-3. Practice the following melodies at the keyboard, simultaneously singing and playing each pitch. Sing the scale-degree numbers that correspond to the pitches. (Because the number "seven" contains two syllables, you may sing "sev" instead.) Men should perform these melodies an octave lower than they are written.

a.

b.

c.

d.

e.

L3-4. The following compositions are for voice (upper staff) and keyboard (lower staff). Sing the scale-degree numbers that correspond to the pitches. At first you may play the vocal part on the keyboard while you sing, in order to solidify your performance. Eventually, however, observe the rests in the accompanying part during your vocal measures. The range of the compositions should be appropriate for most women's voices. Men should perform both the keyboard and vocal parts an octave lower.

a.

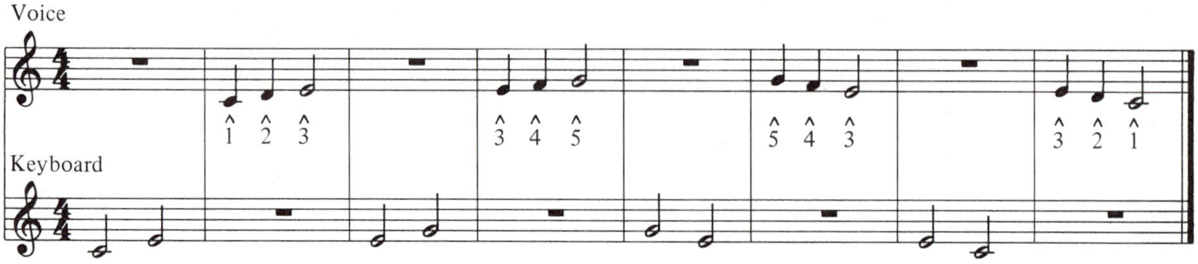

b.

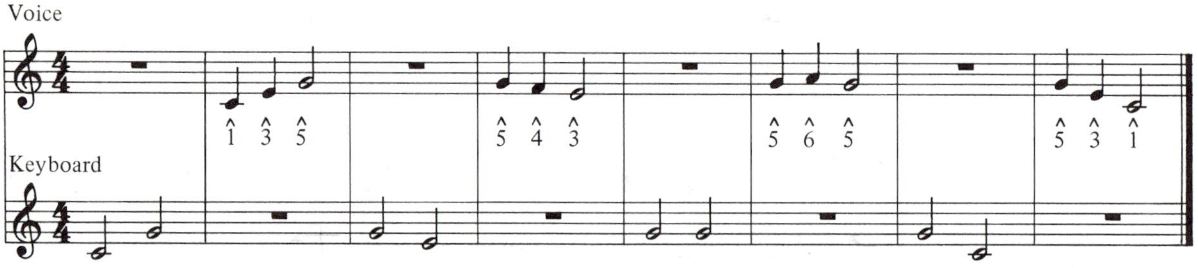

L3-5. The following compositions are for two voices. Sing the scale-degree numbers that correspond to the pitches. Men should perform these melodies an octave lower than they are written.

a.

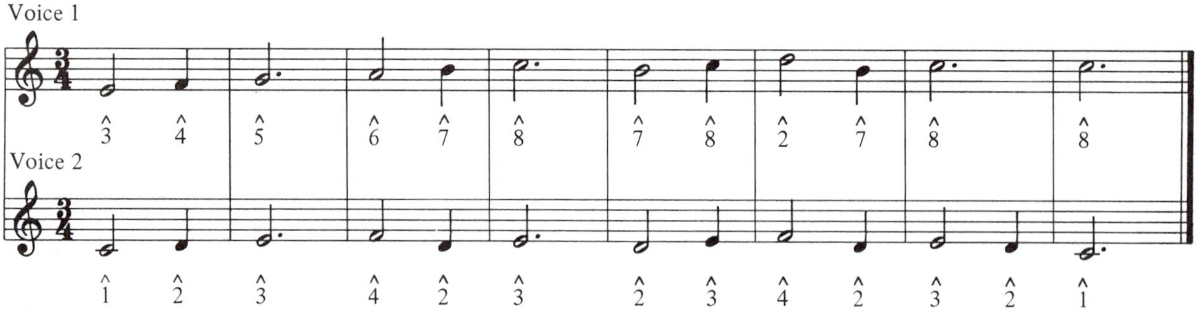

b.

L3-6. Write in the beat numbers below the notated rhythms. Then perform each by clapping the rhythm or playing the pitch F at the keyboard while pronouncing the syllables for the beats aloud. Practice until you can perform each exercise at a tempo of about ♩ = 60.

a.

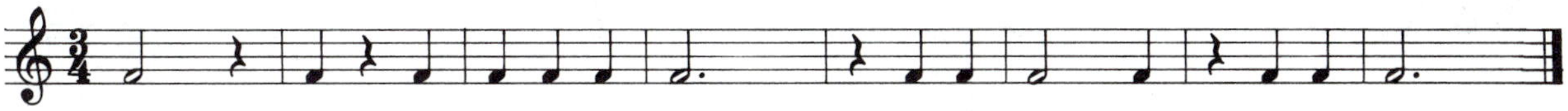

b.

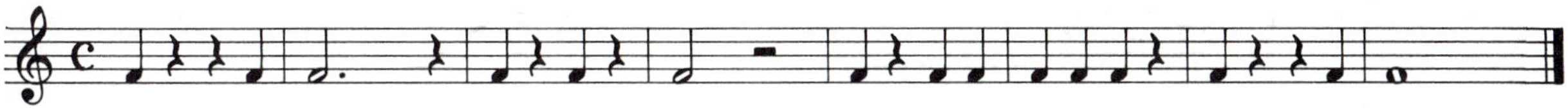

c.

d.

e.

L3-7. Write in the beat numbers below the notated rhythms. Then perform them by dividing the class into two groups, with each group clapping one part while saying the beat numbers aloud. Alternatively, individual students may perform both parts simultaneously at the keyboard, saying the beat numbers aloud while the index finger of the right hand strikes C and the index finger of the left hand strikes F, as notated. Observe that when two rhythmic lines share the same staff and a rest pertains to only one of them, the rest is written near the top or near the bottom of the staff, rather than in its center. If the rest applies to both parts, it is written in its normal position.

a.

b.

c.

d.

e.

L3-8. This exercise requires that a student or the instructor serve as the performer at a keyboard.

a. The performer plays a scale, either ascending or descending and beginning on the pitch C. Indicate whether the scale is or is not a C major scale. The performer's choices of scales for performance are as follows:

1. C D E F G A B C (the C major scale)
2. C D E♭ F G A B C
3. C D E F G A♭ B♭ C
4. C D E F♯ G A B C

b. The performer plays two pitches in either ascending or descending order, and then plays them together. Indicate whether the interval performed is or is not a perfect fifth.

c. The performer places three fingers above keys that sound a major triad and performs them in descending order. Then the performer plays one of the following:

Third–Root
Fifth–Root
Fifth–Third

Indicate which of the three choices is performed.

Audio exercises for Chapter 3 are on pages 94–96.

Name: ______________________

Instructor: ______________________

Date: ______________________

EXERCISES

Pitch Exercises

P3-1. For each of the following patterns of ascending or descending whole and half steps, indicate the scale degrees in the key of C major where the succession occurs. In some cases several answers must be supplied, whereas in others there may be no succession of scale degrees that fits the pattern. Remember that the scale extends beyond a single octave on the keyboard. The circular diagram may be useful for recognizing patterns in which the first scale degree is an internal element.

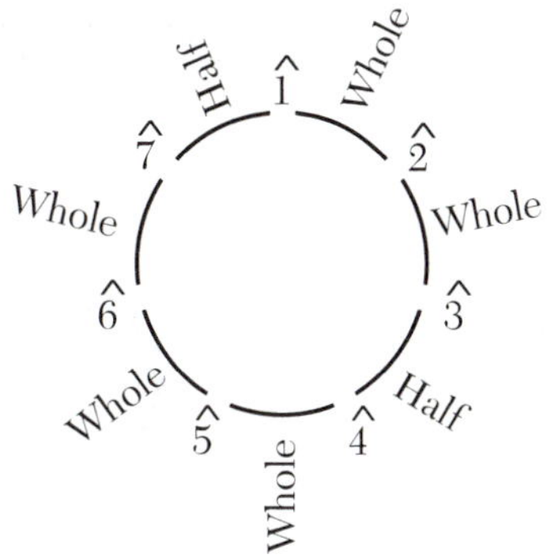

SAMPLE: Half-Whole (Ascending)
SOLUTION: $\hat{3}$–$\hat{4}$–$\hat{5}$; $\hat{7}$–$\hat{1}$–$\hat{2}$

a. Whole-Whole-Half (Ascending)

b. Whole-Half (Ascending)

c. Whole-Whole-Whole (Descending)

d. Half-Whole-Half (Ascending)

e. Whole-Half-Whole (Descending)

f. Half-Whole-Whole (Ascending)

g. Whole-Whole-Whole-Half (Descending)

h. Whole-Half-Half (Descending)

i. Whole-Half-Whole-Whole (Ascending)

j. Half-Whole-Whole-Half (Descending)

k. Whole-Whole-Half-Whole (Ascending)

l. Whole-Half-Whole-Whole-Whole (Ascending)

P3-2. Intervals of C major are presented in staff notation. Above each pitch, indicate its scale degree, using the numbers $\hat{1}$ through $\hat{8}$. Below, indicate the interval quality and size.

a.

b.

c.

d.
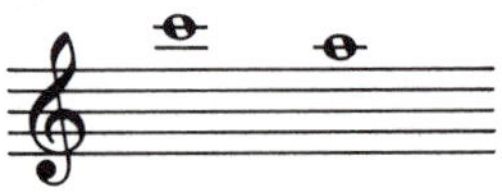

e.

f.

g.

h.

i.

j.
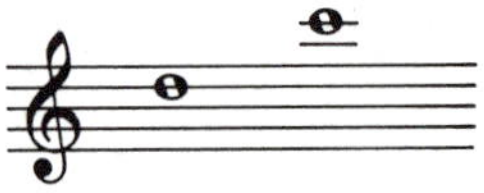
k.

l.

m.
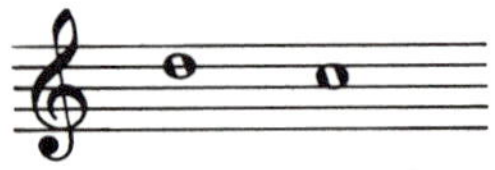
n.
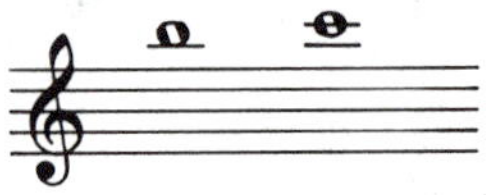
o.

p.

q.

r.

s.

t.

u.

v.

w.
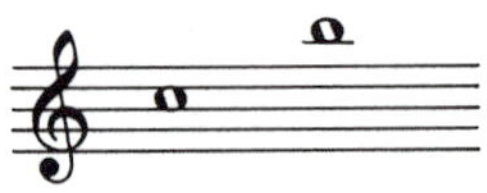
x.
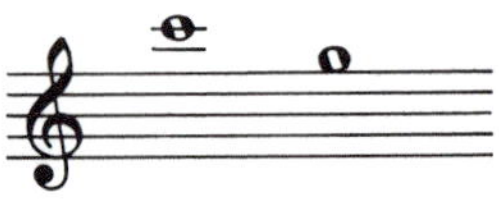

Name: ____________________
Instructor: ____________________
Date: ____________________

P3-3. Fill in the following diagram completely for the key of C major.

	Scale Degrees	*Interval Name*	*Size in Half Steps*	*Consonant/ Dissonant*
a.	$\hat{1} - \hat{3}$	____________	___	____________
b.	___ $- \hat{8}$	Perfect fifth	___	____________
c.	$\hat{1} - \hat{8}$	____________	___	____________
d.	$\hat{2} - \hat{8}$	____________	___	____________
e.	$\hat{1} -$ ___	Perfect fourth	___	____________
f.	$\hat{4} - \hat{8}$	____________	___	____________
g.	$\hat{1} -$ ___	____________	11	____________
h.	___ $- \hat{8}$	Minor second	___	____________
i.	$\hat{1} - \hat{6}$	____________	___	____________
j.	___ $- \hat{8}$	Minor third	___	____________
k.	$\hat{1} -$ ___	____________	4	____________
l.	___ $- \hat{8}$	____________	1	____________
m.	$\hat{1} -$ ___	Major sixth	___	____________
n.	___ $- \hat{8}$	____________	8	____________
o.	$\hat{1} - \hat{7}$	____________	___	____________
p.	___ $- \hat{8}$	____________	5	____________
q.	$\hat{1} -$ ___	Perfect unison	___	____________
r.	$\hat{5} - \hat{8}$	____________	___	____________
s.	$\hat{1} -$ ___	____________	7	____________

	Scale Degrees	*Interval Name*	*Size in Half Steps*	*Consonant/ Dissonant*
t.	___ – $\hat{8}$	Minor seventh	___	___
u.	$\hat{1}$ – ___	___	12	___
v.	___ – $\hat{8}$	___	3	___
w.	$\hat{1}$ – ___	Major second	___	___
x.	___ – $\hat{8}$	___	0	___
y.	$\hat{1}$ – $\hat{2}$	___	___	___
z.	___ – $\hat{8}$	Minor sixth	___	___
aa.	$\hat{1}$ – $\hat{4}$	___	___	___
bb.	$\hat{8}$ – $\hat{8}$	___	___	___
cc.	$\hat{1}$ – ___	Major seventh	___	___
dd.	$\hat{3}$ – $\hat{8}$	___	___	___
ee.	$\hat{1}$ – ___	___	9	___
ff.	___ – $\hat{8}$	Perfect unison	___	___
gg.	$\hat{1}$ – $\hat{5}$	___	___	___
hh.	___ – $\hat{8}$	Perfect fourth	___	___
ii.	$\hat{1}$ – ___	___	2	___
jj.	___ – $\hat{8}$	___	10	___
kk.	$\hat{1}$ – ___	Perfect octave	___	___
ll.	$\hat{7}$ – $\hat{8}$	___	___	___
mm.	$\hat{1}$ – $\hat{1}$	___	___	___
nn.	$\hat{6}$ – $\hat{8}$	___	___	___
oo.	$\hat{1}$ – ___	___	5	___

Name: ______________________
Instructor: ______________________
Date: ______________________

R3-3. Form a melody using the fragments provided. Only one ordering of these fragments results in measures that contain the correct number of beats.

a.

b.

R3-4. Notate the melodies indicated by the positioning of the pitch names in relation to the counting syllables. Use only unisons, seconds, thirds, and fourths as melodic intervals. Do not add rests.

a.

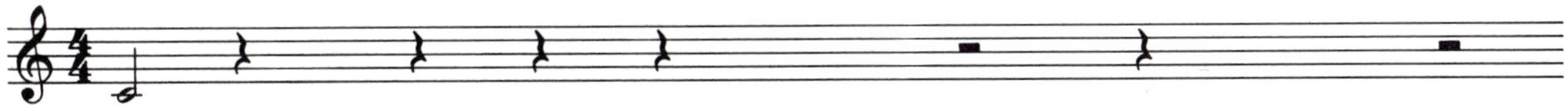

C D F E A G F E D E D C

1 2 3 4 1 2 3 4 1 2 3 4 1 2 3 4 1 2 3 4 1 2 3 4

b.

C C E A G A B C B C

1 2 1 2 1 2 1 2 1 2 1 2 1 2 1 2

c.

C D E G F E A G F D C C

1 2 3 1 2 3 1 2 3 1 2 3 1 2 3 1 2 3 1 2 3 1 2 3

Audio Exercises

A3-1. A succession of eight pitches, ascending or descending and beginning on C, will be performed. Circle "Yes" if these notes form a C major scale, "No" if they do not.

a. Yes	No	f. Yes	No
b. Yes	No	g. Yes	No
c. Yes	No	h. Yes	No
d. Yes	No	i. Yes	No
e. Yes	No	j. Yes	No

A3-2. Ten intervals will be performed, first as two successive pitches, then as two simultaneous pitches. Circle "Yes" if the interval is a perfect fifth, "No" if it is not.

a. Yes	No	f. Yes	No
b. Yes	No	g. Yes	No
c. Yes	No	h. Yes	No
d. Yes	No	i. Yes	No
e. Yes	No	j. Yes	No

A3-3. The three pitches of a major triad will be performed in descending order. Two of the three pitches will be performed a second time. Indicate which two.

a. Third–Root	Fifth–Root	Fifth–Third
b. Third–Root	Fifth–Root	Fifth–Third
c. Third–Root	Fifth–Root	Fifth–Third
d. Third–Root	Fifth–Root	Fifth–Third
e. Third–Root	Fifth–Root	Fifth–Third
f. Third–Root	Fifth–Root	Fifth–Third
g. Third–Root	Fifth–Root	Fifth–Third
h. Third–Root	Fifth–Root	Fifth–Third
i. Third–Root	Fifth–Root	Fifth–Third
j. Third–Root	Fifth–Root	Fifth–Third

Name: ______________________

Instructor: ______________________

Date: ______________________

A3-4. Four melodies that begin on the pitch C will be performed. In each case circle the score that shows the correct pitch notation.

a.

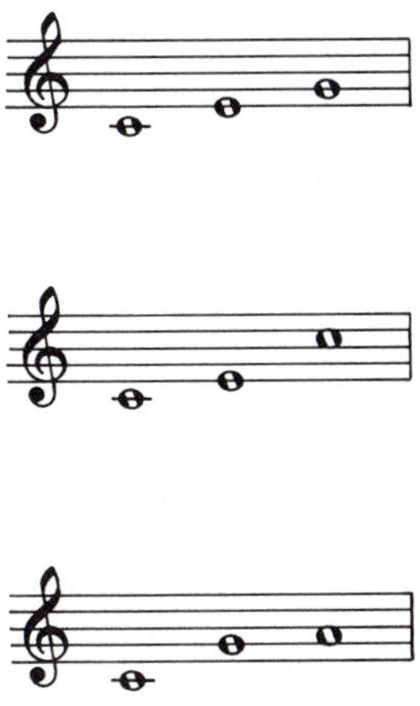

b.

c.

d.

A3-5. Four rhythms will be performed. In each case circle the score that shows the correct notation.

a.

b.

c.

d.

Name: ____________________
Instructor: ____________________
Date: ____________________

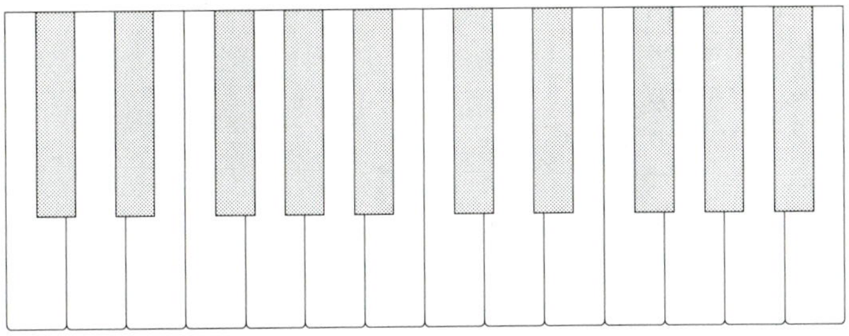

Mastery Test, Chapter 3

________ 1. Which interval contains exactly five half steps?
X. Major Third Y. Major Fourth Z. Perfect Fourth

________ 2. Exactly how many half steps are there in a Major Seventh?
X. Seven Y. Ten Z. Eleven

________ 3. Which interval is the inversion of a Major Third?
X. Minor Sixth Y. Major Sixth Z. Minor Third

________ 4. Which interval is the inversion of a Perfect Fifth?
X. Major Third Y. Perfect Fourth Z. Minor Fifth

________ 5. Is the interval shown consonant or dissonant?
Y. Consonant Z. Dissonant

________ 6. Is the interval shown consonant or dissonant?
Y. Consonant Z. Dissonant

________ 7. In the key of C major, what is the name of the triad whose root is F?
X. Subdominant Triad
Y. Tonic Triad
Z. Dominant Triad

________ 8. In the key of C major, what is the name of the triad whose root is G?
X. Subdominant Triad
Y. Tonic Triad
Z. Dominant Triad

_______ 9. In the C major scale, between which scale degree does one find exactly one half step?
X. Between $\hat{2}$ and $\hat{3}$ and between $\hat{7}$ and $\hat{8}$
Y. Between $\hat{3}$ and $\hat{4}$ and between $\hat{6}$ and $\hat{7}$
Z. Between $\hat{3}$ and $\hat{4}$ and between $\hat{7}$ and $\hat{8}$

_______ 10. Which group of *ascending* pitches in the C major scale follows the pattern Half Step, Whole Step?
X. B C D Y. D E F Z. F G A

_______ 11. Which group of *descending* pitches in the C major scale follows the pattern Whole Step, Whole Step?
X. G F E Y. E D C Z. C B A

_______ 12. How many different pitch classes are used in the C major scale?
X. Seven Y. Eight Z. Nine

_______ 13. In $\frac{4}{4}$ meter, how many beats does the following symbol fill?
X. 2 Y. 3 Z. 4

_______ 14. What kind of rest should be inserted at the arrow to complete the measure?
X. Quarter rest Y. Half rest Z. Whole rest

_______ 15. What kind of rest should be inserted at the arrow to complete the measure?
X. Quarter rest Y. Half rest Z. Whole rest

_______ 16. A succession of eight descending pitches beginning on C will be performed. Do they form a C major scale?
Y. Yes Z. No

_______ 17. An interval will be performed, first as two successive pitches, then as two simultaneous pitches. Is the interval a perfect fifth?
Y. Yes Z. No

Name: ______________________
Instructor: ______________________
Date: ______________________

________ 18. The three pitches of a major triad will be performed in descending order. Two of the three pitches will be performed a second time. Indicate which two.

X. Third and Root
Y. Fifth and Root
Z. Fifth and Third

________ 19. A melody that begins with the pitch C will be performed. Which score shows the correct pitch notation?

X. 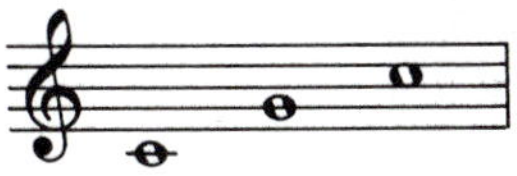

Y. 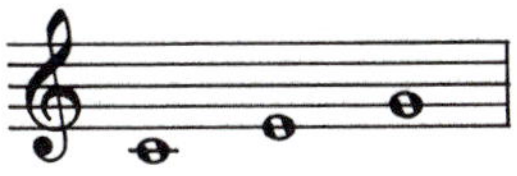

Z. 

________ 20. Which score shows the correct notation for the rhythm performed?

X. 

Y. 

Z. 

4

Key Signatures

Terms and Concepts

key signature
eighth note
beam
flag
dotted quarter note
eighth rest
circle of fifths

PITCH

Any Pitch Class as Tonic

Any melody in the major mode could be notated in the key of C major. Yet if C major were our only option, we might tire of the uniformity that would result. Or perhaps the highest or lowest pitches of a melody, when written in C major, would fall outside the range of the instrument or voice that is to perform it. Moreover, composers have long understood that a melody can have greater appeal if presented in different keys during the course of a composition. For these various reasons, our music system allows a melody to be notated with any of the twelve pitch classes serving as the tonic.

Because the tonal center may change, either within a composition or between compositions, the pitch classes of music must assume a variety of roles. Pitch class C, which functions as $\hat{1}$ in the key of C, plays six other diatonic roles in major keys. It serves as $\hat{2}$ when the tonic is B♭, as $\hat{3}$ when the tonic is A♭, as $\hat{4}$ when the tonic is G, as $\hat{5}$ when the tonic is F, as $\hat{6}$ when the tonic is E♭, and as $\hat{7}$ when the tonic is D♭. Observe in Example 4-1 that the interval formed between the tonic pitch ($\hat{1}$) and C is the same as was formed by the equivalent scale degrees in C major. (Compare with Ex. 3-6.)

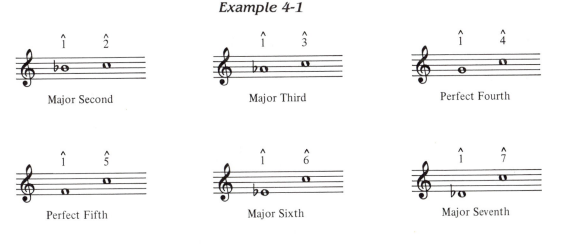

Example 4-1

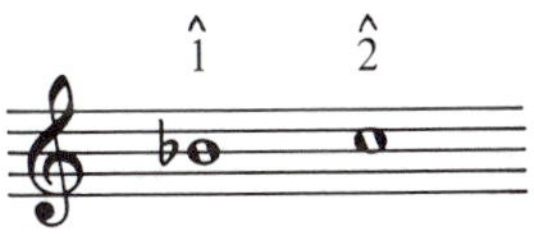

Major Second

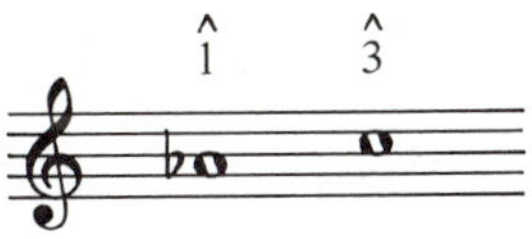

Major Third

Perfect Fourth

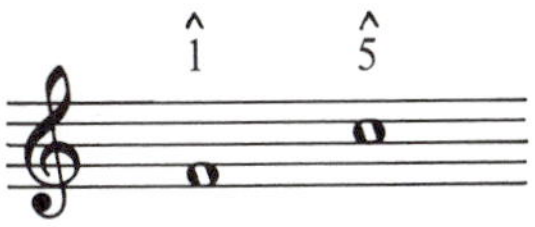

Perfect Fifth

Major Sixth

Major Seventh

We explored the key of C major first because its diatonic pitch classes coincide exactly with the white keys of the piano. The pattern Whole-Whole-Half-Whole-Whole-Whole-Half occurs to the right of every C without the use of accidentals. No other major key possesses this property.

We *could* take each of the eleven remaining pitch classes in turn and apply the characteristic pattern of whole and half steps to form major scales. For example, if D♭ is chosen as $\hat{1}$, then E♭ (a whole step higher) is $\hat{2}$, F (a whole step higher) is $\hat{3}$, G♭ (a half step higher) is $\hat{4}$, and so on. Proceeding in this way we might eventually succeed in forming all the major keys, but it would be difficult to remember how many and which sharps or flats apply to each key. Fortunately, there is an arrangement of the keys that is much easier to learn and remember. It will guide our discussion below.

The Sharp Keys and Their Signatures

Keys whose tonics are separated by the interval of a perfect fifth have six diatonic pitch classes in common. For example, compare C major and G major. If the pattern of whole and half steps that appears in the C major scale is applied with G as tonic, one black key, F♯, must be used. The six remaining pitch classes (A, B, C, D, E, and G) are shared by both scales (Ex. 4-2).

Example 4-2

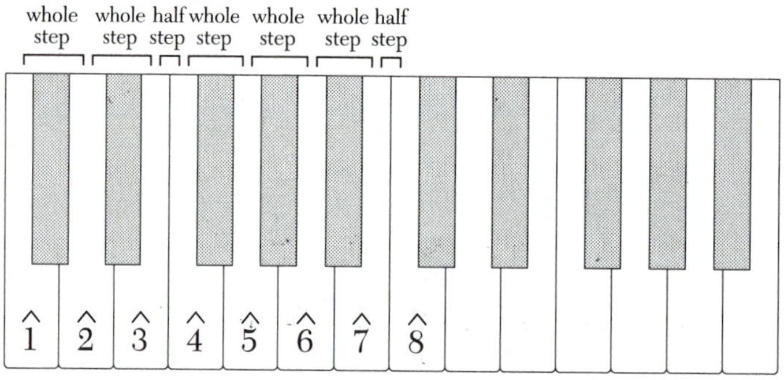

C Major

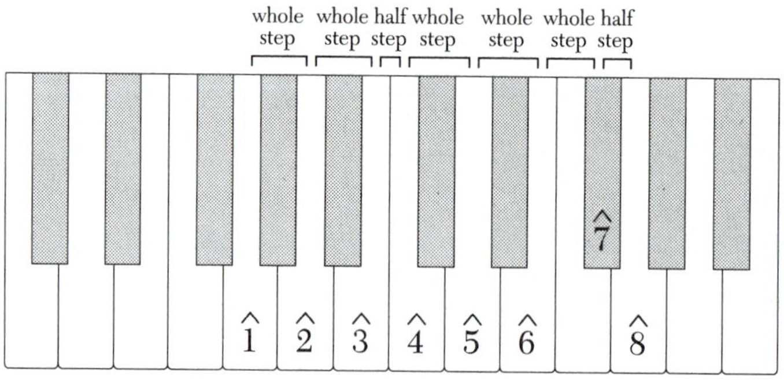

G Major

The pitch F♯ should never be spelled as G♭ in the key of G, because the interval from $\hat{7}$ to $\hat{8}$ is always a minor second (as is F♯ to G), not a type of unison (as is G♭ to G).

The sharp sign *could* be positioned beside the F notehead each time the pitch F♯ occurs in G major, as in Example 4-3. Almost every F notehead that might appear in G major will require a sharp. In some keys, all seven diatonic pitch classes will require an accidental! To avoid a clutter of accidentals on the staff, we manage this aspect of music notation by using a ***key signature***, a symbol that instructs performers to apply sharps or flats automatically to noteheads on specific lines and spaces even though no accidentals actually appear beside these noteheads.

key signature

Example 4-3

All Through the Night

A key signature is an array of sharps or flats. When individual sharps or flats are added within a measure, they pertain only to noteheads written on that line or space. The sharps and flats of the key signature, in contrast, pertain to all noteheads of that pitch class written anywhere on the staff or using ledger lines. Observe that the key signature is placed just to the right of the clef and to the left of the time signature in the renotated melody, Example 4-4. In this case the key signature consists of a sharp sign on the fifth line of the staff. It implies that *all* F's (regardless of whether they are positioned in the first space, on the fifth line, or using ledger lines) are to be read and performed as F♯'s.

Example 4-4

All Through the Night

In summary, we observe that six of the seven diatonic pitch classes are shared between C major and G major. The key signature of G major raises $\hat{4}$ in C major (F) to become $\hat{7}$ in G major (F♯). The two tonics are separated by the interval of a perfect fifth.

We should expect similar results when comparing G major and D major, the key whose tonic is a perfect fifth above G. Indeed, $\hat{4}$ in G major (C) is raised to become $\hat{7}$ in D major (C♯), while the two keys share six diatonic pitch classes (A, B, D, E, F♯, and G). Similar relationships hold between D major and A major, A major and E major, E major and B major, B major and F♯ major, and F♯ major and C♯ major. The scales for these keys are shown in Example 4-5. Observe that in some cases the tonic *pitch* is notated a perfect fourth lower, rather than a perfect fifth higher, than the tonic of the preceding scale. Because the perfect fourth and perfect fifth are inversions of one another, ascending a perfect fifth and descending a perfect fourth from a given pitch lead to the same pitch class.

Example 4-5

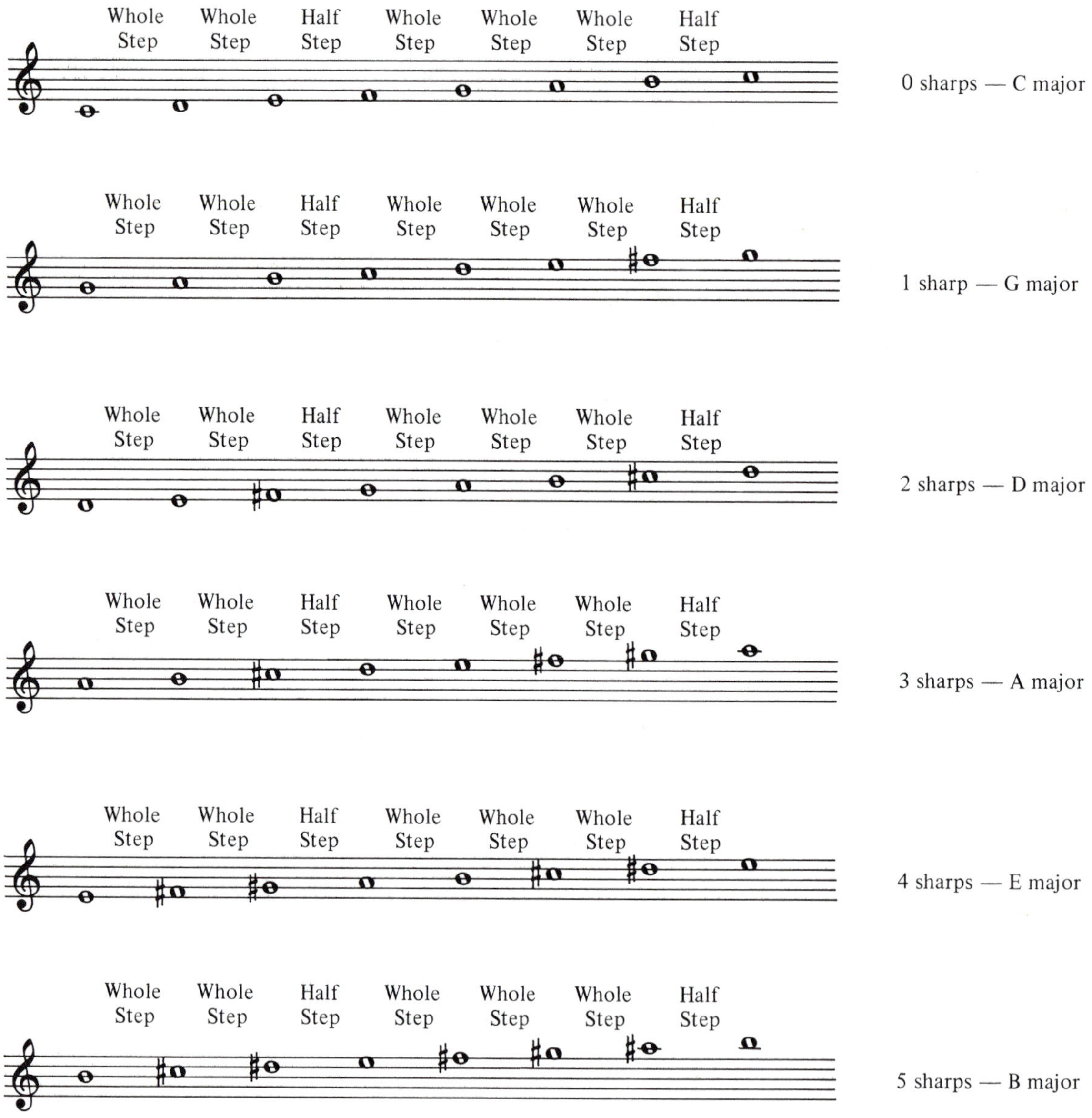

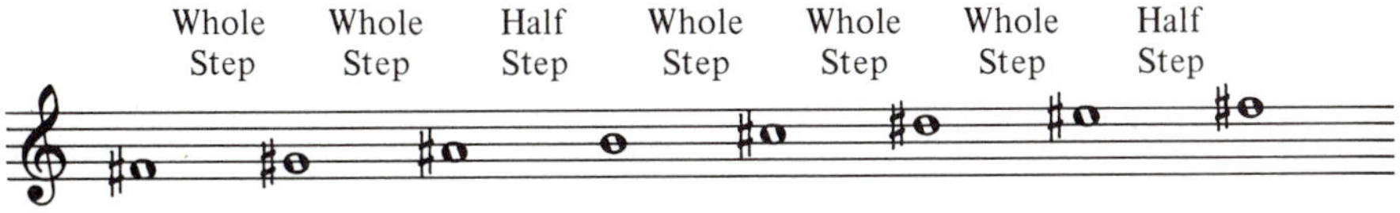

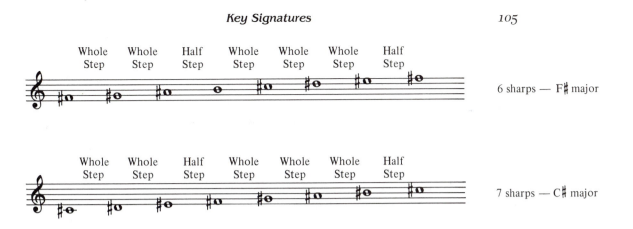

6 sharps — F♯ major

7 sharps — C♯ major

Observe that from zero to seven sharps are applied (not counting the repeat of a sharp for $\hat{1}$ and $\hat{8}$) and that each number of sharps occurs only once. The key signatures that correspond to these scales are shown in Example 4-6.

Example 4-6

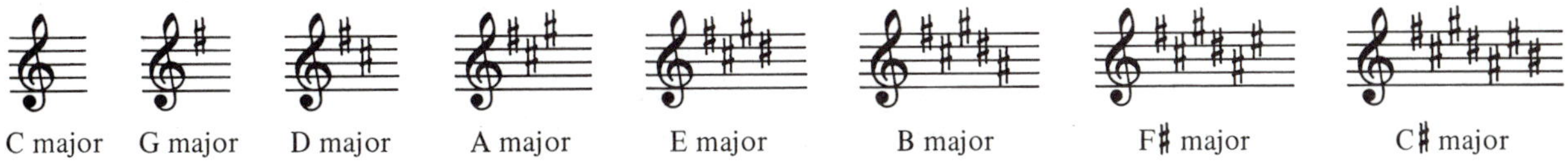

Always write the sharp key signatures in this manner. Never, for example, use the first space rather than the fifth line as the position for F♯. Observe that the signature's last sharp always pertains to $\hat{7}$ in that key (Ex. 4-7). This feature should be of use when you write or read a signature.

Example 4-7

The Flat Keys and Their Signatures

The sharp keys are arranged by ascending fifths starting from C. The flat keys are arranged by descending fifths from C. The key of F major, whose tonic is a perfect fifth below C, shares six pitch classes with C major (A, C, D, E, F, and G). $\hat{7}$ in C major (B) is lowered to become $\hat{4}$ in F major (B♭). Similar relationships hold between F major and B♭ major, B♭ major and E♭ major, E♭ major and A♭ major, A♭ major and D♭ major, D♭ major and G♭ major, and G♭ major and C♭ major. The scales for these keys are shown in Example 4-8.

Example 4-8

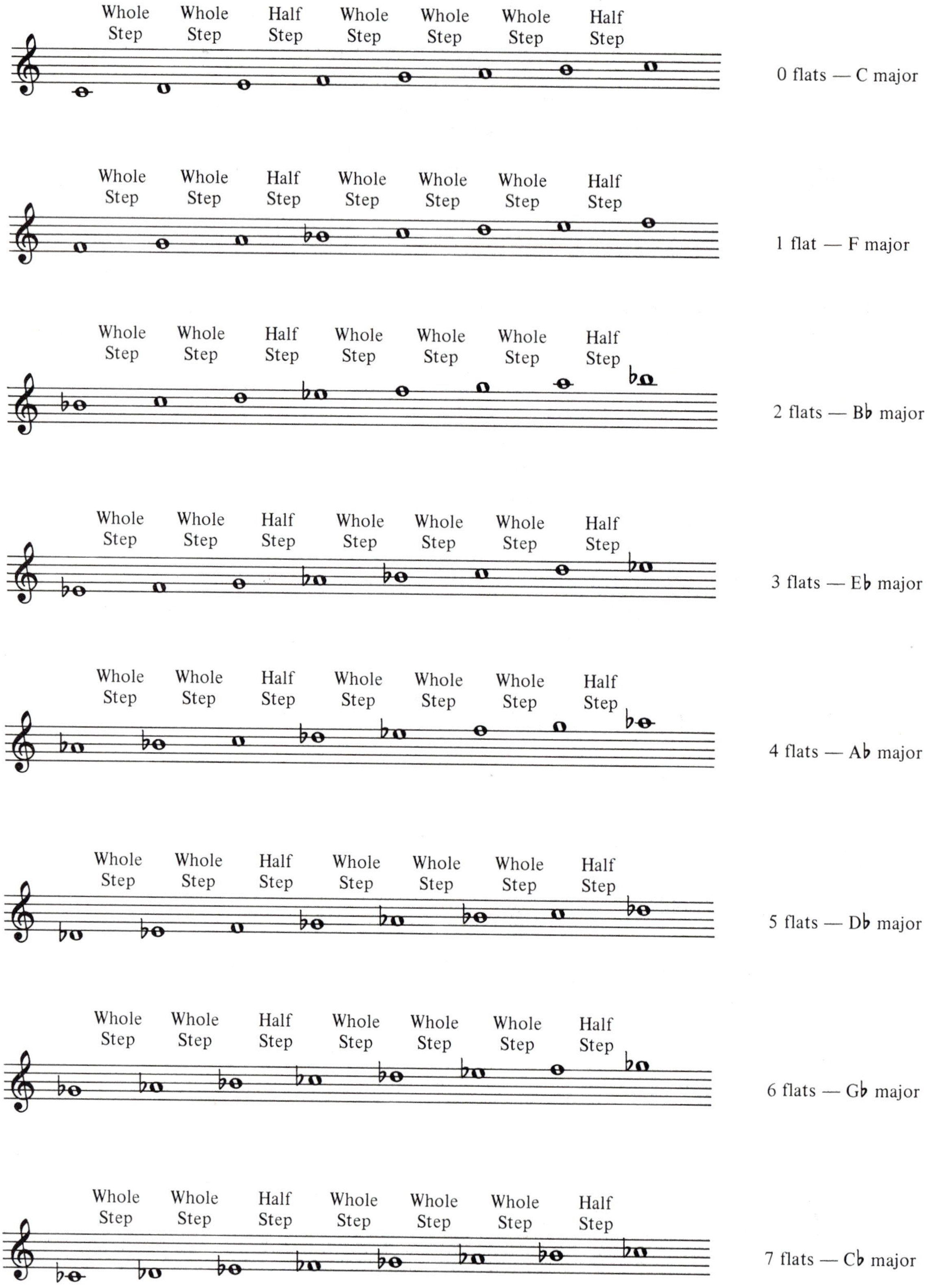
Whole Step Whole Step Half Step Whole Step Whole Step Whole Step Half Step
0 flats — C major
Whole Step Whole Step Half Step Whole Step Whole Step Whole Step Half Step
1 flat — F major
Whole Step Whole Step Half Step Whole Step Whole Step Whole Step Half Step
2 flats — B♭ major
Whole Step Whole Step Half Step Whole Step Whole Step Whole Step Half Step
3 flats — E♭ major
Whole Step Whole Step Half Step Whole Step Whole Step Whole Step Half Step
4 flats — A♭ major
Whole Step Whole Step Half Step Whole Step Whole Step Whole Step Half Step
5 flats — D♭ major
Whole Step Whole Step Half Step Whole Step Whole Step Whole Step Half Step
6 flats — G♭ major
Whole Step Whole Step Half Step Whole Step Whole Step Whole Step Half Step
7 flats — C♭ major

Observe that from zero to seven flats are applied (not counting the repeat of a flat for $\hat{1}$ and $\hat{8}$) and that each number of flats is represented only once. The key signatures that correspond to these scales are shown in Example 4-9.

Example 4-9

Always write the flat key signatures in this manner. Observe that the signature's last flat always pertains to $\hat{4}$ in that key, while its next-to-last flat always pertains to $\hat{1}$ in that key (Ex. 4-10). These features should be of use when you write or read a signature.

Example 4-10

Enharmonically Equivalent Keys

You may have observed that with C major, the seven sharp keys, and the seven flat keys, we have introduced fifteen major keys. But there are only twelve different pitch classes! This riddle is explained by the principle of enharmonic equivalence. For three of the twelve pitch classes, two alternative spellings are used: C♯ or D♭, F♯ or G♭, B or C♭. The musical context usually determines which choice is appropriate. For example, if the first movement of a composition is written in A♭ major and the composer chooses to use the tonal center five half steps higher for the second movement, D♭ (with its similar key signature) would generally be chosen rather than C♯. But the second movement of a composition in the key of F♯ major, if written five half steps lower, would generally be notated in the key of C♯ (with its similar key signature), not D♭.

Charts for Constructing Key Signatures

The charts in Example 4-11 summarize the information you will need when writing key signatures for the fifteen major keys. Observe that the interval formed by adjacent pitch classes on these charts is always a perfect fifth.

Example 4-11

NUMBER OF SHARPS OR FLATS IN THE KEY SIGNATURE

0	1	2	3	4	5	6	7	
	G	D	A	E	B	F♯	C♯	(Sharps)
C								
	F	B♭	E♭	A♭	D♭	G♭	C♭	(Flats)

ARRANGEMENTS OF SHARPS OR FLATS IN THE SIGNATURE

Sharps →

1st	2nd	3rd	4th	5th	6th	7th
F	C	G	D	A	E	B
7th	6th	5th	4th	3rd	2nd	1st

← Flats

POSITIONS OF THE SHARPS AND FLATS ON THE STAFF

Sharps

Flats

New Strategies for Forming Intervals

Intervals are the building blocks of music. Whenever two pitches sound, an interval is formed. Musicians generally think of intervals in relation to specific keys, not in terms of the number of half steps that separate their component pitches. At this point we should begin to abandon the counting method of interval formation.

If asked which pitch is a major third above E♭, you should make use of the fact that $\hat{1}$ and $\hat{3}$ in E♭ major form a major third. Instead of counting four half steps from E♭ to G, you should think, If E♭ is $\hat{1}$, what pitch is $\hat{3}$? The E♭ major key signature and scale come to mind and the pitch G is found without consulting a keyboard diagram or performing any arithmetic calculations (Ex. 4-12).

Example 4-12

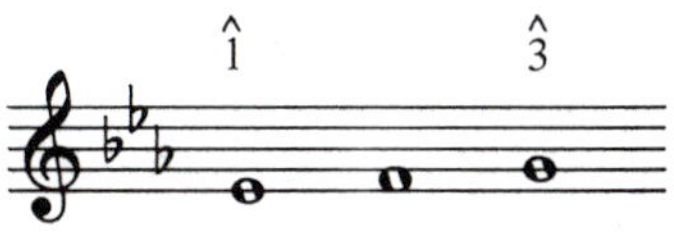

If asked which pitch is a major sixth above F♯, you should make use of the fact that $\hat{1}$ and $\hat{6}$ in F♯ major form a major sixth. Visualizing the F♯ major scale, you find the answer D♯. In consulting this scale, you could either ascend from $\hat{1}$ to $\hat{6}$ or take a shorter route by descending from $\hat{8}$ to $\hat{6}$, as shown in Example 4-13. The ascent of a major sixth and descent of a minor third from the tonic lead to the same pitch class because these two intervals are inversions of one another.

Example 4-13

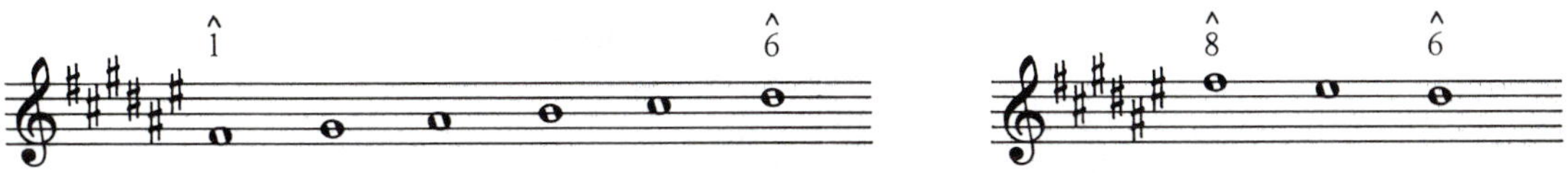

If asked which pitch is a perfect fourth below B, you should make use of the fact that $\hat{5}$ and $\hat{8}$ in the key of B major form a perfect fourth. In other words, a perfect fourth below B is $\hat{5}$ in the key of B major, or F♯.

Example 4-14

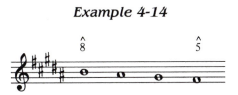

You should use this method when forming intervals, though you may want to check your work by counting half steps at first. All of the intervalic relationships between $\hat{1}$ or $\hat{8}$ and the remaining scale degrees of the fifteen major keys are available to you, supplying numerous examples of all major, minor, and perfect intervals of sizes 1 through 8. When the second of the two modes, the *minor* mode, is introduced in Chapter 6, you will have even more scales from which to draw out the interval you are seeking.

Pitch exercises for Chapter 4 are on pages 121–132.

RHYTHM

Subdivisions of the Quarter-Note Beat

eighth note

beam

Quarter-note beats combine to form half notes, dotted half notes, and whole notes. ***Eighth notes,*** on the other hand, result from the subdivision of a quarter-note beat. Two eighth notes fill the same musical time as one quarter note ($\frac{1}{8} + \frac{1}{8} = \frac{2}{8} = \frac{1}{4}$). When at least two eighth notes appear in succession, they are generally notated by connecting the stems of filled-in noteheads with a solid horizontal or diagonal line called a ***beam.*** Example 4-15 shows that four, six, and eight eighth notes fill measures in $\frac{2}{4}$, $\frac{3}{4}$, and $\frac{4}{4}$ meters, respectively.

Example 4-15

In $\frac{2}{4}$ and $\frac{3}{4}$ meters, each beat may be beamed separately, though if consecutive beats contain nothing but eighth notes, a single beam may connect them all. In $\frac{4}{4}$ meter, a beam that connects more than two eighth notes will never cross the midpoint of the measure. (That is, beats one and two or beats three and four may be beamed together, but not beats two and three.) The stem direction appropriate for the note furthest from the center line of the staff governs the direction of all stems joined by a beam, as shown in Example 4-16. The conventional direction of an individual note's stem may be altered when it is connected to a beam.

Example 4-16

Counting the Beats and Their Eighth-Note Subdivisions

Examples 4-15 and 4-16 show the least complicated usage of eighth notes: that in which no other note values appear. Correct performance requires only that the eighth notes follow one another at a uniform rate, for example two notes per second at a moderate tempo of ♩ = 60. Measures containing notes of diverse rhythms are more challenging to perform. To promote accuracy, you should count the eighth-note subdivisions of the beat whenever eighth notes play an important role in a melody. The syllable "and" (notated as "+" underneath the staff) marks the moment in time when the second half of a beat occurs. By pronouncing the syllables for the beats and their subdivisions at a uniform rate, you will promote accuracy in your performance. For example, an exercise in $\frac{4}{4}$ meter could be counted as "one and two and three and four and one and two and three and four and . . ." At a moderate tempo, you would pronounce two syllables per second.

Example 4-17 shows how to count the beats and their eighth-note subdivisions in $\frac{2}{4}$, $\frac{3}{4}$, and $\frac{4}{4}$ meters.

Example 4-17

1 + 2 + **1** + 2 + 3 + **1** + 2 + **3** + 4 +

Individual Eighth Notes and Rests

Whenever a single eighth note is required (for example, when a $\frac{2}{4}$ measure contains one note of one and one-half beats and another note of one-half beat), beam notation is not feasible. Beams always connect at least two stems. Single eighth notes are formed by attaching a ***flag*** to the stem, as in Example 4-18. Observe that the flag is placed to the right of the stem both when the stem ascends and when it descends.

flag

Example 4-18

An augmentation dot is applied to a quarter note to form a ***dotted quarter note.*** As you will recall from Chapter 2, an augmentation dot increases the time value of a note by one half. In this case the time value of the quarter note is one beat (1), to which half of one (½) is added, resulting in a total value of one and one-half beats (1½). The dotted quarter note and the single eighth note are emphasized in the melody shown in Example 4-19.

dotted quarter note

Example 4-19

1 + 2 + **3** + 4 + **1** + 2 + **3** + 4 + **1** + 2 + **3** + 4 + **1** + 2 + **3** + 4 +

eighth rest

A single eighth note or a dotted quarter note may also appear with an ***eighth rest***, notated as 𝄾. The horizontal portion of an eighth rest fills the third space on the staff, as in Example 4-20.

Example 4-20

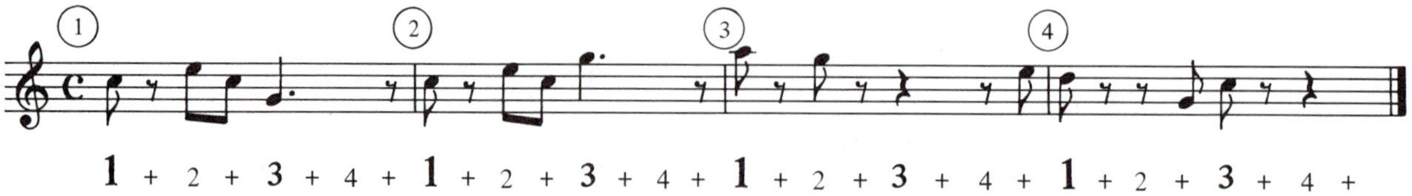

Composers are careful to notate rhythm as clearly as possible. It is important that the notation not obscure the positioning of the beats. Compare measures 3 and 4 of Example 4-20 with the alternative shown in Example 4-21. The two quarter rests in measure 3 of Example 4-21 fill the same musical time as the eighth-quarter-eighth combination of rests in measure 3 of Example 4-20, but they obscure the position of beats 3 and 4. Likewise, the rests in measure 4 of Example 4-21 straddle the beats, promoting confusion and the risk of an incorrect performance. Observe also that the adjacent eighth notes in measure 4 of Example 4-20 are correctly notated using flags. Beam notation (as shown in Example 4-21) would be incorrect because the two eighth notes do not fall within the same beat.

Example 4-21

INCORRECT

Rhythm exercises for Chapter 4 are on pages 133–135.

LABORATORY

L4-1. At the keyboard perform major scales, ascending and descending, so that the given pitch falls on the scale degree indicated. During the ascent, say aloud the words "whole, whole, half, whole, whole, whole, half" at the appropriate times. During the descent, say aloud the words "half, whole, whole, whole, half, whole, whole" at the appropriate times.

Performance suggestion: Use both hands. Each finger (excluding the thumbs) can be assigned its own pitch to perform. Before you begin, position the little finger of your left hand on $\hat{1}$ and the little finger of your right hand on $\hat{8}$.

a.

C as $\hat{1}$

E as $\hat{1}$

F♯ as $\hat{1}$

D as $\hat{1}$

B as $\hat{1}$

A as $\hat{1}$

D♭ as $\hat{1}$

A♭ as $\hat{1}$

F as $\hat{1}$

B♭ as $\hat{1}$

E♭ as $\hat{1}$

G as $\hat{1}$

b.

E as $\hat{6}$

G as $\hat{3}$

D♭ as $\hat{4}$

A as $\hat{6}$

B♭ as $\hat{3}$

C as $\hat{2}$

F♯ as $\hat{6}$

B as $\hat{2}$

D♯ as $\hat{3}$

A♭ as $\hat{4}$

E♭ as $\hat{2}$

C♯ as $\hat{5}$

L4-2.a. Perform each of the following triads at the keyboard using your right hand.

1.

2.

3.

4.

5.

6.

7.

8.
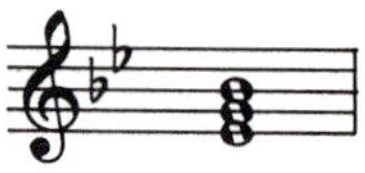

9.

b. Perform each of the following melodies at the keyboard using your right hand. Recommended fingerings are included.

Beethoven: "Archduke" Trio

1.

Schubert: Symphony No. 9

2.

Haydn: Symphony No. 45

3.
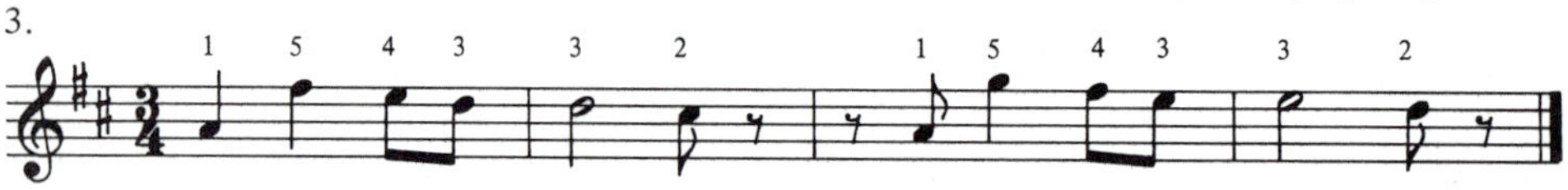

Beethoven: Piano Concerto No. 5

4.
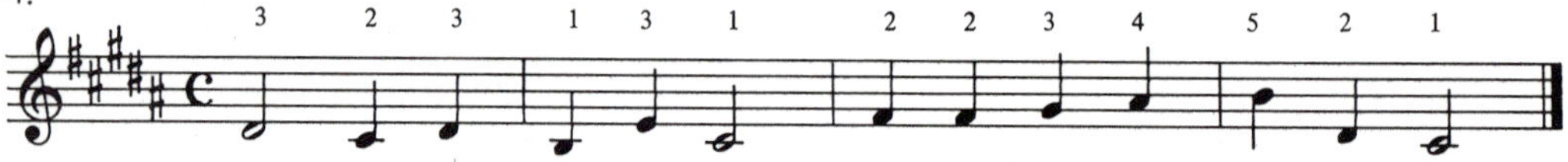

L4-3. Mark the lowest and highest notes you can sing on the diagram below. Do not let your fingers extend beyond these boundaries.

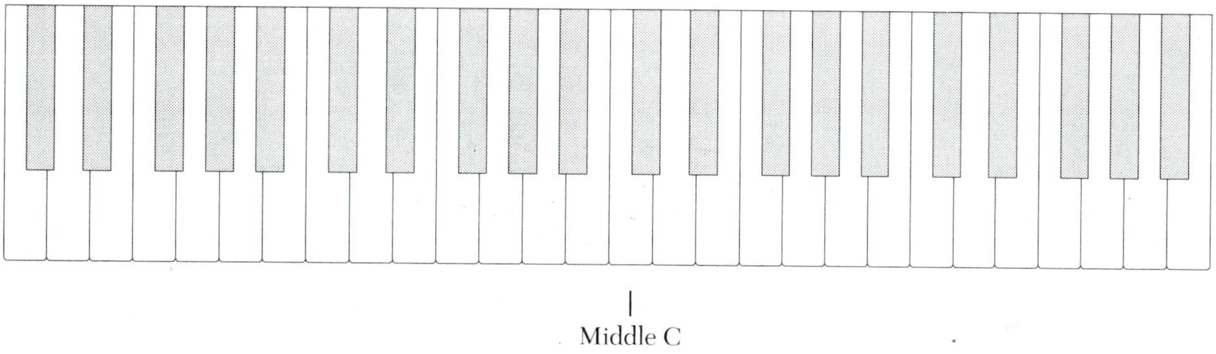

a. Practice the following exercise until you have mastered it perfectly.

- Position two fingers on top of keys that are a major third apart, but do not strike them.
- Strike the lower key.
- Sing that pitch.
- Sing the pitch a major third higher.
- Strike the higher key and confirm that it is what you have sung.

b. Once the above exercise is going well, add the following steps.

- Position two fingers on top of keys that are a major third apart, but do not strike them.
- Strike the upper key.
- Sing that pitch.
- Sing the pitch a major third lower.
- Strike the lower key and confirm that it is what you have sung.

L4-4. Practice the following melodies at the keyboard, simultaneously singing and playing each pitch. Sing the scale-degree numbers that correspond to the pitches. Men should perform these melodies an octave lower than they are written.

a.

b.

c.

d.

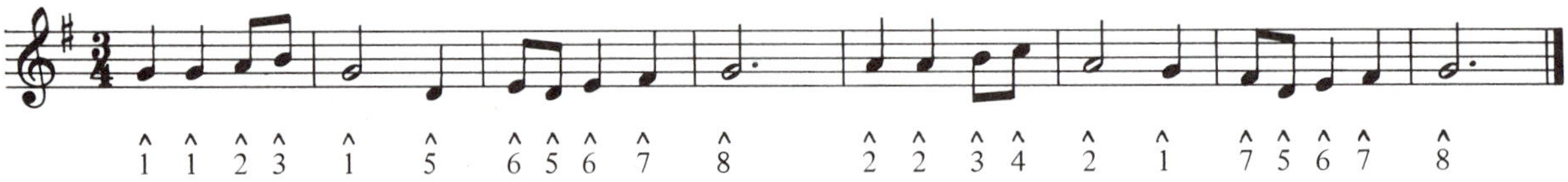

e.

L4-5. The following compositions are for voice (upper staff) and keyboard (lower staff). Sing the scale-degree numbers that correspond to the pitches. At first you may play the vocal part on the keyboard while you sing, in order to solidify your performance. Eventually, however, observe the rests in the accompanying part during your vocal measures. The range of the compositions should be appropriate for most women's voices. Men should perform both the keyboard and vocal parts an octave lower.

a. Voice

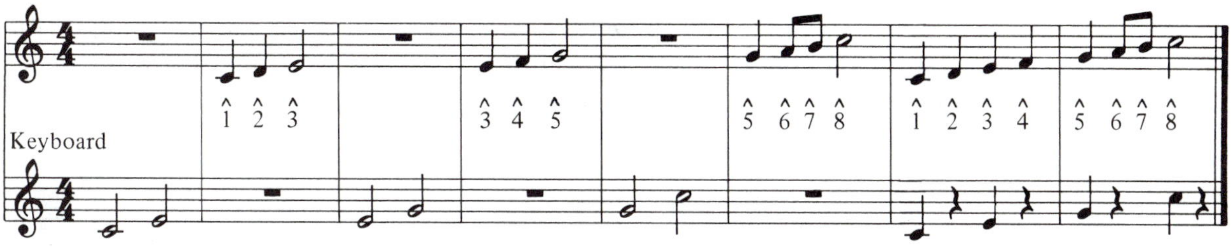

b. Voice

L4-6. The following compositions are for two voices. Sing the scale-degree numbers that correspond to the pitches. Men should perform these melodies an octave lower than they are written.

a. Voice 1

b. Voice 1

L4-7. Write in the counting syllables (1 + 2 + 3 +, etc.) below the notated rhythms. Then perform each by clapping the rhythm or playing the pitch F at the keyboard while pronouncing the counting syllables aloud. Practice until you can perform each exercise at a tempo of about ♩ = 60.

SAMPLE

a.

b.

c.

d.

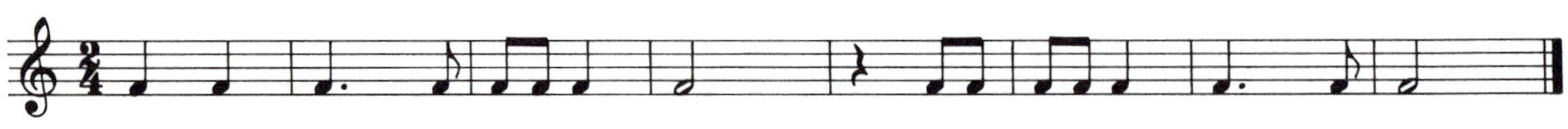

L4-8. Write in the counting syllables below the notated rhythms. Then perform them by dividing the class into two groups, with each group clapping one part while pronouncing the counting syllables aloud. Alternatively, individual students may perform both parts simultaneously at the keyboard, pronouncing the counting syllables aloud while the index finger of the right hand strikes C and the index finger of the left hand strikes F, as notated.

Sample

a.

b.

c.

d.

L4-9. This exercise requires that a student or the instructor serve as the performer at a keyboard.

a. The performer places three fingers above keys that sound a major triad and strikes the three keys simultaneously. Then the performer plays either the major third (root and third) or perfect fifth (root and fifth) either ascending or descending. Indicate which interval is performed.

b. The performer plays two pitches in either ascending or descending order, and then plays them together. Indicate whether the interval performed is or is not a major third.

c. The performer plays ascending or descending scales that either are major scales or have one or two pitches altered by a half step. Indicate whether the scale performed is or is not a major scale.

Audio exercises for Chapter 4 are on pages 136–138.

Name: ____________________

Instructor: ____________________

Date: ____________________

EXERCISES

Pitch Exercises

P4-1. Cut this page along the dotted lines. Form these slips into a pile and examine each in turn, identifying the key signature as you view it. (The answer is on the reverse.) Reshuffle the slips frequently. Practice until you can go through the pile with no errors in one minute or less. Also practice by turning the pile over and, upon seeing the name of a major key, visualize the sharps or flats in its key signature.

Hint: At first you may want to include only a few of the slips, for example, all slips that contain zero, one, or two sharps or flats. Eventually add to your pile until it contains all of the slips.

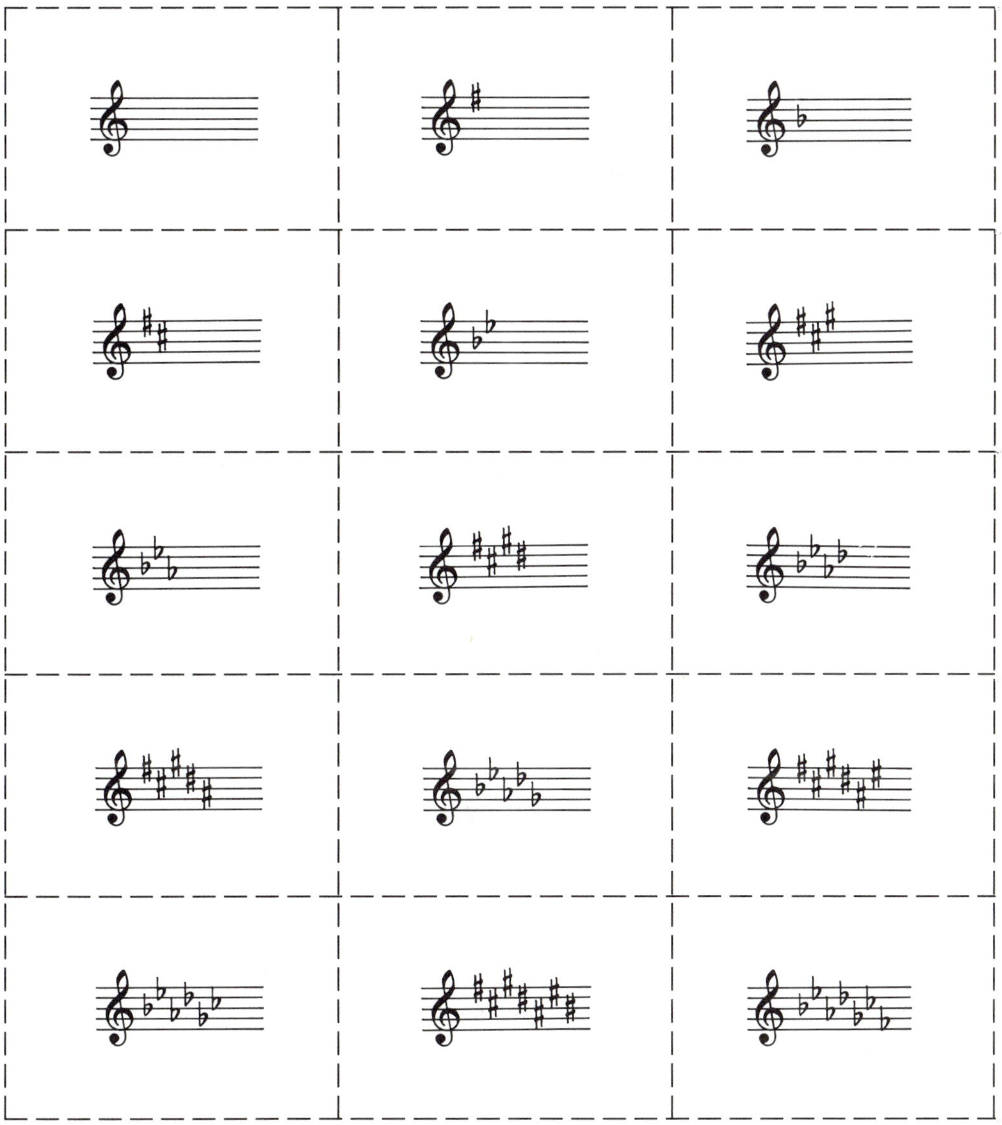

G♭ major

C♯ major

C♭ major

B major

D♭ major

F♯ major

E♭ major

E major

A♭ major

D major

B♭ major

A major

C major

G major

F major

Name: ______________________________
Instructor: __________________________
Date: _______________________________

P4-2. Name each pitch of the following melodies in the space underneath the staff, including all appropriate accidentals.

a.

b.

c.

d.

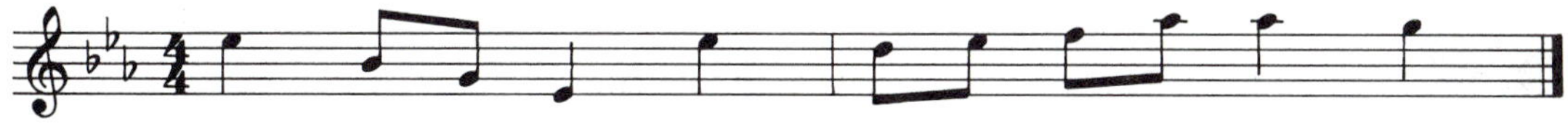

e.

f.

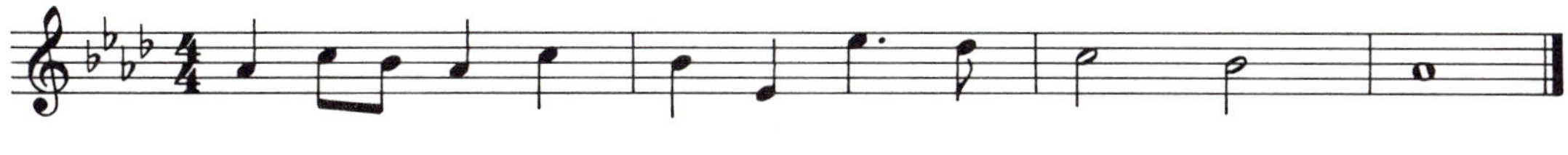

g.

h.

i.

j.

k.

l.

Name: ______________________________

Instructor: __________________________

Date: _______________________________

P4-3. The major keys are often arranged in a ***circle of fifths***, so named because the diagram is circular and all adjacent keys are a perfect fifth apart. Add the remaining key names in the boxes to complete the figure. Observe how the enharmonically equivalent keys are positioned within the circle of fifths.

circle of fifths

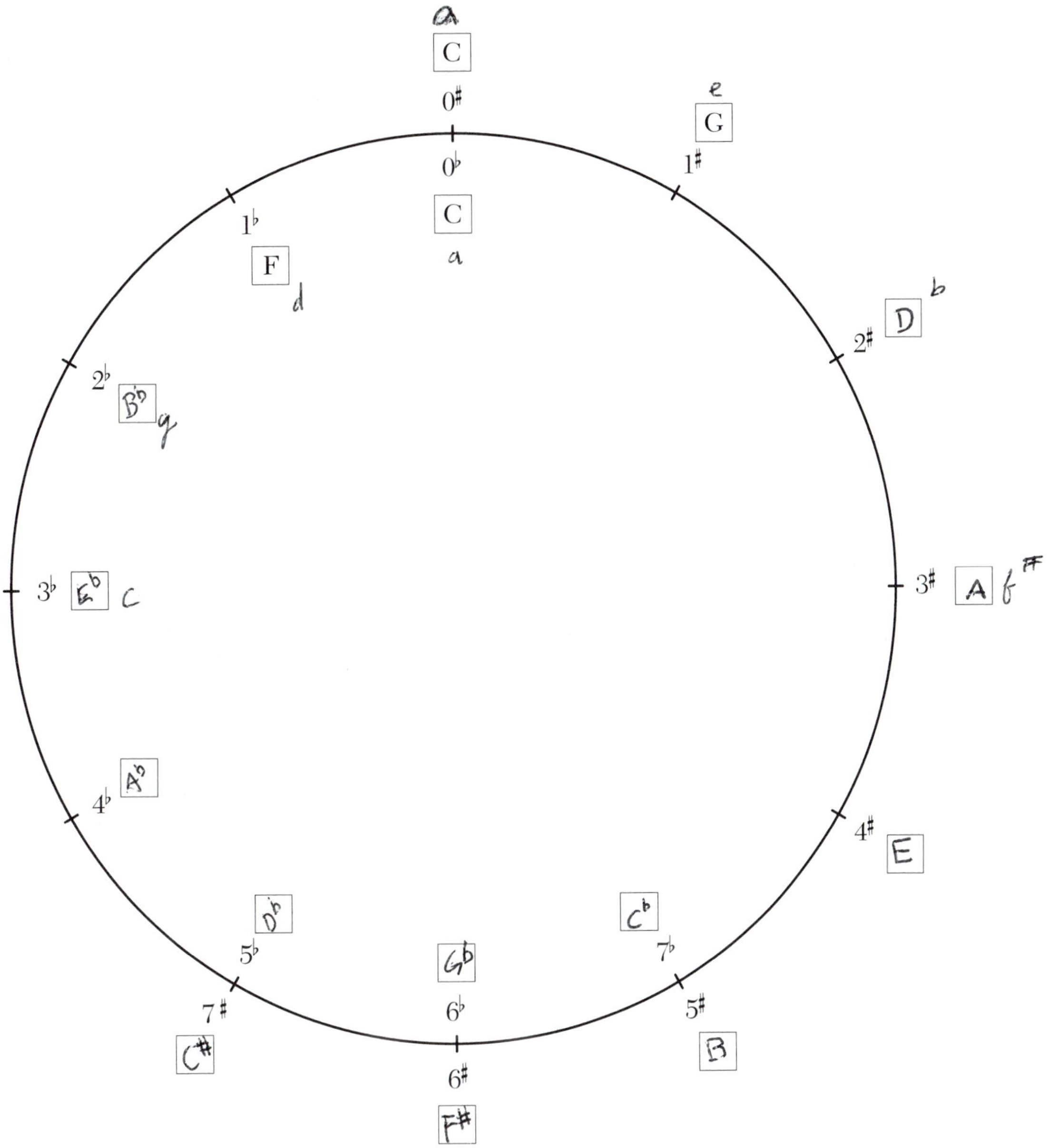

P4-4. Form the ascending intervals requested by treating the given pitch as $\hat{1}$, drawing the appropriate key signature for that major key on the staff, and ascending the major scale until you find the desired pitch.

Sample: Major sixth above E.
Solution: The major sixth appears between $\hat{1}$ and $\hat{6}$ in key of E major, whose key signature contains four sharps. $\hat{6}$ is C♯.

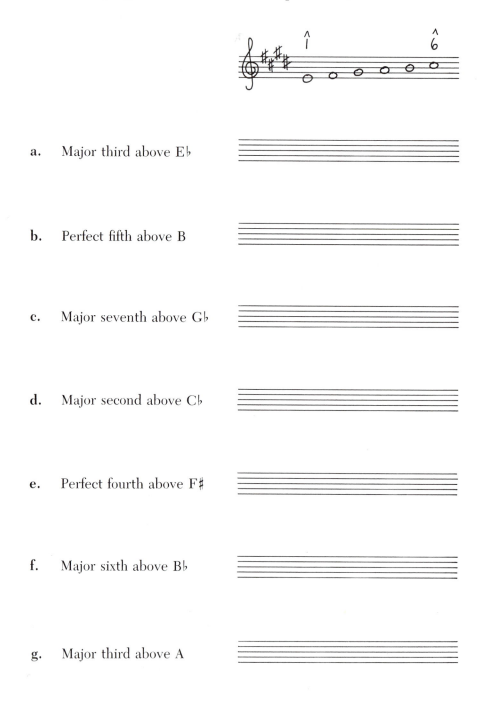

a. Major third above E♭

b. Perfect fifth above B

c. Major seventh above G♭

d. Major second above C♭

e. Perfect fourth above F♯

f. Major sixth above B♭

g. Major third above A

Name: ______________________

Instructor: ______________________

Date: ______________________

A4-4. Six melodies will be performed. The starting pitch for each will be stated before the melody is performed. In each case circle the score that shows the correct pitch notation.

a.

b.

c.

d.

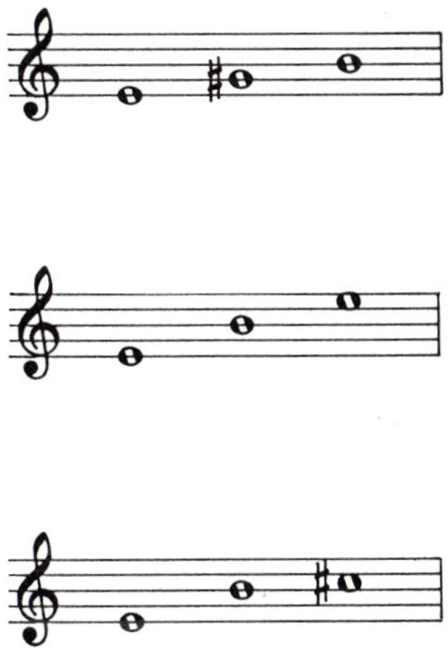

e.

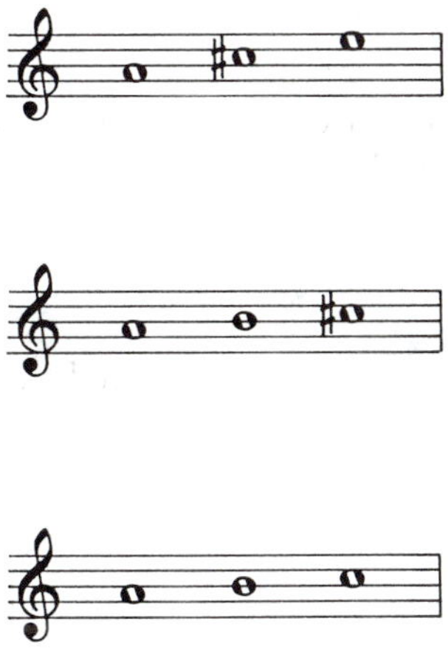

f.

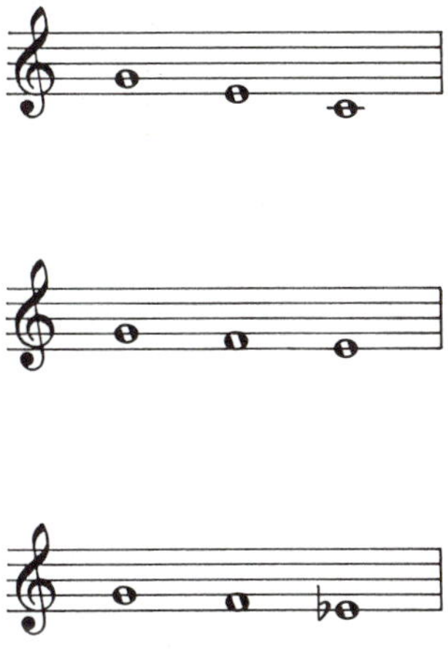

A4-5. Four rhythms will be performed. In each case circle the score that shows the correct notation.

a.

b.

c.

d.

Name: ______________________
Instructor: ______________________
Date: ______________________

Mastery Test, Chapter 4

________ 1. Exactly how many sharps appear in the key signature for F♯ major?
X. Five Y. Six Z. Seven

________ 2. Exactly how many flats appear in the key signature for A♭ major?
X. Four Y. Five Z. Six

________ 3. Which key signature contains exactly three sharps?
X. A major Y. B major Z. E major

________ 4. Which key signature contains exactly seven flats?
X. B♭ major Y. C♭ major Z. G♭ major

________ 5. Which of the key signatures shown is that of D♭ major?

X. 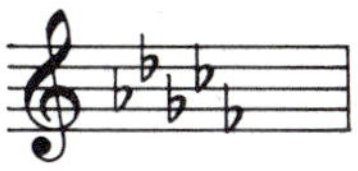
Y. 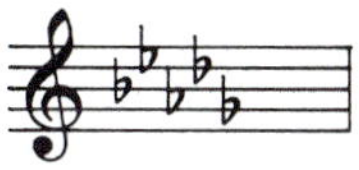
Z. 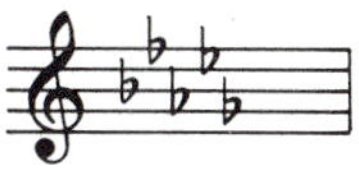

________ 6. Which of the key signatures shown is that of C♯ major?

X. 
Y. 
Z. 

________ 7. Which major key is the enharmonic equivalent of B major?
X. A♯ major Y. B♭ major Z. C♭ major

________ 8. Which major key is the enharmonic equivalent of G♭ major?
X. G♯ major Y. F♯ major Z. E♭ major

________ 9. In which major key does the pitch G function as $\hat{4}$?
X. C major Y. D♭ major Z. D major

________ 10. In which major key does the pitch B♭ function as $\hat{5}$?
X. E♭ major Y. E major Z. F major

________ 11. Which pitch functions as $\hat{7}$ in the key of F♯ major?
X. E Y. E♯ Z. F

________ 12. Which pitch functions as $\hat{3}$ in the key of C♭ major?
X. D♯ Y. E♭ Z. E

________ 13. In $\frac{4}{4}$ meter, how many beats does the following symbol fill?
X. 1½ Y. 2½ Z. 3

________ 14. What kind of note should be inserted at the arrow to complete the measure?
X. Eighth note
Y. Quarter note
Z. Dotted quarter note

________ 15. What kind of rest should be inserted at the arrow to complete the measure?
X. Eighth rest Y. Quarter rest
Z. Half rest

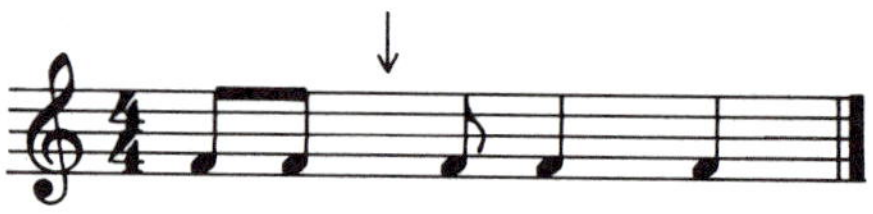

________ 16. An interval will be performed, first as two successive pitches, then as two simultaneous pitches. Is the interval a major third?
Y. Yes Z. No

________ 17. A succession of eight ascending pitches will be performed. Is it a major scale?
Y. Yes Z. No

Name: ____________________________

Instructor: ________________________

Date: _____________________________

__________ 18. A major triad will be performed, followed by a melodic statement of one of its intervals, the major third or the perfect fifth. Which of these intervals is performed?

X. Major third   Y. Perfect fifth

__________ 19. A melody that begins with the pitch G will be performed. Which score shows the correct pitch notation?

X. 

Y. 

Z. 

__________ 20. Which score shows the correct notation for the rhythm performed?

X. 

Y. 

Z. 

5

Bass Clef and Transposition

Terms and Concepts

bass clef	*downbeat*	*pickup*
transposition	*upbeat*	*repeat sign*

PITCH

Bass Clef

bass clef

The treble clef is ideal for melodies that sound primarily above middle C. For melodies that sound primarily below middle C, the ***bass clef*** is generally used instead. The bass clef shows which line on the staff corresponds to the pitch F below middle C. Once that pitch is fixed, notes on all other lines and spaces (and, by extension, notes written above or below the staff using ledger lines) fall into place as well.

The two dots of the bass clef symbol surround the fourth line of the staff to mark the position of the pitch F below middle C (Ex. 5-1).

Example 5-1

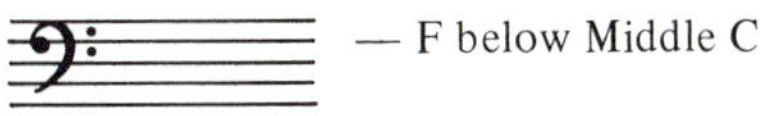

Pitches named using the letters C, E, and G over a span of two octaves below middle C are notated using the bass clef on the staff in Example 5-2.

Example 5-2

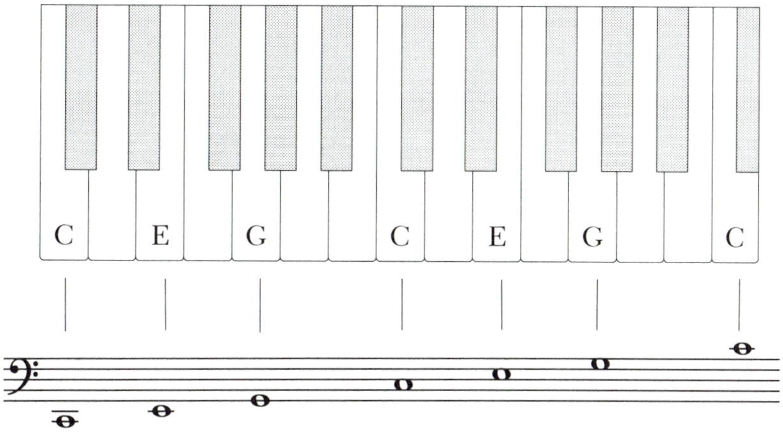

The remaining white-key pitches appear in staff notation as shown in Example 5-3.

Example 5-3

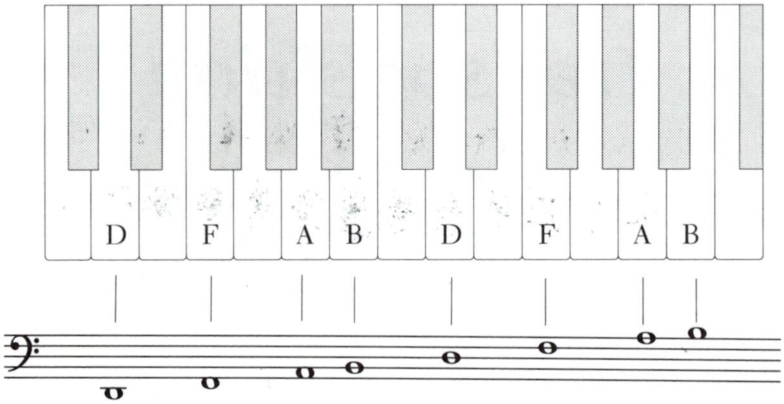

The treble and bass clefs offer two alternative meanings for the lines and spaces of the staff. Observe that in both clefs, the pitch middle C is drawn on a ledger line: below the staff in treble clef, above the staff in bass clef (Ex. 5-4).

Example 5-4

You might wish to learn the notes in the two groupings displayed or in terms of notes that fall on lines (G B D F A) and in spaces (A C E G). Remember that additional notes can be drawn using ledger lines above and below the staff. The application of accidentals does not differ from the conventions of treble clef.

Key Signatures in Bass Clef

The sharps and flats of key signatures in the bass clef are added in the same order as in the treble clef, but their positions on the staff are lower, as shown in Example 5-5. For example, the F♯ of treble-clef key signatures appears on the fifth line, while in bass-clef key signatures it appears on the fourth line. All other sharps and flats are written in a correspondingly lower position on the staff as well.

Example 5-5

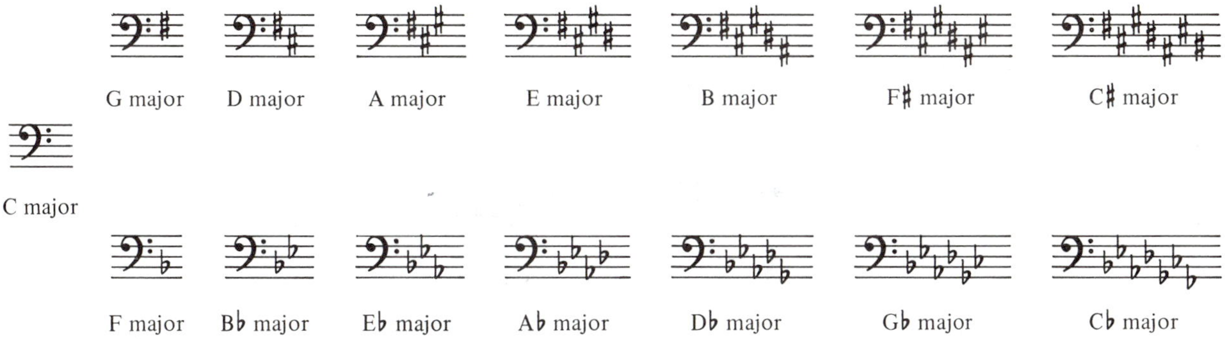

Transposition

transposition

Transposition is the operation of moving a melody higher or lower, either with or without a change of key. The simplest form of transposition is *octave transposition*, in which the original key is retained. In Example 5-6, a melody in the key of B♭ major is shown, followed by an octave transposition (one octave lower).

Example 5-6

Beethoven: Symphony No. 9

Each notehead of the initial melody is notated exactly one octave lower in the transposition. We could, of course, transpose the melody yet another octave lower, or an octave higher.

Composers frequently enliven a composition through statements of the same melody in both high and low registers. Octave transposition may also occur spontaneously when a man sings a melody notated in the treble clef or a woman sings a melody notated in the bass clef.

A more complex type of transposition is used when, for example, a melody is just slightly too high for a vocalist. To move the melody an entire octave lower would not solve the problem, for then some notes would likely be too low. In such cases we transpose the melody into a different key, one slightly lower than the key in which it was written originally.

As an example, we transpose a melody from the key of C major to the key of A♭ major, a major third lower. The original melody appears in Example 5-7.

Example 5-7

Schubert: Symphony No. 9

Every pitch of this melody has been notated a major third lower in Example 5-8. Thus C is replaced by A♭, D is replaced by B♭, E is replaced by C, and so on. Observe that the key signature for A♭ major replaces that for C major.

Example 5-8

Schubert: Symphony No. 9 (transposed)

The succession of scale degrees is the same in both versions of this melody, as shown. A *successful transposition will never alter the scale degree of a pitch in the context of the prevailing tonal center.*

Sometimes we must change the key signature and clef simultaneously, as in the transposition of the melody shown in Example 5-9. Here, notating the melody a perfect fifth lower would require the use of many ledger lines in the treble clef. In the bass clef, on the other hand, only a few ledger lines are required.

Example 5-9

Beethoven: Piano Sonata Op. 13

When chromatic pitches—pitches requiring accidentals other than those of the prevailing key signature—appear in a melody, we must be careful to maintain both the size and quality of the transposing interval when renotating each pitch. For example, the melody in C major shown in Example 5-10 uses the sharp sign to change the diatonic pitch F into F♯ ($\hat{4}$ into $\uparrow\hat{4}$), emphasizing the G with an approach by half step ($\uparrow\hat{4}$–$\hat{5}$) rather than by whole step ($\hat{4}$–$\hat{5}$). $\uparrow\hat{4}$ (read "raised four") is probably the most utilized chromatic pitch in the major mode.

Example 5-10

Haydn: Symphony No. 94

The transposition of this melody into the key of F major (a perfect fourth higher) requires a natural sign where the sharp sign was used originally, because a perfect fourth above F♯ (the chromatic pitch $\uparrow\hat{4}$ in the original melody) is B♮. This natural is obligatory; without it, a notehead on that line would be read as B♭, the only flat in the key signature of F major (Ex. 5-11). To confirm that this transposition is correct, observe that the interval formed by corresponding pitches of the two melodies is always a perfect fourth.

Example 5-11

Haydn: Symphony No. 94 (transposed)

Transposition will never affect the status of a pitch within the prevailing tonal center: diatonic pitches will remain diatonic, chromatic pitches will remain chromatic; $\hat{3}$ will remain $\hat{3}$, $\hat{7}$ will remain $\hat{7}$, $\uparrow\hat{4}$ will remain $\uparrow\hat{4}$.

Three Methods for Performing Transposition

The operation of transposition depends upon intervals. The succession of intervals formed by each pair of adjacent pitches in a melody will remain unchanged in its transposition. A specific interval—the *interval of transposition*—will always be formed by corresponding pitches of the original melody and its transposition. The scale degrees of the pitches in a melody will correspond to those of its transposition. Each of these properties can be called upon when transposing a melody. We shall explore them in turn, using the same melody and transposing to the same new key in each case to confirm that each method produces the same result.

Adjacent pitches of a melody form specific intervals, which are useful tools for transposition. In Example 5-12, the intervals between adjacent pitches are as follows: descending perfect fourth, perfect unison, perfect unison, descending minor third, ascending minor sixth, descending perfect fourth, descending minor second, ascending minor second, perfect unison, descending minor third.

Example 5-12

Mozart: Symphony No. 35

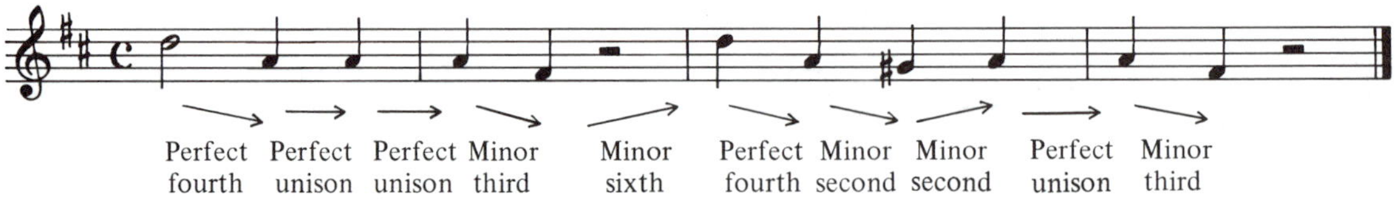

When transposing to any other key, these intervalic relationships should not change. For example, if we transpose the melody from D major to B♭ major, every pitch will be different, but all of the intervals between adjacent pitches will be the same. Confirm that in the transposition to B♭ major, shown in Example 5-13, B♭ and F form a descending perfect fourth, F and D form a descending minor third, and so on.

Example 5-13

Mozart: Symphony No. 35

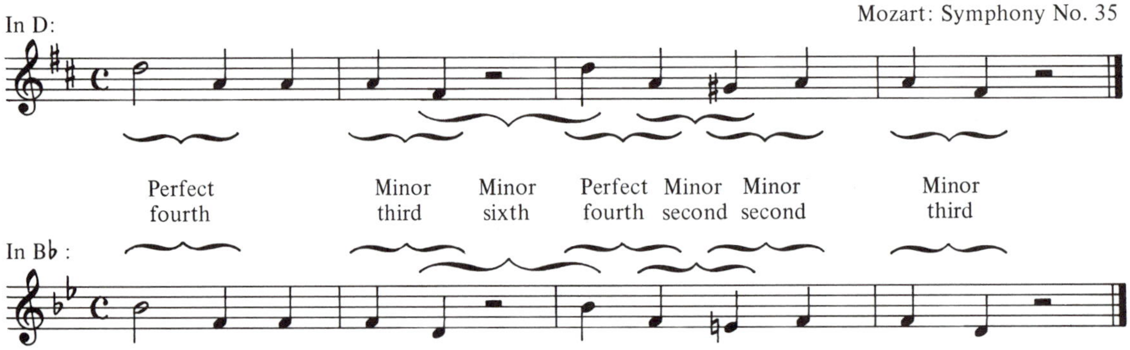

The method of transposition shown in Example 5-13 will always produce the desired transposition if performed correctly. Its main disadvantage is that if a single error is made, then all of the notes following that error will be wrong as well.

In the second method (shown in Ex. 5-14), we find the interval of transposition and then raise or lower every pitch of the original melody by that interval. In Example 5-13, we have transposed the melody from D major down a major third to B♭ major. In the second method, we lower every pitch of the original melody by a major third to achieve the same result. D becomes B♭, A becomes F, F♯ becomes D, and so on.

You must be very careful whenever a chromatic pitch is used. A major third below G♯ (measure 3) is E. Since the key signature for B♭ major includes E♭, a natural must be placed to the left of this E. Though diatonic pitches remain diatonic and chromatic pitches remain chromatic in a transposition, the accidentals that must be used to notate the chromatic pitches will not necessarily remain the same.

Example 5-14

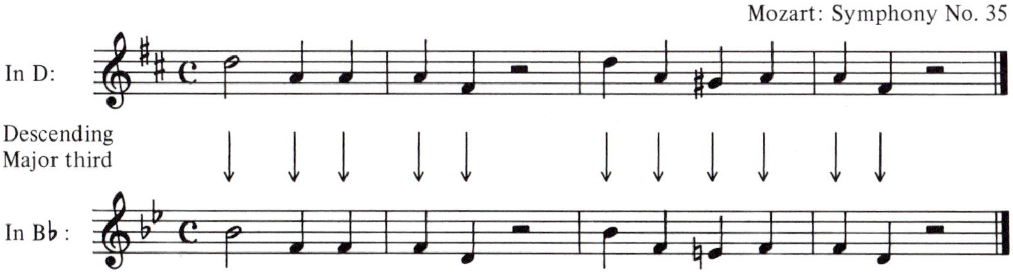

In the third method of transposition (Ex. 5-15), we relate every pitch of the melody to the tonic pitch of the key, using scale degree numbers. Since a transposition will never change the scale degree of a pitch, you can perform a transposition without finding the intervals between adjacent pitches or even knowing the interval of transposition. For example, in converting the melody shown in Example 5-12 from D major to B♭ major, you might first make a chart of all diatonic scale degrees in both keys, as follows:

Scale Degree:	$\hat{1}$	$\hat{2}$	$\hat{3}$	$\hat{4}$	$\hat{5}$	$\hat{6}$	$\hat{7}$	$\hat{8}$
D major:	D	E	F♯	G	A	B	C♯	D
B♭ major:	B♭	C	D	E♭	F	G	A	B♭

Using this chart, we see that every D should be converted to B♭, every E to C, every F♯ to D, and so on. By taking a few moments to construct this chart, you save much time in computing intervals, as is required in the other methods.

In this method of transposition, you must give special attention whenever an accidental that is not found in the key signature is used. In measure 3 of the melody shown in Example 5-15 the pitch G♯ occurs. It is not $\hat{4}$ but $\uparrow\hat{4}$. Since $\hat{4}$ in the key of B♭ major is E♭, $\uparrow\hat{4}$ is E♮. The pitch letter, E, remains the same, while the accidental that raises the pitch one half step is applied. Observe that the resulting transposition, shown in Example 5-15, is the same as that produced by the other methods, shown in Examples 5-13 and 5-14. The position of each pitch class on the staff corresponds to the ascending and descending contours of the original melody.

Example 5-15

Mozart: Symphony No. 35

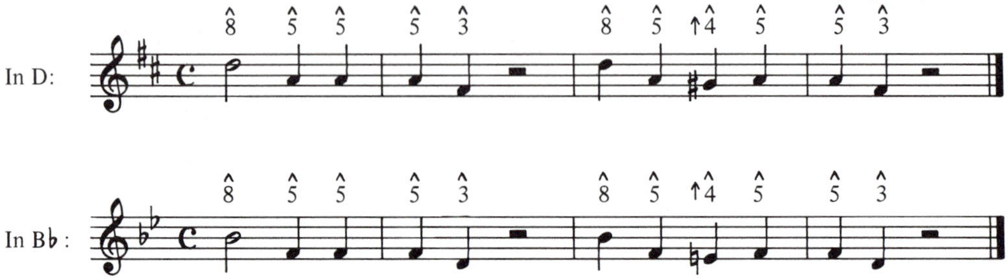

Pitch exercises for Chapter 5 are on pages 161–168.

RHYTHM

Downbeats and Upbeats

downbeat
upbeat
pickup

Melodies often begin on a ***downbeat,*** the first beat of a measure. Of course, composers are not restricted to this one choice. They may begin a melody on any beat, or even between beats. A note that precedes a downbeat is called an ***upbeat*** or ***pickup.*** Though an upbeat often fills one beat, it may also fill half a beat, two beats, or any other number of beats. Also, more than one upbeat may precede a downbeat. The downbeat is the moment of the first strong metrical pulse. Performers should be careful not to make an upbeat sound accented, like a downbeat.

When an upbeat precedes the first measure of a melody, the label "measure 1" refers to the first complete measure, not to the upbeat. This convention both saves space on the page (by eliminating the need for rests before the upbeat) and allows the number of measures of music and the number of measures used to display it to match. Observe in Example 5-16 how four measures of music are notated within what would be labeled measures 1, 2, 3, and 4 of a melody when the upbeat precedes the first measure. The measure numbers are enclosed in circles above the staff. The incorrect alternative requires five measures to display four measures of music, with the first perceived downbeat occurring in measure 2 rather than in measure 1.

Example 5-16

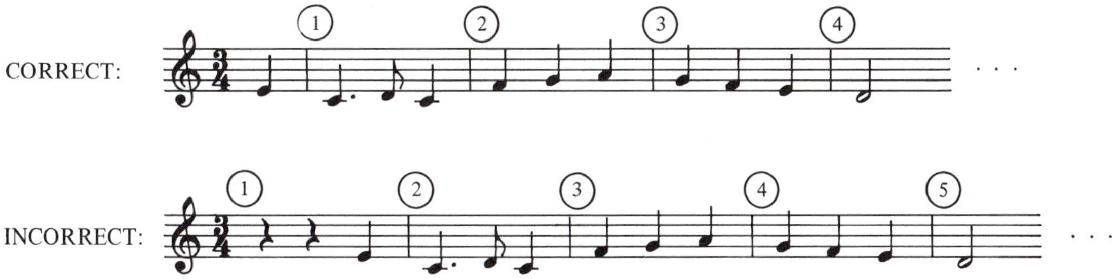

By convention, the last measure of a melody that begins with an upbeat is usually shortened by the number of beats that precede the first measure. For example, a melody of eight measures might be notated with only seven *complete* measures, as in Example 5-17.

Example 5-17

A melody that begins with an upbeat generally will use similar rhythmic gestures throughout. For example, if measure 1 is preceded by an eighth note, measure 5 might be also, as in the example below.

Example 5-18

The Repeat Sign

The ***repeat sign*** is a common notational device that saves a composer's time and reduces the expense of publication. If the double bar that typically designates the end of a melody is preceded by two vertically aligned dots in the second and

repeat sign

third spaces of the staff, as shown in Example 5-19, it designates that the performer should go back to the beginning of the melody and repeat all of the music that precedes the sign.

Example 5-19

NOTATED:

PERFORMED:

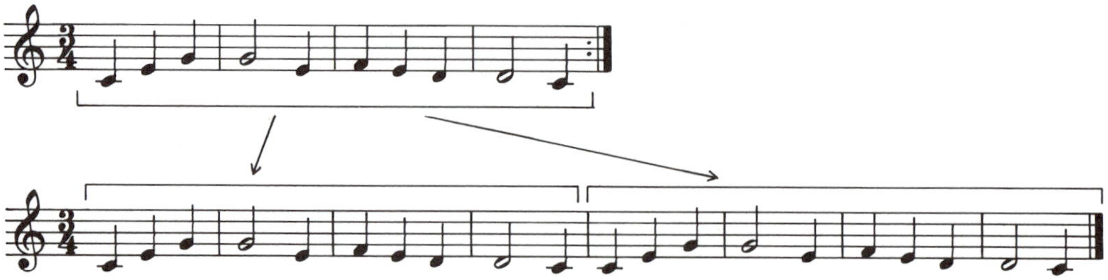

When a composer wants only the latter part of the music that precedes a repeat sign to be performed twice, another repeat sign, the mirror image of that shown in Example 5-19, is positioned at the point where the music to be repeated begins. In all cases, the two dots appear on the side of the double bar adjacent to the repeated music, while the thicker vertical line of the double bar is the one more distant from the repeated music. Example 5-20 demonstrates how these symbols should be interpreted. Observe especially that repeat signs do not always coincide with bar lines.

Example 5-20

NOTATED:

PERFORMED:

Occasionally two adjacent sections of a melody are both repeated. In that case, the point between the sections is notated using a special variant of the repeat sign. This symbol includes one thick and two thin vertical lines, rather than one thick and one thin, and two dots appear on *both* sides of this group of lines, as illustrated in Example 5-21.

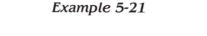

Example 5-21

Rhythm exercises for Chapter 5 are on pages 169–171.

LABORATORY

L5-1.a. Perform each of the following triads at the keyboard using your left hand.

a.

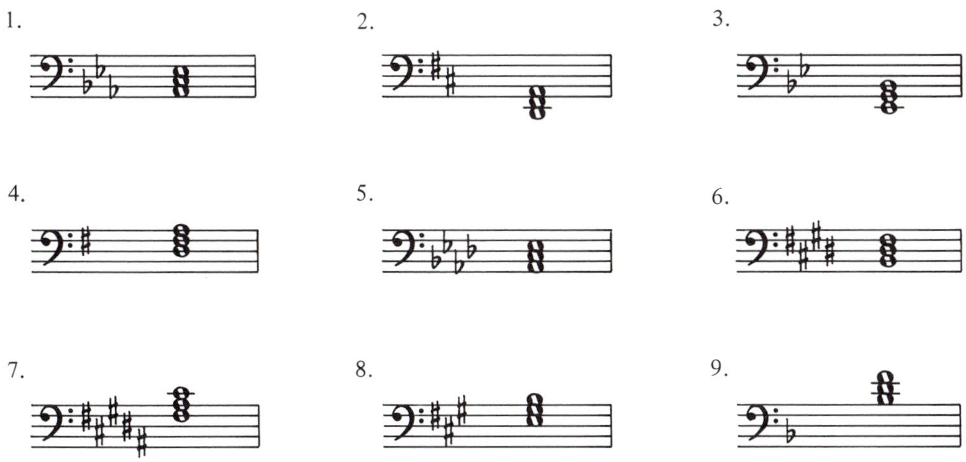

b. Perform each of the following melodies at the keyboard. When the melody is notated in bass clef, use your left hand; when notated in treble clef, use your right hand. Recommended fingerings are included. (The left thumb is "1," index finger is "2," etc.)

b.

Liszt: Consolation No. 2

1.

Beethoven: Quartet Op. 59, No. 1

2.

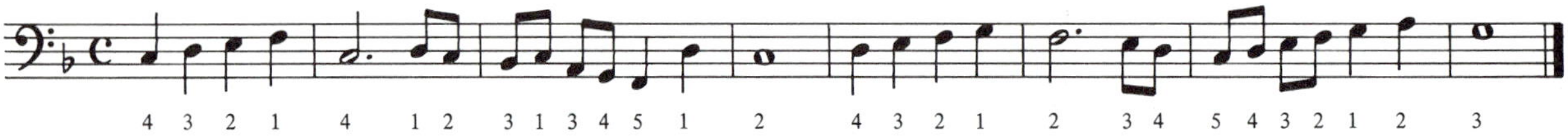

Johann Strauss, Jr.: *Morgenblätter* Waltz

3.

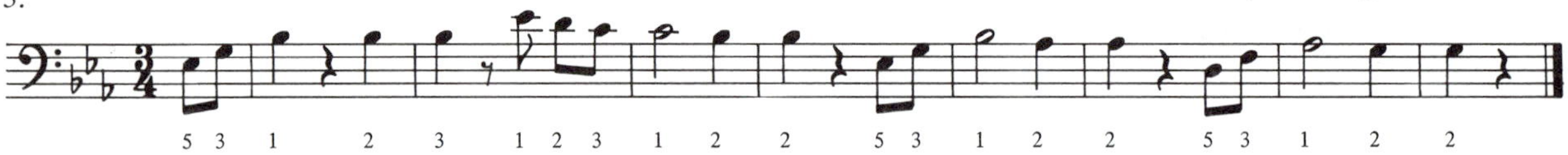

Schumann: The Happy Farmer, Op. 68, No. 10

4.

L5-2. At the keyboard, perform each of the following melodies first as written and then in transpositions such that several of the other eleven pitch classes serve as the starting pitch. The scale degrees have been written in to assist you.

a.

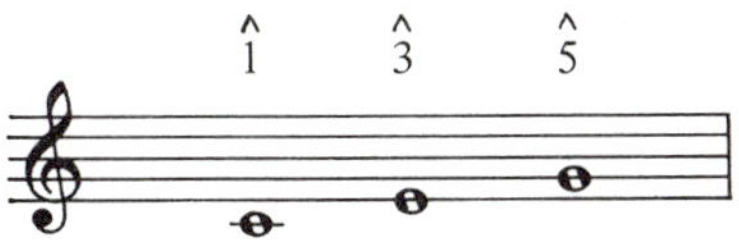

b.

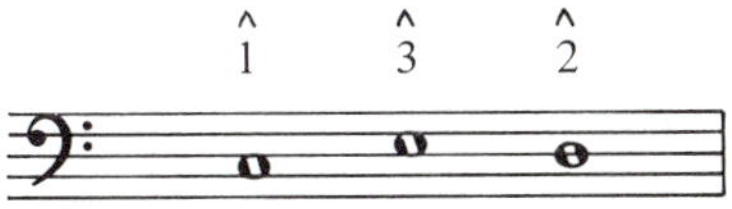

c.

d.

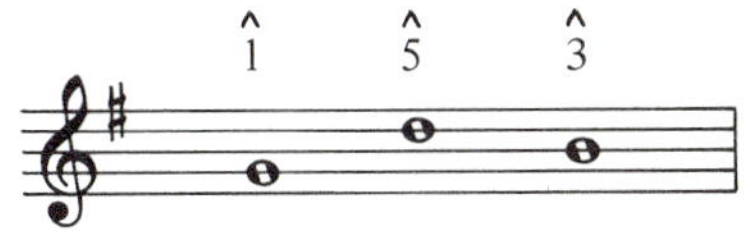

e.

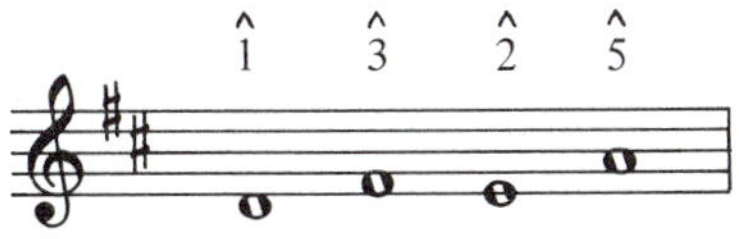

f.

g.

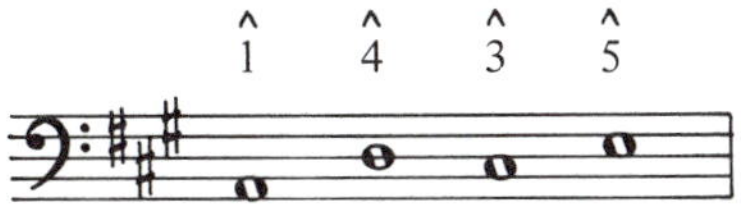

h.

L5-3. Starting on a pitch low in your vocal range, simultaneously sing and play an ascending major scale. Then strike scale degrees $\hat{1}$, $\hat{3}$, and $\hat{5}$ simultaneously. In this way, the key you have selected is solidly established in your ear. Now sing each melodic succession below in turn, confirming what you have sung by playing the appropriate pitches on the keyboard after each succession. Practice both in the order presented and in random order.

$\hat{1}$–$\hat{3}$

$\hat{1}$–$\hat{5}$

$\hat{3}$–$\hat{1}$

$\hat{3}$–$\hat{5}$

$\hat{5}$–$\hat{1}$

$\hat{5}$–$\hat{3}$

L5-4. Practice the following melodies at the keyboard, simultaneously singing and playing each pitch. Sing the scale-degree numbers that correspond to the pitches. Women should perform these melodies an octave higher than they are written. To do so, transpose the entire score up one octave.

a.

b.

c.

L5-5. The following compositions are for voice (upper staff) and keyboard (lower staff). Sing the scale-degree numbers that correspond to the pitches. At first you may play the vocal part on your keyboard while you sing, in order to solidify your performance. Eventually, however, observe the rests in the accompanying part during your vocal measures. The range of the compositions should be appropriate for most men's voices. Women should perform both the keyboard and vocal parts an octave higher.

a.

b.

L5-6. The following compositions are for two voices. Sing the scale-degree numbers that correspond to the pitches. Women should perform these melodies an octave higher than they are written.

a.

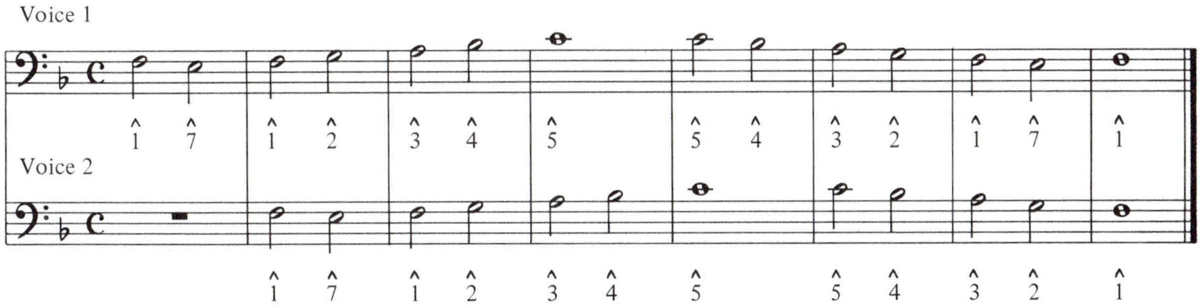

b.

L5-7. Write in the counting syllables below the notated rhythms. Then perform each by clapping the rhythm or playing the pitch C at the keyboard while pronouncing the counting syllables aloud. Practice until you can perform each exercise at a tempo of about ♩ = 60.

a.

b.

c.

d.

e.

L5-8. Write in the counting syllables below the notated rhythms. Then perform them by dividing the class into two groups, with each group clapping one part while pronouncing the counting syllables aloud. Alternatively, individual students may perform both parts simultaneously at the keyboard, pronouncing the counting syllables aloud while the index finger of the right hand strikes G and the index finger of the left hand strikes C, as notated.

a.

b.
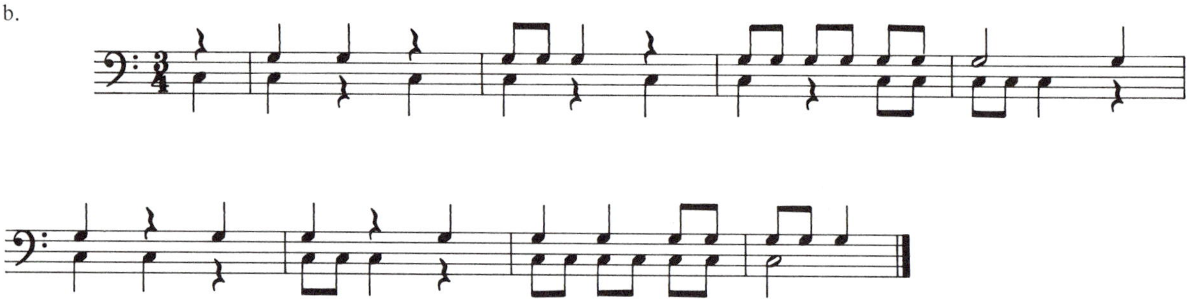

c.

L5-9. This exercise requires that a student or the instructor serve as the performer at a keyboard.

a. The performer plays an ascending major third or perfect fifth. Indicate which interval is performed.

b. The performer plays a descending major third or perfect fifth. Indicate which interval is performed.

c. The performer plays a major triad and then a melodic succession of two of its pitches. Indicate which two scale degrees are performed, from the choices provided below.

$\hat{1}$–$\hat{3}$
$\hat{1}$–$\hat{5}$
$\hat{3}$–$\hat{1}$
$\hat{3}$–$\hat{5}$
$\hat{5}$–$\hat{1}$
$\hat{5}$–$\hat{3}$

d. The performer plays a melody of three or four pitches, carefully noting the intervalic relationships. Then the performer chooses another starting pitch for the melody and either plays an exact transposition of the melody or an altered melody. Indicate whether an exact transposition occurs.

SAMPLE : Performer plays C D E C and then F G A♭ F. Your response is "No."

Audio exercises for Chapter 5 are on pages 172–174.

Name: ______________________

Instructor: ______________________

Date: ______________________

EXERCISES

Pitch Exercises

P5-1. Cut this page along the dotted lines. Form these slips into a pile and examine them one by one, identifying each note as you view it. (The answer is on the reverse.) Reshuffle the slips frequently. Practice until you can go through the pile with no errors in thirty seconds or less.

Hint: In the beginning, you may want to include only a few of the slips, for example all slips that contain C, E, or G. Eventually add to your pile until it contains all of the slips.

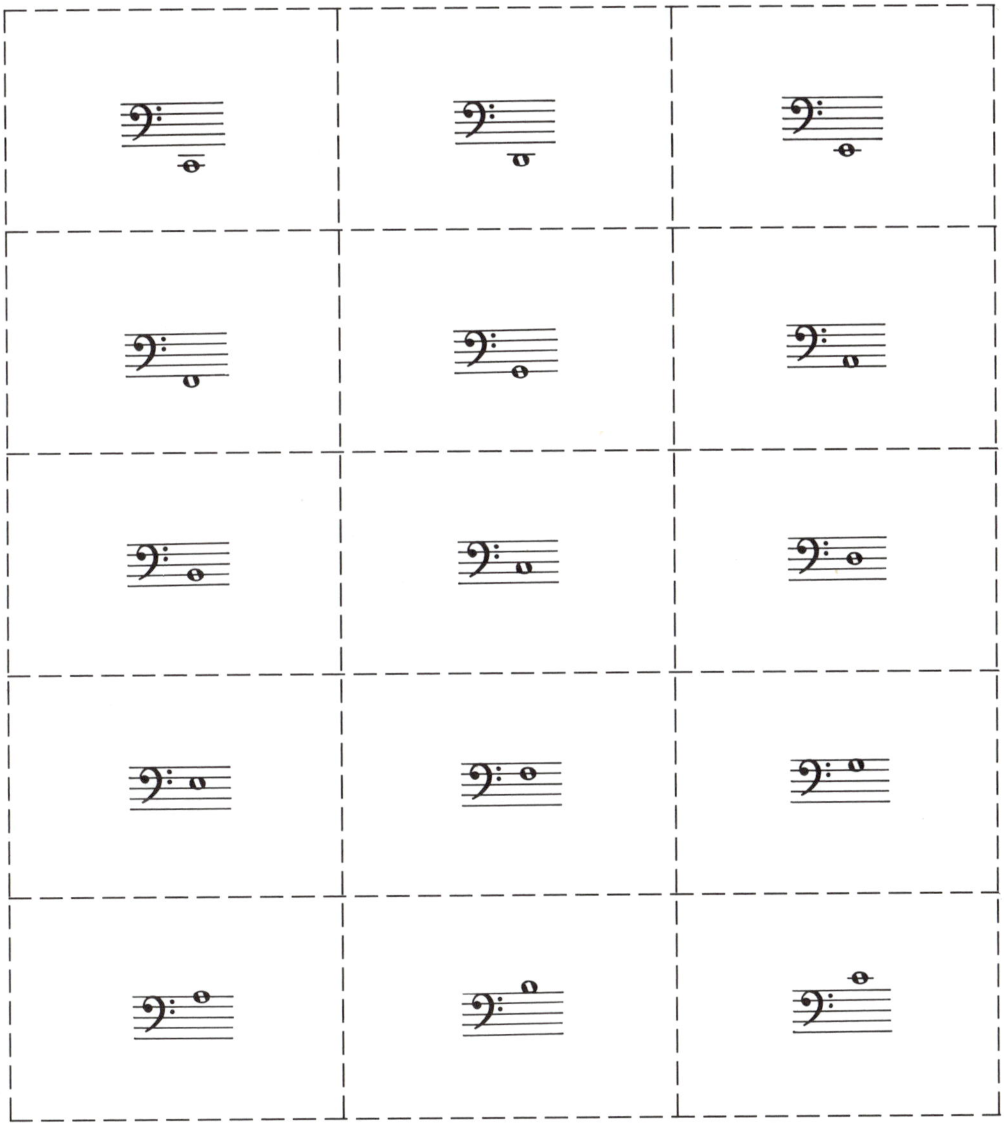

E	D	C
A	G	F
D	C	B
G	F	E
C	B	A

Name: ______________________

Instructor: ______________________

Date: ______________________

Rhythm Exercises

R5-1. Modify the time value of the last notehead in each of the following rhythms so that it represents the correct number of beats.

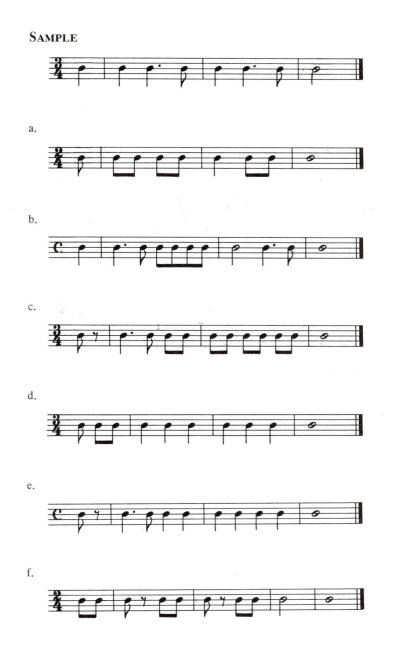

SAMPLE

a.

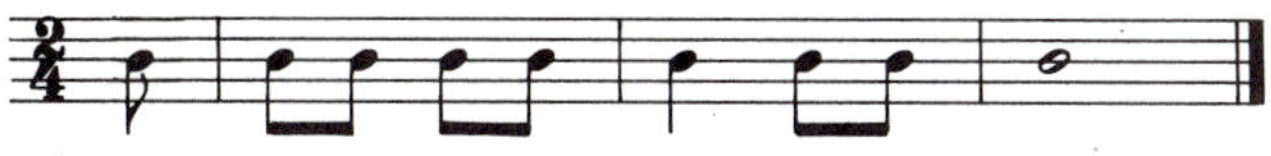

b.

c.

d.

e.

f.

R5-2. For each melody notated using repeat signs, write an equivalent score notation that does not use repeat signs.

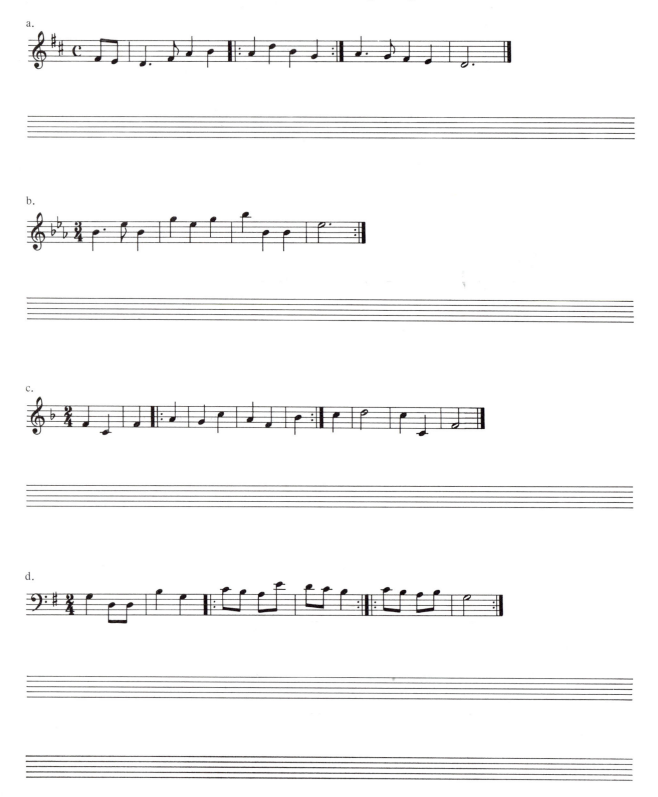

a.

b.

c.

d.

Name: ______________________

Instructor: ______________________

Date: ______________________

R5-3. Form a melody using the fragments provided. Only one ordering of these fragments results in measures that contain the correct number of beats.

a.

b.

R5-4. Notate the melodies indicated by the positioning of the pitch names in relation to the counting syllables. Use only unisons, seconds, thirds, and fourths as melodic intervals. Do not add rests.

a.

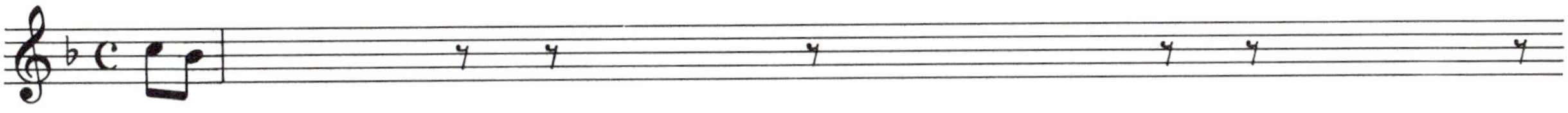

C Bb A G A C Bb A G Bb A G A Bb G F E F

4 + 1 + 2 + 3 + 4 + 1 + 2 + 3 + 4 + 1 + 2 + 3 + 4 + 1 + 2 + 3 +

b.

G A B A B C B A G F♯ G A B C D C B G A G F♯ G

2 + 1 + 2 + 1 + 2 + 1 + 2 + 1 + 2 + 1 + 2 + 1 + 2 + 1 + 2 + 1 +

c.

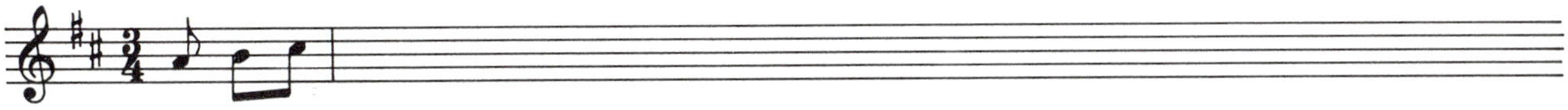

A B C♯ D A A C♯ D E B C♯ D E F♯ E D C♯ D

+ 3 + 1 + 2 + 3 + 1 + 2 + 3 + 1 + 2 + 3 + 1 + 2

Audio Exercises

A5-1. Two pitches will be performed in ascending order. Indicate whether they form the interval of a major third or a perfect fifth.

a. Major Third Perfect Fifth
b. Major Third Perfect Fifth
c. Major Third Perfect Fifth
d. Major Third Perfect Fifth
e. Major Third Perfect Fifth
f. Major Third Perfect Fifth
g. Major Third Perfect Fifth
h. Major Third Perfect Fifth
i. Major Third Perfect Fifth
j. Major Third Perfect Fifth

A5-2. Two pitches will be performed in descending order. Indicate whether they form the interval of a major third or a perfect fifth.

a. Major Third Perfect Fifth
b. Major Third Perfect Fifth
c. Major Third Perfect Fifth
d. Major Third Perfect Fifth
e. Major Third Perfect Fifth
f. Major Third Perfect Fifth
g. Major Third Perfect Fifth
h. Major Third Perfect Fifth
i. Major Third Perfect Fifth
j. Major Third Perfect Fifth

A5-3. A major triad will be performed, followed by a melodic succession of two of its pitches. Circle the choice of scale degrees that corresponds to the pitches performed.

a. $\hat{1}$–$\hat{3}$ $\hat{1}$–$\hat{5}$ $\hat{3}$–$\hat{5}$
b. $\hat{3}$–$\hat{1}$ $\hat{5}$–$\hat{1}$ $\hat{5}$–$\hat{3}$
c. $\hat{1}$–$\hat{3}$ $\hat{1}$–$\hat{5}$ $\hat{3}$–$\hat{5}$
d. $\hat{3}$–$\hat{1}$ $\hat{5}$–$\hat{1}$ $\hat{5}$–$\hat{3}$
e. $\hat{1}$–$\hat{3}$ $\hat{1}$–$\hat{5}$ $\hat{3}$–$\hat{5}$
f. $\hat{3}$–$\hat{1}$ $\hat{5}$–$\hat{1}$ $\hat{5}$–$\hat{3}$
g. $\hat{1}$–$\hat{3}$ $\hat{1}$–$\hat{5}$ $\hat{3}$–$\hat{5}$
h. $\hat{3}$–$\hat{1}$ $\hat{5}$–$\hat{1}$ $\hat{5}$–$\hat{3}$
i. $\hat{1}$–$\hat{3}$ $\hat{1}$–$\hat{5}$ $\hat{3}$–$\hat{5}$
j. $\hat{3}$–$\hat{1}$ $\hat{5}$–$\hat{1}$ $\hat{5}$–$\hat{3}$

Name: ______________________

Instructor: ______________________

Date: ______________________

A5-4. Two melodies will be performed. Circle "Yes" if the second is an exact transposition of the first, "No" if it is not.

a.	Yes	No	**f.**	Yes	No
b.	Yes	No	**g.**	Yes	No
c.	Yes	No	**h.**	Yes	No
d.	Yes	No	**i.**	Yes	No
e.	Yes	No	**j.**	Yes	No

A5-5. Six melodies will be performed. The starting pitch for each will be stated before the melody is performed. In each case circle the score that shows the correct pitch notation.

a.

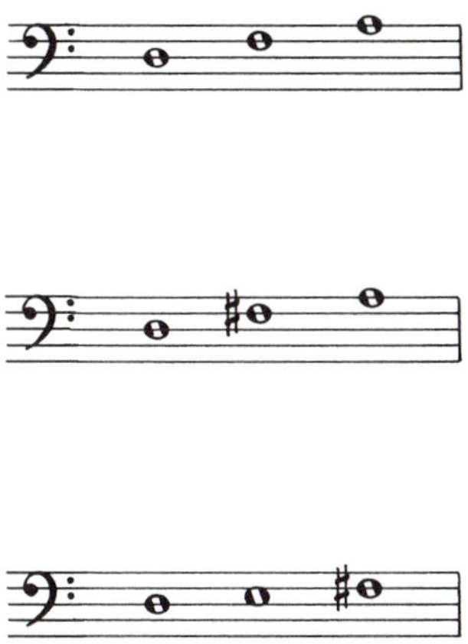

b.

c.

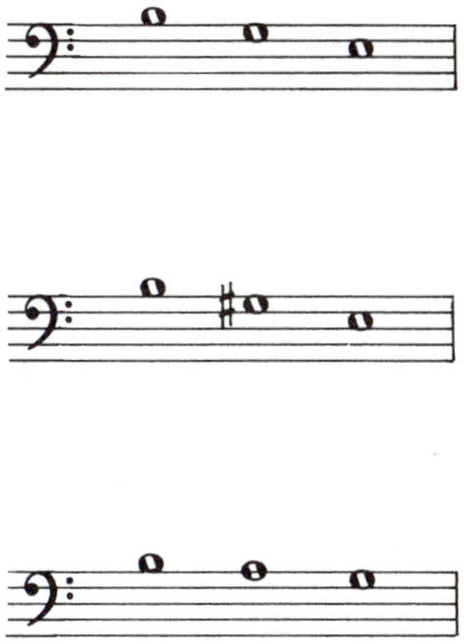

d.

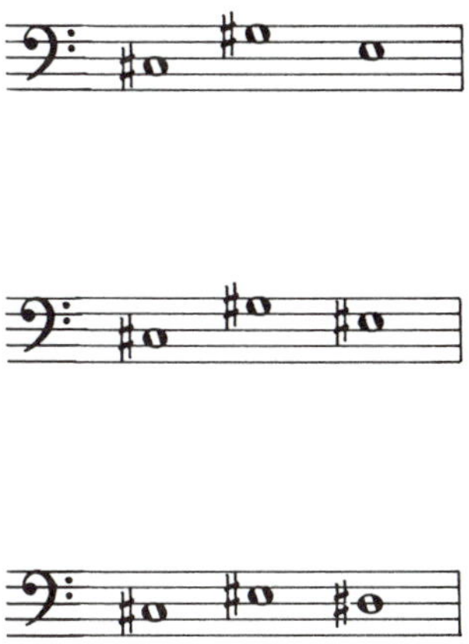

e.

f.

A5-6. Four rhythms will be performed. In each case circle the score that shows the correct notation.

a.

b.

c.

d.

Name: ______________________
Instructor: ______________________
Date: ______________________

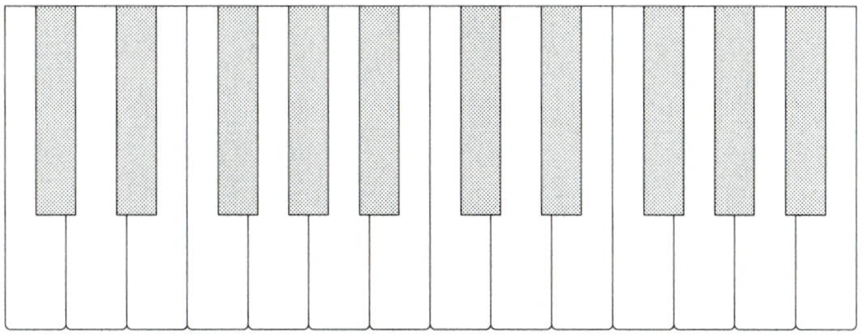

Mastery Test, Chapter 5

_______ 1. Which notehead corresponds to the pitch D?

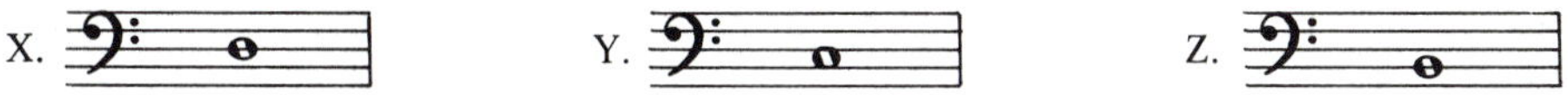

_______ 2. Which notehead corresponds to the pitch B♭?

_______ 3. Which one of the major triads shown includes the pitch E♭?

_______ 4. Which one of the major triads shown includes the pitch F♯?

_______ 5. Which one of the triads shown is a major triad?

__________ 6. Which one of the triads shown is a major triad?

X. 
Y. 
Z. 

__________ 7. Which one of the key signatures shown is that of G♭ major?

X. 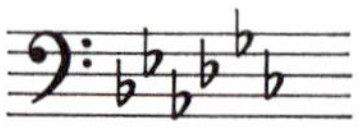
Y. 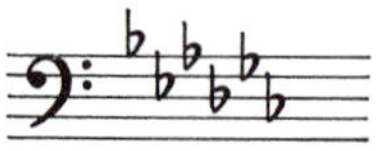
Z. 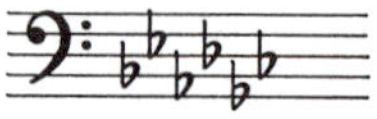

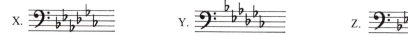

__________ 8. Which one of the key signatures shown is that of B major?

X. 
Y. 
Z. 

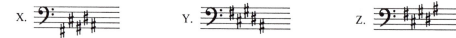

__________ 9. Which of the three alternatives is a correct transposition of the given melody an octave higher?

GIVEN:

X. 
Y. 
Z. 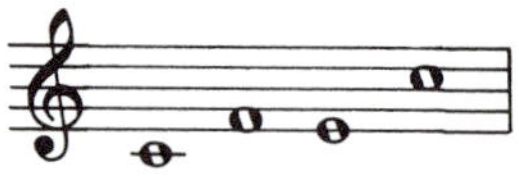

__________ 10. Which of the three alternatives is a correct transposition of the given melody a perfect fifth lower?

GIVEN:

X. 
Y. 
Z. 

__________ 11. Which of the three alternatives is a correct transposition of the given melody a perfect fifth higher?

GIVEN:

X. 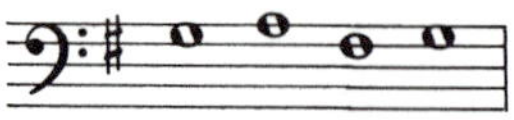
Y. 
Z. 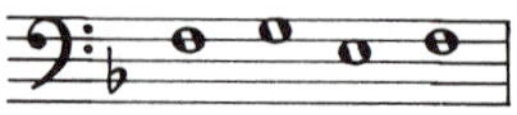

Name: ____________________
Instructor: ____________________
Date: ____________________

_________ 12. Which of the three alternatives is a correct transposition of the given melody a major third lower?

GIVEN:

X.  Y.  Z. 

_________ 13. Which of the three alternatives is the most likely ending for a melody that begins as shown?

X.  Y.  Z. 

_________ 14. Which of the three alternatives is the most likely ending for a melody that begins as shown?

X.  Y.  Z. 

_________ 15. Does the following symbol appear before or after material that is to be repeated?

Y. Before Z. After

_________ 16. Indicate whether the interval performed is a major third or a perfect fifth.

Y. Major third Z. Perfect fifth

_________ 17. A major triad will be performed, followed by a melodic succession of two of its pitches. Which scale degrees are performed?

X. $\hat{3}$–$\hat{1}$ Y. $\hat{5}$–$\hat{1}$ Z. $\hat{5}$–$\hat{3}$

_________ 18. Two melodies will be performed. Is the second an exact transposition of the first?

Y. Yes Z. No

__________ 19. A melody that begins with the pitch E will be performed. Which score shows the correct pitch notation?

X. 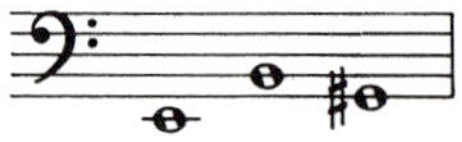

Y. 

Z. 

__________ 20. Which score shows the correct notation for the rhythm performed?

X. 

Y. 

Z. 

6

The Natural Minor Mode

Terms and Concepts

natural minor	*parallel keys*	*simple meter*
minor triad	*relative keys*	*compound meter*

PITCH

The Natural Minor Mode and Its Scale

Well over half of all tonal music is written in the major mode. The major third between $\hat{1}$ and $\hat{3}$ not only motivates the name of that mode but also reinforces a prominent overtone of the tonic pitch class. The other mode used in tonal music, the ***natural minor*** mode, features a minor third between $\hat{1}$ and $\hat{3}$. The word *natural* distinguishes the form of the minor mode introduced in this chapter from the variant forms considered in Chapter 10. Though there are exceptions, the major mode is traditionally associated with cheerful sentiments, while the natural minor mode is associated with sad ones. Compare the wedding march and funeral march illustrated in Example 6-1a and b.

natural minor

Example 6-1

Wagner: Wedding March from *Lohengrin*
(Rhythmic notation simplified)

a.

Chopin: Piano Sonata No. 2, Op. 35, Funeral March
(Transposed; Rhythmic notation simplified)

b.

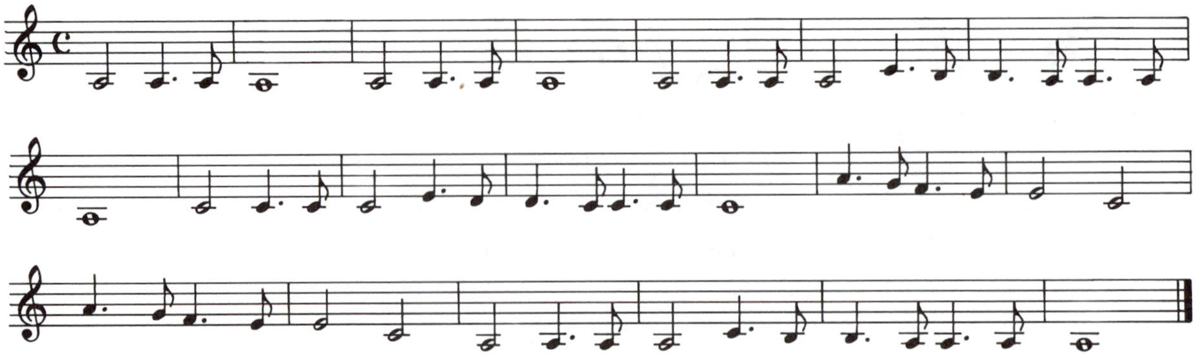

The minor third between $\hat{1}$ and $\hat{3}$ endows the tonic triad in natural minor with a quality that differs from that of major's tonic. A triad in which the root and third form a minor third, the third and fifth form a major third, and root and fifth form a perfect fifth is called a ***minor triad.*** Two examples of minor triads are shown in Example 6-2.

minor triad

Example 6-2

The minor triad is found in the major mode, but rooted only on some of the less prominent scale degrees—$\hat{2}$, $\hat{3}$, and $\hat{6}$—as shown in Example 6-3.

Example 6-3

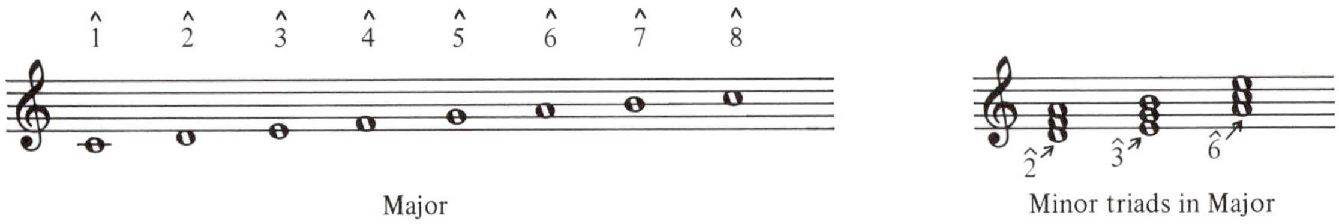

The diatonic pitch classes of the natural minor mode form minor triads rooted not only on tonic, but on the dominant and subdominant as well. In A minor, none of these pitch classes require accidentals, as shown in Example 6-4.

Example 6-4

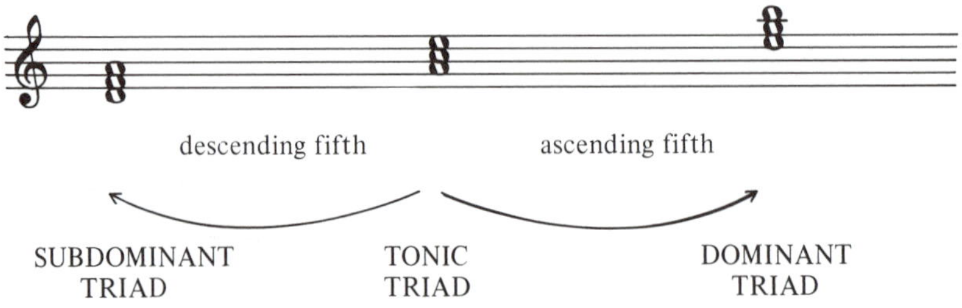

The diatonic pitch classes of natural minor keys, like those of major keys, are often arranged as scales. Ascending and descending natural minor scales for tonic A are shown in Example 6-5.

Example 6-5

Example 6-6 shows the relationships between adjacent scale degrees in the natural minor mode.

Example 6-6

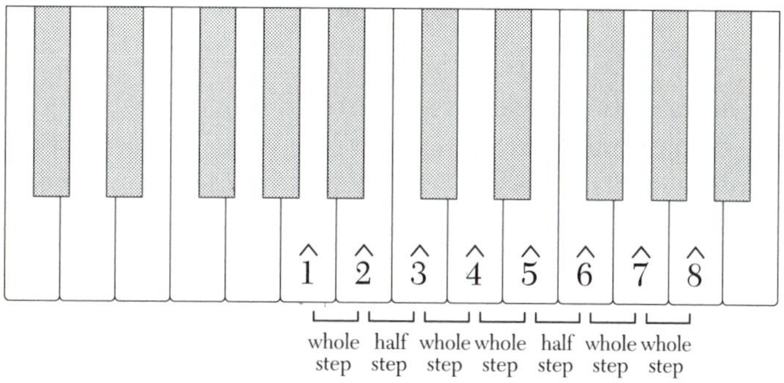

These relationships give the natural minor mode its distinctive character. Between most adjacent scale degrees, there is a whole step. But between $\hat{2}$ and $\hat{3}$ and between $\hat{5}$ and $\hat{6}$, there is only a half step. Any change in this set of interrelationships would contradict the mode.

Intervals of the Natural Minor Mode

If we compare major and natural minor scales starting on the same pitch, we discover that several scale degrees correspond. Both major and natural minor scales contain a major second, perfect fourth, perfect fifth, and perfect octave above the tonic pitch. But where the major scale contains a major third, major sixth, and major seventh, the natural minor scale contains intervals that are a half step smaller: the minor third, minor sixth, and minor seventh. These differences are what darken the tonic, subdominant, and dominant triads into their more somber guises in the natural minor mode. Natural minor and major scales are compared in Example 6-7, with pitch class A serving as tonic.

Example 6-7

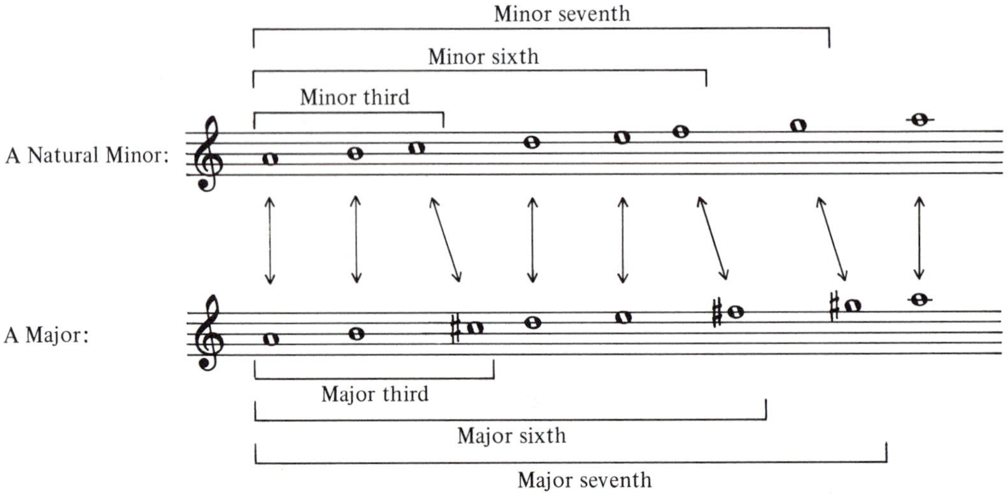

The chart in Example 6-8 shows all intervals that can be formed using $\hat{1}$ or $\hat{8}$ and one of the remaining diatonic scale degrees in the natural minor mode. Each interval is paired with its inversion. Most of the information on the chart matches that given for the major scale in Chapter 3. That which differs is shown in italics.

Example 6-8

Scale Degrees	*Interval Name*	*Size in Half Steps*	*Consonant/ Dissonant*
$\hat{1}$ $\hat{1}$	Perfect unison	0	Consonant
$\hat{1}$ $\hat{8}$	Perfect octave	12	Consonant
$\hat{1}$ $\hat{2}$	Major second	2	Dissonant
$\hat{2}$ $\hat{8}$	Minor seventh	10	Dissonant
$\hat{1}$ $\hat{3}$	*Minor* third	3	Consonant
$\hat{3}$ $\hat{8}$	*Major* sixth	9	Consonant
$\hat{1}$ $\hat{4}$	Perfect fourth	5	Dissonant
$\hat{4}$ $\hat{8}$	Perfect fifth	7	Consonant
$\hat{1}$ $\hat{5}$	Perfect fifth	7	Consonant
$\hat{5}$ $\hat{8}$	Perfect fourth	5	Dissonant

Scale Degrees	Interval Name	Size in Half Steps	Consonant/ Dissonant
$\hat{1}$ $\hat{6}$	*Minor* sixth	*8*	Consonant
$\hat{6}$ $\hat{8}$	*Major* third	*4*	Consonant
$\hat{1}$ $\hat{7}$	*Minor* seventh	*10*	Dissonant
$\hat{7}$ $\hat{8}$	*Major* second	*2*	Dissonant
$\hat{1}$ $\hat{8}$	Perfect octave	12	Consonant
$\hat{8}$ $\hat{8}$	Perfect unison	0	Consonant

Keys in the Natural Minor Mode

Natural minor scales can be built using each of the twelve pitch classes as tonic. As with the major keys, any two natural minor keys whose tonic pitches form the interval of a perfect fifth have key signatures that differ by only one sharp or flat. For example, A natural minor, as we know, contains no sharps or flats. E, the pitch class a perfect fifth above A, is the tonic of the natural minor key with one sharp, while D, the pitch class a perfect fifth below A, is the tonic of the natural minor key with one flat, as shown in Example 6-9.

Example 6-9

A Natural Minor

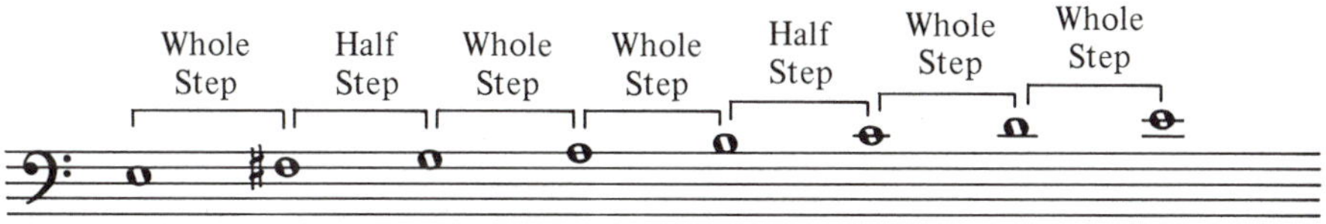

E Natural Minor

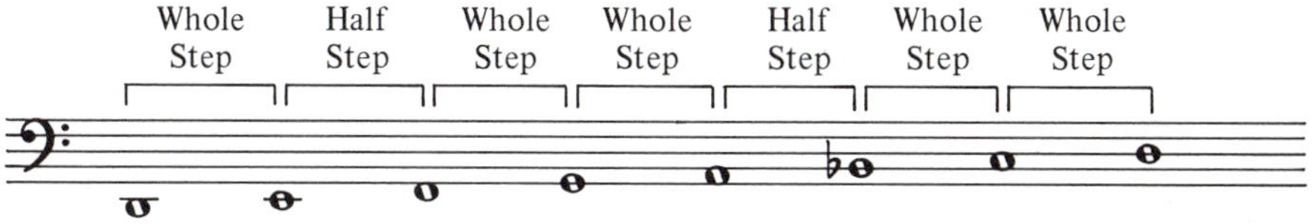

D Natural Minor

An account of all natural minor keys and their signatures will follow a brief discussion of the relationships between major and natural minor keys, below, because one of those relationships helps simplify learning the natural minor signatures.

Parallel and Relative Keys

parallel keys

Two keys that share the same tonic pitch class but are of different modes are called ***parallel keys.*** The key of A major is the parallel major of A natural minor; A natural minor is the parallel minor of A major. Likewise, D major and D natural minor are parallel keys, as are E♭ major and E♭ natural minor. Composers occasionally juxtapose a major key and its parallel minor, as Example 6-10 demonstrates.

Example 6-10

Mozart: Clarinet Quintet,
Minuet and Trio

(Rhythmic notation simplified)

A Major:

A Natural Minor:

relative keys

Two keys that use the same collection of diatonic pitch classes but are of different modes are called ***relative keys.*** The diatonic pitch classes of A natural minor and of C major both correspond to the white keys on the piano. For this reason, C major is the relative major of A natural minor, and A natural minor is the relative minor of C major. Likewise, D major and B natural minor are relative keys, as are E♭ major and C natural minor, as shown in Example 6-11.

Example 6-11

D major (two sharps)

B natural minor (two sharps)

E♭ major (three flats)

C natural minor (three flats)

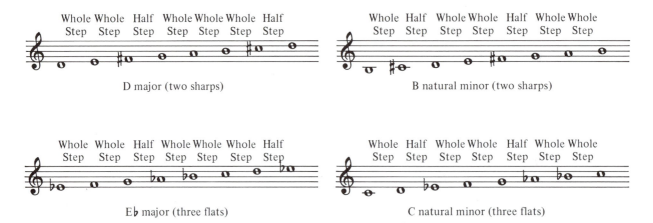

Though relative keys share the same set of pitch classes, a different pitch class serves as tonic in each. The tonics of relative keys will always form the interval of a minor third, that of the natural minor key corresponding to the lower note of the third, that of the major key to the higher.

Because relative keys share the same diatonic pitch classes, *all natural minor keys have the same key signatures as their relative majors*. Relative keys are often juxtaposed in musical compositions. In the last movement of Dvořák's "New World" Symphony, the first theme is in E minor, but later a theme in G major is introduced. These two themes are shown in Example 6-12.

Example 6-12

Dvořák: Themes from "New World" Symphony

E minor:

G major:

Major and Natural Minor Key Signatures Compared

A listing of all major and natural minor keys and their signatures is displayed in Example 6-13. Observe that most of this information was first introduced in Chapter 4. If you know how to find the relative major of any natural minor key (by ascending a minor third from the natural minor tonic), and if you have learned the major key signatures, the natural minor key signatures will not present a challenge.

Example 6-13

SHARP SIGNATURES

Major:	C	G	D	A	E	B	F♯	C♯
Natural Minor:	A	E	B	F♯	C♯	G♯	D♯	A♯

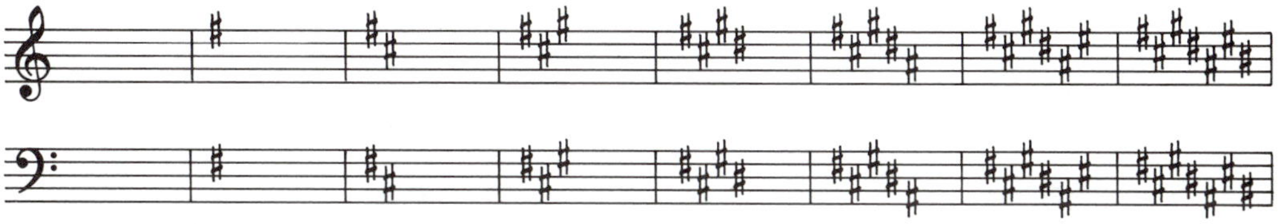

FLAT SIGNATURES

Major:	C	F	B♭	E♭	A♭	D♭	G♭	C♭
Natural Minor:	A	D	G	C	F	B♭	E♭	A♭

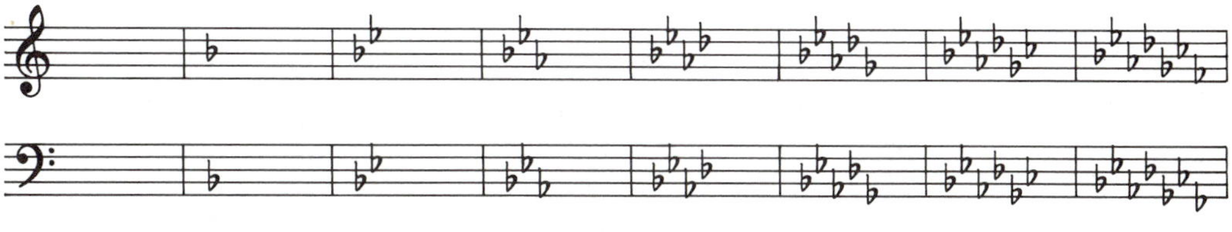

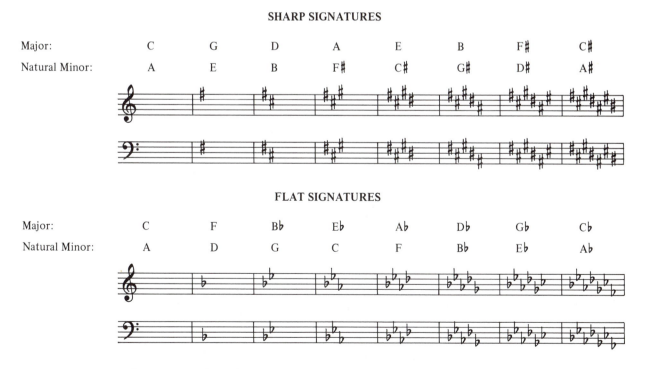

Pitch exercises for Chapter 6 are on pages 195–204.

RHYTHM

Simple versus Compound Meter

Though the $\frac{2}{4}$, $\frac{3}{4}$, and $\frac{4}{4}$ meters each contain a different number of beats per measure, these beats share a basic characteristic: they subdivide into halves. Composers often write two eighth notes to fill a quarter-note beat, or a dotted quarter note followed by an eighth note to fill two beats. Because their beats subdivide into halves, $\frac{2}{4}$, $\frac{3}{4}$, and $\frac{4}{4}$ are called ***simple meters.***

simple meter

compound meter

In ***compound meters*** beats subdivide into thirds rather than halves. The most common compound meters are $\frac{6}{8}$, $\frac{9}{8}$, and $\frac{12}{8}$, containing two, three, and four beats per measure, respectively. In each case, *three* eighth notes fill a beat. In $\frac{6}{8}$ a measure can hold two groups of three eighth notes (six eighth notes); in $\frac{9}{8}$ a measure can hold three such groups (nine eighth notes); and in $\frac{12}{8}$ a measure can hold four such groups (twelve eighth notes).

A comparison of $\frac{3}{4}$ and $\frac{6}{8}$ meters, both of which can hold six eighth notes within a measure, reveals the essential difference between simple and compound meters. In $\frac{3}{4}$ there are three beats, each of which is divided into two parts; in $\frac{6}{8}$ there are two beats, each of which is divided into three parts. As shown in Example 6-14, the eighth notes of simple meters are beamed in pairs, while the eighth notes of compound meters are beamed in groups of three. When counting, each syllable fills the same span of time, as usual. In compound meters the syllable "uh" is used for the third portion of each beat, as in "One and uh two and uh."

Example 6-14

NOTATED	COUNTED
	1 + 2 + 3 +
	1 + uh 2 + uh

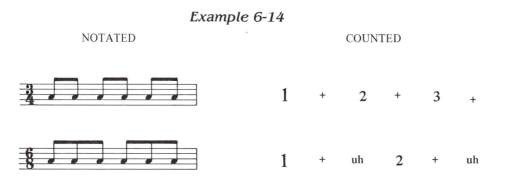

Dotted Quarter Note as Representative of the Beat

The quarter note is unsuitable as the representative of the beat in compound meters, because each beat contains three eighth notes. Instead, the dotted quarter note represents the beat. In simple meters, the dotted quarter note fills one and one-half beats, but in compound meters it fills exactly one beat. The melodies in Example 6-15 show how the dotted quarter note, groupings of three eighth notes, and the pattern of a quarter note plus an eighth note are ideally suited to meters whose beats subdivide into thirds. Observe that, unlike the simple meters we have employed, the upper number of compound time signatures does *not* indicate the number of beats per measure. For example, $\frac{6}{8}$ contains two (not six) beats per measure.

Example 6-15

Though most music notation is clear and unambiguous, $\frac{3}{4}$ meter includes one situation that composers and publishers have notated in a less than ideal manner over the centuries. When a measure in $\frac{3}{4}$ meter contains a dotted quarter note and three eighth notes, the preferred notation is that in Example 6-16a.

Example 6-16

Separating the first eighth note from the beam of the remaining eighth notes clarifies that the second of the three eighth notes is on the beat, while the first and third are off the beat. Unfortunately, the notation shown in Example 6-16b, in which the eighth note that falls on the beat is the middle of the three notes beamed together, occurs occasionally. You should avoid it in your work, because it looks like $\frac{6}{8}$ meter, not $\frac{3}{4}$.

In compound meters such as $\frac{6}{8}$, $\frac{9}{8}$, and $\frac{12}{8}$, a beat of silence is notated using a quarter rest followed by an eighth rest (Ex. 6-17a). When the first two thirds of a beat are silent, a quarter rest is used (Ex. 6-17b). When the last two thirds of a beat are silent, two eighth rests are used (Ex. 6-17c).

Example 6-17

Rhythm exercises for Chapter 6 are on pages 204–205.

LABORATORY

L6-1.a. Perform each of the following triads at the keyboard, using your right hand for those notated in treble clef and your left hand for those notated in bass clef.

1.
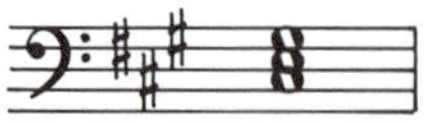

2.

3.

4.

5.

6.

7.

8.

9.

b. Perform each of the following melodies at the keyboard. Recommended fingerings for the left hand (below the staff) or right hand (above the staff) are included.

Mozart: Symphony No. 40

1.
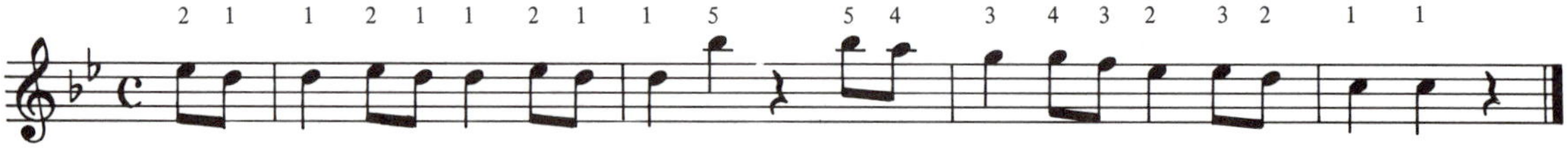

Mendelssohn: Symphony No. 4

2.

Bach: "Brandenburg" Concerto No. 6

3.
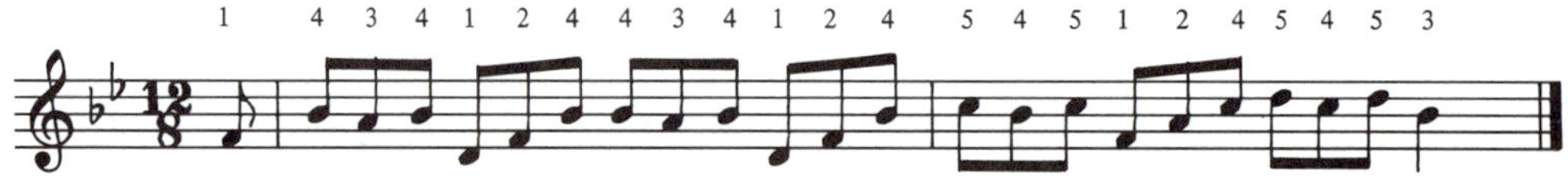

4.

Chopin: Valse brillante, Op. 34, No. 2

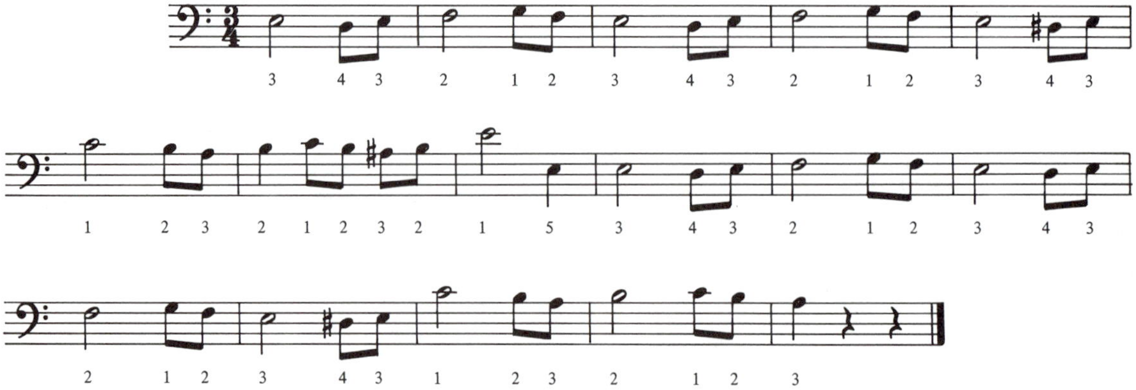

L6-2. At the keyboard, perform natural minor scales, ascending and descending, so that the given pitch falls on the scale degree indicated. During the ascent, say aloud the words "whole, half, whole, whole, half, whole, whole" at the appropriate times. During the descent, say aloud the words "whole, whole, half, whole, whole, half, whole" at the appropriate times.

Performance suggestion: Use both hands. Each finger (excluding the thumbs) can be assigned its own pitch to perform. Before you begin, position the little finger of your left hand on $\hat{1}$ and the little finger of your right hand on $\hat{8}$.

a.	C as $\hat{1}$	G♯ as $\hat{1}$	**b.**	E as $\hat{4}$	F♯ as $\hat{5}$
	B as $\hat{1}$	F♯ as $\hat{1}$		G as $\hat{6}$	B as $\hat{6}$
	F as $\hat{1}$	C♯ as $\hat{1}$		D♭ as $\hat{6}$	D♯ as $\hat{5}$
	A as $\hat{1}$	B♭ as $\hat{1}$		A♭ as $\hat{4}$	G♯ as $\hat{4}$
	G as $\hat{1}$	D as $\hat{1}$		B♭ as $\hat{3}$	E♭ as $\hat{3}$
	E as $\hat{1}$	D♯ as $\hat{1}$		C♯ as $\hat{2}$	A♯ as $\hat{5}$

L6-3.a. Practice the following exercise over a period of days or weeks until you have mastered it perfectly.

- Position two fingers on top of keys that are a minor third apart, but do not strike them. Make sure that these keys correspond to pitches within your vocal range.
- Strike the lower key.
- Sing that pitch.
- Sing the pitch a minor third higher.
- Strike the higher key and confirm that it is what you have sung.

b. Once the above exercise is going well, add the following steps.

- Position two fingers on top of keys that are a minor third apart, but do not strike them.
- Strike the upper key.
- Sing that pitch.
- Sing the pitch a minor third lower.
- Strike the lower key and confirm that it is what you have sung.

L6-4. Starting on a pitch low in your vocal range, sing and play an ascending natural minor scale. Then strike scale degrees $\hat{1}$, $\hat{3}$, and $\hat{5}$ simultaneously. In this way, the key you have selected is solidly established in your ear. Now sing each melodic succession below in turn, confirming what you have sung by playing the appropriate pitches on the keyboard after each succession. Practice both in the order presented and in random order.

$\hat{1}$–$\hat{3}$
$\hat{1}$–$\hat{5}$
$\hat{3}$–$\hat{1}$
$\hat{3}$–$\hat{5}$
$\hat{5}$–$\hat{1}$
$\hat{5}$–$\hat{3}$

L6-5. Four segments of major and natural minor scales are shown. Sing each segment, either in the order given or in random order. Also attempt to perform the exercise using transpositions. For example, perform (a) in C major, (b) in D minor, (c) in E major, and (d) in F minor.

a.

b.

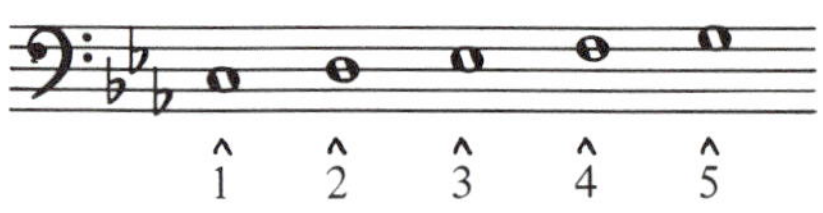

c.

d.

L6-6. Practice the following melodies at the keyboard, simultaneously singing and playing each pitch. Sing the scale-degree numbers that correspond to the pitches. If necessary, transpose the entire score up or down one octave.

a.

b.

c.

L6-7. The following compositions are for voice (upper staff) and keyboard (lower staff). Sing the scale-degree numbers that correspond to the pitches. At first you may wish to play the vocal part on the keyboard as well, in order to solidify your performance. Eventually, however, observe the rests in the accompanying part during your vocal measures. If necessary, transpose the entire score up or down one octave.

a. Voice

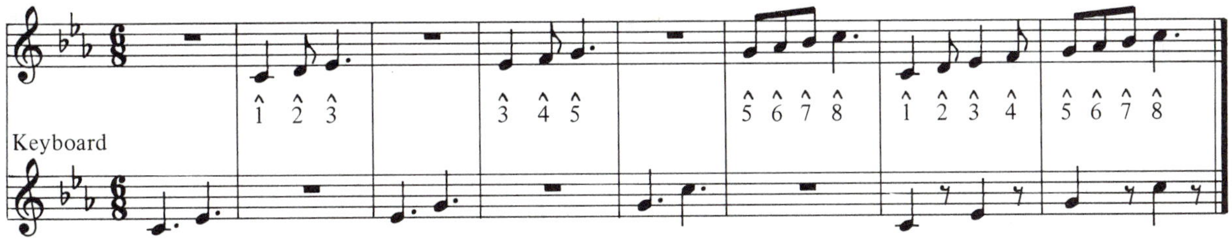

b. Voice

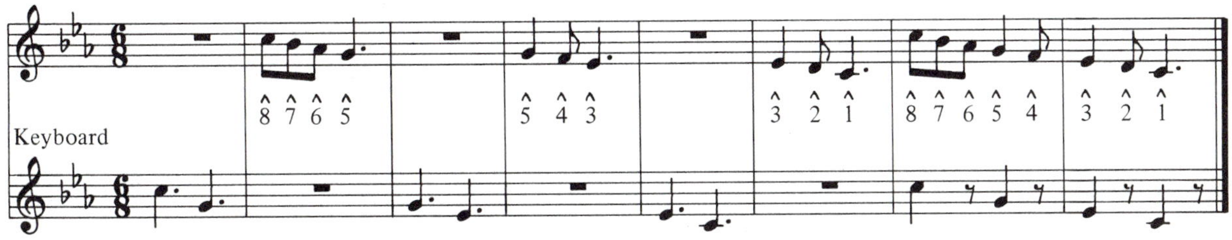

c. Voice

d. Voice

L6-8. The following compositions are for two voices. Sing the scale-degree numbers that correspond to the pitches. If necessary, transpose the entire score up or down one octave.

a.

b.

L6-9. Write in the counting syllables below the notated rhythms. Then perform each by clapping the rhythm or playing the pitch C or F at the keyboard, as notated, while pronouncing the counting syllables aloud. Practice until you can perform each exercise at a tempo of about ♩ = 60.

SAMPLE

a.

b.

c.

d.

L6-10. Write in the counting syllables below the notated rhythms. Then perform them by dividing the class into two groups, with each group clapping one part while pronouncing the counting syllables aloud. Alternatively, individual students may perform both parts simultaneously at the keyboard, pronouncing the counting syllables aloud while the index fingers strike the notated pitches.

a.

b.

c.

L6-11. This exercise requires that a student or the instructor serve as the performer at a keyboard.

a. The performer plays two pitches in either ascending or descending order, then plays them together. Indicate whether the interval performed is or is not a minor third.

b. The performer plays an ascending major third or minor third. Indicate which interval is performed.

c. The performer plays a descending major third or minor third. Indicate which interval is performed.

d. The performer plays a minor triad and then a melodic succession of two of its pitches. Indicate which two scale degrees are performed, from the choices presented below.

$\hat{1}$–$\hat{3}$
$\hat{1}$–$\hat{5}$
$\hat{3}$–$\hat{1}$
$\hat{3}$–$\hat{5}$
$\hat{5}$–$\hat{1}$
$\hat{5}$–$\hat{3}$

e. The performer plays a scale, either ascending or descending. Indicate whether the scale performed is C major, C natural minor, or neither. The performer's choices of scales for performance are as follows.

1. C D E F G A B C (major)
2. C D E♭ F G A♭ B♭ C (natural minor)
3. C D E♭ F G A B C
4. C D E F G A♭ B♭ C

Audio exercises for Chapter 6 are on pages 206–208.

Name: ____________________
Instructor: ____________________
Date: ____________________

	Scale Degrees	Interval Name	Size in Half Steps	Consonant/ Dissonant
v.	$\hat{1}$ – ___	Perfect fourth	___	___
w.	$\hat{4}$ – $\hat{8}$	___	___	___
x.	$\hat{1}$ – ___	___	10	___
y.	___ – $\hat{8}$	Major second	___	___
z.	$\hat{1}$ – ___	Minor seventh	___	___
aa.	$\hat{3}$ – $\hat{8}$	___	___	___
bb.	$\hat{1}$ – $\hat{7}$	___	___	___
cc.	$\hat{1}$ – $\hat{6}$	___	___	___
dd.	___ – $\hat{8}$	Major third	___	___
ee.	$\hat{1}$ – ___	___	3	___
ff.	___ – $\hat{8}$	___	2	___
gg.	$\hat{1}$ – ___	Minor sixth	___	___
hh.	___ – $\hat{8}$	___	4	___
ii.	$\hat{1}$ – ___	Major second	___	___
jj.	___ – $\hat{8}$	___	0	___
kk.	$\hat{1}$ – $\hat{2}$	___	___	___
ll.	$\hat{1}$ – ___	___	2	___
mm.	___ – $\hat{8}$	___	10	___
nn.	$\hat{1}$ – ___	Perfect octave	___	___
oo.	$\hat{7}$ – $\hat{8}$	___	___	___
pp.	$\hat{1}$ – $\hat{1}$	___	___	___

P6-3. Like the major keys, the natural minor keys can be arranged in a circle of fifths. Add the remaining key names in the boxes to complete the figure. Observe how the enharmonically equivalent keys are positioned within the circle of fifths.

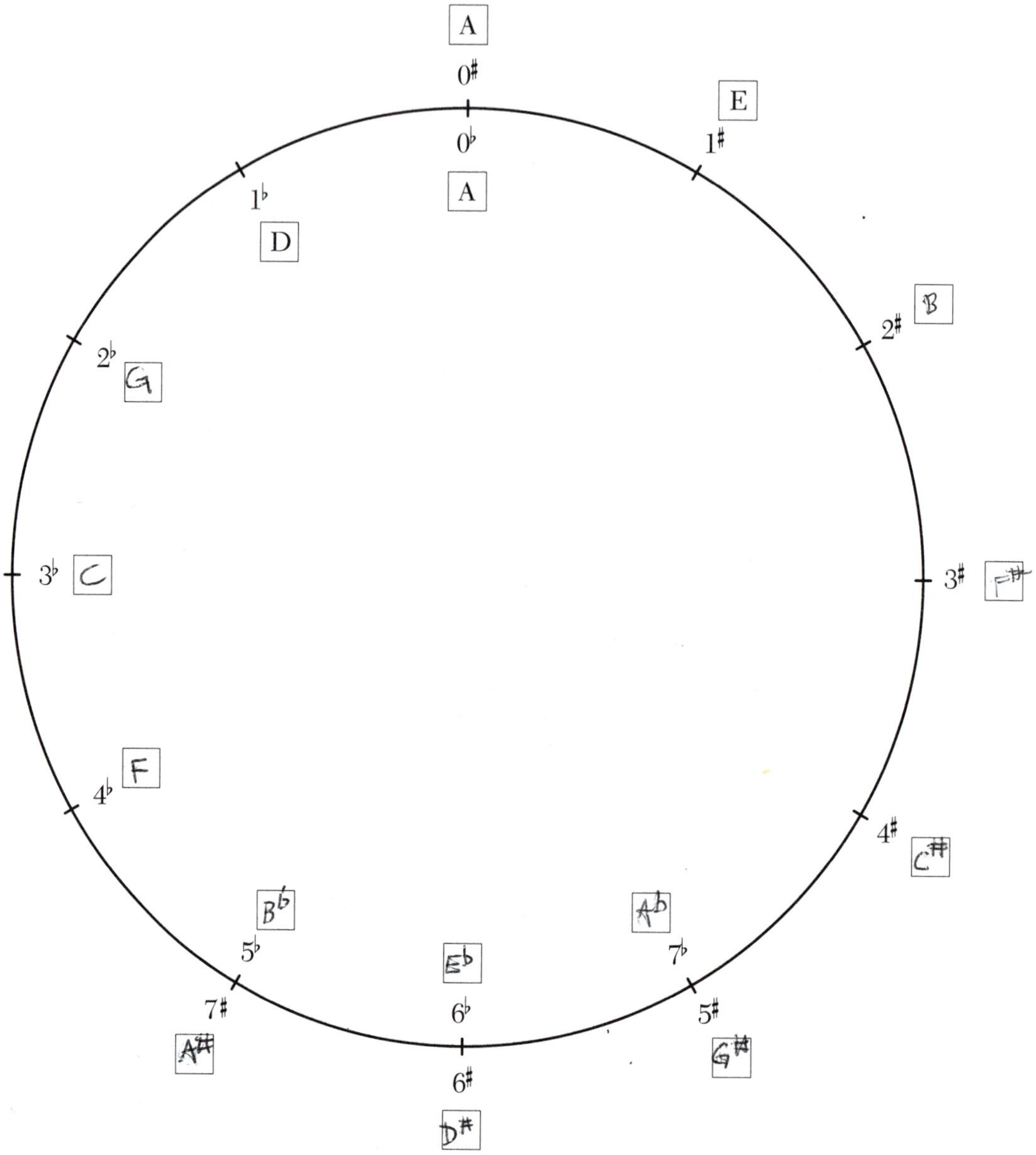

P6-4. Form the ascending intervals requested by treating the given pitch as $\hat{1}$, drawing the appropriate key signature for that natural minor key on the staff, and ascending the minor scale until you find the desired pitch.

Sample: Minor third above D♯.
Solution: The minor third appears between $\hat{1}$ and $\hat{3}$ in the key of D♯ natural minor, whose key signature contains six sharps. $\hat{3}$ is F♯.

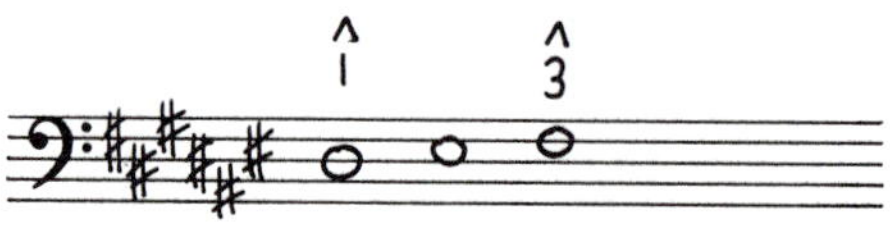

Name: ______________________
Instructor: ______________________
Date: ______________________

l. Major third below C♯

m. Major second below D

n. Major sixth below G♯

o. Major third below F

P6-6. A pitch and its scale degree in the natural minor mode are given. Find which pitch serves as the tonic by descending or ascending the scale, using the appropriate succession of whole and half steps to reach $\hat{1}$ or $\hat{8}$. The pattern of whole and half steps is shown below.

$\hat{1}$		$\hat{2}$		$\hat{3}$		$\hat{4}$		$\hat{5}$		$\hat{6}$		$\hat{7}$		$\hat{8}$
	Whole		Half		Whole		Whole		Half		Whole		Whole	

Sample: G as $\hat{6}$
Solution: B

Descend $\hat{6}$–$\hat{5}$–$\hat{4}$–$\hat{3}$–$\hat{2}$–$\hat{1}$ (G–F♯–E–D–C♯–B) or ascend $\hat{6}$–$\hat{7}$–$\hat{8}$ (G–A–B) to find tonic B. Be careful to use consecutive letters for adjacent pitches.

a. B♭ as $\hat{4}$

b. E as $\hat{6}$

c. D♭ as $\hat{4}$

d. A as $\hat{2}$

e. B as $\hat{4}$

f. F♯ as $\hat{6}$

g. F as $\hat{4}$

h. A as $\hat{7}$

i. G♭ as $\hat{3}$

j. E as $\hat{3}$

k. F as $\hat{5}$

l. A as $\hat{4}$

m. F as $\hat{3}$

P6-7. A notehead and its scale degree within a natural minor key are given. Decide which natural minor key is appropriate, using the method of Exercise P6-6. Then write its key signature beside the clef and add the remaining notes of the scale.

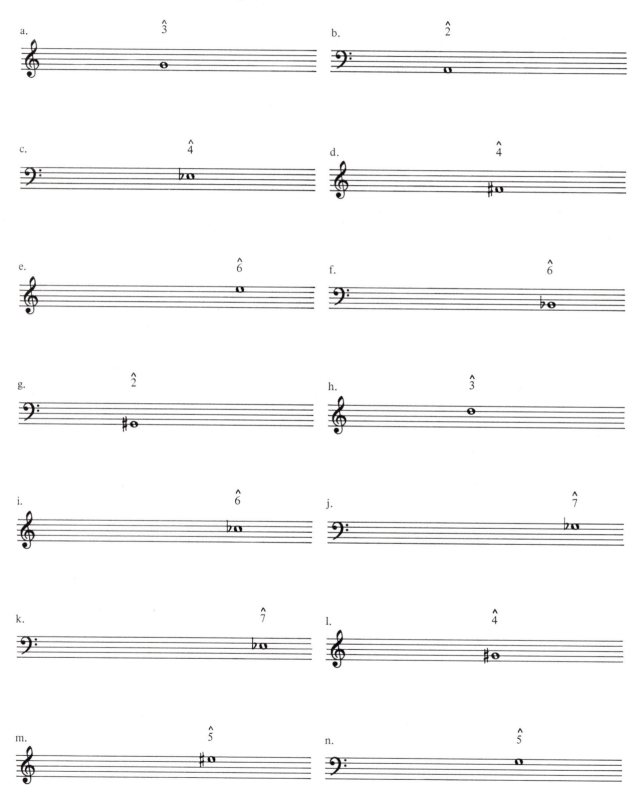

a.

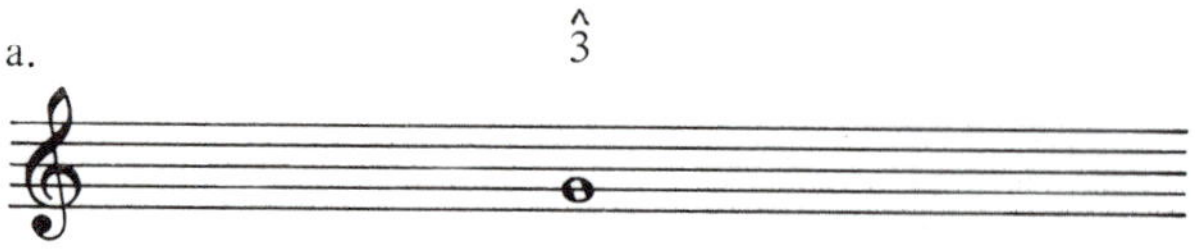

b.

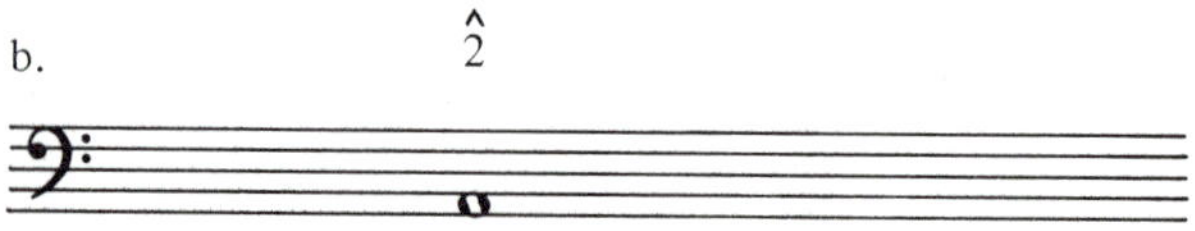

c.

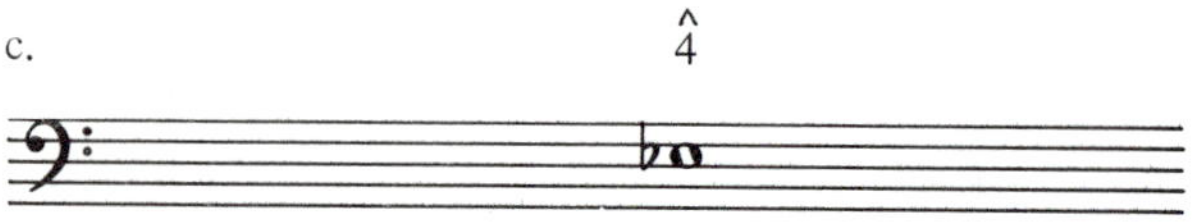

d.

e.

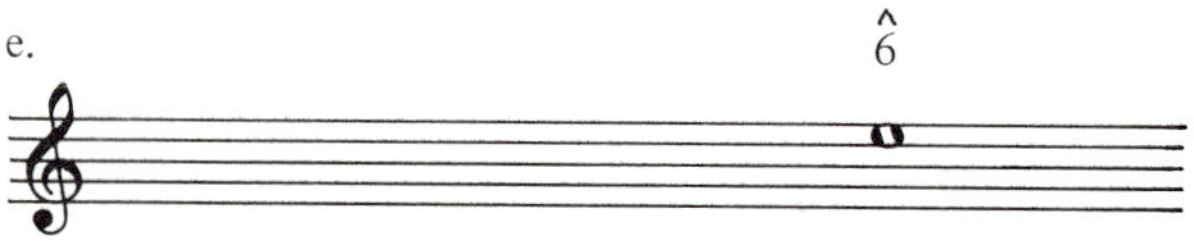

f.

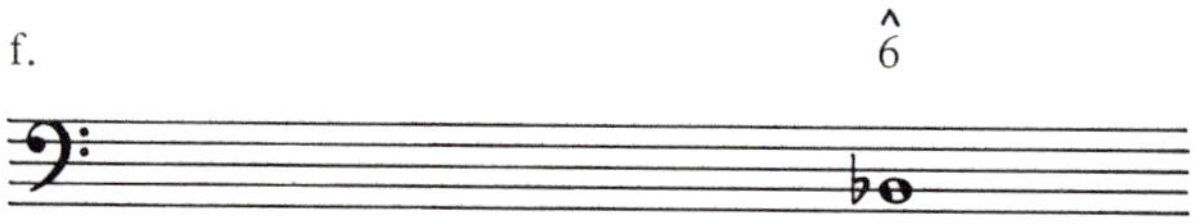

g.

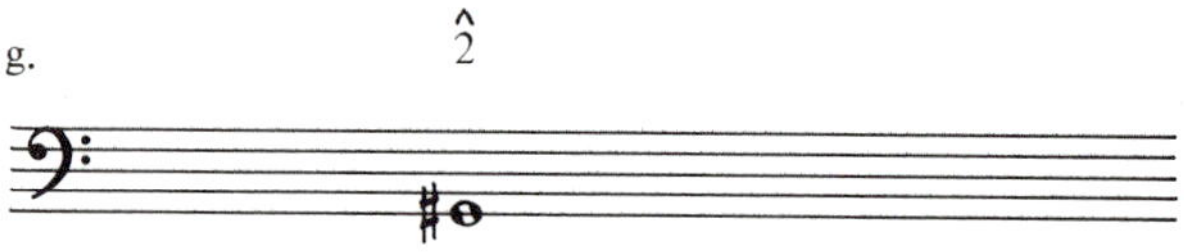

h.

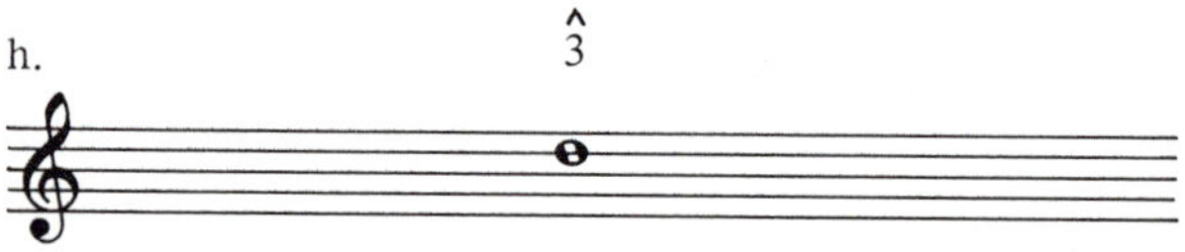

i.

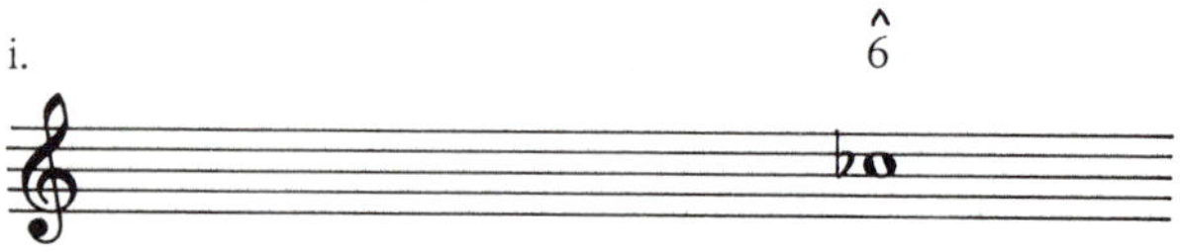

j.

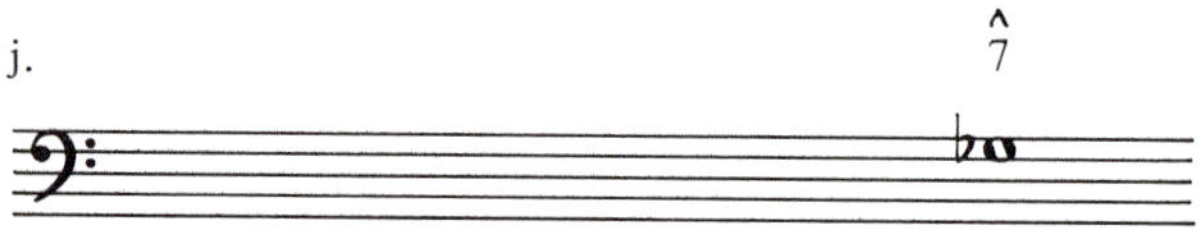

k.

l.

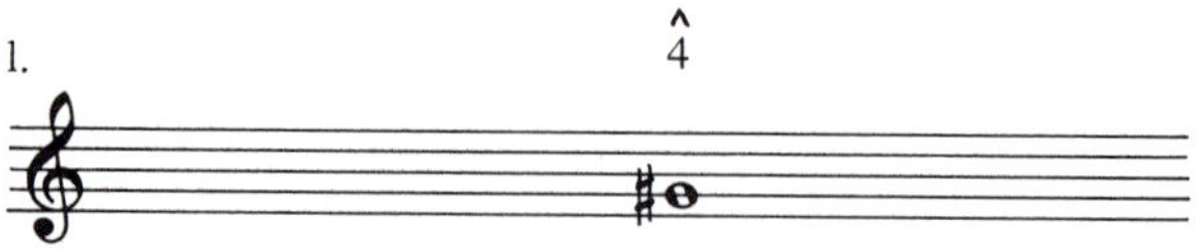

m.

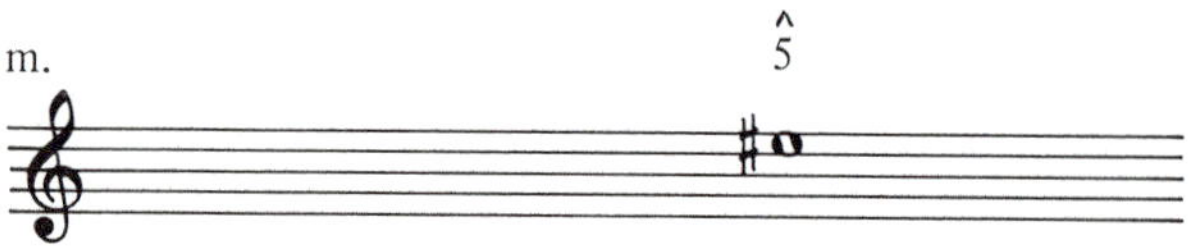

n.

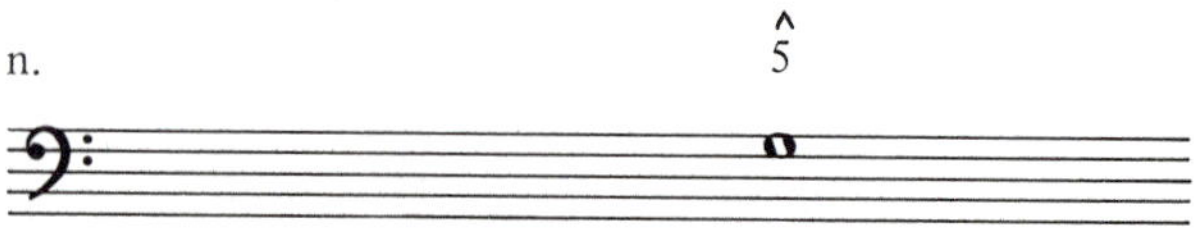

Name: ______________________
Instructor: ______________________
Date: ______________________

P6-8. Complete the following chart.

Natural Minor	*Parallel Major*	*Relative Major*	*Sharps or Flats in Key Signature*
D	___	___	___________
___	___	G♭	___________
B	___	___	___________
___	___	___	7 flats
C♯	___	___	___________
___	___	___	3 sharps
___	___	A♭	___________
___	C	___	___________
E	___	___	___________
___	___	B♭	___________
___	___	___	5 flats
___	___	C	___________
___	___	___	4 sharps
___	E♭	___	___________
___	___	A	___________
B♭	___	___	___________
___	___	___	4 flats
___	B	___	___________
___	___	___	1 sharp

P6-9. For three natural minor keys, there are no parallel major keys with the same letter names. One of them is G♯ natural minor. Because there is no key of G♯ major, we would have to use the enharmonic equivalent, A♭ major, as the parallel major. Which other natural minor keys lack a parallel major with the same letter name? What key would substitute as parallel major?

Natural minor key: Substitute parallel major:

Natural minor key: Substitute parallel major:

P6-10. For three major keys, there are no parallel minor keys with the same letter names. One of them is D♭ major. Because there is no key of D♭ natural minor, we would have to use the enharmonic equivalent, C♯ natural minor, as the parallel minor. Which other major keys lack a parallel minor with the same letter name? What key would substitute as parallel minor?

Major key: Substitute parallel minor:

Major key: Substitute parallel minor:

Rhythm Exercises

R6-1. Modify the noteheads indicated by arrows to form complete measures containing the appropriate number of beats. Wherever possible, incorporate the existing beam notation.

a.

b.

c.

d.
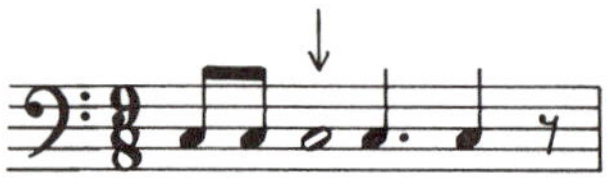

e.
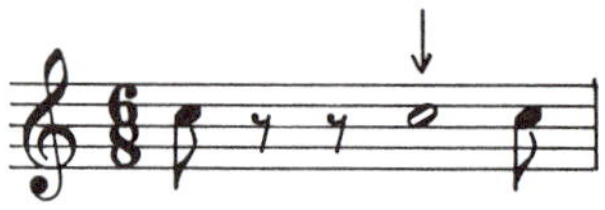

f.

g.
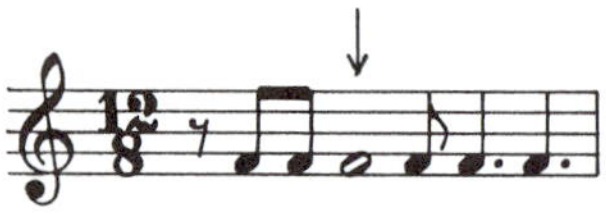

h.
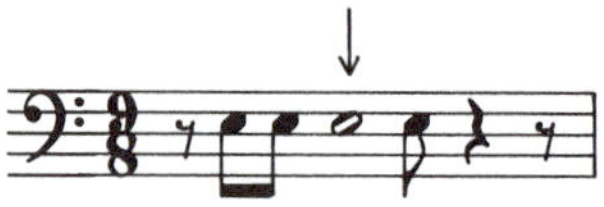

i.
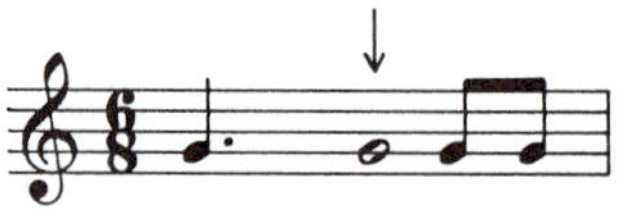

j.
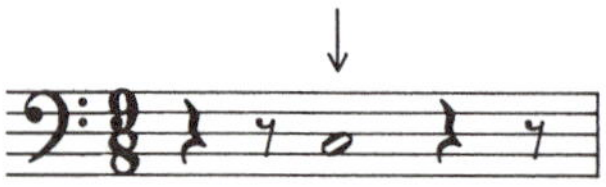

k.
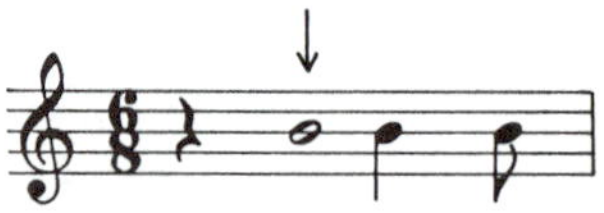

l.

m.

n.

o.

Name: ______________________

Instructor: ______________________

Date: ______________________

R6-2. Form a melody using the fragments provided. Only one ordering of these fragments results in measures that contain the correct number of beats.

a.

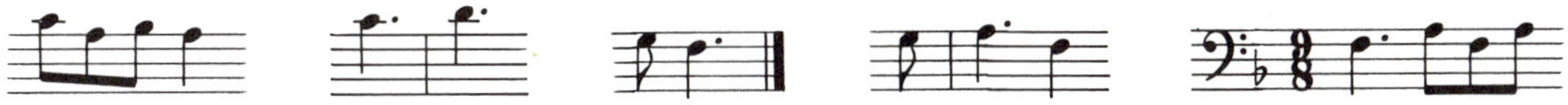

b.

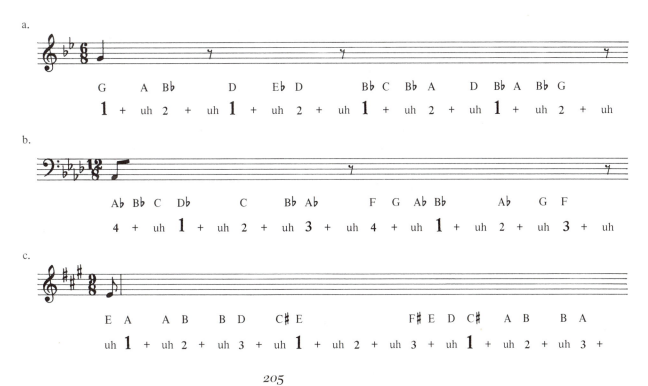

R6-3. Notate the melodies indicated by the positioning of the pitch names in relation to the counting syllables. Use only unisons, seconds, thirds, and fourths as melodic intervals. Do not add rests.

a.

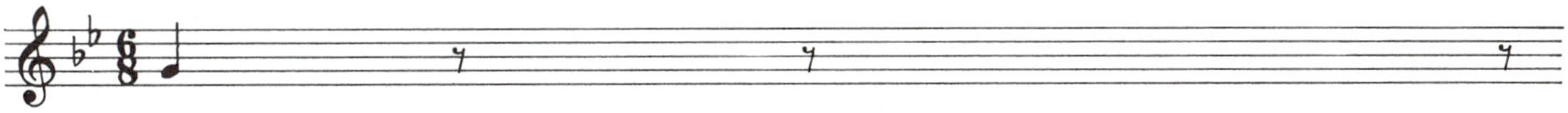

G A B♭ D E♭ D B♭ C B♭ A D B♭ A B♭ G

1 + uh 2 + uh **1** + uh 2 + uh **1** + uh 2 + uh **1** + uh 2 + uh

b.

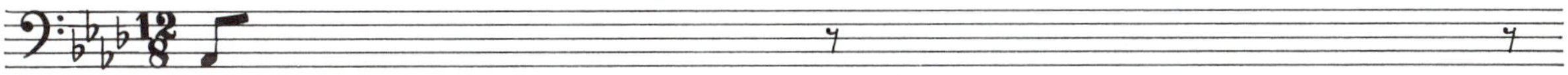

A♭ B♭ C D♭ C B♭ A♭ F G A♭ B♭ A♭ G F

4 + uh **1** + uh 2 + uh **3** + uh 4 + uh **1** + uh 2 + uh **3** + uh

c.

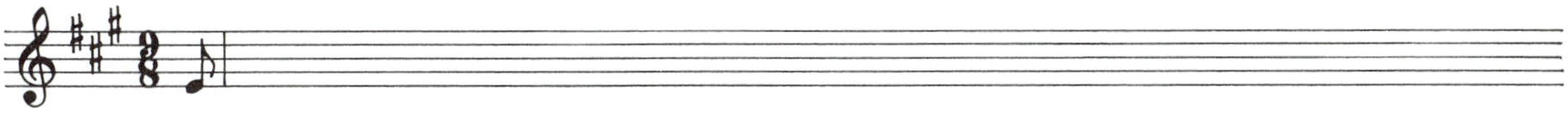

E A A B B D C♯ E F♯ E D C♯ A B B A

uh **1** + uh 2 + uh 3 + uh **1** + uh 2 + uh 3 + uh **1** + uh 2 + uh 3 +

Audio Exercises

A6-1. Ten intervals will be performed, first as two successive pitches, then as two simultaneous pitches. Circle "Yes" if the interval is a minor third, "No" if it is not.

a. Yes	No	**f.** Yes	No
b. Yes	No	**g.** Yes	No
c. Yes	No	**h.** Yes	No
d. Yes	No	**i.** Yes	No
e. Yes	No	**j.** Yes	No

A6-2. A major third or a minor third will be performed, either ascending or descending. Indicate which of these two intervals is performed.

a. Major Third	Minor Third
b. Major Third	Minor Third
c. Major Third	Minor Third
d. Major Third	Minor Third
e. Major Third	Minor Third
f. Major Third	Minor Third
g. Major Third	Minor Third
h. Major Third	Minor Third
i. Major Third	Minor Third
j. Major Third	Minor Third

A6-3. A minor triad will be performed, followed by a melodic statement of two of its pitches. Circle the choice of scale degrees that corresponds to the pitches performed.

a. $\hat{1}$–$\hat{3}$	$\hat{1}$–$\hat{5}$	$\hat{3}$–$\hat{5}$	**f.** $\hat{3}$–$\hat{1}$	$\hat{5}$–$\hat{1}$	$\hat{5}$–$\hat{3}$
b. $\hat{3}$–$\hat{1}$	$\hat{5}$–$\hat{1}$	$\hat{5}$–$\hat{3}$	**g.** $\hat{1}$–$\hat{3}$	$\hat{1}$–$\hat{5}$	$\hat{3}$–$\hat{5}$
c. $\hat{1}$–$\hat{3}$	$\hat{1}$–$\hat{5}$	$\hat{3}$–$\hat{5}$	**h.** $\hat{3}$–$\hat{1}$	$\hat{5}$–$\hat{1}$	$\hat{5}$–$\hat{3}$
d. $\hat{3}$–$\hat{1}$	$\hat{5}$–$\hat{1}$	$\hat{5}$–$\hat{3}$	**i.** $\hat{1}$–$\hat{3}$	$\hat{1}$–$\hat{5}$	$\hat{3}$–$\hat{5}$
e. $\hat{1}$–$\hat{3}$	$\hat{1}$–$\hat{5}$	$\hat{3}$–$\hat{5}$	**j.** $\hat{3}$–$\hat{1}$	$\hat{5}$–$\hat{1}$	$\hat{5}$–$\hat{3}$

A6-4. A scale will be performed, either ascending or descending. Indicate whether the scale is the major scale, the natural minor scale, or neither by circling the appropriate response.

a. Major	Natural Minor	Neither
b. Major	Natural Minor	Neither
c. Major	Natural Minor	Neither
d. Major	Natural Minor	Neither
e. Major	Natural Minor	Neither
f. Major	Natural Minor	Neither
g. Major	Natural Minor	Neither
h. Major	Natural Minor	Neither
i. Major	Natural Minor	Neither
j. Major	Natural Minor	Neither

Name: ______________________

Instructor: ______________________

Date: ______________________

A6-5. Six melodies will be performed. The starting pitch for each will be stated before the melody is performed. In each case circle the score that shows the correct pitch notation.

a.

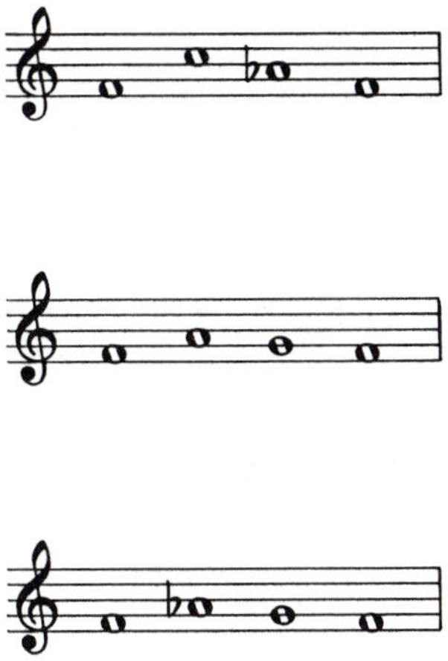

b.

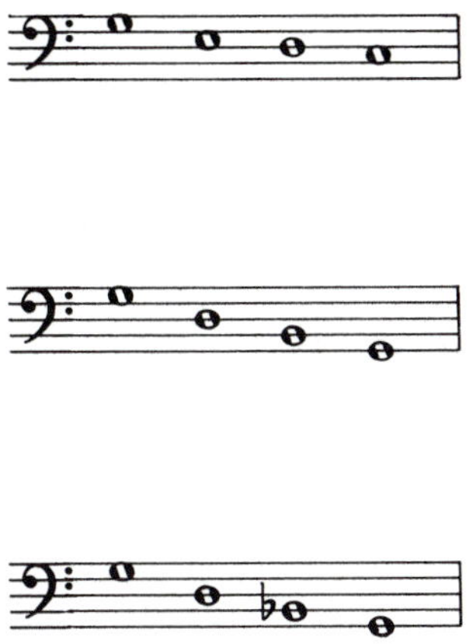

c.

d.

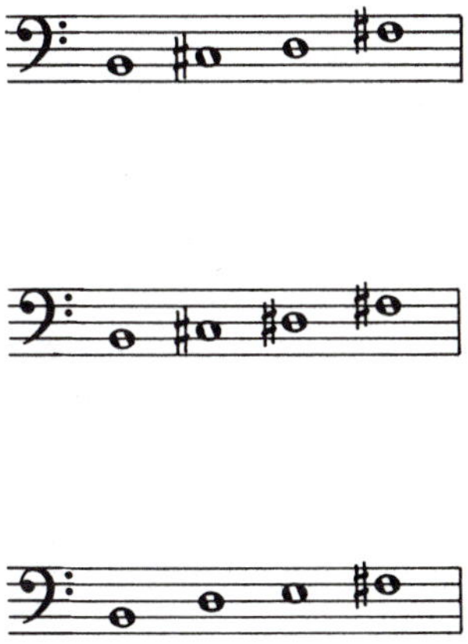

e.

f.

A6-6. Four rhythms will be performed. In each case circle the score that shows the correct notation.

a.

b.

c.

d.

Name: ______________________
Instructor: ______________________
Date: ______________________

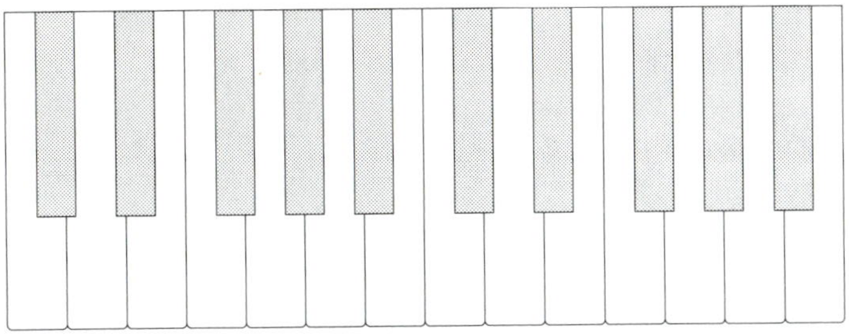

Mastery Test, Chapter 6

______ 1. In the natural minor mode, which scale degrees serve as roots for minor triads?
X. $\hat{1}$, $\hat{5}$, and $\hat{6}$ Y. $\hat{2}$, $\hat{3}$, and $\hat{6}$ Z. $\hat{1}$, $\hat{4}$, and $\hat{5}$

______ 2. In the major mode, which scale degrees serve as roots for minor triads?
X. $\hat{1}$, $\hat{5}$, and $\hat{6}$ Y. $\hat{2}$, $\hat{3}$, and $\hat{6}$ Z. $\hat{1}$, $\hat{4}$, and $\hat{5}$

______ 3. Which key is the relative minor of F major?
X. D minor Y. F minor Z. A♭ minor

______ 4. Which key is the parallel major of C minor?
X. E♭ major Y. A major Z. C major

______ 5. Which scale degrees in the *ascending* natural minor scale form the relationship Half Step, Whole Step, Whole Step, Half Step?
X. $\hat{4}$–$\hat{5}$–$\hat{6}$–$\hat{7}$–$\hat{8}$ Y. $\hat{7}$–$\hat{1}$–$\hat{2}$–$\hat{3}$–$\hat{4}$ Z. $\hat{2}$–$\hat{3}$–$\hat{4}$–$\hat{5}$–$\hat{6}$

______ 6. Which one of the triads shown is a minor triad?

X. Y. Z.

______ 7. Which pitch is a minor seventh higher than the pitch F♯?
X. E Y. E♯ Z. E♭

______ 8. Which pitch is a minor sixth lower than the pitch B?
X. D Y. D♯ Z. E♭

_________ 9. Exactly how many sharps appear in the key signature for G♯ minor?
X. Five Y. Six Z. Seven

_________ 10. Exactly how many flats appear in the key signature for E♭ minor?
X. Four Y. Five Z. Six

_________ 11. Which pitch functions as $\hat{6}$ in the key of G♯ natural minor?
X. E Y. E♯ Z. F

_________ 12. Which pitch functions as $\hat{7}$ in the key of E♭ natural minor?
X C♯ Y. D♭ Z. D

_________ 13. If the dotted quarter note represents the beat, then how many beats occur within one measure in $\frac{12}{8}$ meter?
X. 3 Y. 4 Z. 12

_________ 14. What kind of note should be inserted at the arrow to complete the measure?
X. Eighth note
Y. Quarter note
Z. Dotted quarter note

_________ 15. What kind of note should be inserted at the arrow to complete the measure?
X. Eighth note
Y. Quarter note
Z. Dotted quarter note

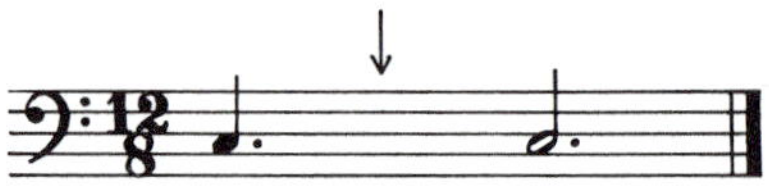

_________ 16. An interval will be performed, first as two successive pitches, then as two simultaneous pitches. Is the interval a minor third?
Y. Yes Z. No

_________ 17. A minor triad will be performed, followed by a melodic statement of two of its pitches. Which scale degrees are performed?
X. $\hat{1}$–$\hat{3}$ Y. $\hat{1}$–$\hat{5}$ Z. $\hat{3}$–$\hat{5}$

_________ 18. A succession of eight descending pitches will be performed. Is it a natural minor scale?
Y. Yes Z. No

Name: ____________________
Instructor: ____________________
Date: ____________________

________ 19. A melody that begins with the pitch B will be performed. Which score shows the correct pitch notation?

X. 

Y. 

Z. 

________ 20. Which score shows the correct notation for the rhythm performed?

X. 

Y. 

Z. 

7

Interval Relationships and the Chromatic Scale

Terms and Concepts

compound interval	*chromatic scale*
simple interval	*double sharp*
augmented	*double flat*
diminished	*sixteenth note*
tritone	*dotted eighth note*
diatonic half step	*dotted eighth rest*
chromatic half step	*sixteenth rest*

PITCH

Compound Intervals

Many of the intervals used in music were introduced during our study of the major and natural minor scales. Each interval that can be formed between $\hat{1}$ or $\hat{8}$ and one of the other diatonic pitches of either mode has been named, paired with its inversion, and classified as consonant or dissonant. An interval's name depends both upon what letters are used to spell it and upon the distance, as measured in half steps and whole steps, between its two pitches. For example, A and the C♯ above it form a major third. The interval size is three because the letters *A* and *C* are used. (A and D♭, though they might sound the same as A and C♯, make a fourth, not a third.) The quality of the third is major because two whole steps separate A and C♯.

The C♯ directly above A is not the only C♯ that forms an interval with A. Consider the two alternatives shown in Example 7-1.

Example 7-1

Major Third   Alternative 1   Alternative 2

Both of these alternatives are related to the major third, because they use the same two pitch classes and because composers employ them in similar ways.

compound interval

simple interval

Alternative 1 differs from the major third only in that an octave has been added to the interval size. Any interval larger than an octave is called a ***compound interval*** (in contrast to a ***simple interval,*** which falls within the range of an octave). Because the relationship between the two pitches remains similar to that of the major third, Alternative 1 is called a compound major third. It could also be called a major tenth, to reflect the interval size between its two pitches (because ten lines and spaces in staff notation separate the two noteheads). Observe that the quality of the interval has not changed, only its size. *The quality of any compound interval is determined by finding the quality of its simple counterpart.*

In Alternative 2, two octaves, rather than one octave, have been added to the major third. As with Alternative 1, this interval could be called a compound major third. It could also be called a major seventeenth, to reflect the number of lines and spaces that separate its two noteheads. (For each octave added, we must add seven to the interval size. The compounds of the third are $3 + 7 = 10$; $10 + 7 = 17$; $17 + 7 = 24$; etc.) In practice, intervals larger than a tenth are rarely named according to their actual interval sizes. Instead, they are named as compound versions of the corresponding simple intervals—as a "compound major third" rather than a "major seventeenth," for example.

Interval Inversion Revisited

When we form a compound interval, the relationship between the upper and lower pitch classes does not change. As shown in Example 7-1, C♯ remains the upper and A remains the lower of the two pitch classes. If we reverse this relationship, we invert the interval. In Example 7-2a the C♯ of the major third is moved down an octave to form the inversion, a minor sixth. The two intervals both employ pitch classes A and C♯. In the major third, C♯ is above A, while in the minor sixth C♯ is below A. Alternatively, the major third could be inverted by moving its lower pitch class A up an octave, as shown (Ex. 7-2b).

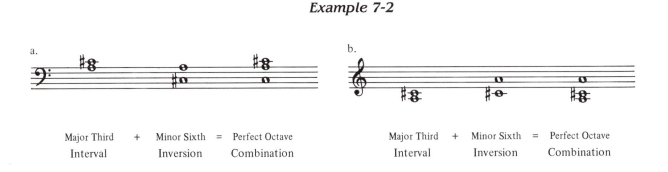

Example 7-2

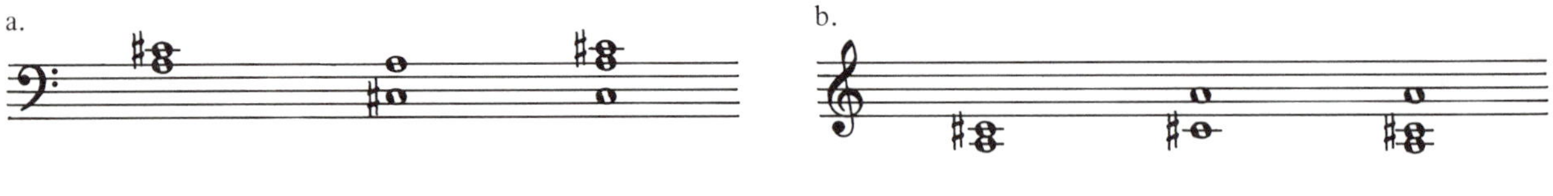

a. Major Third Interval + Minor Sixth Inversion = Perfect Octave Combination

b. Major Third Interval + Minor Sixth Inversion = Perfect Octave Combination

Example 7-2 demonstrates two general principles of interval inversion first mentioned in Chapter 3: (1) the sum of the interval sizes of two inversionally related intervals always equals nine; and (2) the inversion of a major interval is of minor quality. Example 7-3 demonstrates two additional general principles: (3) the inversion of a minor interval is of major quality; and (4) the inversion of a perfect interval is of perfect quality.

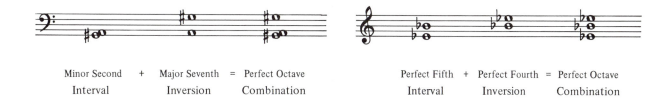

Example 7-3

Minor Second Interval	+	Major Seventh Inversion	=	Perfect Octave Combination

Perfect Fifth Interval	+	Perfect Fourth Inversion	=	Perfect Octave Combination

Intervals Formed Using Diatonic Scale Degrees

The fifteen major and fifteen natural minor keys offer numerous examples of the various intervals we have encountered. The major third, for example, occurs not only between $\hat{1}$ and $\hat{3}$ in the major keys but also between $\hat{4}$ and $\hat{6}$ and between $\hat{5}$ and $\hat{7}$ in major keys, and between $\hat{3}$ and $\hat{5}$, $\hat{6}$ and $\hat{8}$, and $\hat{7}$ and $\hat{2}$ in natural minor keys, as shown in Example 7-4.

Example 7-4

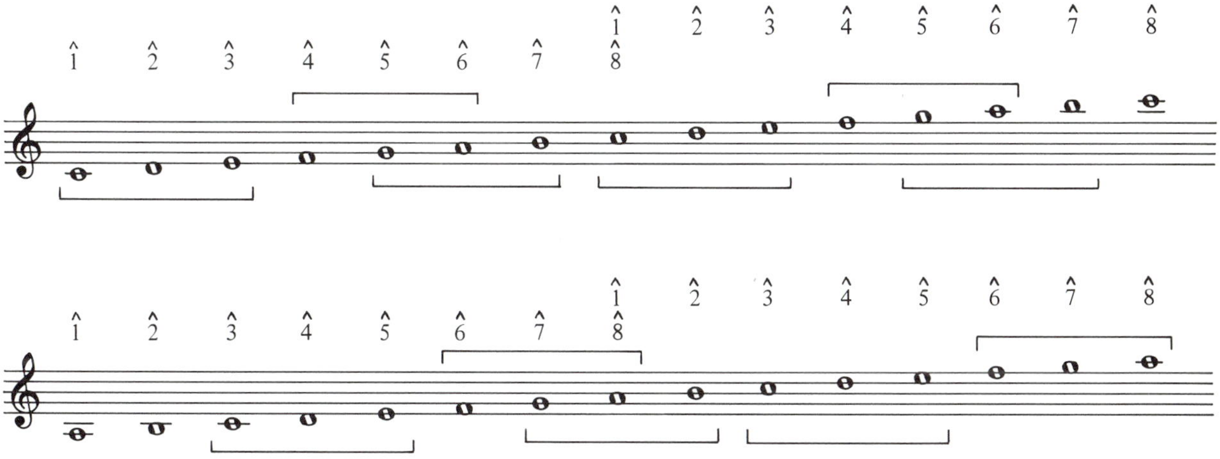

Only two intervals that can be formed using the diatonic pitch classes of these modes have yet to be introduced: the augmented fourth and the diminished fifth.

The terms ***augmented*** and ***diminished*** are the labels for interval qualities one half step larger and smaller, respectively, than perfect. In major, an augmented fourth appears between $\hat{4}$ and the $\hat{7}$ above it; a diminished fifth appears between

augmented

diminished

$\hat{7}$ and the $\hat{4}$ above it. In natural minor, an augmented fourth appears between $\hat{6}$ and the $\hat{2}$ above it; a diminished fifth appears between $\hat{2}$ and the $\hat{6}$ above it. These intervals are displayed in Example 7-5.

Example 7-5

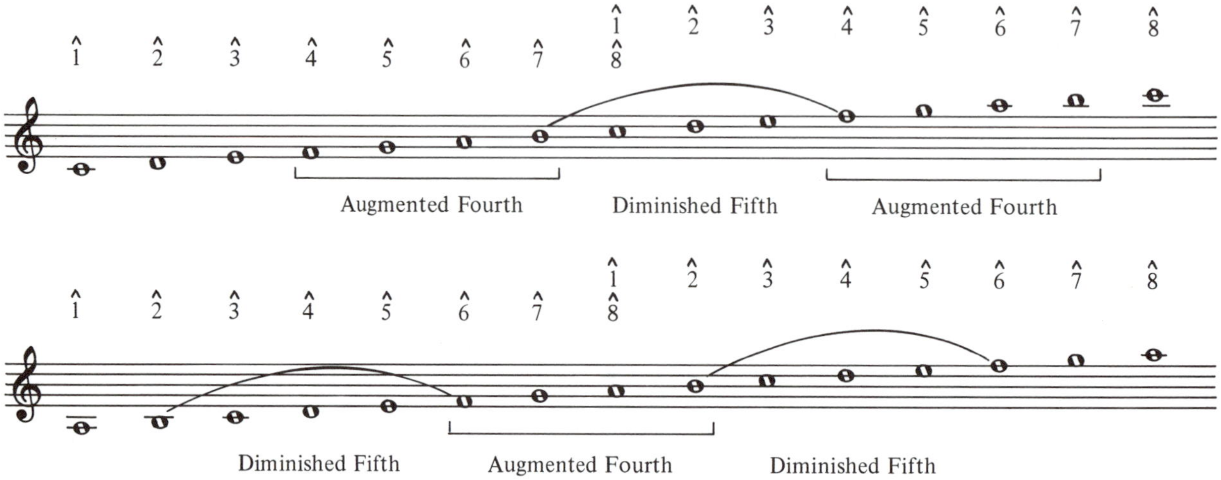

tritone

Both the augmented fourth and the diminished fifth span six half steps, exactly half an octave. The augmented fourth is sometimes called a ***tritone*** ("three tones") because three whole steps separate $\hat{4}$ and $\hat{7}$ in major, or $\hat{6}$ and $\hat{2}$ in natural minor. These intervals are classified as dissonances due to their distinctly unstable characters.

The augmented fourth and diminished fifth are inversions of one another. In fact, because these intervals contain the same number of half steps—six—they are also enharmonic equivalents of one another. Example 7-6 demonstrates these properties.

Example 7-6

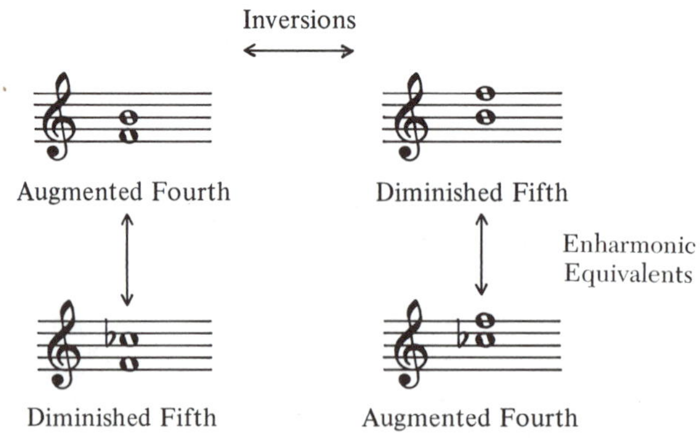

A summary of the sizes and qualities of all intervals that can be formed using the diatonic pitch classes of major and natural minor keys is shown in Example 7-7.

Each interval's inversion and status as a consonance or dissonance are listed. The standard abbreviations *P* for perfect, *M* for major, *m* for minor, *A* for augmented, and *d* for diminished are used.

Example 7-7

Interval	*Size in Half Steps*	*Inversion*	*Consonance/ Dissonance*
P1	0	P8	Consonant
m2	1	M7	Dissonant
M2	2	m7	Dissonant
m3	3	M6	Consonant
M3	4	m6	Consonant
P4	5	P5	Dissonant
A4	6	d5	Dissonant
d5	6	A4	Dissonant
P5	7	P4	Consonant
m6	8	M3	Consonant
M6	9	m3	Consonant
m7	10	M2	Dissonant
M7	11	m2	Dissonant
P8	12	P1	Consonant

The Chromatic Scale

The minor second is called a ***diatonic half step*** because its two pitches appear as adjacent diatonic scale degrees in some major or natural minor key. For example, C–D♭ appears as $\hat{3}$–$\hat{4}$ in A♭ major and as $\hat{5}$–$\hat{6}$ in F natural minor. In contrast, a ***chromatic half step***—for example, C–C♯—is spelled using notes with the same letter name. Chromatic half steps do not appear as adjacent diatonic scale degrees in any major or natural minor key. They must always be formed using an accidental that is not part of the key signature.

diatonic half step

chromatic half step

chromatic scale

The ***chromatic scale***, which ascends and descends entirely in half steps, is shown in Example 7-8. The chromatic pitches appear as filled-in noteheads, while the diatonic pitches appear as open noteheads.

Example 7-8

Ascending Chromatic Scale (Key of C Major)

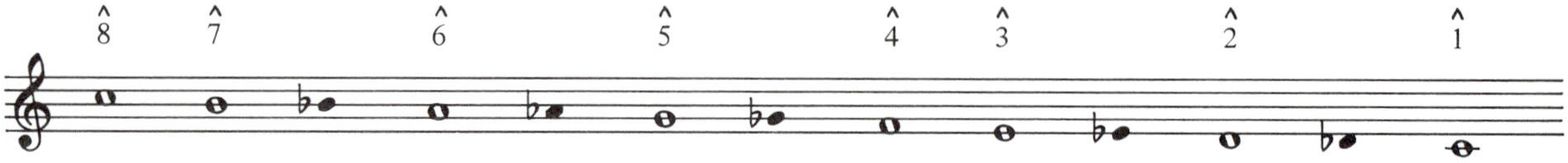

Descending Chromatic Scale (Key of C Major)

Observe that when two half steps fill a diatonic whole step, *the chromatic half step precedes the diatonic half step*. For example, in ascending chromatically from $\hat{1}$ to $\hat{2}$ in the key of C, the pitches would generally be spelled C, C♯, D rather than C, D♭, D. But in descending from $\hat{2}$ to $\hat{1}$, the correct spelling would be D, D♭, C rather than D, C♯, C.

This rule is motivated by the way accidentals apply to noteheads within a measure. (Remember that once an accidental is written on the staff, it applies to all noteheads written on that line or space until the next bar line, unless its effect is canceled by a natural.) If the chromatic pitch were spelled using the same letter name as the following pitch, then *both* noteheads would require accidentals if they appear within the same measure. By following the rule, only the chromatic notehead requires an accidental. The correct version in Example 7-9 employs one accidental whenever a chromatic pitch is used, while the incorrect version employs two: one for the chromatic pitch and one for the diatonic pitch that follows it. Tchaikovsky's melody includes all the pitches between B♭ and F (a chromatic ascent from $\hat{5}$ to $\hat{2}$ in E♭ major), relieved by an occasional leap to a pitch above this chromatic line. The presence of these higher pitches (G and A♭) does not affect the spellings of the chromatic pitches.

Example 7-9

Tchaikovsky: Symphony No. 2

CORRECT (Tchaikovsky's version)

INCORRECT (*not* how Tchaikovsky notated it)

In some chromatic scales, pitches that are already sharp or flat as a result of the key signature must be raised or lowered an additional half step. For example, consider how chromatic pitches should be applied to the diatonic ascent from $\hat{1}$ to $\hat{3}$ in E major, shown in Example 7-10a.

Example 7-10

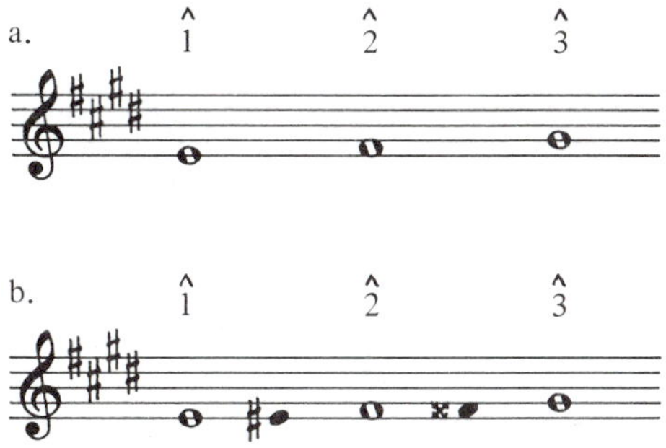

The chromatic pitch that connects E and F♯ is spelled E♯ (*not* F♮), in conformity with the rule that the chromatic half step should precede the diatonic half step. What pitch should come between F♯ and G♯? Certainly G♮ is incorrect, since F♯–G♮ forms a diatonic half step and G♮–G♯ forms a chromatic half step, the opposite of what should occur. Instead, we use the enharmonic equivalent of G♮, called F ***double sharp*** (F𝄪). The symbol 𝄪 implies a double application of a sharp. F𝄪 is *two* half steps higher than F. The chromatic ascent from E to G♯ using E♯ and F𝄪 is shown in Example 7-10b.

double sharp

Likewise, in descending chromatically from $\hat{3}$ to $\hat{1}$ in D♭ major, we employ the chromatic pitches F♭ (*not* E♮) and E♭♭ (E ***double flat***) to fill in the diatonic whole steps F–E♭ and E♭–D♭. Observe that there is no special symbol, but simply two flats placed side by side, to indicate the double flat. This chromatic descent is shown in Example 7-11.

double flat

Example 7-11

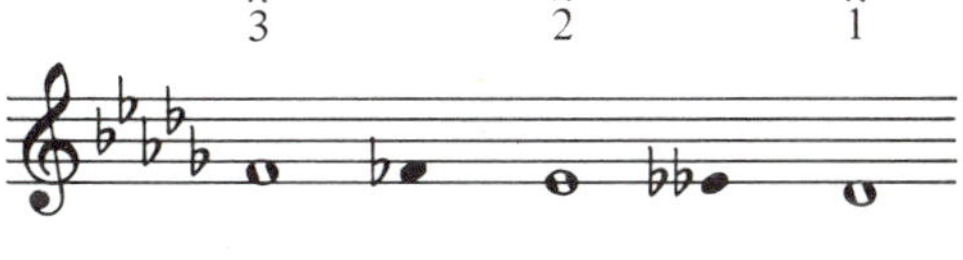

Intervals Formed Using Chromatic Pitches

The chromatic pitches significantly increase the variety of intervals that can be formed. For example, C and G♯, which appear in the ascending chromatic scale of C major, form an interval of size five. But what is its quality? Since C and G♯

exceed the perfect fifth by one half step, they form an augmented fifth (Ex. 7-12a). The term *augmented* applies to intervals one half step larger than perfect or major. Likewise, the term *diminished* applies to intervals one half step smaller than perfect or minor. For example, B and the A♭ above it form the interval of a diminished seventh, one half step smaller than B and the A above it, the minor seventh (Ex. 7-12b).

Example 7-12

a.

Augmented Fifth

One half step larger than Perfect Fifth

b.

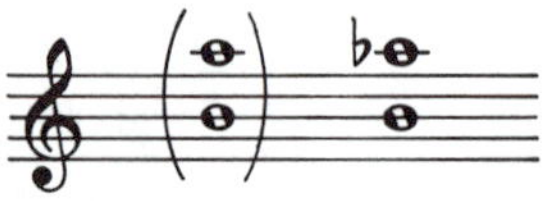

Diminished Seventh

One half step smaller than Minor Seventh

The chart in Example 7-13 should assist you in finding the qualities of intervals formed using chromatic pitches. All augmented and diminished intervals are dissonant. The inversion of an augmented interval is always diminished. The inversion of a diminished interval is always augmented.

Example 7-13

Qualities Applied to the Unison, Fourth, Fifth, and Octave

Diminished +1 half step Perfect +1 half step Augmented

Qualities Applied to the Second, Third, Sixth, and Seventh

Diminished +1 half step Minor +1 half step Major +1 half step Augmented

Pitch exercises for Chapter 7 are on pages 229–236.

RHYTHM

Sixteenth Notes and Rests

In simple meters such as $\frac{2}{4}$, $\frac{3}{4}$, and $\frac{4}{4}$, the beat may be divided into four parts. Just as one quarter note ($\frac{1}{4}$) or two eighth notes ($\frac{1}{8} + \frac{1}{8} = \frac{2}{8} = \frac{1}{4}$) fill a beat, so also do four ***sixteenth notes*** ($\frac{1}{16} + \frac{1}{16} + \frac{1}{16} + \frac{1}{16} = \frac{4}{16} = \frac{1}{4}$). *Two* beams or flags are attached to the stems of darkened noteheads to notate sixteenth notes, as shown in Example 7-14.

sixteenth note

Example 7-14

Four sixteenth notes fill a beat, just as four quarter notes fill a measure in $\frac{4}{4}$ meter. The four subdivisions of a beat share with the four beats of a measure the metrical pattern "Strongly accented, *U*naccented, *M*oderately accented, *U*naccented," displayed in Example 7-15.

Example 7-15

Symbols for notes and rests that fill one through four quarters of a beat are displayed in Example 7-16.

Example 7-16

Duration	*Notes* Symbol	*Notes* Name	*Rests* Symbol	*Rests* Name
$\frac{1}{4}$ of a beat	𝅘𝅥𝅯	Sixteenth note	𝄿	Sixteenth rest
$\frac{1}{2}$ of a beat	𝅘𝅥𝅮	Eighth note	𝄾	Eighth rest
$\frac{3}{4}$ of a beat	𝅘𝅥𝅮.	Dotted eighth note	𝄾.	Dotted eighth rest
1 beat	𝅘𝅥	Quarter note	𝄽	Quarter rest

dotted eighth note

dotted eighth rest

sixteenth rest

The ***dotted eighth note*** and ***dotted eighth rest*** are formed by placing an augmentation dot to the right of the eighth note and eighth rest, respectively. The ***sixteenth rest*** resembles the eighth rest but has two flaglike swirls attached to the straight diagonal line instead of one.

Conventions of Notation and Counting

Several examples of how these symbols appear in context are displayed in Example 7-17. Observe especially how the combination of a dotted eighth note and a sixteenth note is beamed.

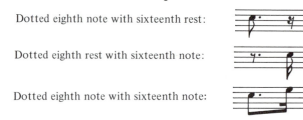

Example 7-17

Dotted eighth note with sixteenth rest: 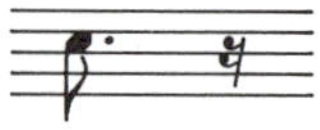

Dotted eighth rest with sixteenth note: 

Dotted eighth note with sixteenth note: 

When sixteenth notes are employed, each beat is beamed separately, as in Example 7-18. Syllables for the beats and their subdivisions are shown. Observe that the syllable "ee" is used for the unaccented second and fourth quarters of the beat. When you pronounce these syllables out loud, give more emphasis to the numbers and the word "and" than to the syllable "ee."

Example 7-18

1 ee + ee 2 ee + ee 3 ee + ee 4 ee + ee 1 ee + ee 2 ee + ee 3 ee + ee 4 ee + ee

1 ee + ee 2 ee + ee 3 ee + ee 1 ee + ee 2 ee + ee 3 ee + ee 1 ee + ee 2 ee + ee 3 ee + ee

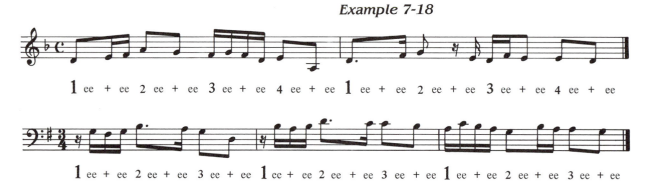

Sixteenth Notes in Compound Meters

Two sixteenth notes may fill the time of an eighth note in compound meters, just as in simple meters. Though the beat in compound meters (notated with a dotted quarter note) divides into three parts (eighth notes), those parts in turn divide into halves (sixteenth notes) rather than thirds. Thus six sixteenth notes may fill a beat in a compound meter, as shown in Example 7-19. Since the eighth-note values are counted "one and uh two and uh . . .," when sixteenth notes are employed you should count "one ee and ee uh ee two ee and ee uh ee . . . ."

Example 7-19

1 ee + ee uh ee 2 ee + ee uh ee 1 ee + ee uh ee 2 ee + ee uh ee 1 ee + ee uh ee 2 ee + ee uh ee

Rhythm exercises for Chapter 7 are on pages 237–239.

LABORATORY

L7-1. Perform each of the following melodies at the keyboard. Recommended fingerings for the left hand (below the staff) or right hand (above the staff) are included.

a.

Bruckner: Symphony No. 4

b.

Berlioz: Harold in Italy

c.

Dvořák: "New World" Symphony

d.

Beethoven: Minuet in G

e.

Beethoven: Quartet Op. 130

f.

Beethoven: Symphony No. 8

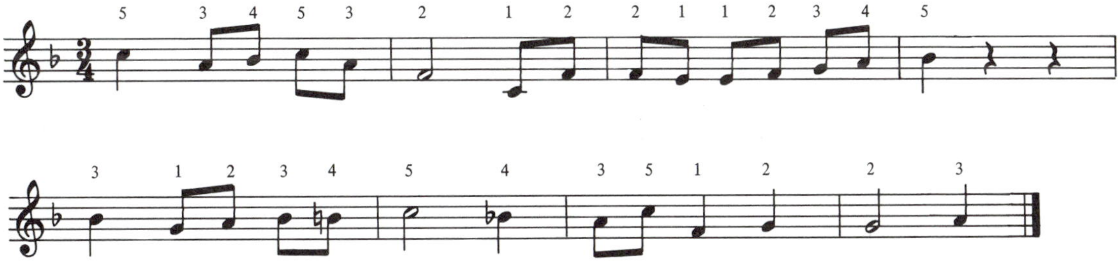

Note: The flat symbol beside B♭ in measure 6 of L7-1f is not required, because a bar line follows the B♮ of measure 5. However, composers often insert such precautionary accidentals to prevent misreading by performers. In this case, the flat reaffirms that the B notehead should be read as B♭. It does *not* imply lowering the B♭ (flat because of the key signature) by another flat, resulting in B♭♭.

L7-2. Starting on a pitch low in your vocal range, simultaneously sing and play an ascending major or natural minor scale. Then strike scale degrees $\hat{1}$, $\hat{3}$, $\hat{5}$, and $\hat{8}$ simultaneously. In this way, the key you have selected is solidly established in your ear. Now sing each melodic succession below in turn, confirming what you have sung by playing the appropriate pitches on the keyboard after each succession. Practice both in the order presented and in random order.

$\hat{1}$–$\hat{3}$

$\hat{8}$–$\hat{3}$

$\hat{1}$–$\hat{5}$

$\hat{8}$–$\hat{5}$

$\hat{3}$–$\hat{1}$

$\hat{3}$–$\hat{8}$

$\hat{5}$–$\hat{1}$

$\hat{5}$–$\hat{8}$

L7-3. Practice the following melodies at the keyboard, simultaneously singing and playing each pitch. Sing the scale-degree numbers that correspond to the pitches. If necessary, transpose the entire score up or down one octave.

a.

b.

c.

L7-4. The following compositions are for voice (upper staff) and keyboard (lower staff). Sing the scale-degree numbers that correspond to the pitches. At first you may wish to play the vocal part on the keyboard as well, in order to solidify your performance. Eventually, however, observe the rests in the accompanying part during your vocal measures. If necessary, transpose the entire score up or down one octave.

a.

b.

L7-5. The following compositions are for two voices. Sing the scale-degree numbers that correspond to the pitches. If necessary, transpose the entire score up or down one octave.

a.

b.

L7-6. Write in the counting syllables below the notated rhythms. Then perform each by clapping the rhythm or playing the pitch C or F at the keyboard, as notated, while pronouncing the counting syllables aloud. Practice until you can perform each exercise at a tempo of about ♩ = 40 or ♩. = 40.

Sample

a.

b.

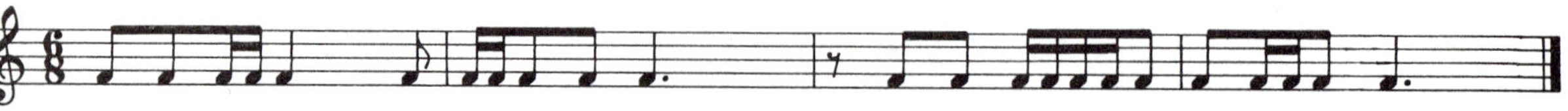

c.

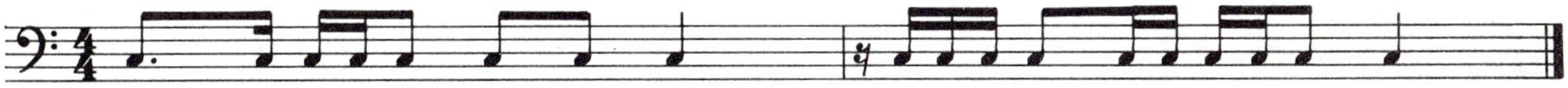

d.

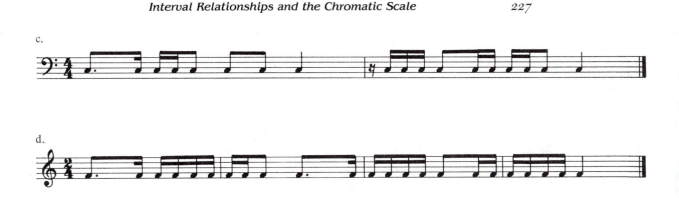

L7-7. Write in the counting syllables below the notated rhythms. Then perform them by dividing the class into two groups, with each group clapping one part while pronouncing the counting syllables aloud. Alternatively, individual students may perform both parts simultaneously at the keyboard, pronouncing the counting syllables aloud while the index fingers strike the notated pitches.

a.

b.

c.

L7-8. This exercise requires that a student or the instructor serve as the performer at a keyboard.

a. The performer plays a triad. Indicate whether it is a major triad, a minor triad, or neither. The performer's choices of triads for performance are as follows.

1. Root with major third and perfect fifth (major)
2. Root with minor third and perfect fifth (minor)
3. Root with minor third and diminished fifth
4. Root with major third and augmented fifth

b. The performer plays an ascending major or natural minor scale and then two of its pitches in ascending melodic succession. Indicate which two scale degrees are performed. The choices for scale degrees in the ascending melodic succession are as follows.

$\hat{1}$–$\hat{3}$
$\hat{1}$–$\hat{5}$
$\hat{1}$–$\hat{8}$
$\hat{3}$–$\hat{5}$
$\hat{3}$–$\hat{8}$
$\hat{5}$–$\hat{8}$

c. The performer plays a descending major or natural minor scale and then two of its pitches in descending melodic succession. Indicate which two scale degrees are performed. The choices for scale degrees in the descending melodic succession are as follows.

$\hat{3}$–$\hat{1}$
$\hat{5}$–$\hat{1}$
$\hat{8}$–$\hat{1}$
$\hat{5}$–$\hat{3}$
$\hat{8}$–$\hat{3}$
$\hat{8}$–$\hat{5}$

d. The performer plays an ascending or descending simple interval, and then another interval. Indicate whether the second interval is a compound version of the first interval.

e. The performer plays an ascending or descending simple interval, and then another interval. Indicate whether the second interval is the inversion of the first interval.

Audio exercises for Chapter 7 are on pages 239–242.

Name: ______________________

Instructor: ______________________

Date: ______________________

Rhythm Exercises

R7-1. Modify the noteheads indicated by arrows to form complete measures containing the appropriate number of beats. Wherever possible, incorporate the existing beam notation.

a.

b.

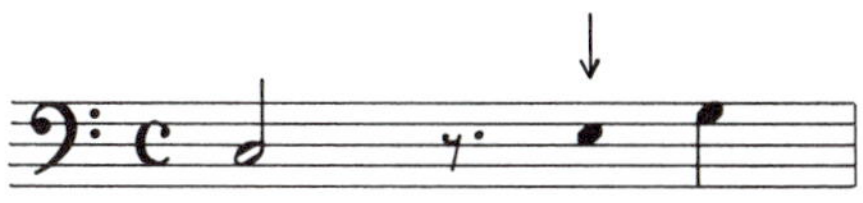

c.

d.

e.

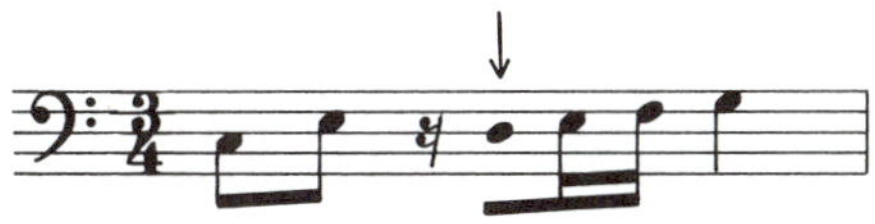

f.

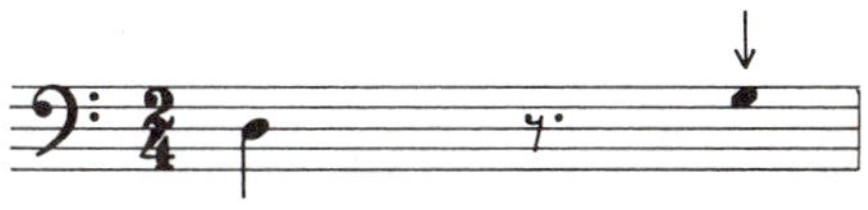

g.

h.

i.

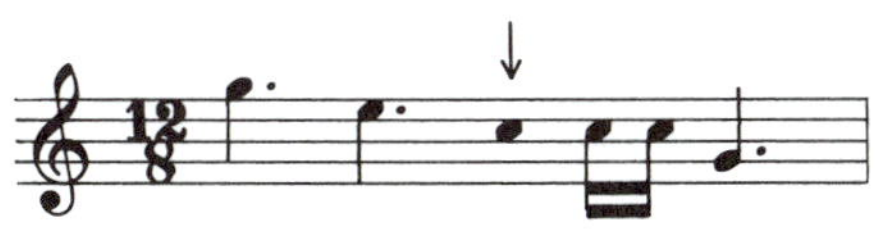

j.

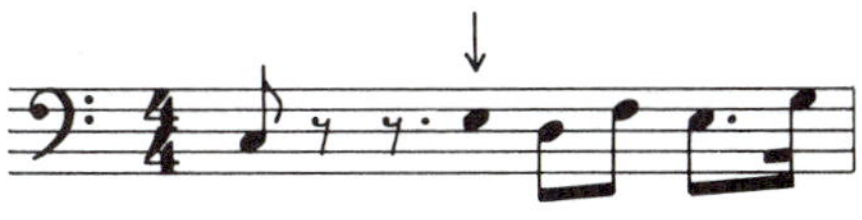

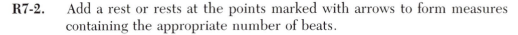

R7-2. Add a rest or rests at the points marked with arrows to form measures containing the appropriate number of beats.

a.
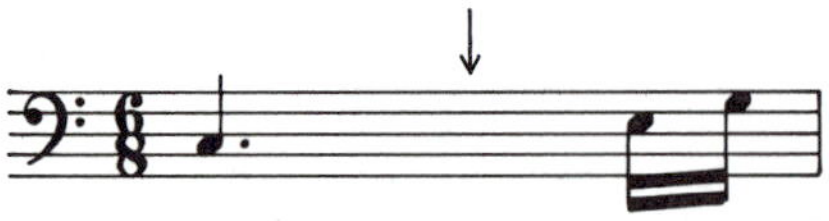

b.
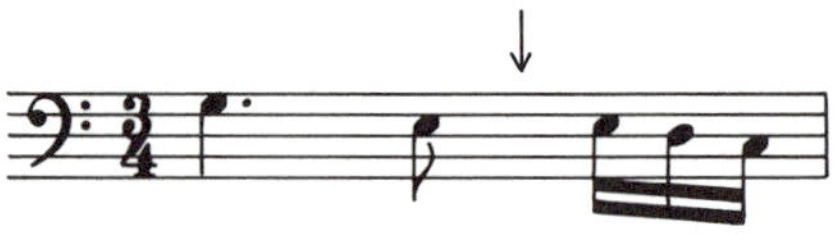

c.
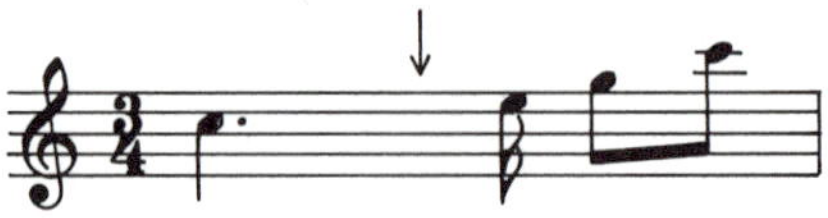

d.
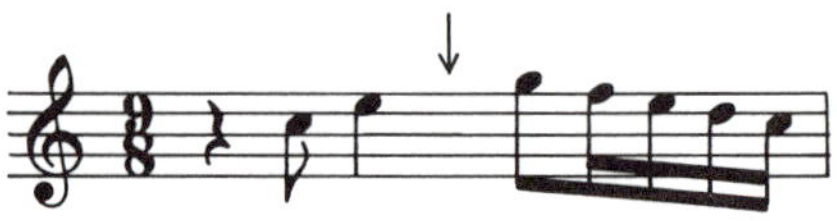

e.

f.

g.

h.

i.

j.

R7-3. Form a melody using the fragments provided. Only one ordering of these fragments results in measures that contain the correct number of beats.

a.

b.

Name: ______________________

Instructor: ______________________

Date: ______________________

R7-4. Notate the melodies indicated by the positioning of the pitch names in relation to the counting syllables. Use only unisons, seconds, thirds, and fourths as melodic intervals. Do not add rests.

a.

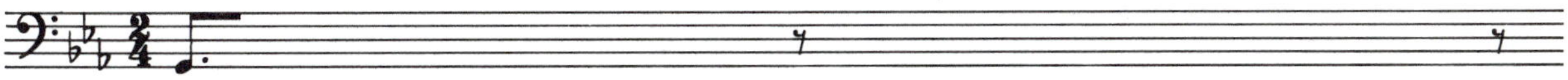

G G C C D E♭ C D G F E♭ E♭ C D E♭ C

2 ee + ee 1 ee + ee 2 ee + ee 1 ee + ee 2 ee + ee 1 ee + ee 2 ee + ee 1 ee + ee

b.

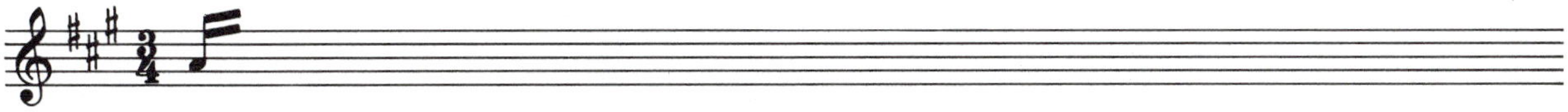

A G♯ A C♯ E E F♯ F♯ E D C♯ B E C♯ B A

1 ee + ee 2 ee + ee 3 ee + ee 1 ee + ee 2 ee + ee 3 ee + ee

c.

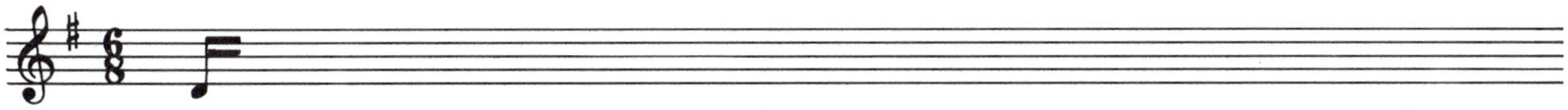

D D G G F♯ G B A D D E D C B A B G

uh ee 1 ee + ee uh ee 2 ee + ee uh ee 1 ee + ee uh ee 2 ee + ee

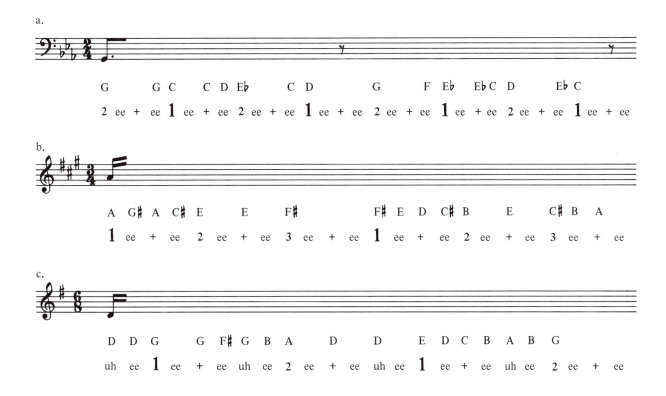

Audio Exercises

A7-1. A triad will be performed. Indicate whether its quality is major, minor, or neither.

a. Major Minor Neither
b. Major Minor Neither
c. Major Minor Neither
d. Major Minor Neither
e. Major Minor Neither
f. Major Minor Neither
g. Major Minor Neither
h. Major Minor Neither
i. Major Minor Neither
j. Major Minor Neither

A7-2. An ascending major or natural minor scale will be performed, followed by an ascending melodic succession of two of its pitches. Circle the choice of scale degrees that corresponds to the pitches performed.

a. $\hat{1}$–$\hat{3}$ $\hat{1}$–$\hat{5}$ $\hat{1}$–$\hat{8}$ $\hat{3}$–$\hat{5}$ $\hat{3}$–$\hat{8}$ $\hat{5}$–$\hat{8}$
b. $\hat{1}$–$\hat{3}$ $\hat{1}$–$\hat{5}$ $\hat{1}$–$\hat{8}$ $\hat{3}$–$\hat{5}$ $\hat{3}$–$\hat{8}$ $\hat{5}$–$\hat{8}$
c. $\hat{1}$–$\hat{3}$ $\hat{1}$–$\hat{5}$ $\hat{1}$–$\hat{8}$ $\hat{3}$–$\hat{5}$ $\hat{3}$–$\hat{8}$ $\hat{5}$–$\hat{8}$
d. $\hat{1}$–$\hat{3}$ $\hat{1}$–$\hat{5}$ $\hat{1}$–$\hat{8}$ $\hat{3}$–$\hat{5}$ $\hat{3}$–$\hat{8}$ $\hat{5}$–$\hat{8}$
e. $\hat{1}$–$\hat{3}$ $\hat{1}$–$\hat{5}$ $\hat{1}$–$\hat{8}$ $\hat{3}$–$\hat{5}$ $\hat{3}$–$\hat{8}$ $\hat{5}$–$\hat{8}$
f. $\hat{1}$–$\hat{3}$ $\hat{1}$–$\hat{5}$ $\hat{1}$–$\hat{8}$ $\hat{3}$–$\hat{5}$ $\hat{3}$–$\hat{8}$ $\hat{5}$–$\hat{8}$
g. $\hat{1}$–$\hat{3}$ $\hat{1}$–$\hat{5}$ $\hat{1}$–$\hat{8}$ $\hat{3}$–$\hat{5}$ $\hat{3}$–$\hat{8}$ $\hat{5}$–$\hat{8}$
h. $\hat{1}$–$\hat{3}$ $\hat{1}$–$\hat{5}$ $\hat{1}$–$\hat{8}$ $\hat{3}$–$\hat{5}$ $\hat{3}$–$\hat{8}$ $\hat{5}$–$\hat{8}$
i. $\hat{1}$–$\hat{3}$ $\hat{1}$–$\hat{5}$ $\hat{1}$–$\hat{8}$ $\hat{3}$–$\hat{5}$ $\hat{3}$–$\hat{8}$ $\hat{5}$–$\hat{8}$
j. $\hat{1}$–$\hat{3}$ $\hat{1}$–$\hat{5}$ $\hat{1}$–$\hat{8}$ $\hat{3}$–$\hat{5}$ $\hat{3}$–$\hat{8}$ $\hat{5}$–$\hat{8}$

A7-3. A descending major or natural minor scale will be performed, followed by a descending melodic succession of two of its pitches. Circle the choice of scale degrees that corresponds to the pitches performed.

a. $\hat{3}$–$\hat{1}$ $\hat{5}$–$\hat{1}$ $\hat{8}$–$\hat{1}$ $\hat{5}$–$\hat{3}$ $\hat{8}$–$\hat{3}$ $\hat{8}$–$\hat{5}$
b. $\hat{3}$–$\hat{1}$ $\hat{5}$–$\hat{1}$ $\hat{8}$–$\hat{1}$ $\hat{5}$–$\hat{3}$ $\hat{8}$–$\hat{3}$ $\hat{8}$–$\hat{5}$
c. $\hat{3}$–$\hat{1}$ $\hat{5}$–$\hat{1}$ $\hat{8}$–$\hat{1}$ $\hat{5}$–$\hat{3}$ $\hat{8}$–$\hat{3}$ $\hat{8}$–$\hat{5}$
d. $\hat{3}$–$\hat{1}$ $\hat{5}$–$\hat{1}$ $\hat{8}$–$\hat{1}$ $\hat{5}$–$\hat{3}$ $\hat{8}$–$\hat{3}$ $\hat{8}$–$\hat{5}$
e. $\hat{3}$–$\hat{1}$ $\hat{5}$–$\hat{1}$ $\hat{8}$–$\hat{1}$ $\hat{5}$–$\hat{3}$ $\hat{8}$–$\hat{3}$ $\hat{8}$–$\hat{5}$
f. $\hat{3}$–$\hat{1}$ $\hat{5}$–$\hat{1}$ $\hat{8}$–$\hat{1}$ $\hat{5}$–$\hat{3}$ $\hat{8}$–$\hat{3}$ $\hat{8}$–$\hat{5}$
g. $\hat{3}$–$\hat{1}$ $\hat{5}$–$\hat{1}$ $\hat{8}$–$\hat{1}$ $\hat{5}$–$\hat{3}$ $\hat{8}$–$\hat{3}$ $\hat{8}$–$\hat{5}$
h. $\hat{3}$–$\hat{1}$ $\hat{5}$–$\hat{1}$ $\hat{8}$–$\hat{1}$ $\hat{5}$–$\hat{3}$ $\hat{8}$–$\hat{3}$ $\hat{8}$–$\hat{5}$
i. $\hat{3}$–$\hat{1}$ $\hat{5}$–$\hat{1}$ $\hat{8}$–$\hat{1}$ $\hat{5}$–$\hat{3}$ $\hat{8}$–$\hat{3}$ $\hat{8}$–$\hat{5}$
j. $\hat{3}$–$\hat{1}$ $\hat{5}$–$\hat{1}$ $\hat{8}$–$\hat{1}$ $\hat{5}$–$\hat{3}$ $\hat{8}$–$\hat{3}$ $\hat{8}$–$\hat{5}$

A7-4. Two intervals will be performed melodically. Circle "Yes" if the second interval is a compound version of the first interval, "No" if it is not.

a. Yes No
b. Yes No
c. Yes No
d. Yes No
e. Yes No
f. Yes No
g. Yes No
h. Yes No
i. Yes No
j. Yes No

A7-5. Two simple intervals will be performed melodically. Circle "Yes" if they are inversions of one another, "No" if they are not.

a. Yes No
b. Yes No
c. Yes No
d. Yes No
e. Yes No
f. Yes No
g. Yes No
h. Yes No
i. Yes No
j. Yes No

Name: ____________________
Instructor: ____________________
Date: ____________________

A7-6. Six melodies will be performed. The starting pitch for each will be stated before the melody is performed. In each case circle the score that shows the correct pitch notation.

a.

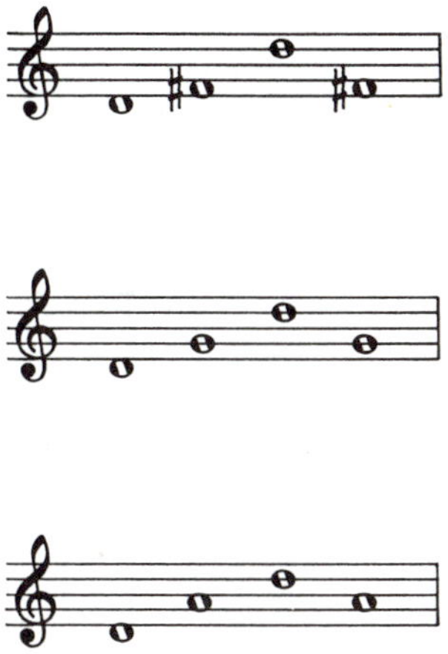

b.

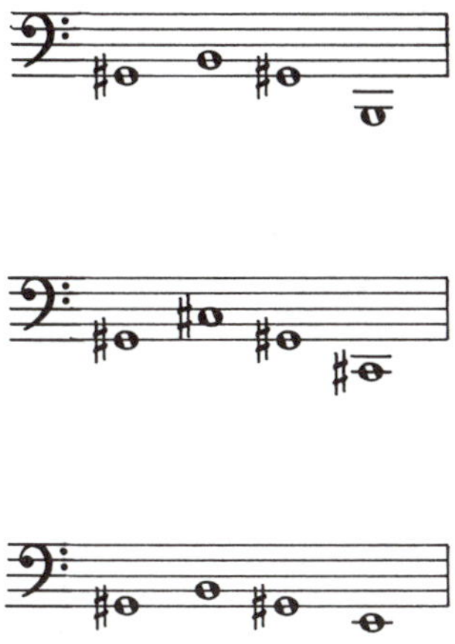

c.

d.

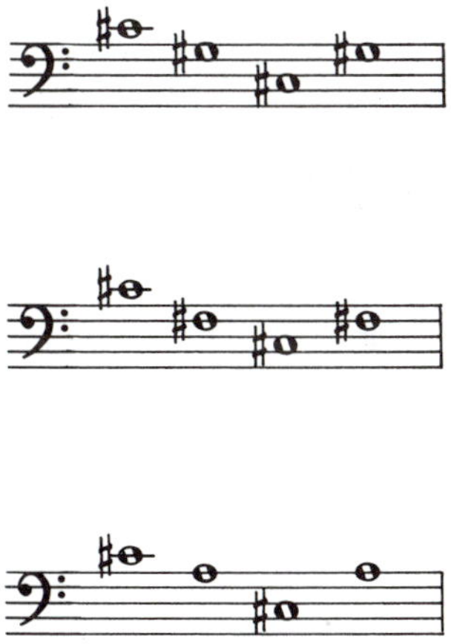

e.

f.

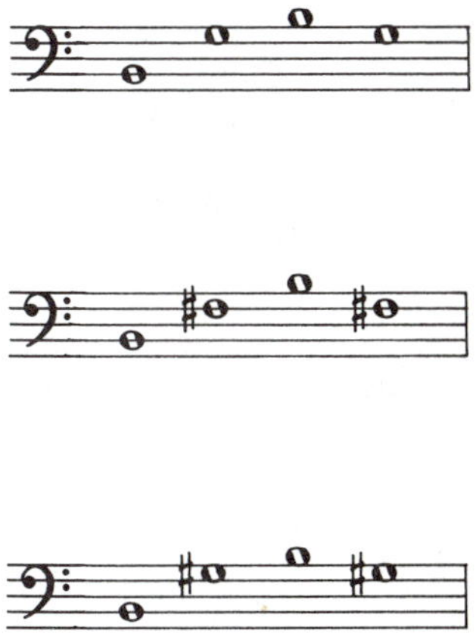

A7-7. Four rhythms will be performed. In each case circle the score that shows the correct notation.

a.

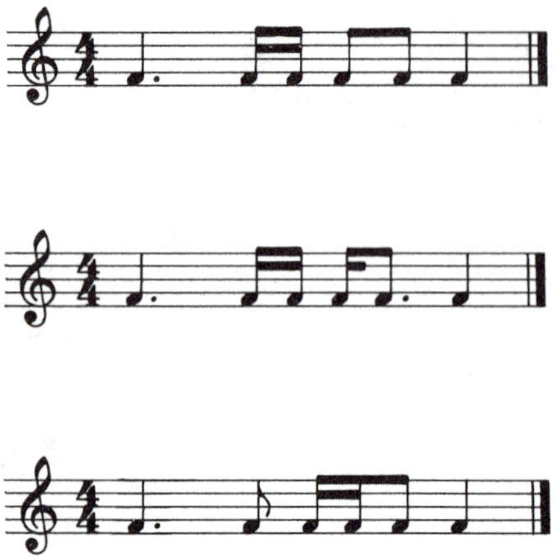

b.

c.

d.

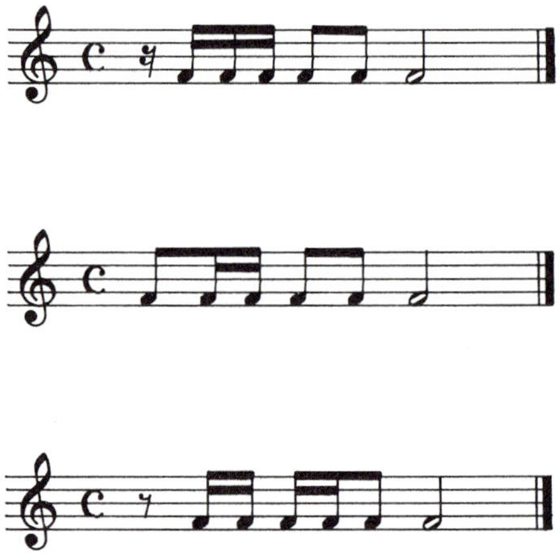

Name: ______________________
Instructor: ______________________
Date: ______________________

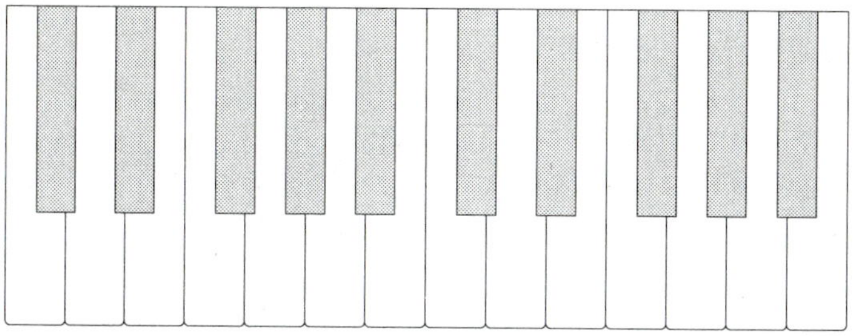

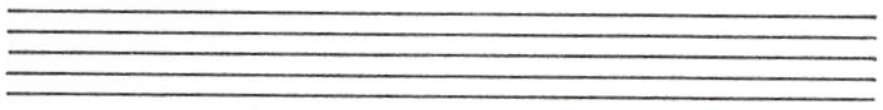

Mastery Test, Chapter 7

_______ 1. Which one of the intervals shown is a diminished fifth?

_______ 2. Which one of the intervals shown is a minor second?

_______ 3. Which one of the intervals shown is a compound minor third?

_______ 4. Which one of the intervals shown is a compound major sixth?

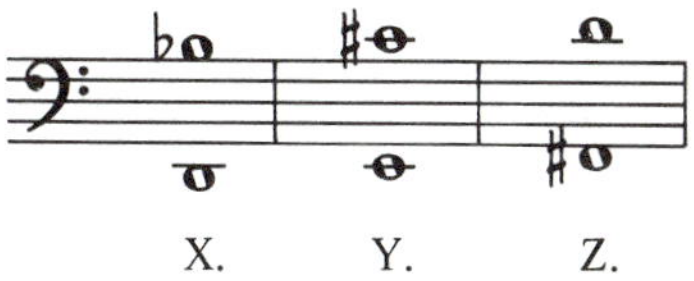

_______ 5. Which one of the intervals shown is an inversion of a minor seventh?

_______ 6. Which one of the intervals shown is an inversion of a diminished fifth?

______ 7. Exactly how many *half steps* are contained in the combination of an interval and its inversion?

X. Nine Y. Twelve Z. Thirteen

______ 8. The first three notes in the ascending chromatic scale in the key of D major are displayed. Which note comes next?

X. E♯ Y. F Z. F♯

______ 9. The first two notes in the descending chromatic scale in the key of C♭ major are displayed. Which note comes next?

X. B♭ Y. A Z. B♭♭

______ 10. Which one of the intervals shown is called a tritone?

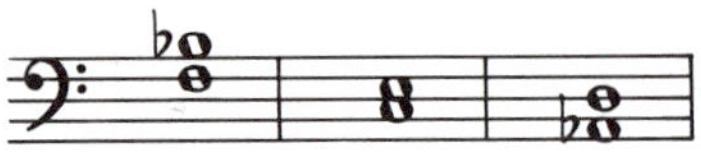

X. Y. Z.

______ 11. Which one of the following intervals is consonant?

X. Augmented fifth
Y. Major sixth
Z. Minor seventh

______ 12. Which one of the following intervals is dissonant?

X. Major second
Y. Minor third
Z. Minor sixth

______ 13. What is the maximum number of sixteenth notes that may occur within a measure in $\frac{6}{8}$ meter?

X. 9 Y. 12 Z. 16

______ 14. What kind of note should be inserted at the arrow to complete the measure?

X. Sixteenth note
Y. Eighth note
Z. Dotted eighth note

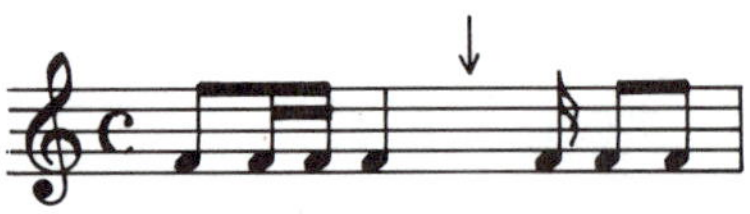

______ 15. What kind of rest should be inserted at the arrow to complete the measure?

X. Sixteenth rest
Y. Eighth rest
Z. Dotted eighth rest

Name: ____________________

Instructor: ____________________

Date: ____________________

_________ 16. A descending natural minor scale will be performed, followed by a descending melodic succession of two of its pitches. Which pitches are performed?

X. $\hat{5}$–$\hat{3}$ Y. $\hat{8}$–$\hat{3}$ Z. $\hat{8}$–$\hat{5}$

_________ 17. Two intervals will be performed melodically. Is the second interval a compound version of the first interval?

Y. Yes Z. No

_________ 18. Two simple intervals will be performed melodically. Are they inversions of one another?

Y. Yes Z. No

_________ 19. A melody that begins with the pitch E will be performed. Which score shows the correct pitch notation?

X. 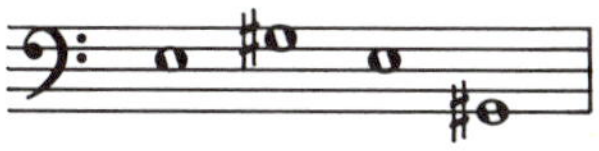

Y. 

Z. 

_________ 20. Which score shows the correct notation for the rhythm performed?

X. 

Y. 

Z. 

8

Chords and Their Inversions

Terms and Concepts

triad	*second inversion*	*figured bass*
chord	*doubling*	*arpeggiation*
system	*soprano*	*triplets*
root position	*inner voices*	*bracket*
first inversion	*bass*	

PITCH

Compound Intervals and Inversion Applied to Triads

When a simple interval is expanded into a compound interval or inverted, its pitch classes remain the same. Triads, which are made up of simple intervals, can also be expanded or inverted. They too retain the same pitch classes when either or both of these operations are performed.

The term ***triad*** refers to a combination of three simultaneously sounding pitches notated on three adjacent lines or three adjacent spaces. A triad always contains two intervals of size three and one interval of size five. The more general term ***chord*** refers to any combination of three or more simultaneously sounding pitches. All triads are chords, but many chords are not triads.

triad

chord

Example 8-1 shows how a triad can be transformed using compound intervals. One or both of the pitches above the root may be replaced by the same pitch class one or more octaves higher. Or the root may be moved one or more octaves lower. Either way, the root remains the lowest pitch. The last two chords of the example are notated on a ***system,*** or combination of staves. Observe that the vertical lines at the left edge of a system extend from the bottom of the lower staff to the top of the upper staff. This will also be true of bar lines. A system is ideal when both high and low notes are to be read simultaneously, as in keyboard music.

system

Example 8-1

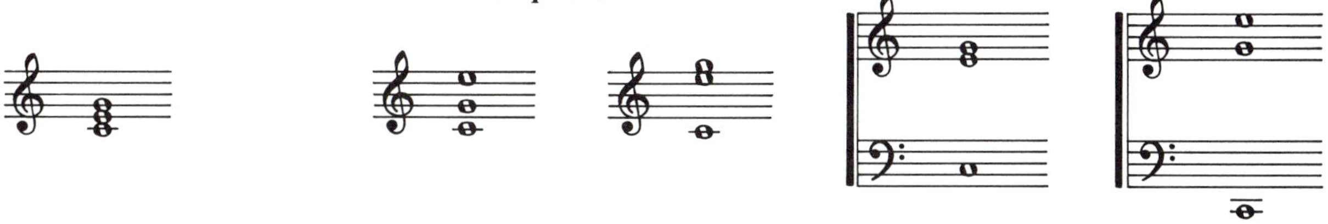

Triad

Expansion using Compound Intervals

root position

first inversion

second inversion

When an interval undergoes inversion, what was formerly the higher of the two pitches becomes the lower. Similarly, when a triad undergoes inversion, what was formerly the middle or highest of the three pitches becomes the lowest. Because a triad has three pitches, the process of inversion can be applied to the basic triad twice without duplicating its original configuration (that is, two thirds within the frame of a fifth). In order to keep track of the different arrangements of the triad's pitch classes; we name the inversions according to whether the basic triad has been inverted once, twice, or not at all. In its original arrangement, with the root as the lowest pitch, the triad is in ***root position.*** If inverted once, leaving the third as the lowest pitch, the triad is in ***first inversion.*** If inverted again, leaving the fifth as the lowest pitch, the triad is in ***second inversion.*** Example 8-2 illustrates this principle for both major and minor triads. Observe that the first inversion is formed by moving the root of the triad an octave higher, while the second inversion is formed by moving both the root and the third of the triad an octave higher.

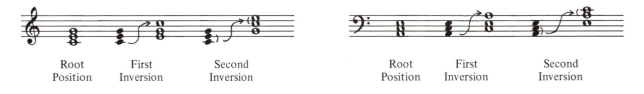

Example 8-2

Root Position — First Inversion — Second Inversion — Root Position — First Inversion — Second Inversion

Like triads, inverted chords can be transposed to another octave or expanded using compound intervals, as shown in Example 8-3. The bottom pitch class must remain the same if the inversion is to remain the same.

Example 8-3

a. b.

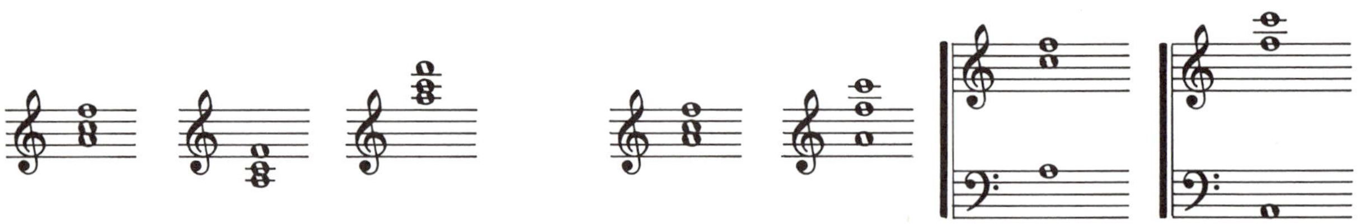

Octave Transpositions of an Inverted Chord

Compound Intervals Applied to an Inverted Chord

Triads and their inversions, as shown in Examples 8-2 and 8-3a, appear in music much less frequently than do their transformations using compound intervals, as shown in Example 8-3b. Composers favor the fuller sound that results when the pitches are further apart from one another and, as we shall see later in this chapter, when a fourth pitch is added. Most chords used in music are derived from some triad. Composers, arrangers, and performers need to understand which triad has been transformed to create a given chord, because only then can they correctly interpret the succession from one chord to another, a topic that we shall explore in Chapters 9 and 10.

Example 8-4 shows how to apply compound intervals and inversion to a triad simultaneously and, conversely, how to transform such chords back to their triadic forms. Observe especially the order in which the operations are performed.

Example 8-4

a. Convert the given triad into first inversion, using at least one compound interval.

STEP ONE: Convert the triad into first inversion.

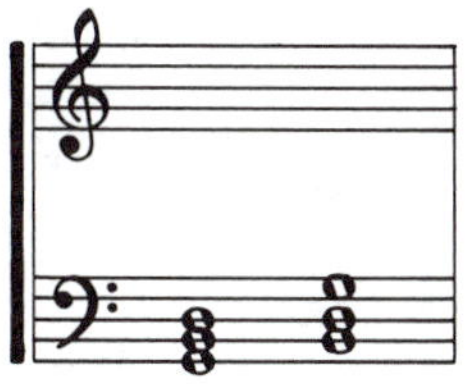

STEP TWO: Expand using at least one compound interval.

b. Convert the given triad into second inversion, using at least one compound interval.

STEP ONE: Convert the triad into second inversion.

STEP TWO: Expand using at least one compound interval.

c. Convert the given inverted chord using at least one compound interval into a triad.

STEP ONE: Reduce all compound intervals into simple intervals.

STEP TWO: Rearrange the pitch classes to form root position.

d. Convert the given chord using at least one compound interval into a triad.

STEP ONE: Reduce all compound intervals into simple intervals.

STEP TWO: Rearrange the pitch classes to form root position.

Keyboard Accompaniment

Triads and their inversions contain three pitches. Most music, however, is written using four pitches for each chord. For example, most music for choir is scored for two groups of women (sopranos and altos) and two groups of men (tenors and basses), and the most favored combination of string instruments is the quartet—two violins, a viola, and a violoncello. In either of these typical combinations, two voices or instruments must sound simultaneously, or ***double***, one of

doubling

the pitch classes of a triad or its inversion. Possible doublings include two roots, a third, and a fifth; a root, two thirds, and a fifth; and a root, a third, and two fifths.

In each of the chords shown in Example 8-5, three noteheads are drawn on the system's upper staff, while the bottom notehead of the chord appears alone on the system's lower staff. This arrangement of the four pitches of a chord is convenient for keyboard accompaniment both because the chords sound good in this arrangement and because the fingers can play them with ease. So that the right hand (which must strike three different keys on the keyboard at once) does not overstretch, all three of the notes on the upper staff must fall within the span of an octave. The highest note of each chord is called the ***soprano.*** All stems applied to soprano notes point upward. The two lower notes on the upper staff are called the ***inner voices.*** They share stems that point downward. The lower staff contains the ***bass,*** the lowest note of each chord. Its stems point up or down, depending upon where the notehead is placed on the staff. Procedures for selecting and connecting chords for a keyboard accompaniment will be explored in Chapters 11 through 13.

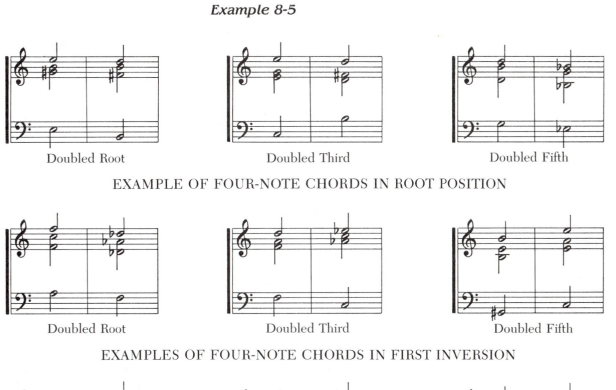

soprano

inner voices

bass

Example 8-5

Doubled Root — Doubled Third — Doubled Fifth

EXAMPLE OF FOUR-NOTE CHORDS IN ROOT POSITION

Doubled Root — Doubled Third — Doubled Fifth

EXAMPLES OF FOUR-NOTE CHORDS IN FIRST INVERSION

Doubled Root — Doubled Third — Doubled Fifth

EXAMPLES OF FOUR-NOTE CHORDS IN SECOND INVERSION

Figured Bass

The terms *root position, first inversion,* and *second inversion* are a useful means for describing how the notes of a chord are arranged. In an alternative system, called ***figured bass,*** the interval content of chords is displayed using numbers, or "figures," which indicate the sizes of all intervals formed against the bass. In figured bass, compound intervals are usually numbered as if they were simple intervals. As Example 8-6 demonstrates, all root-position chords have the figures $^{5}_{3}$, all first-inversion chords have the figures $^{6}_{3}$, and all second-inversion chords have the figures $^{6}_{4}$.

figured bass

Example 8-6

Figured bass:	5/3	5/3	5/3	6/3	6/3	6/3	6/4	6/4	6/4

Interval sizes from which the figures above are derived (measuring upward from the bass)

A–A = 8	G–B = 3	G–G = 8
A–E = 5	G–G = 8	G–E = 6
A–C = 3	G–E = 6	G–C = 4
F–A = 3	F–D = 6	D–B = 6
F–F = 8	F–A = 3	D–G = 4
F–C = 5	F–D = 6	D–D = 8
D–F = 3	B–D = 3	E–A = 4
D–D = 8	B–G = 6	E–E = 8
D–A = 5	B–D = 3	E–C = 6

Observe that the numbers used in figured bass are always arranged with the higher number on top, regardless of the arrangement of the pitch classes within the chord. Doublings, including the doubling of the bass at the octave, are seldom notated in the figures. The symbol $^{6}_{3}$, for example, specifies that there are intervals of a simple or compound sixth and a simple or compound third above the bass. It does not indicate whether the pitch that forms a sixth with the bass is higher or lower than the pitch that forms a third with the bass, nor does it indicate which of the three pitches is doubled.

Comparison of $^5_3$, $^6_3$, and $^6_4$ Positions

The $^5_3$ position is the most stable arrangement of a chord because, unlike $^6_3$ and $^6_4$ positions, it contains a perfect fifth, the most stable interval after the unison and octave. The $^6_3$ position, lacking a perfect fifth, is less stable. Still, because it contains only consonant intervals (third and sixth above the bass), it is more stable than the $^6_4$ position, which contains a fourth against the bass.

Even though the $^6_4$ position is the least stable of a chord's three possible arrangements, there are certain situations where it can occur. Consider, for example, the excerpt from "My Country, 'Tis of Thee" in Example 8-7.

Example 8-7

In this context, the interval of a fourth between the bass (G) and the C above it (beat 3 of the first measure) does not sound dissonant. In fact, the bass pitches of the three chords in this measure ***arpeggiate***, or present successively, the three pitch classes that usually occur simultaneously as members of the tonic triad in the key of C major. The ear remembers the earlier pitches when the $^6_4$-position chord sounds. For this reason, there is no tendency for the C that appears above the G to move to any other pitch.

arpeggiation

Pitch exercises for Chapter 8 are on pages 263–269.

RHYTHM

Triplets

triplets

The beats of simple meters may be divided into two or four parts using eighth and sixteenth notes, as we have seen. Subdivision of the beat into three parts, though more characteristic of compound meters, is also possible. Three notes of equal duration that fill a beat in a simple meter are called ***triplets.*** When used judiciously, they attract special attention because they contradict the typical division of the beat. If overused, triplets can begin to imply compound meter.

Triplets that fill a beat in $\frac{2}{4}$, $\frac{3}{4}$, or $\frac{4}{4}$ meter are notated as eighth notes. They are distinguished from normal eighth notes by placing the number "3" along their beam. This notation indicates that all three, rather than just two, of the notes beamed together are to be performed within the time of one beat. Example 8-8 contains three groups of triplets.

Example 8-8

bracket

Triplets appear most often as three eighth notes. Sometimes, however, one or two of these eighth notes may be replaced by rests, or two eighth notes may be merged into a quarter note. A ***bracket,*** a horizontal line placed beyond the stems of the noteheads involved, is drawn to group the appropriate stems whenever a beam does not extend through the beat, as Example 8-9 demonstrates.

Example 8-9

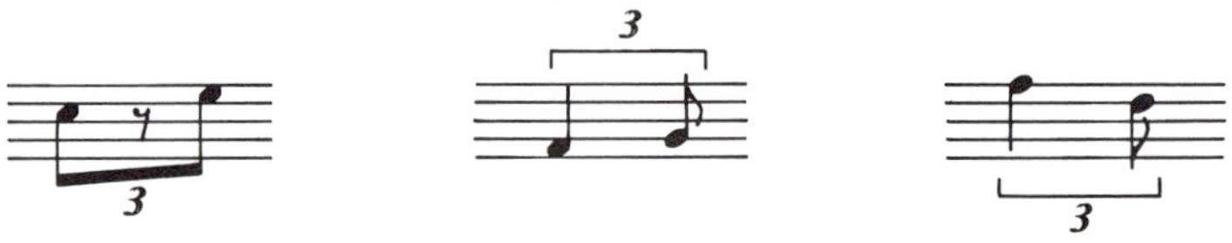

Performance Strategy for Triplets

Because triplets contradict the method of beat division that we have used for counting in simple meters up to this point, a new performance strategy is required. We must alternate between elements of the counting techniques used for simple and compound meters, adjusting the submetrical syllables to the type of subdivision found within each beat. *The syllables for numbers must be evenly spaced in time, even though the syllables that come between these numbers will occur at varying rates.* A good strategy for assuring that this happens is to tap your foot on every beat, making sure that these taps are evenly spaced in time, whether what comes between them is "1 +" or "1 ee + ee" or "1 + uh," etc. Example 8-10 shows suitable counting syllables for a melody that alternates between duple and triple subdivisions of the beat. The asterisks indicate when the foot should tap. Remember that the eighth notes of triplets are performed faster than normal eighth notes.

Example 8-10

Rhythm exercises for Chapter 8 are on pages 270–272.

LABORATORY

L8-1.a. Perform each of the following chords at the keyboard using your right hand for those notated in treble clef, your left hand for those notated in bass clef, and both hands for those notated on a system.

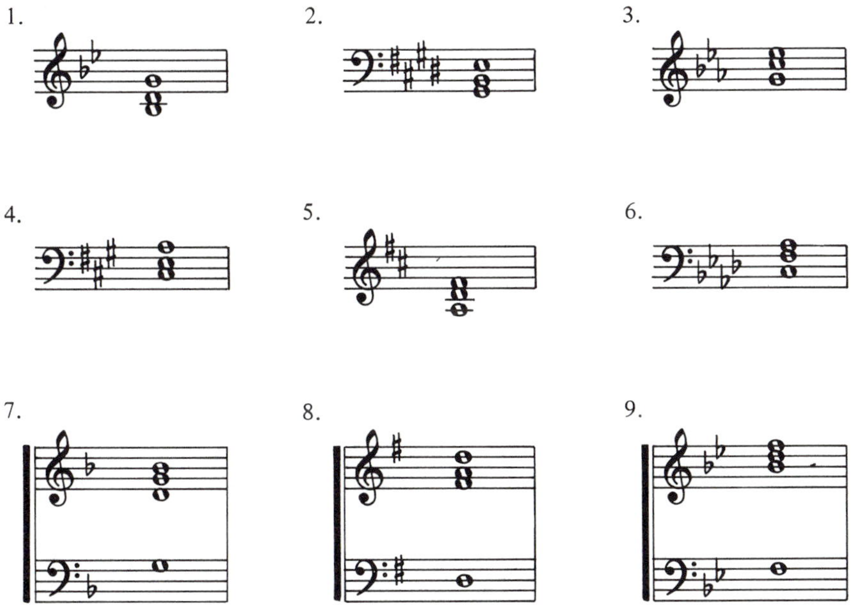

b. Perform each of the following melodies at the keyboard. Recommended fingerings are included.

Debussy: *Pour le piano*, Sarabande

1.

Mahler: Symphony No. 2

2.

Schubert: Scherzo in B♭ major

3.

Chopin: Waltz Op. 69, No. 1

4.

L8-2. Practice the following exercise, changing the reference scale after every two or three attempts.

- Simultaneously sing and play an ascending major or natural minor scale beginning on a pitch low in your vocal range. Extend the scale up a tenth instead of the customary octave.
- Using both hands, strike scale degrees $\hat{1}$, $\hat{3}$, $\hat{5}$, $\hat{8}$ ($\hat{1}$), and $\hat{10}$ ($\hat{3}$) simultaneously. In this way, the tonal center and mode you have selected are solidly established in your ear, and the five pitches required to create the triad and its two inversions are sounding.
- Now strike any one of the three lowest keys ($\hat{1}$, $\hat{3}$, or $\hat{5}$) and sing the corresponding ascending melodic succession, as indicated below.

  If you strike $\hat{1}$, arpeggiate $\hat{1}$–$\hat{3}$–$\hat{5}$ (the $^{5}_{3}$ position).
  If you strike $\hat{3}$, arpeggiate $\hat{3}$–$\hat{5}$–$\hat{8}$ (the $^{6}_{3}$ position).
  If you strike $\hat{5}$, arpeggiate $\hat{5}$–$\hat{8}$–$\hat{10}$ (the $^{6}_{4}$ position).

- Confirm what you have sung by playing the appropriate pitches on the keyboard.

L8-3. Practice the following melodies at the keyboard, simultaneously singing and playing each pitch. Sing the scale-degree numbers that correspond to the pitches. If necessary, transpose the entire score up or down one octave.

a.

b.

c.

L8-4. The following compositions are for voice and keyboard. A student or the instructor could play the keyboard part while other students sing the melody. The keyboard part should be performed as written, but the vocal line may be moved down an octave if necessary.

a.

b.

L8-5. The following compositions are for two voices. Sing the scale-degree numbers that correspond to the pitches. If necessary, transpose the entire score up or down one octave.

a.

b.

L8-6. Write in the counting syllables below the notated rhythms. Some beats will require duple subdivisions (1 + 2 +), others triple subdivisions (1 + uh 2 + uh), and others quadruple subdivisions (1 ee + ee 2 ee + ee). Then perform each by clapping the rhythm or playing the pitch C or F at the keyboard, as notated, while pronouncing the counting syllables aloud. Practice until you can perform each exercise at a tempo of about ♩ = 60.

Hint: When an exercise contains both duple and quadruple subdivisions in alternation with triplets, count quadruple subdivisions even during those beats which contain only duple subdivisions.

Sample

a.

b.

c.

d.

L8-7. Write in the counting syllables below the notated rhythms. Then perform them by dividing the class into two groups, with each group clapping one part while pronouncing the counting syllables aloud. Alternatively, individual students may perform both parts simultaneously at the keyboard, pronouncing the counting syllables aloud while the index fingers strike the notated pitches.

a.

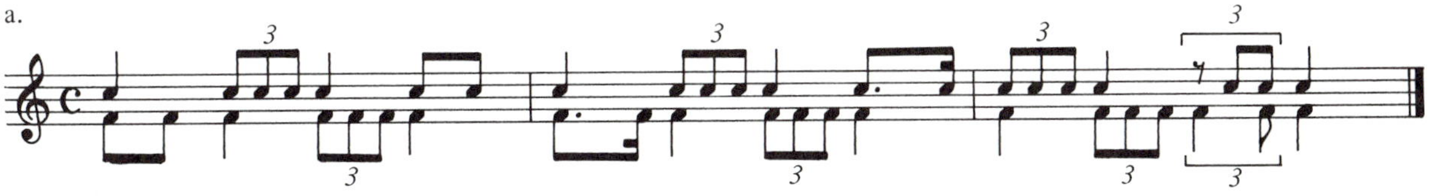

b.

c.

L8-8. This exercise requires that a student or the instructor serve as the performer at a keyboard.

a. The performer places three fingers above keys that sound a major or minor triad and strikes the three keys simultaneously. Then the performer plays one of the three pitches alone. Indicate whether that pitch is the root, the third, or the fifth.

b. The performer places five fingers above keys that represent scale degrees $\hat{1}$, $\hat{3}$, $\hat{5}$, $\hat{8}$ ($\hat{1}$), and $\hat{10}$ ($\hat{3}$) in any major or minor key and strikes them simultaneously. The performer arpeggiates one of the following three ascending patterns and then strikes those three keys simultaneously.

$\hat{1}$–$\hat{3}$–$\hat{5}$

$\hat{3}$–$\hat{5}$–$\hat{8}$

$\hat{5}$–$\hat{8}$–$\hat{10}$

Indicate whether the three notes performed represent the $^5_3$, $^6_3$, or $^6_4$ position of the chord.

Audio exercises for Chapter 8 are on pages 273–275.

Name: ______________________
Instructor: ______________________
Date: ______________________

P8-12. Above each bass note, add three additional half notes that conform to the given symbols of figured bass and follow the conventions of keyboard accompaniment outlined in this chapter.

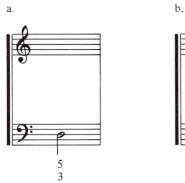

a.

b.

c.

d.

e.

f.

g.

h.

i.

j.

k.

l.

Rhythm Exercises

R8-1. For each melody below, supply the appropriate counting syllables.

a.

b.

c.

d.

e.

Name: ______________________
Instructor: ______________________
Date: ______________________

R8-2. Form a melody using the fragments provided. Only one ordering of the fragments results in measures that contain the correct number of beats.

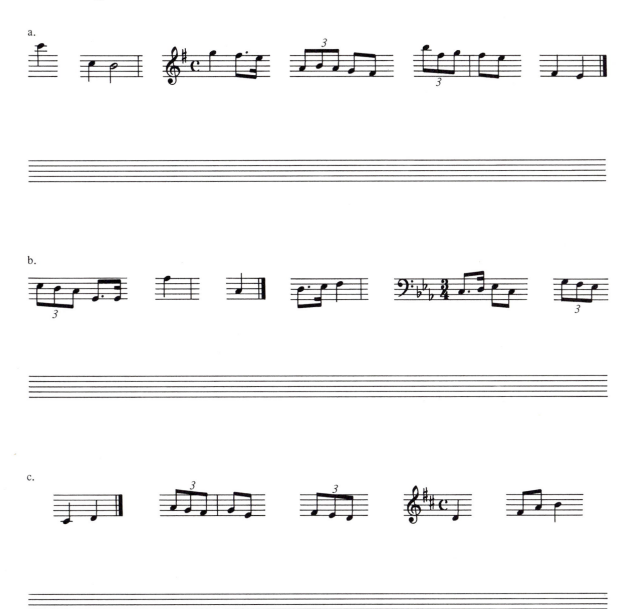

a.

b.

c.

R8-3. Notate the melodies indicated by the positioning of the pitch names in relation to the counting syllables. Use only unisons, seconds, thirds, and fourths as melodic intervals. Do not add rests.

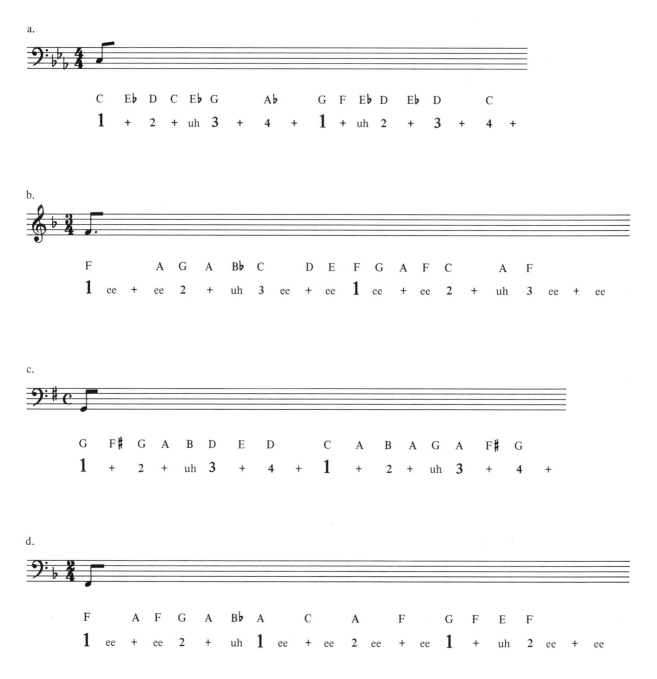

a.

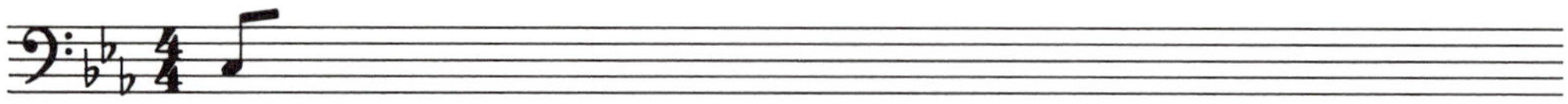

C Eb D C Eb G Ab G F Eb D Eb D C

1 + 2 + uh 3 + 4 + 1 + uh 2 + 3 + 4 +

b.

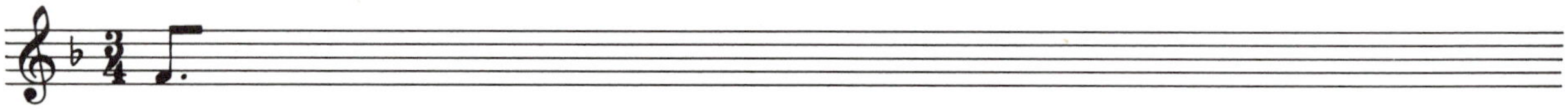

F A G A Bb C D E F G A F C A F

1 ee + ee 2 + uh 3 ee + ee 1 ee + ee 2 + uh 3 ee + ee

c.

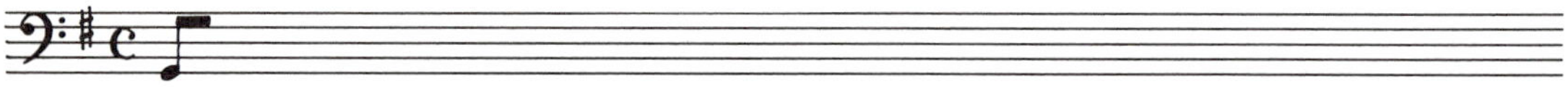

G F♯ G A B D E D C A B A G A F♯ G

1 + 2 + uh 3 + 4 + 1 + 2 + uh 3 + 4 +

d.

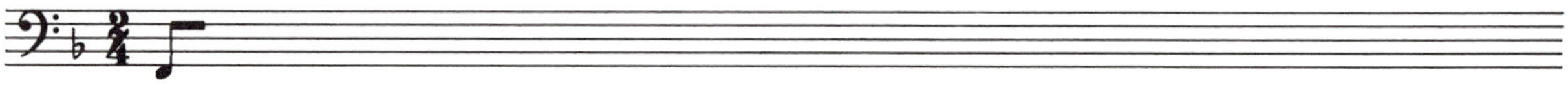

F A F G A Bb A C A F G F E F

1 ee + ee 2 + uh 1 ee + ee 2 ee + ee 1 + uh 2 ee + ee

Name: ______________________________

Instructor: ___________________________

Date: ______________________________

Audio Exercises

A8-1. A major triad will be performed, followed by one of its three pitches. Indicate whether the single pitch is the triad's root, third, or fifth.

a. Root Third Fifth
b. Root Third Fifth
c. Root Third Fifth
d. Root Third Fifth
e. Root Third Fifth
f. Root Third Fifth
g. Root Third Fifth
h. Root Third Fifth
i. Root Third Fifth
j. Root Third Fifth

A8-2. A reference chord consisting of scale degrees $\hat{1}$, $\hat{3}$, $\hat{5}$, $\hat{8}$ ($\hat{1}$), and $\hat{10}$ ($\hat{3}$) will be performed, followed by an ascending arpeggiation and then simultaneous performance of three of these pitches. Indicate whether these pitches represent the $^5_3$ position ($\hat{1}$–$\hat{3}$–$\hat{5}$), the $^6_3$ position ($\hat{3}$–$\hat{5}$–$\hat{8}$), or the $^6_4$ position ($\hat{5}$–$\hat{8}$–$\hat{10}$) of the chord.

a. $^5_3$ $^6_3$ $^6_4$
b. $^5_3$ $^6_3$ $^6_4$
c. $^5_3$ $^6_3$ $^6_4$
d. $^5_3$ $^6_3$ $^6_4$
e. $^5_3$ $^6_3$ $^6_4$
f. $^5_3$ $^6_3$ $^6_4$
g. $^5_3$ $^6_3$ $^6_4$
h. $^5_3$ $^6_3$ $^6_4$
i. $^5_3$ $^6_3$ $^6_4$
j. $^5_3$ $^6_3$ $^6_4$

A8-3. Six melodies will be performed. The starting pitch for each will be stated before the melody is performed. In each case circle the score that shows the correct pitch notation.

a.

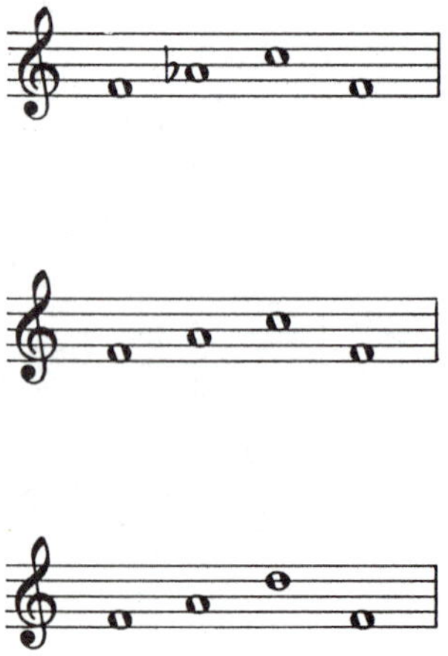

b.

c.

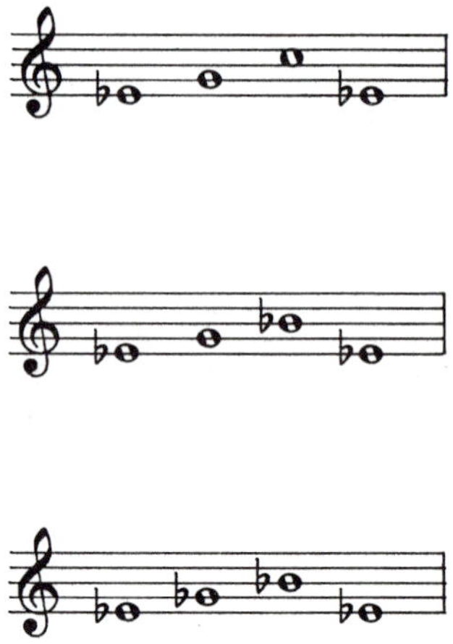

d.

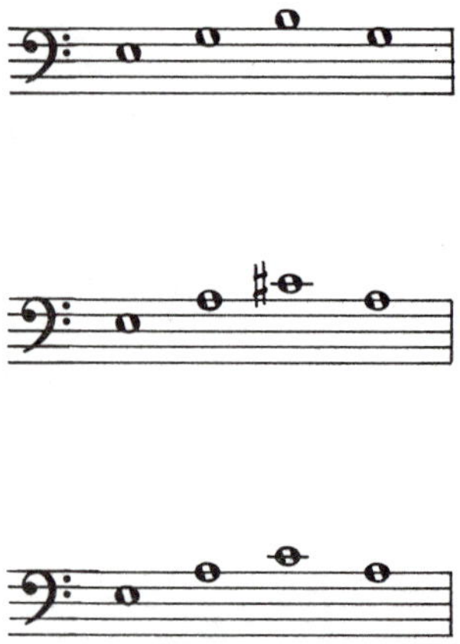

e.

f.

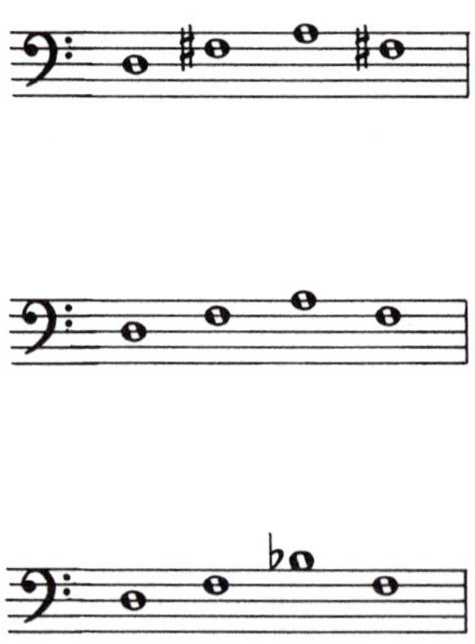

Name: ______________________________
Instructor: ___________________________
Date: _______________________________

A8-4. Four rhythms will be performed. In each case circle the score that shows the correct notation.

a.

b.

c.

d.

Name: ____________________
Instructor: ____________________
Date: ____________________

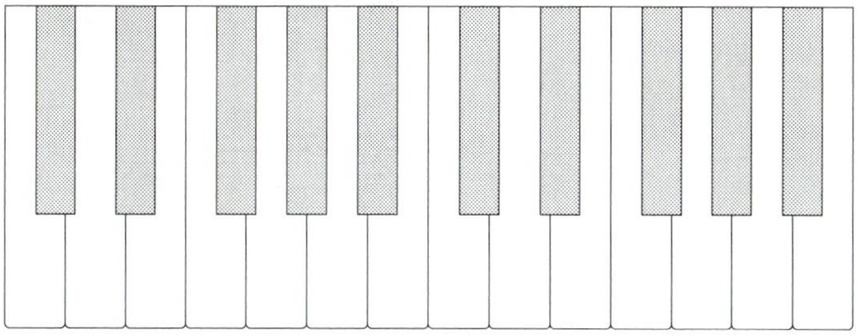

Mastery Test, Chapter 8

______ 1. Which one of the chords shown is in root position?

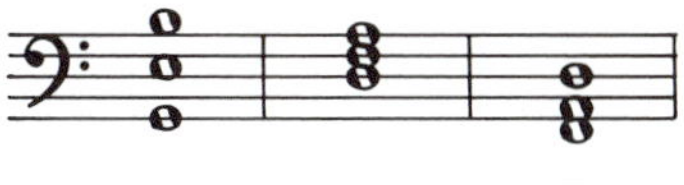

X. Y. Z.

______ 2. Which one of the chords shown is in first inversion?

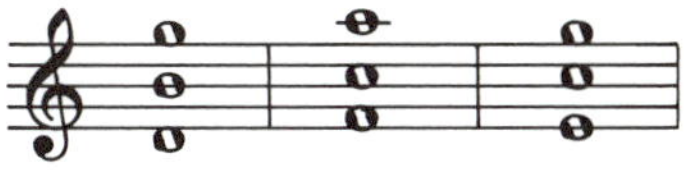

X. Y. Z.

______ 3. Which one of the chords shown is in second inversion?

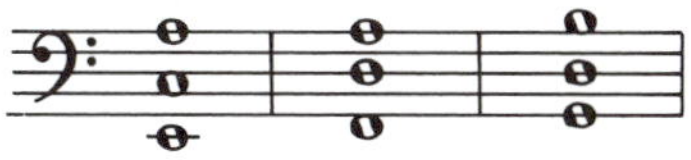

X. Y. Z.

______ 4. Which one of the chords shown could be described as the first inversion of a C major triad?

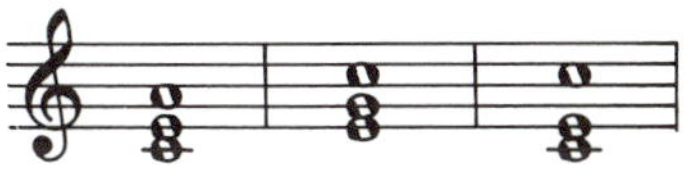

X. Y. Z.

______ 5. Which one of the chords shown could be described as the second inversion of an F minor triad?

X. Y. Z.

______ 6. Which name is used for the *bottom note* of any chord in a keyboard accompaniment?
X. Root Y. Bass Z. Soprano

_________ 7. Which one of the chords shown displays the correct placement of stems for the soprano, inner voices, and bass in a keyboard accompaniment?

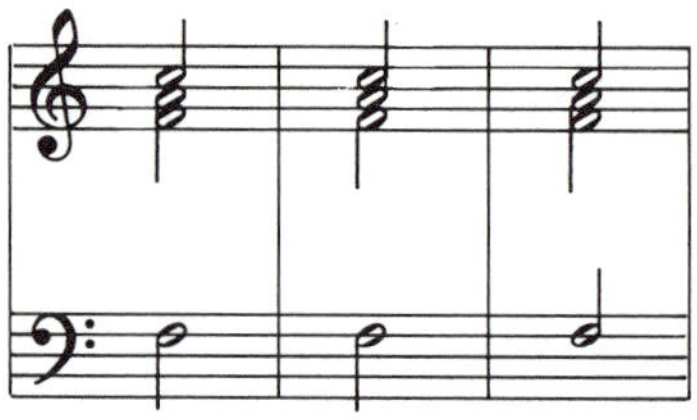

X. Y. Z.

_________ 8. What is the figured bass for the second inversion of a triad?

X. $^{5}_{3}$ Y. $^{6}_{4}$ Z. $^{6}_{3}$

_________ 9. Which one of the chords shown is in $^{6}_{4}$ position?

X. Y. Z.

_________ 10. Which one of the chords shown is in $^{6}_{3}$ position?

X. Y. Z.

_________ 11. Which one of the chords shown is in $^{5}_{3}$ position?

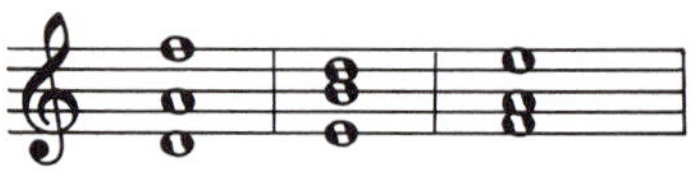

X. Y. Z.

_________ 12. Which one of the chords shown is in $^{6}_{3}$ position?

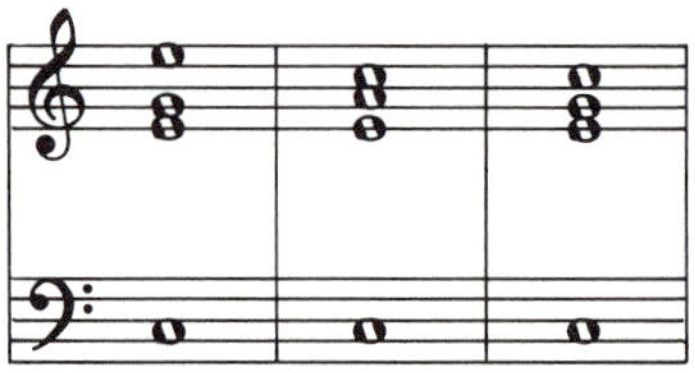

X. Y. Z.

_________ 13. How many beats does the following symbol fill in $^{4}_{4}$ meter?

X. ½ Y. 1 Z. 1½

Name: ______________________
Instructor: ______________________
Date: ______________________

______ 14. What kind of note should be inserted at the arrow to complete the measure?
X. Eighth note
Y. Quarter note
Z. Dotted quarter note

______ 15. What kind of rest should be inserted at the arrow to complete the measure?
X. Eighth rest
Y. Quarter rest
Z. Dotted quarter rest

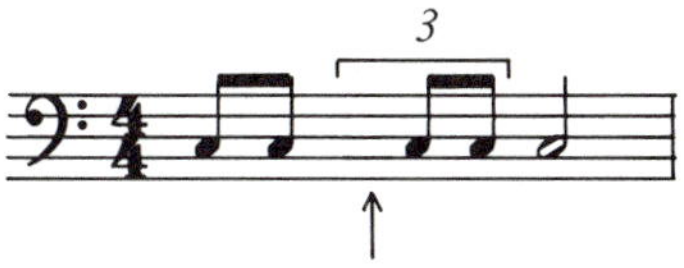

______ 16. A major triad will be performed. Then one of its three pitches will be performed again. Which pitch is performed a second time?
X. Root Y. Third Z. Fifth

A reference chord consisting of $\hat{1}$, $\hat{3}$, $\hat{5}$, $\hat{8}$, and $\hat{10}$ will be performed, followed by an ascending arpeggiation and then simultaneous performance of three of these pitches. Indicate which figured bass position these pitches represent.

______ 17. X. $^5_3$ Y. $^6_3$ Z. $^6_4$

______ 18. X. $^5_3$ Y. $^6_3$ Z. $^6_4$

______ 19. A melody that begins with the pitch G will be performed. Which score shows the correct pitch notation?

X. 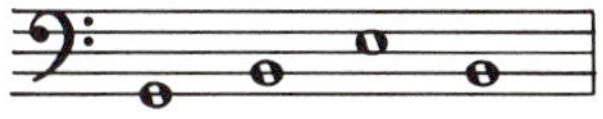

Y. 

Z. 

__________ 20. Which score shows the correct notation for the rhythm performed?

X. 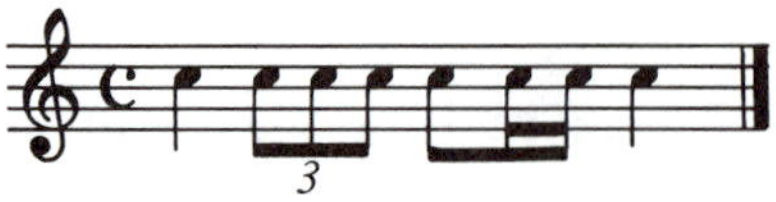

Y. 

Z. 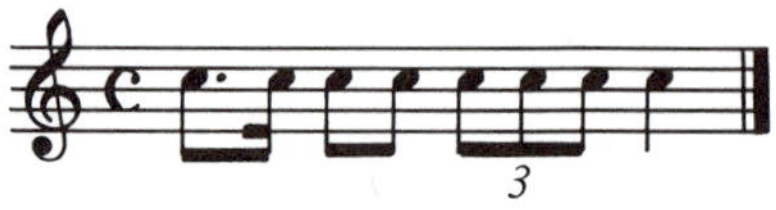

9

Chord Identification and Cadences

Terms and Concepts

mediant	*full cadence*
submediant	*authentic cadence*
supertonic	*half cadence*
leading tone	*semicadence*
Roman numerals	*perfect authentic cadence*
diminished triad	*imperfect authentic cadence*
dominant seventh chord	*plagal cadence*
phrase	*perfect plagal cadence*
harmony	*imperfect plagal cadence*
cadence	*deceptive cadence*
period	*syncopation*
parallel period	*slur*
antecedent and consequent phrases	

PITCH

Diatonic Triads in Major Keys

Each of the diatonic pitch classes of a major key serves as the root of a triad. These seven triads perform distinct roles within the key, interacting with one another in various ways that affect how we come to recognize the tonal center of a composition. We have already named three of these triads: the tonic triad (rooted on $\hat{1}$), the subdominant triad (rooted on $\hat{4}$), and the dominant triad (rooted on $\hat{5}$). In fact, all seven diatonic triads have names. The triad rooted on $\hat{3}$ is called the ***mediant*** triad. Its root divides the ascending fifth between $\hat{1}$ and $\hat{5}$ into two thirds. Likewise, the triad rooted on $\hat{6}$ is called the ***submediant*** triad. Its root divides the descending fifth between $\hat{1}$ and $\hat{4}$ into two thirds. These triads are shown in Example 9-1 in the context of C major.

mediant

submediant

Example 9-1

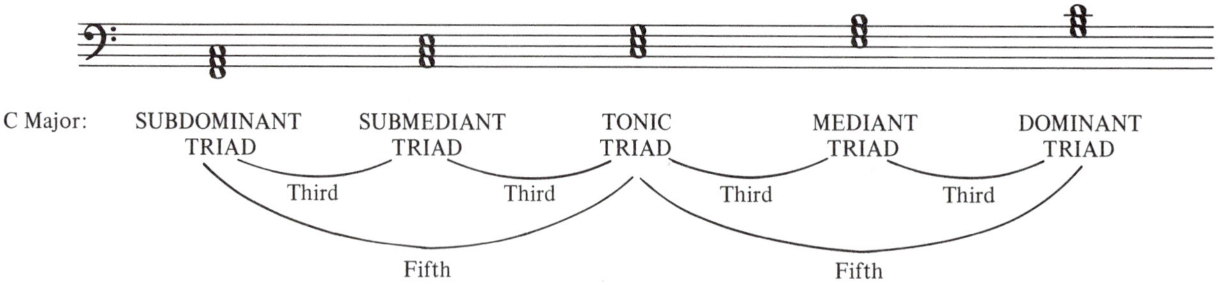

supertonic

leading tone

The remaining two scale degrees, $\hat{2}$ and $\hat{7}$, are the roots of the ***supertonic*** and ***leading tone*** triads, respectively. These roots are both a second away from tonic, as shown in Example 9-2.

Example 9-2

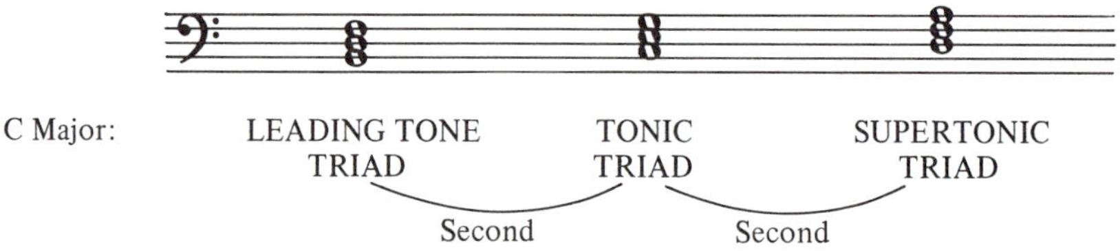

Roman numerals

Musicians also label these seven triads numerically, using ***Roman numerals.*** The Roman-numeral label indicates which scale degree functions as the triad's root, in the context of a specific major or natural minor key. The Roman numerals that apply to the seven diatonic triads in two of the fifteen major keys are displayed in Example 9-3. Observe that a triad may have different labels in different keys. For example, the C-major triad is I in the key of C but IV in the key of G.

Example 9-3

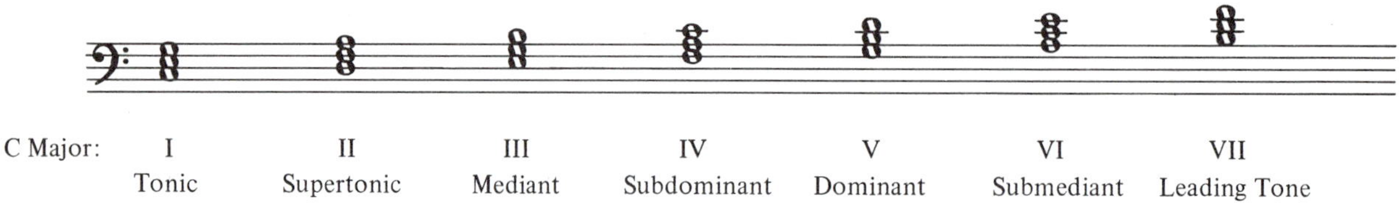

G Major:	I	II	III	IV	V	VI	VII
	Tonic	Supertonic	Mediant	Subdominant	Dominant	Submediant	Leading Tone

The same Roman numerals apply to the triads of all other major keys as well. For example, the II triad in the key of A♭ major is spelled using pitch classes B♭, D♭, and F, because B♭ serves as $\hat{2}$ in A♭ major and the diatonic third and fifth above B♭ in that key are D♭ and F, as shown in Example 9-4.

Example 9-4

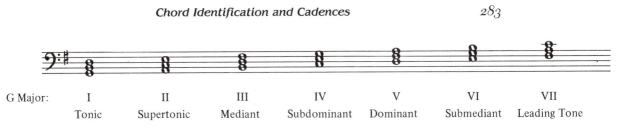

A♭ Major: II

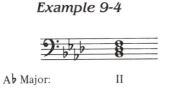

A triad's third and fifth appear as simple intervals above its root. As we have seen, a triad may be expanded into a chord containing compound intervals. In either case, the Roman numeral indicates the scale degree of the chord's root, which in any root-position chord is also the bass. The first three chords in Example 9-5 would be labeled as IV in the key of A major, because their *root* is D, the fourth scale degree in A major. The next three chords would not be labeled as IV. Though the *bass* is D in each case, the *root* is not, because these chords are not in root position.

Example 9-5

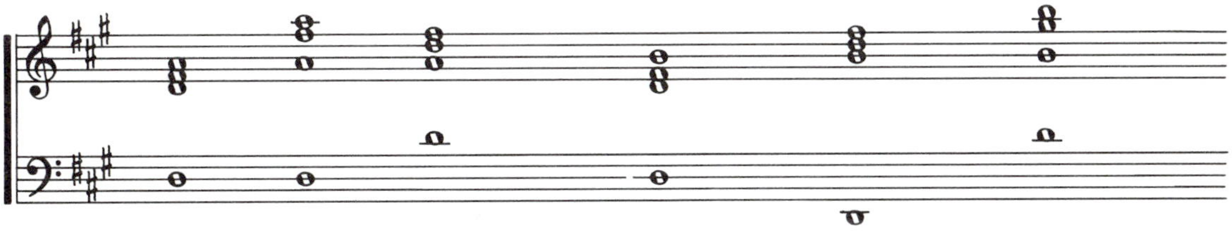

A Major: IV IV IV *not* IV *not* IV *not* IV

Roman Numerals Applied to Inverted Chords

When we apply Roman numerals to inverted chords, we must remember that the *root* (the lowest pitch of the triad from which the inverted chord is derived) and the *bass* (the lowest pitch of the inverted chord itself) are not the same. *The Roman numeral always indicates the scale degree of a chord's root.* In an inverted chord, the root may be in the soprano or in an inner voice, but never in the bass. To find the Roman numeral, convert the inverted chord into a triad and observe which scale degree functions as its root. Example 9-6 illustrates this procedure.

Example 9-6

a. Find the Roman numeral for the given inverted chord in the context of C major.

STEP ONE: Convert the inverted chord into a triad.

STEP TWO: Observe which scale degree functions as the root of the triad in the context of C major, and provide the inverted chord with the corresponding Roman numeral.

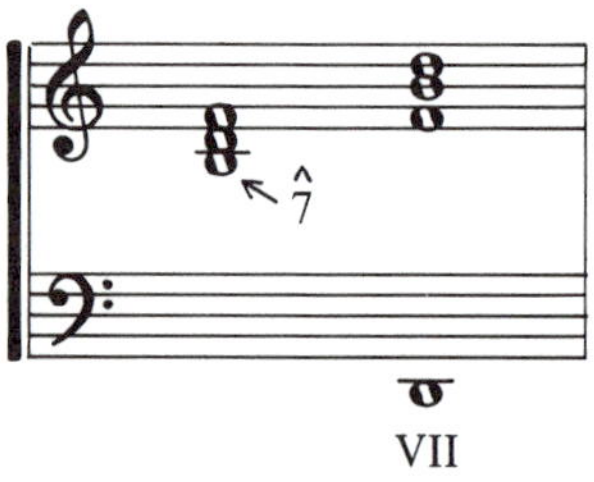

b. Find the Roman numeral for the given inverted chord in the context of G major.

STEP ONE: Convert the inverted chord into a triad.

STEP TWO: Observe which scale degree functions as the root of the triad in the context of G major, and provide the inverted chord with the corresponding Roman numeral.

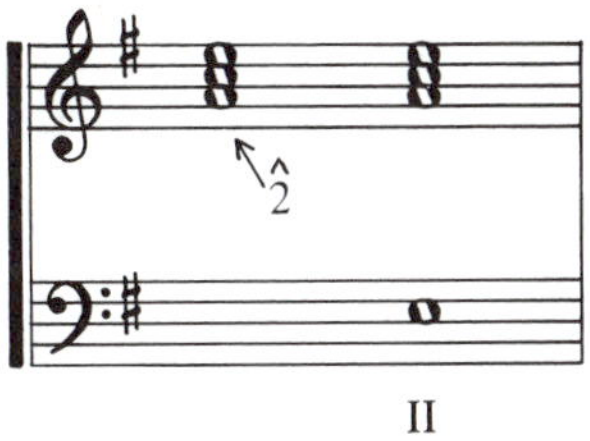

Once you understand Example 9-6, you may adopt the following shortcut: the root of a first-inversion chord is always a simple or compound sixth above the chord's bass, while the root of a second-inversion chord is always a simple or compound fourth above the chord's bass. Use this information to find the root without first converting the chord into a triad. You must, of course, first decide whether the chord is in root position, first inversion, or second inversion.

The Diminished Triad

The diatonic triads in major keys are of three qualities. The I, IV, and V triads are major. The II, III, and VI triads are minor. The VII triad's intervals match neither the major nor the minor triad's. Instead, the VII triad contains two minor thirds within the span of a diminished fifth, forming a ***diminished triad.*** Representatives of each triad quality are displayed in Example 9-7.

diminished triad

Example 9-7

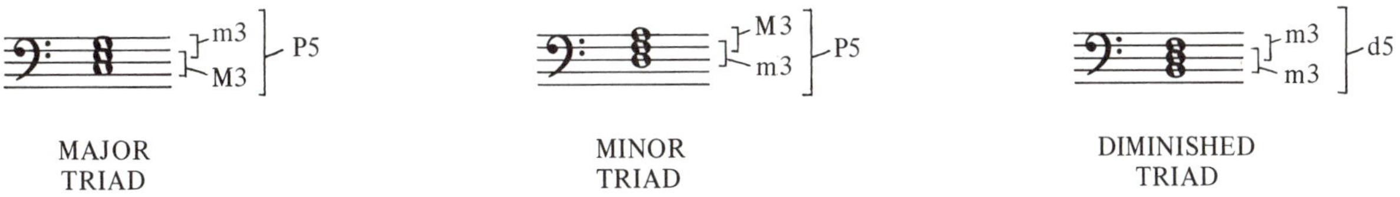

Dissonance in the Leading-Tone and Dominant Seventh Chords

Unlike the major and minor triads, the diminished triad is dissonant, due to the diminished fifth between its root and fifth. Dissonance, which is characterized by instability and a tendency toward resolution, can have a very positive effect when used judiciously. It can create contrast. It can propel a succession of chords toward a goal. The VII chord contains the two scale degrees, $\hat{4}$ and $\hat{7}$, that form a diminished fifth or augmented fourth in the major mode. When these two pitches sound simultaneously, their effect on one another determines how each pitch will resolve. The diminished fifth usually contracts into a third, while the augmented fourth usually expands into a sixth. Each dissonant pitch moves *by step* to a consonant pitch in the following chord. Example 9-8 displays these resolutions. Whether a diminished fifth or augmented fourth appears in a VII chord depends upon whether the chord is in root position or inverted and upon how the pitches above the bass are arranged. (Observe that when two of the three parts notated on the upper staff share the same pitch, its notehead is written only once. In these examples, the B and D of the first chord converge on C in the second chord.)

Example 9-8

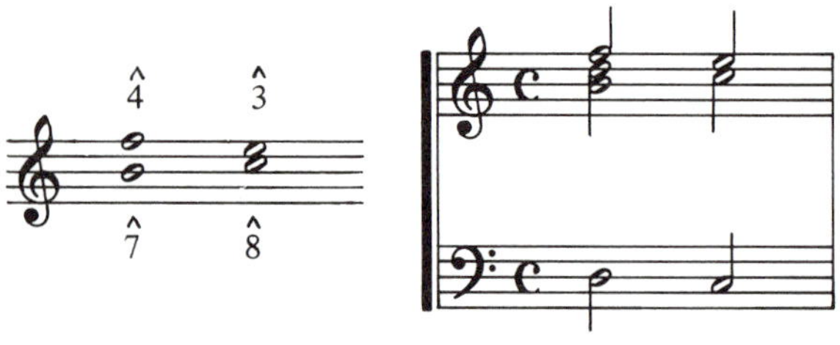

d5 into M3

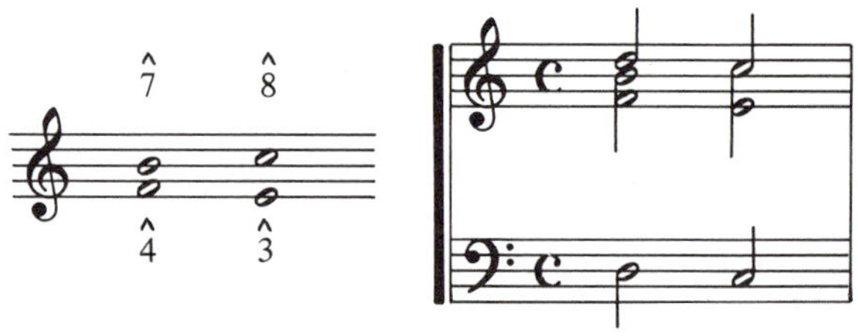

A4 into m6

The names of these intervals suggest their tendencies toward resolution: that which is diminished collapses inward; that which is augmented expands outward. In both cases, $\hat{4}$ resolves to $\hat{3}$ and $\hat{7}$ resolves to $\hat{8}$. In fact, the name of $\hat{7}$—"leading tone"—is merely a description of its tendency to move up a half step to the tonic pitch.

Dissonance is such a powerful and useful force in music that composers apply it to various other triads as well. The dominant triad is particularly well suited to the addition of a dissonant pitch. Like VII, the V triad contains the leading tone, $\hat{7}$. Composers often add $\hat{4}$ to the dominant triad, forming the ***dominant seventh chord,*** which consists of not only a major third and a perfect fifth above the dominant root, but also a minor seventh. In fact, the dominant seventh chord contains all the pitch classes of both the V and the VII triads, as shown in Example 9-9.

dominant seventh chord

Example 9-9

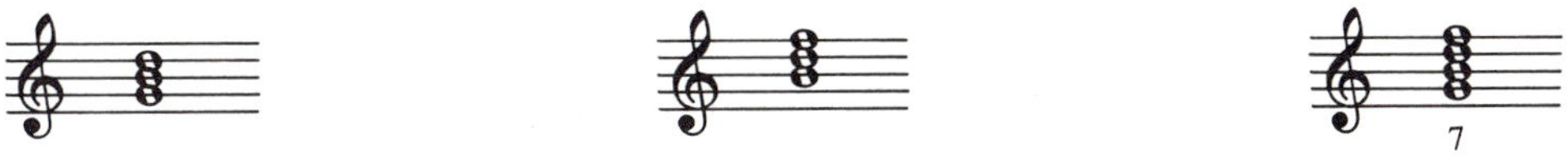

	$\substack{5\\3}$	$\substack{5\\3}$	$\substack{7\\5\\3}$
C Major:	V	VII	V

Observe that the appropriate figured-bass notation for the dominant seventh chord is $\substack{7\\5\\3}$, because a simple or compound diatonic seventh appears above the bass, in addition to the fifth and third. Observe also that the dominant seventh chord contains four different pitch classes. Many of the more advanced chords in music contain four different pitch classes, often through the addition of a seventh above the root.

Incomplete Chords

Composers occasionally omit the fifth when writing a chord in $\substack{5\\3}$ or $\substack{7\\5\\3}$ position. Two roots and two thirds or three roots and a third are sufficient to express the $\substack{5\\3}$ position. Two roots, a third, and a seventh are sufficient to express the $\substack{7\\5\\3}$ position. Because the third and seventh of the dominant seventh chord form a dissonant diminished fifth or augmented fourth, they are almost never doubled. Observe in Example 9-10 that even when the fifth is omitted, the figured bass remains $\substack{5\\3}$ or $\substack{7\\5\\3}$. You should never omit the third of a triad or seventh chord, because the third defines the chord's quality. Because of their comparative instability, inverted chords must always contain all of their component pitch classes.

Example 9-10

$\substack{5\\3}$ $\substack{5\\3}$ $\qquad$ $\substack{7\\5\\3}$ $\substack{7\\5\\3}$ $\substack{7\\5\\3}$

Phrases and Their Cadences

Music is often composed in segments called ***phrases.*** Phrases are typically two, four, or eight measures in length. They are shaped by clearly perceptible beginnings and endings. Melody, ***harmony***—the aspect of music involved with chord construction and succession—and rhythm help the performer and the listener understand how a phrase is shaped. For example, the melody will often descend

phrase

harmony

cadence

period

at the end of a phrase, accompanied by a ***cadence***: a succession of chords that invokes a sense of closure in much the same way that a semicolon or period marks divisions within a sentence.

Often two phrases work together as a pair, forming what is called a ***period.*** In the period shown in Example 9-11, each phrase is four measures in length. As you listen to this example, consider why you sense that measure 5 begins a new phrase, even though there is no rest or other obvious visual clue to indicate the end of the first phrase in measure 4.

Example 9-11

One of the reasons why measure 5 seems like the beginning of a new phrase is that from the beginning of measure 5 through the first chord of measure 7, Mozart uses exactly the same music as is found in the opening measures. A period whose two phrases begin identically is called a ***parallel period.*** What distinguishes the two phrases from one another is how each ends.

parallel period

Both of Mozart's phrases begin with the pitches A, C♯, and E, which form a I chord in the key of A major. The last chord of measure 4 contains the pitches E, G♯, and B, the V chord. The last chord of measure 8 contains the pitches A, C♯, and E, the I chord. This contrast between the endings of the two phrases is critical to the organization of the period. In the first phrase the melody and its accompanying chords lead to $\hat{2}$ over the V chord. Though they end the phrase adequately, neither $\hat{2}$ nor V gives a sense of completion. The composition *must* continue. In the second phrase, on the other hand, the melody and its accompanying chords lead to $\hat{1}$ over the I chord. Both $\hat{1}$ and I give a sense of completion. In this case, they conclude the period but not the composition. Rhythmic factors confirm this sense of closure, since the second half of measure 8 is the only half measure in the period where only one chord appears.

antecedent & consequent phrases

full cadence

authentic cadence

half cadence

semicadence

When the two phrases of a period are structured so that the first phrase requires, for melodic and harmonic reasons, that the second phrase follow, they are called ***antecedent*** and ***consequent phrases.*** Only the consequent phrase resolves fully. A cadence from a root-position V chord to a root-position I chord, as in measure 8 of the excerpt, is called a ***full cadence,*** or ***authentic cadence.*** Though the cadence at the end of an antecedent phrase may adequately conclude the harmonic progression of that phrase, it does not have the strength or finality of a full cadence. For this reason, a cadence on a root-position V chord, as in measure 4 of the excerpt, is called a ***half cadence,*** or ***semicadence.*** A typical antecedent/consequence phrase pair forming a parallel period contains two cadences: the first a half cadence on V, the second a full cadence on I.

perfect authentic cadence

imperfect authentic cadence

The full cadence that ends the Mozart excerpt in Example 9-12 derives part of its finality from the fact that the soprano pitches of the last four chords lead downward by step to $\hat{1}$ in coordination with the harmonic cadence on I. When $\hat{1}$ resides in both the soprano and bass at the end of a phrase, the cadence is called *perfect.* The end of Mozart's period is, then, a ***perfect authentic cadence.*** Later in the composition, Mozart ends a similar phrase on $\hat{3}$ instead of $\hat{1}$ in the soprano, as shown in Example 9-12. Even though the harmonic progression is V–I, this cadence is an ***imperfect authentic cadence*** because a scale degree other than $\hat{1}$ ends the melody. The dissonant B and G♯ that appear above the bass pitch A at this cadence are remnants of the preceding V chord. At the very end of the measure, the consonant C♯ and A (chord members of I) arrive.

Example 9-12

Mozart: Sonata in A Major K. 331

The authentic cadence, V to I, gives a strong sense of closure at the end of a phrase. The leading tone (the third of the V chord) resolves by step to $\hat{1}$. When the dominant seventh chord is used, as in the last measure of Example 9-11, a dissonant augmented fourth or diminished fifth appears against the leading tone and resolves by step to $\hat{3}$. Virtually every tonal composition will contain at least one authentic cadence.

plagal cadence

The progression from IV to I lacks both the leading tone and the capacity to include a dissonant interval that would resolve to pitches of the tonic chord. When this progression occurs at the end of a phrase, a ***plagal cadence*** results. The plagal cadence offers a solemn alternative to the V–I authentic cadence. Though it might be intriguing to regard the subdominant–tonic progression as a sort of mirror of the dominant–tonic progression (since both begin with a chord rooted a perfect fifth from tonic), in practice composers do not use the plagal cadence with nearly the same frequency as they use the authentic cadence. In fact, the plagal cadence rarely occurs except in the immediate context of an authentic cadence.

perfect plagal cadence

imperfect plagal cadence

A plagal cadence appears in the "Amen" endings of many Protestant hymns, *after* the verse has concluded with an authentic cadence. As with the authentic cadence, the plagal cadence is ***perfect*** if the soprano voice of the I chord is $\hat{1}$ and ***imperfect*** if it is $\hat{3}$ or $\hat{5}$. Example 9-13 shows a perfect plagal cadence after a perfect authentic cadence in a Protestant hymn (Ex. 9-13a), and an imperfect plagal cadence in a nocturne by Chopin (Ex. 9-13b). This phrase by Chopin both begins and ends the nocturne. Observe that F♭ and B♭ embellish the succession from the diatonic IV chord to the I chord. The insertion of such pitches into a harmonic context will be explored in Chapter 13. (The squiggly line that appears to the left of the first and last chords is the symbol for arpeggiation, which means that these chords are to be played with each note in rapid succession from bottom to top. The symbol does not alter the *content* of the chord but merely specifies how it should be performed.)

Example 9-13

a. Hyfrydol

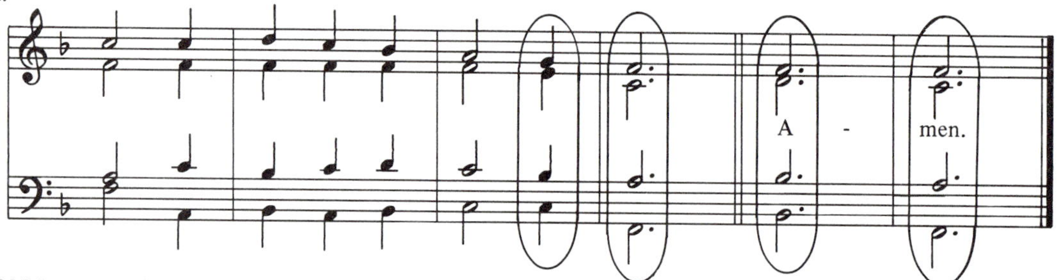

F Major: V I IV I

b. Chopin: Nocturne Op. 32, No. 2

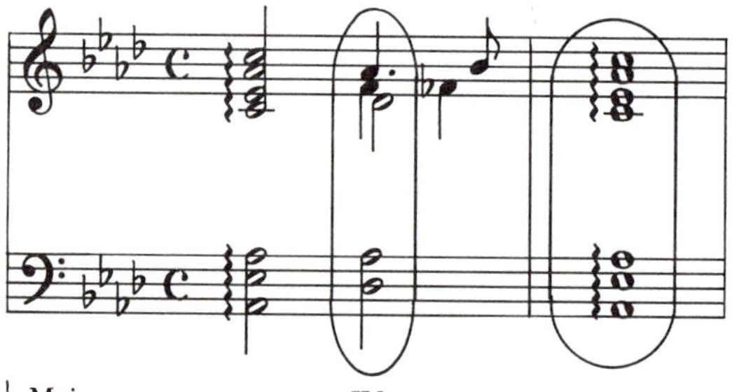

A♭ Major: IV I

The excerpt from Handel's opera *Xerxes*, shown in Example 9-14, contains a surprise. Observe that the melodic line of the passage starts on $\hat{8}$ and proceeds through all the scale degrees down to $\hat{2}$, which is supported by the V harmony in measure 5 of the passage. With this precedent—and because a phrase earlier in the movement began with this same descent and concluded with a perfect authentic cadence—$\hat{1}$ supported by I is the expected continuation. We anticipate that Handel will again conclude the phrase with a perfect authentic cadence. He instead moves the bass from $\hat{5}$ to $\hat{6}$, supporting the IV chord in $^{6}_{3}$ position instead of I. This type of cadence, where VI in $^{5}_{3}$ position or IV in $^{6}_{3}$ position (or, rarely, some other substitute for the tonic) is used, is called a ***deceptive cadence.*** It is the least final of the cadence types discussed in this chapter. The chord that substitutes for I—the IV chord in the Handel excerpt—typically leads into another succession of chords that ends in a perfect authentic cadence, as in measure 8 of the Handel excerpt.

deceptive cadence

Example 9-14

Handel: *Xerxes*, Ombra mai fù (Adapted)

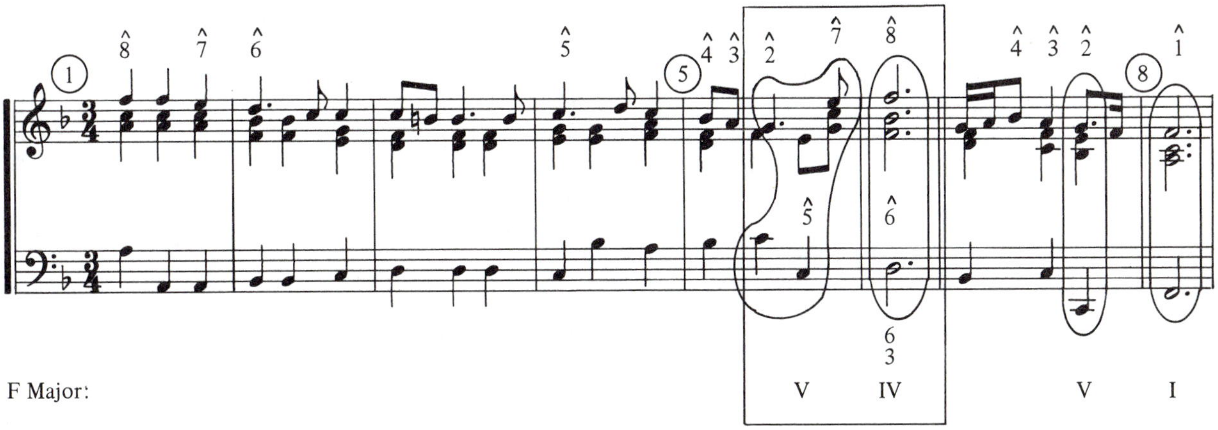

Pitch exercises for Chapter 9 are on pages 305–311.

RHYTHM

Syncopation

Meter is the framework upon which the rhythmic life of music unfolds. It sets up the listener's expectations regarding when various musical events will occur. Because of meter we expect that the first beat of a measure will be the strongest and that what happens on a beat will be stronger than what happens between beats. One of the composer's most powerful tools for enhancing musical expression is the purposeful contradiction of these expectations—confounding the listener by making strong that which is normally weak, or by making weak that which is normally strong.

The temporary contradiction of the prevailing meter is called ***syncopation.*** Though no new types of noteheads or rests are required to notate syncopation, the irregular positioning of notes often warrants the use of a tie (introduced in Chapter 2) to bind two noteheads together. The curved lines connecting the G♯'s in

syncopation

measures 28 and 29 and the B's in measure 30 of Example 9-15 are ties. They instruct the performer to continue sounding the G♯ and B without articulating them again.

Example 9-15

Brahms: Symphony No. 1

The syncopation in the melody shown in Example 9-15 depends upon the regular pattern of normal accentuation established by the opening beats, a pattern that continues in the orchestral accompaniment during the remainder of the melody. After the expected placement of strong notes on each beat for five consecutive beats, measure 29 is a surprising contrast, for *none* of the beats coincide with the articulation of a pitch, while *all* of the midpoints between beats do. As the melody works its way upward to a climax, the expressive forces of syncopated rhythms and chromatic pitches unite.

Ties versus Slurs

slur

Observe that ties connect only two adjacent noteheads, and that those noteheads represent the same pitch. Another curved line, called a ***slur,*** connects noteheads that represent different pitches. A slur may connect adjacent noteheads or span a number of noteheads. Whereas the tie is a symbol of rhythmic notation, the slur is a performance indication pertaining either to legato (smooth) connections among pitches or to phrasing, that is, the grouping of notes into coherent units. The excerpt shown in Example 9-16 contains one tie (connecting two G's) and three slurs.

Example 9-16

Beethoven: Piano Sonata Op. 10 No. 2 (Adapted)

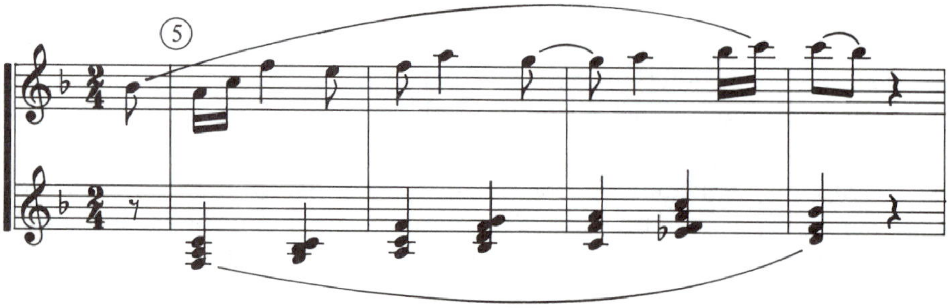

Syncopation as Contrast to Existing Pulse

Syncopation has an effect only if the normal metrical pattern has been established in previous measures or coexists with the syncopated material. If the example by Beethoven (Ex. 9-16) included only the upper line, and if measures 1 through 4 of the movement (not shown) did not contain a more regular accentuation, most of the effect of the syncopation would be lost. Performers must be careful to avoid an interpretation that would correspond to the notation shown in Example 9-17. Fortunately, the vigorous chords projected by the left hand in Example 9-16 leave little doubt regarding the melody's syncopated nature.

Example 9-17

Syncopation among Submetrical Rhythmic Values

As was mentioned in Chapter 7, the four subdivisions of a beat in simple meter share with the four beats of a $\frac{4}{4}$ measure the metrical pattern "Strongly accented, Unaccented, Moderately accented, Unaccented" (*SuMu*). When this hierarchy among *submetrical* notes—notes of less than one beat in duration—is upset, syncopation results. Example 9-18a contains numerous instances of syncopation. An unsyncopated version of the same melody is displayed in 9-18b for comparison.

Example 9-18

Rhythm exercises for Chapter 9 are on pages 312–314.

LABORATORY

L9-1.a. Play the following chord progressions at the keyboard. What type of cadence ends each?

1.

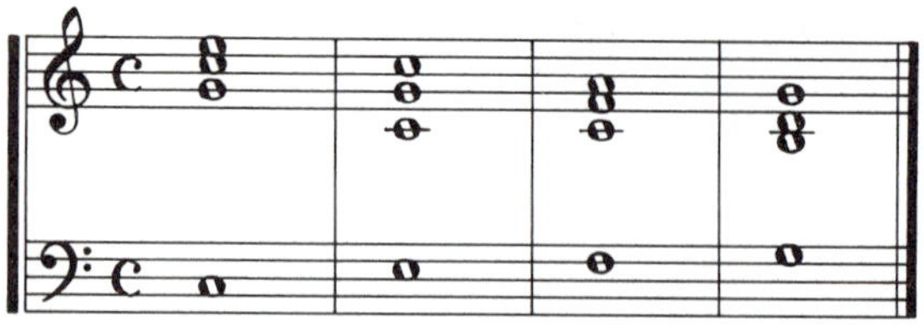

2.

3.

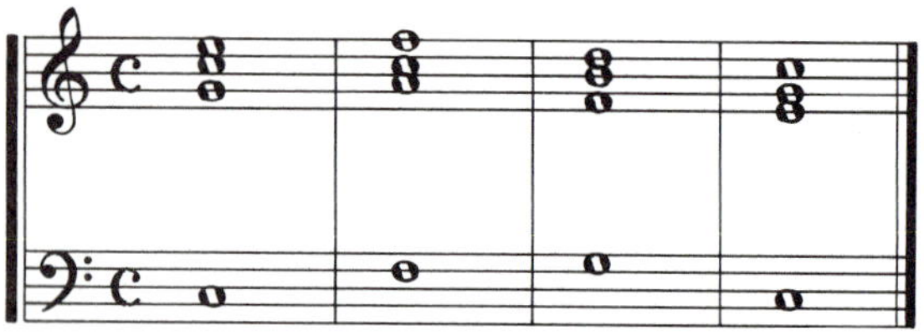

4.

5.

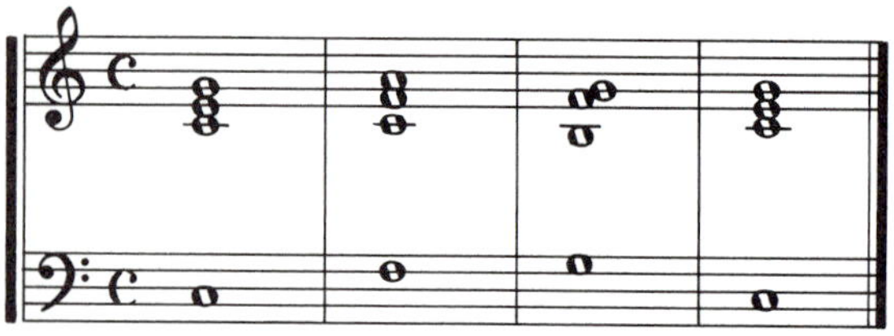

b. Perform each of the following melodies at the keyboard. Recommended fingerings for the right hand are included.

Berlioz: Symphonie fantastique

1.

Beethoven: Symphony No. 7

2.

Albéniz: Tango No. 2

3.

Brahms: Piano Concerto No. 2

4.

L9-2.a. At the keyboard, perform a chord that corresponds to the given Roman numeral and figured bass. The key signature (major mode) and bass note are supplied. Play one note with the left hand and three notes with the right hand.

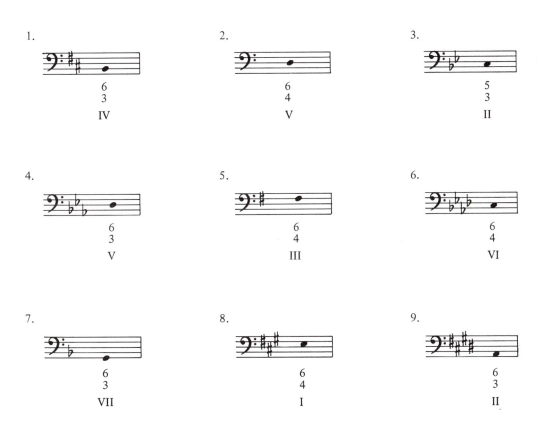

1.

6
3
IV

2.

6
4
V

3.

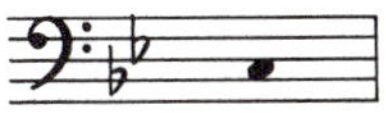

5
3
II

4.

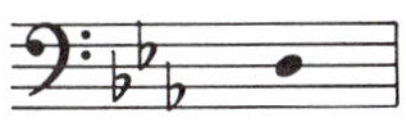

6
3
V

5.

6
4
III

6.

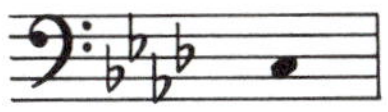

6
4
VI

7.

6
3
VII

8.

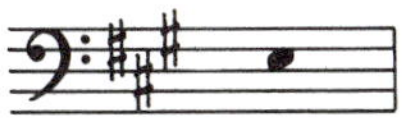

6
4
I

9.

6
3
II

b. At random, select a key from the left column, a Roman numeral from the middle column, and a figured bass from the right column. Then, at the keyboard, perform the chord. Play one note with the left hand and three notes with the right hand. Repeat the exercise until you have developed absolute security with chord construction.

Key	*Roman Numeral*	*Position*
C major	I	$^{5}_{3}$
D♭ major	II	$^{6}_{3}$
D major	III	$^{6}_{4}$
E♭ major	IV	$^{7}_{\substack{5\\3}}$ (with V only)
E major	V	
F major	VI	
F♯ major	VII	
G major		
A♭ major		
A major		
B♭ major		
B major		

L9-3. Practice the following exercise, changing the reference scale after every two or three attempts.

- Simultaneously sing and play an ascending major scale beginning on a pitch low in your vocal range. Extend up a tenth instead of the customary octave.
- Using both hands, strike scale degrees $\hat{1}$, $\hat{3}$, $\hat{5}$, $\hat{8}$ ($\hat{1}$), and $\hat{10}$ ($\hat{3}$) simultaneously. In this way, the tonal center you have selected is solidly established in your ear.
- Now strike again any one of these five keys and sing the pitch.

- Sing one of the four melodic successions below that corresponds to the pitch performed and then confirm what you have sung by playing the appropriate pitches on the keyboard.

$\hat{1}$	$\hat{3}$	$\hat{5}$	$\hat{8}$	$\hat{10}$
$\hat{1}$–$\hat{3}$	$\hat{3}$–$\hat{1}$	$\hat{5}$–$\hat{1}$	$\hat{8}$–$\hat{1}$	$\hat{10}$–$\hat{1}$
$\hat{1}$–$\hat{5}$	$\hat{3}$–$\hat{5}$	$\hat{5}$–$\hat{3}$	$\hat{8}$–$\hat{3}$	$\hat{10}$–$\hat{3}$
$\hat{1}$–$\hat{8}$	$\hat{3}$–$\hat{8}$	$\hat{5}$–$\hat{8}$	$\hat{8}$–$\hat{5}$	$\hat{10}$–$\hat{5}$
$\hat{1}$–$\hat{10}$	$\hat{3}$–$\hat{10}$	$\hat{5}$–$\hat{10}$	$\hat{8}$–$\hat{10}$	$\hat{10}$–$\hat{8}$

L9-4. Practice the following exercise first in C major, then in various other major keys whose scales fall within your vocal range.

- Strike a tonic pitch that appears near the bottom of your vocal range and, starting with that pitch, sing an ascending major scale, using scale degree numbers.
- Place three fingers over keys that form any triad in the key (II, III, IV, etc.), positioning the root higher than the initial tonic pitch. Strike the root.
- Sing the sounded pitch and, arpeggiating upward, sing the third and fifth of the triad.
- Confirm what you have sung by playing the triadic pitches at the keyboard.

Once the above exercise is going well, add the following steps.

- Strike a tonic pitch that appears in the middle to upper region of your vocal range and, starting with that pitch, sing a descending major scale, using scale-degree numbers.
- Place three fingers over keys that form any triad in the key (VII, VI, V, etc.), positioning the root lower than the initial tonic pitch. Strike the root.
- Sing the sounded pitch and, arpeggiating upward, sing the third and fifth of the triad.
- Confirm what you have sung by playing the triadic pitches at the keyboard.

L9-5. Practice the following melodies at the keyboard, simultaneously singing and playing each pitch. Sing the scale-degree numbers that correspond to the pitches. If necessary, transpose the entire score down one octave. The first melody contains chromatic pitches. At those points, sing "raised" instead of a scale degree number, as indicated.

a.

Wait Till the Sun Shines, Nellie

b.

Swing Low, Sweet Chariot

c.

The Marines' Hymn

L9-6. The following compositions are for voice and keyboard. A student or the instructor could play the keyboard part while other students sing the melody. The keyboard part should be performed as written, but the vocal line may be moved down an octave if necessary.

a.

b.

L9-7. The following compositions are for two voices. Sing the scale-degree numbers that correspond to the pitches. If necessary, transpose the entire score up or down one octave.

a. Voice 1

b. Voice 1

L9-8. Write in the counting syllables below the notated rhythms. Then perform each by clapping the rhythm or playing the pitch C or F at the keyboard, as notated, while pronouncing the counting syllables aloud. Practice until you can perform each exercise at a tempo of about ♩ = 40.

a.

b.

c.

d.

e.

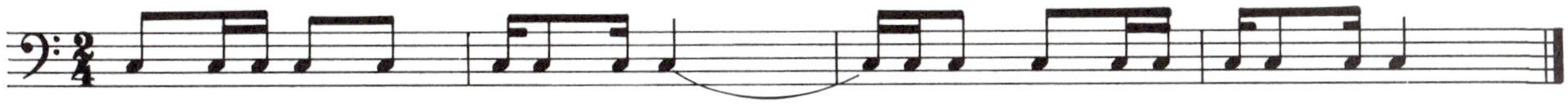

L9-9. Write in the counting syllables below the notated rhythms. Then perform them by dividing the class into two groups, with each group clapping one part while pronouncing the counting syllables aloud. Alternatively, individual students may perform both parts simultaneously at the keyboard, pronouncing the counting syllables aloud while the index fingers strike the notated pitches.

a.

b.

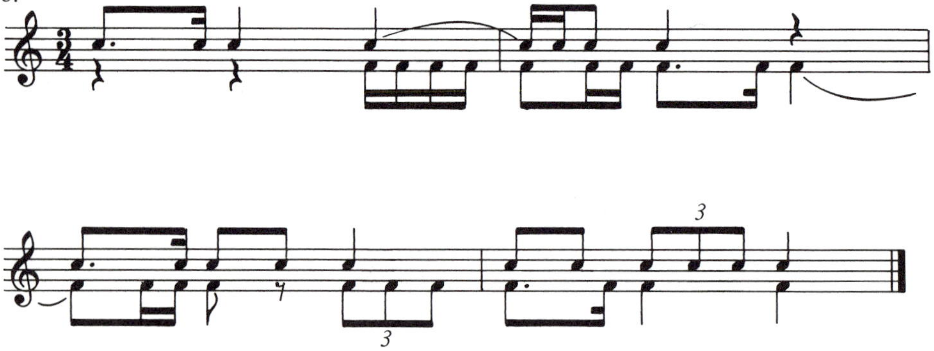

c.

L9-10. This exercise requires that a student or the instructor serve as the performer at a keyboard.

a. The performer plays a triad. Indicate whether it is major, minor, or diminished. The performer's choices of triads for performance are as follows.

1. Bass with major third and perfect fifth (major)
2. Bass with minor third and perfect fifth (minor)
3. Bass with minor third and diminished fifth (diminished)

b. In any major key, the performer strikes scale degree $\hat{1}$ alone and then strikes scale degrees $\hat{1}$, $\hat{3}$, and $\hat{5}$ simultaneously. The performer then strikes scale degree $\hat{2}$, $\hat{3}$, $\hat{4}$, $\hat{5}$, $\hat{6}$, or $\hat{7}$ (either above or below the original $\hat{1}$), followed by the diatonic triad built on that scale degree. Indicate the Roman numeral of the triad performed.

Hint: In major, the I, IV, and V chords are major; the II, III, and VI chords are minor; and the VII chord is diminished.

Audio exercises for Chapter 9 are on pages 315–317.

Name: ______________________
Instructor: ______________________
Date: ______________________

EXERCISES

Pitch Exercises

P9-1. Interpret each chord below in the major key whose key signature is supplied. Specify whether the chord is major, minor, or diminished. Indicate its name (tonic, supertonic, etc.). Supply its Roman numeral.

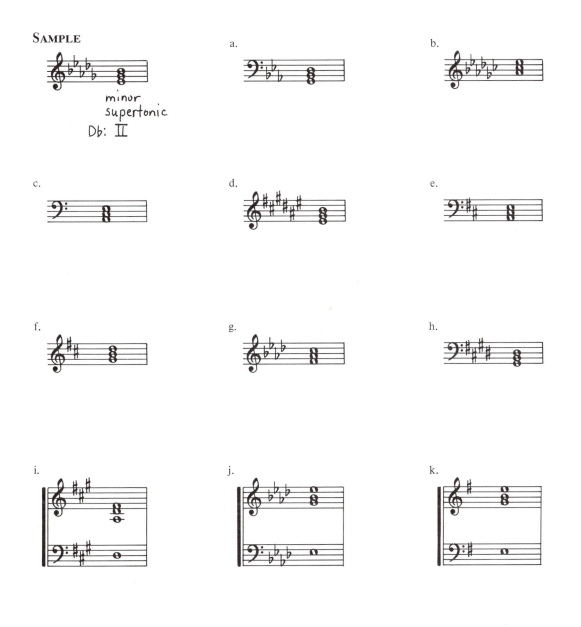

SAMPLE

minor
supertonic
D♭: II

a.

b.

c.

d.

e.

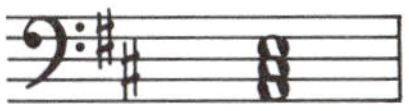

f.

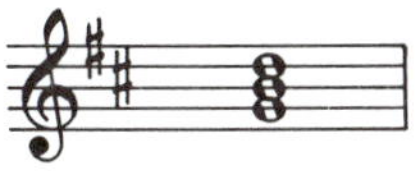

g.

h.

i.

j.

k.

P9-2. Form triads that correspond to the keys and Roman numerals given by writing key signatures and appropriate noteheads on the staves.

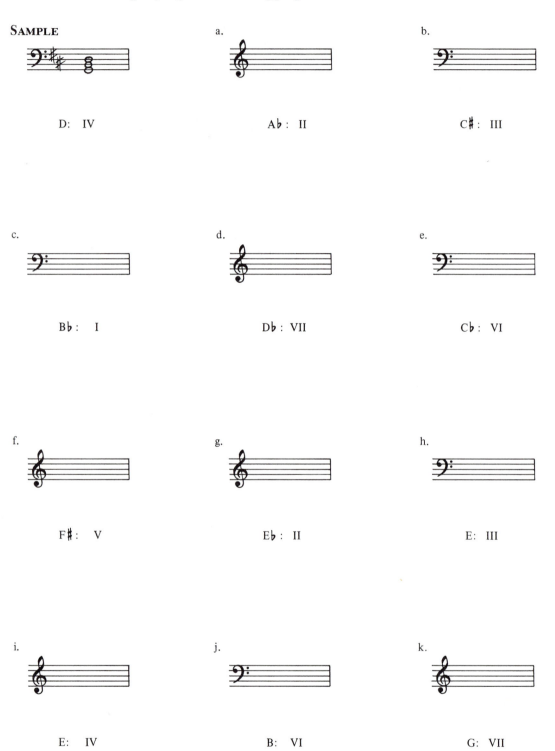

Sample

D: IV

a.

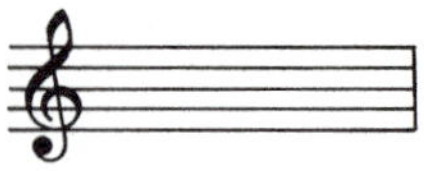

A♭: II

b.

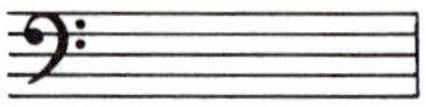

C♯: III

c.

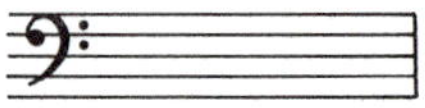

B♭: I

d.

D♭: VII

e.

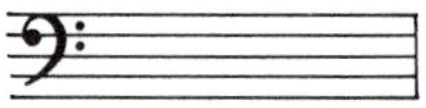

C♭: VI

f.

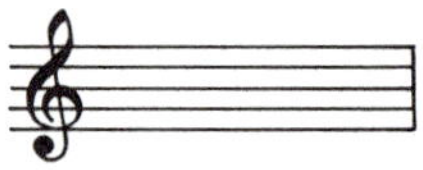

F♯: V

g.

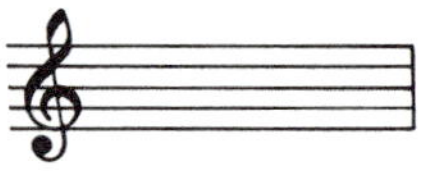

E♭: II

h.

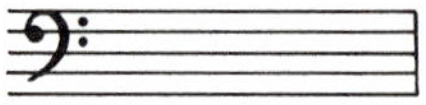

E: III

i.

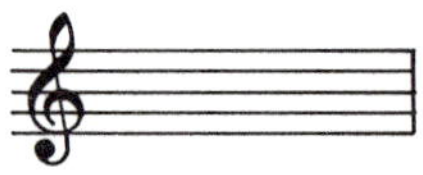

E: IV

j.

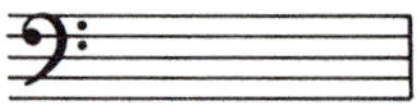

B: VI

k.

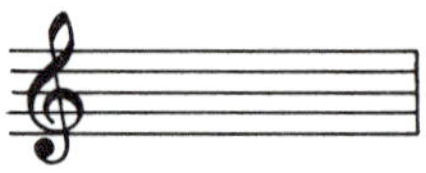

G: VII

Name: ____________________

Instructor: ____________________

Date: ____________________

P9-3. Interpret each chord below in the major key whose key signature is supplied. Specify the figured bass of the chord ($\begin{smallmatrix}5\\3\end{smallmatrix}$, $\begin{smallmatrix}7\\5\\3\end{smallmatrix}$, $\begin{smallmatrix}6\\3\end{smallmatrix}$, or $\begin{smallmatrix}6\\4\end{smallmatrix}$). Supply its Roman numeral. You may use the space to the right of each chord to rewrite it in root position, using simple intervals.

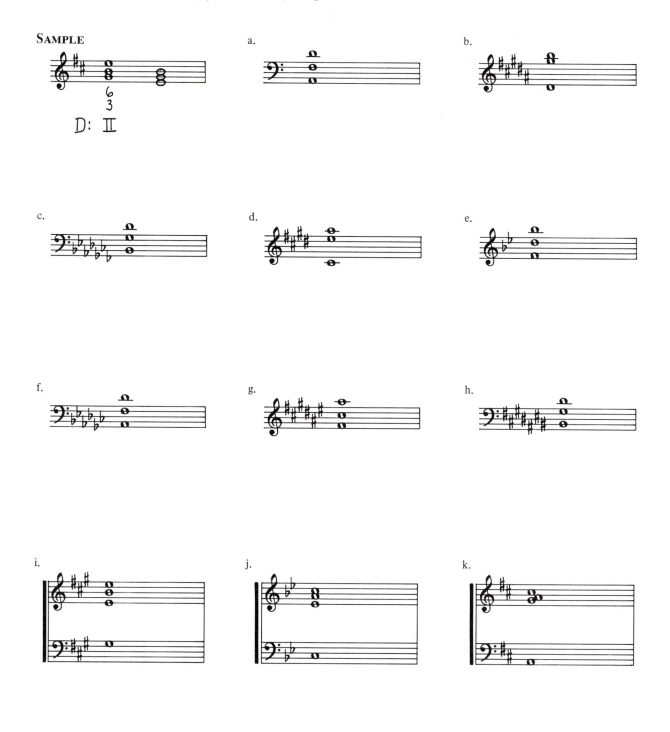

SAMPLE

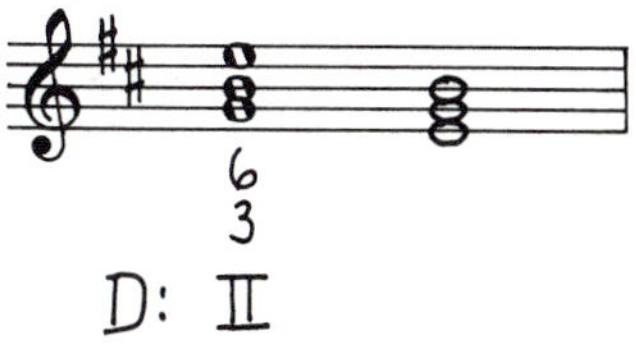

a.

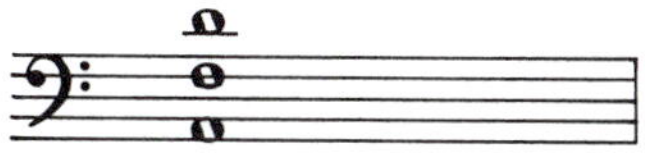

b.

c.

d.

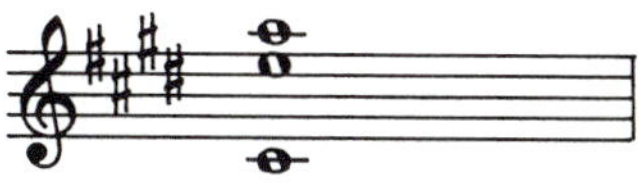

e.

f.

g.

h.

i.

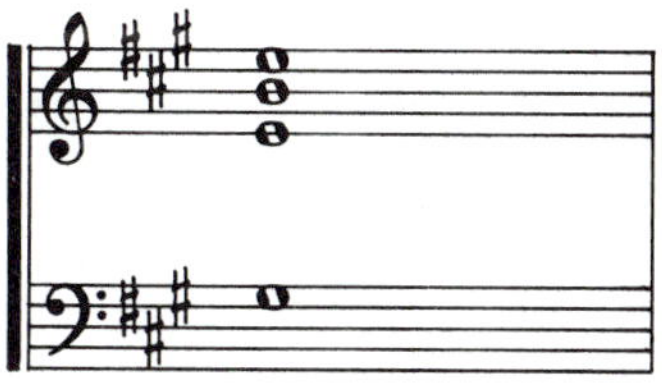

j.

k.

P9-4. For each Roman numeral, figured bass, and major key given, add the key signature and form an appropriate chord on the system. Use half notes notated as a keyboard accompaniment.

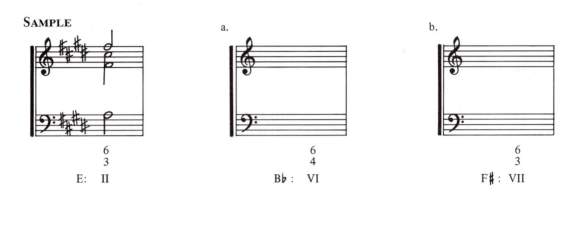

Sample

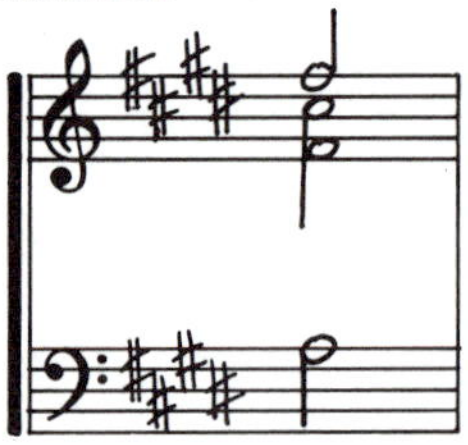

6
3
E: II

a.

6
4
B♭: VI

b.

6
3
F♯: VII

c.

5
3
E♭: IV

d.

6
3
A♭: III

e.

7
5
3
C♭: V

6
3
C♯: VI

5
3
F: II

6
4
B: I

Name: ______________________

Instructor: ______________________

Date: ______________________

P9-5. Each chord below contains a diminished fifth or augmented fourth. Fill in the noteheads that correspond to the pitches of these dissonant intervals. On the right half of each system, show the most appropriate pitches of resolution for these pitches. Remember that $\hat{7}$ leads to $\hat{8}$ and $\hat{4}$ leads to $\hat{3}$.

Sample

a.

b.

c.

d.

e.

f.

g.

h.

i.

j.

k.

P9-6. Determine the major key in which each example is composed from its key signature. Supply figured-bass and Roman-numeral labels for each chord. Then indicate the type of cadence that ends each phrase. Some examples contain two phrases.

SAMPLE

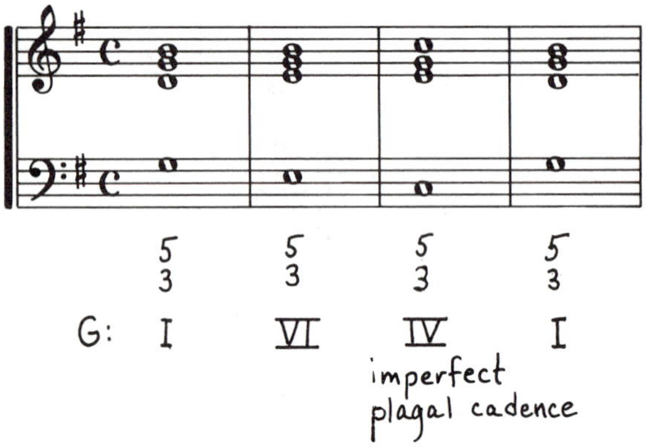

a.

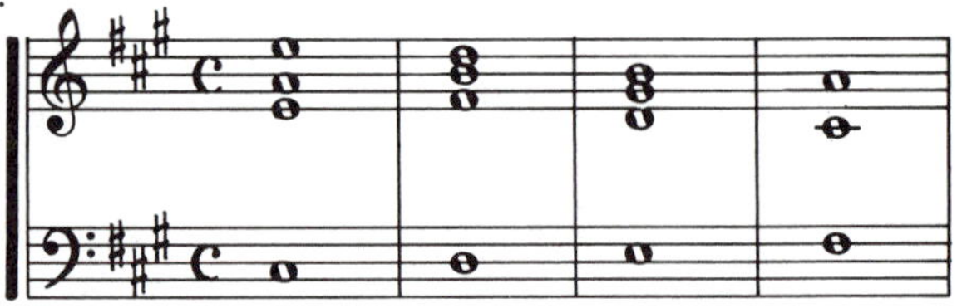

b.

c.

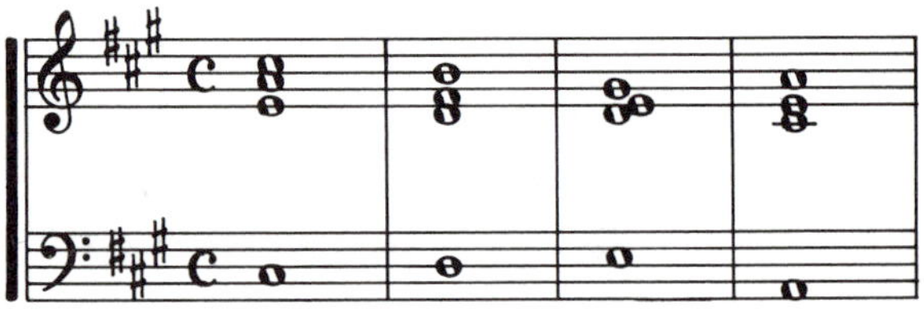

d.

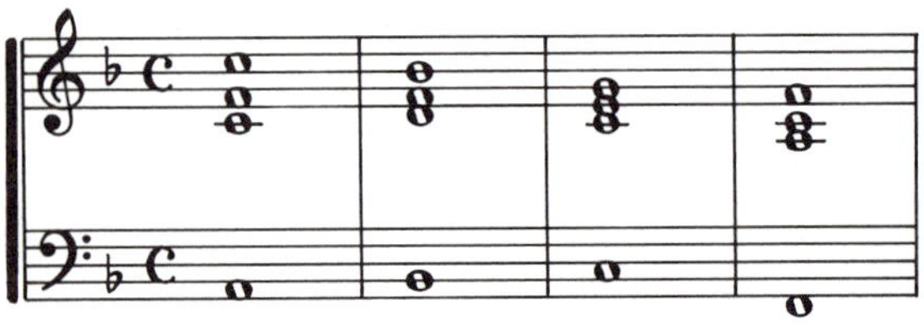

e.

Name: ______________________

Instructor: ______________________

Date: ______________________

f.

g.

h.

i.

Rhythm Exercises

R9-1. For each melody below, supply the appropriate counting syllables.

a.

b.

c.

d.

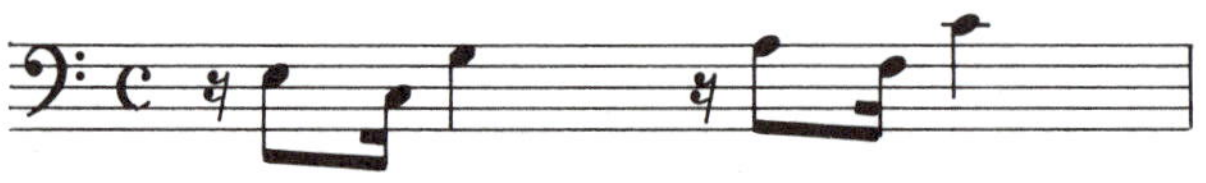

e.

Name: ______________________

Instructor: ______________________

Date: ______________________

R9-2. Form a melody using the fragments provided. Only one ordering of these fragments results in measures that contain the correct number of beats.

a.

b.

c.

R9-3. Notate the melodies indicated by the positioning of the pitch names in relation to the counting syllables. Use only unisons, seconds, thirds, and fourths as melodic intervals. Do not add rests.

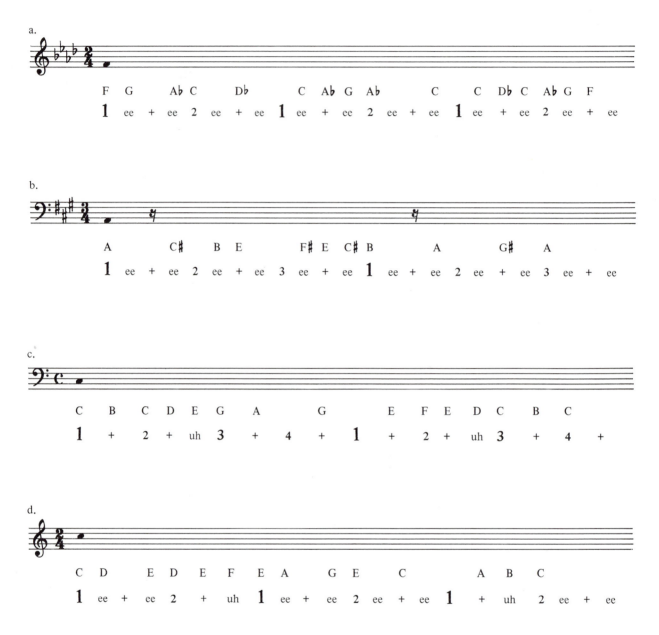

a.

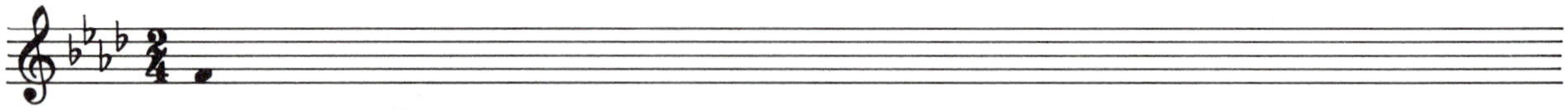

F G A♭ C D♭ C A♭ G A♭ C C D♭ C A♭ G F

1 ee + ee 2 ee + ee 1 ee + ee 2 ee + ee 1 ee + ee 2 ee + ee

b.

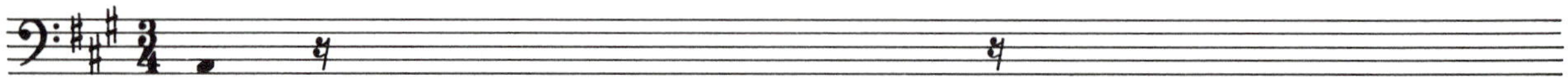

A C♯ B E F♯ E C♯ B A G♯ A

1 ee + ee 2 ee + ee 3 ee + ee 1 ee + ee 2 ee + ee 3 ee + ee

c.

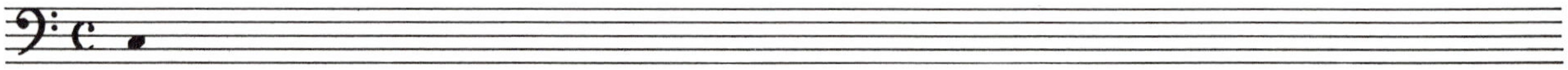

C B C D E G A G E F E D C B C

1 + 2 + uh 3 + 4 + 1 + 2 + uh 3 + 4 +

d.

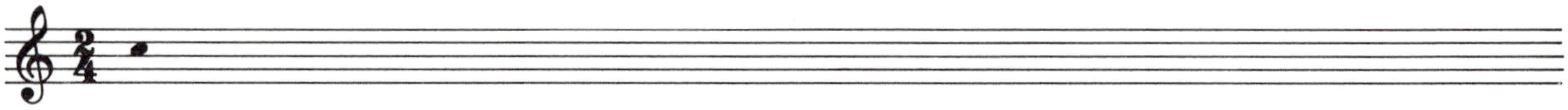

C D E D E F E A G E C A B C

1 ee + ee 2 + uh 1 ee + ee 2 ee + ee 1 + uh 2 ee + ee

Name: ______________________

Instructor: ______________________

Date: ______________________

Audio Exercises

A9-1. A triad will be performed. Indicate whether its quality is major, minor, or diminished.

a.	Major	Minor	Diminished
b.	Major	Minor	Diminished
c.	Major	Minor	Diminished
d.	Major	Minor	Diminished
e.	Major	Minor	Diminished
f.	Major	Minor	Diminished
g.	Major	Minor	Diminished
h.	Major	Minor	Diminished
i.	Major	Minor	Diminished
j.	Major	Minor	Diminished

A9-2. Two triads will be performed in root position, each preceded by a performance of its root alone. If the first triad is interpreted as tonic (I), what label should be applied to the second triad?

a.	II	III	IV	V	VI	VII
b.	II	III	IV	V	VI	VII
c.	II	III	IV	V	VI	VII
d.	II	III	IV	V	VI	VII
e.	II	III	IV	V	VI	VII
f.	II	III	IV	V	VI	VII
g.	II	III	IV	V	VI	VII
h.	II	III	IV	V	VI	VII
i.	II	III	IV	V	VI	VII
j.	II	III	IV	V	VI	VII

A9-3. Six melodies will be performed. The starting pitch for each will be stated before the melody is performed. In each case circle the score that shows the correct pitch notation.

a.

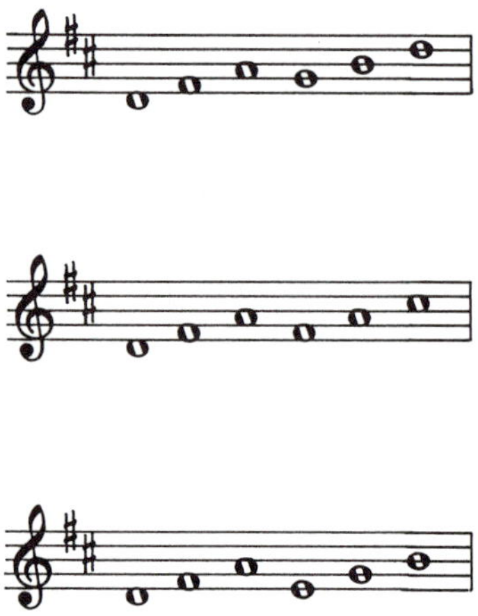

b.

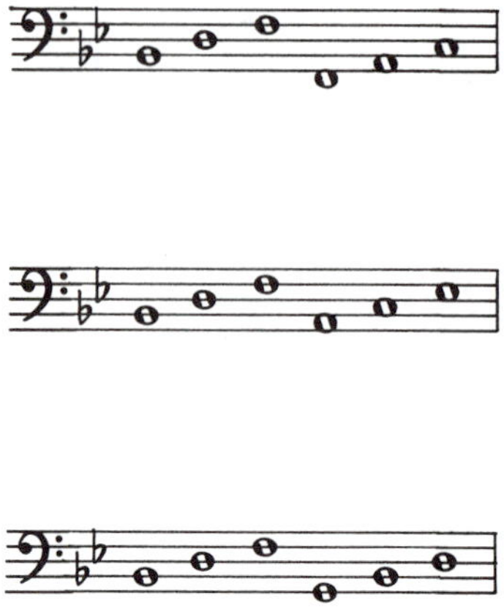

c.

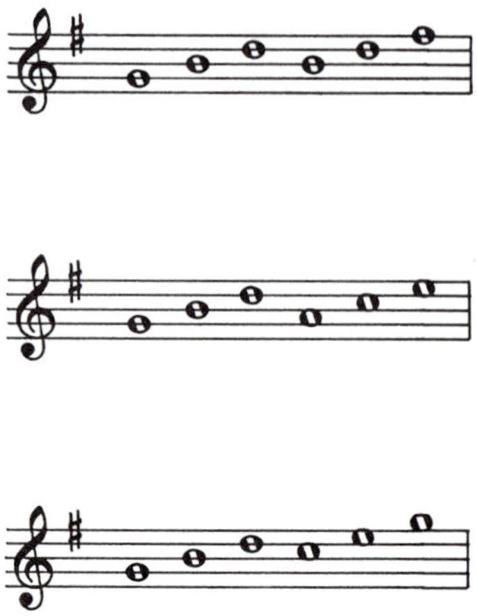

d.

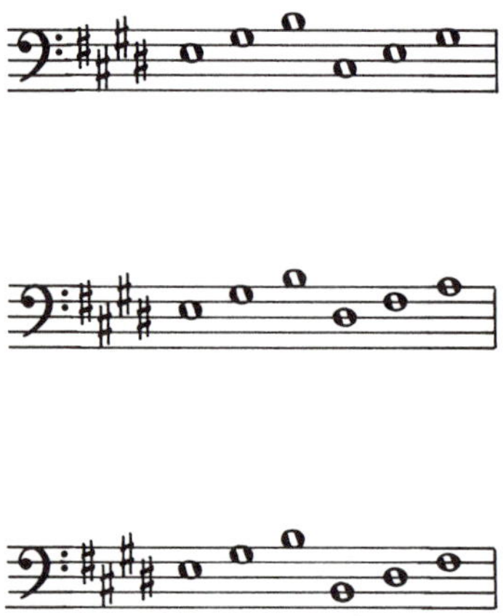

e.

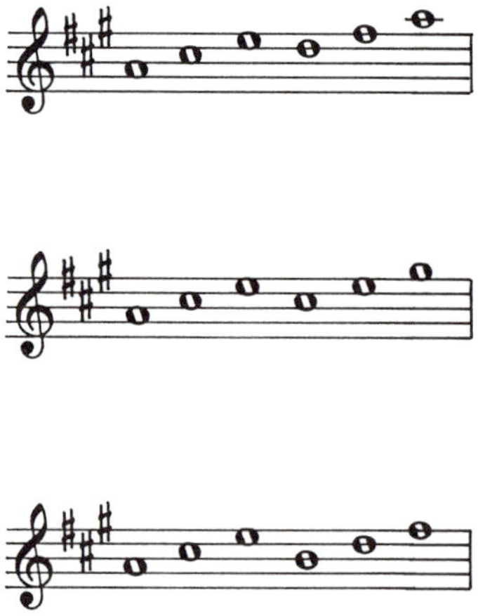

f.

Name: ______________________

Instructor: ______________________

Date: ______________________

A9-4. Four rhythms will be performed. In each case circle the score that shows the correct notation.

a.

b.

c.

d.

Name: ______________________
Instructor: ______________________
Date: ______________________

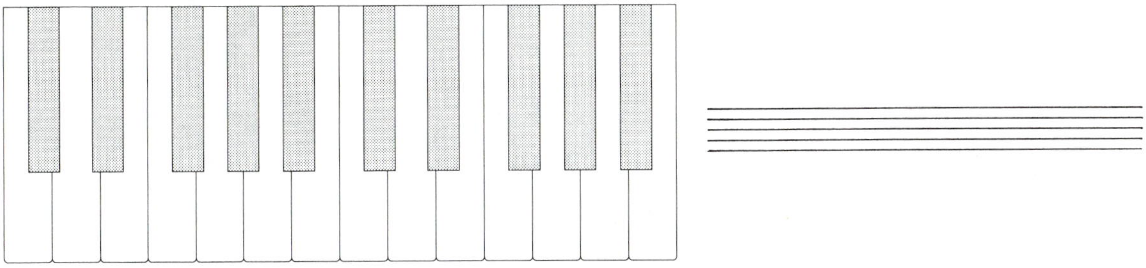

Mastery Test, Chapter 9

_______ 1. Which one of the triads shown functions as the submediant triad in the key of D major?

X. Y. Z.

_______ 2. Which one of the triads shown functions as the supertonic triad in the key of A♭ major?

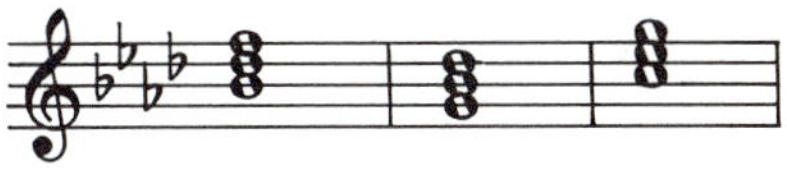

X. Y. Z.

_______ 3. Which one of the triads shown is of diminished quality?

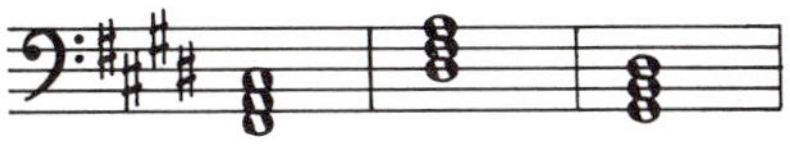

X. Y. Z.

For Questions 4 and 5:

A major

_______ 4. What Roman numeral pertains to the chord shown?

X. III Y. IV Z. V

_______ 5. What figured bass pertains to the chord shown?

X. $^{5}_{3}$ Y. $^{6}_{3}$ Z. $^{6}_{4}$

For Questions 6–10:

B♭ major

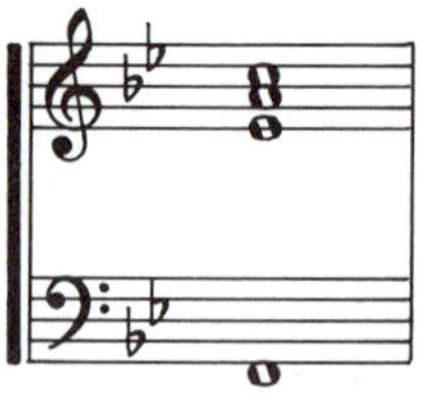

_________ 6. What Roman numeral pertains to the chord shown?

X. IV Y. V Z. VI

_________ 7. What figured bass pertains to the chord shown?

X. $\substack{5\\3}$ Y. $\substack{6\\3}$ Z. $\substack{7\\5\\3}$

_________ 8. To what pitch would the A most likely resolve?

X. B Y. B♭ Z. G

_________ 9. To what pitch would the E♭ most likely resolve?

X. D Y. F Z. B♭

_________ 10. To what chord would the given chord resolve in an authentic cadence?

X. IV Y. VI Z. I

_________ 11. Which cadence type is characterized by the progression IV–I?

X. Half Y. Plagal Z. Deceptive

_________ 12. Where is a half cadence most likely to occur?

X. The end of a parallel period
Y. The end of a consequent phrase
Z. The end of an antecedent phrase

_________ 13. Which symbol is occasionally used in the notation of syncopation?

X. Slur
Y. Repeat sign
Z. Tie

_________ 14. What kind of note should be inserted at the arrow to complete the measure?

X. Sixteenth note
Y. Eighth note
Z. Dotted eighth note

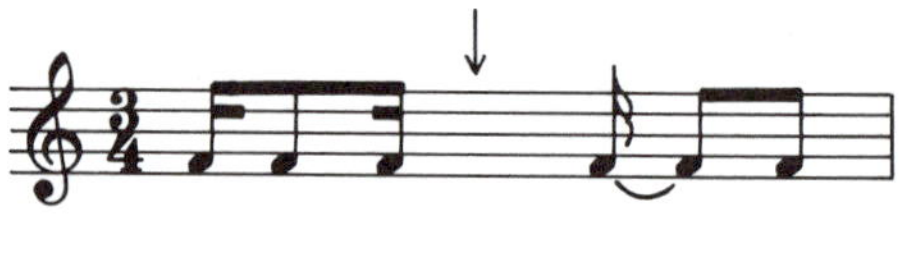

_________ 15. What kind of rest should be inserted at the arrow to complete the measure?

X. Eighth rest
Y. Quarter rest
Z. Dotted eighth rest

Name: ______________________

Instructor: ______________________

Date: ______________________

_________ 16. A triad will be performed. Indicate whether its quality is major, minor, or diminished.

X. Major Y. Minor Z. Diminished

Two triads will be performed in root position, each preceded by a performance of its root alone. If the first triad is interpreted as tonic (I), what label should be applied to the second triad?

_________ 17. X. II Y. III Z. IV

_________ 18. X. V Y. VI Z. VII

_________ 19. A melody that begins with the pitch G will be performed. Which score shows the correct pitch notation?

X. 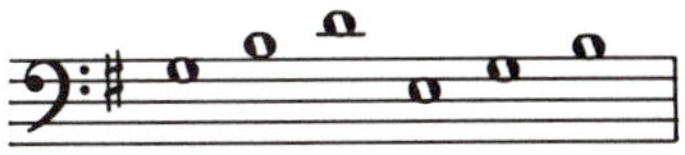

Y. 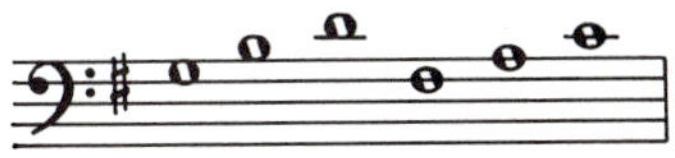

Z. 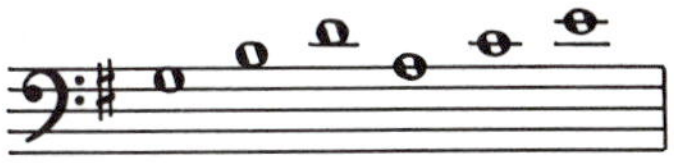

_________ 20. Which score shows the correct notation for the rhythm performed?

X. 

Y. 

Z. 

10

Chords and Scales in the Minor Mode

Terms and Concepts

subtonic	*cut time*
modal mixture	*dotted whole note*
harmonic minor scale	*double whole note*
melodic minor scale	*double whole rest*
alla breve	

PITCH

Diatonic Triads in Natural Minor Keys

Though each natural minor key shares four diatonic pitch classes with its parallel major, all seven diatonic triads in minor differ in quality from their counterparts in major. Three of these triads—III, VI, and VII—are rooted a half step lower in the natural minor mode than in major. For example, in C major the root of the mediant triad (III) is E, above which G and B form a triad of minor quality. But in C natural minor the mediant triad's root is E♭, above which G and B♭ form a triad of major quality. The seven diatonic triads in two of the fifteen natural minor keys are displayed in Example 10-1 along with their names and Roman-numeral labels. The same names and labels apply to the triads of all other natural minor keys as well.

Example 10-1

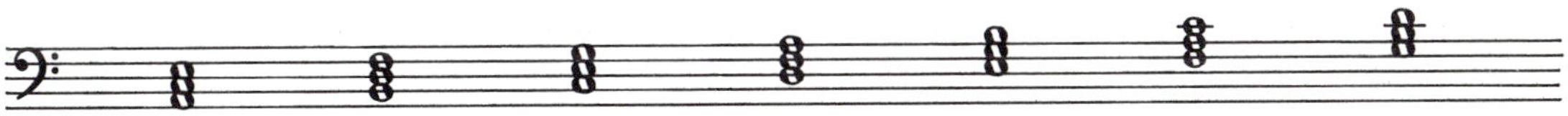

A Natural Minor:	I	II	III	IV	V	VI	VII
	Tonic	Supertonic	Mediant	Subdominant	Dominant	Submediant	Subtonic

C Natural Minor:	I	II	III	IV	V	VI	VII
	Tonic	Supertonic	Mediant	Subdominant	Dominant	Submediant	Subtonic

The diatonic triads in natural minor keys are of three qualities. The I, IV, and V triads are minor. The III, VI, and VII triads are major. The II triad is diminished. The diatonic triads in A natural minor and A major are compared in Example 10-2.

Example 10-2

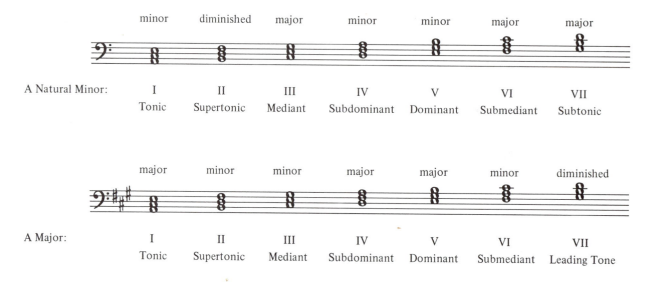

	minor	diminished	major	minor	minor	major	major

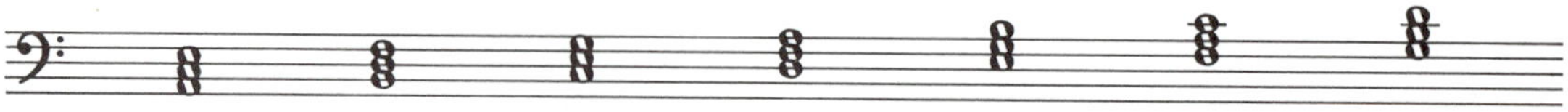

A Natural Minor:	I	II	III	IV	V	VI	VII
	Tonic	Supertonic	Mediant	Subdominant	Dominant	Submediant	Subtonic

	major	minor	minor	major	major	minor	diminished

A Major:	I	II	III	IV	V	VI	VII
	Tonic	Supertonic	Mediant	Subdominant	Dominant	Submediant	Leading Tone

subtonic

Observe that one of these seven triads has a name not used in major. We call VII the ***subtonic*** in natural minor. It is rooted a whole step below the tonic, as far below the tonic as is the supertonic above. This additional name is warranted because of the sharply contrasting functions of VII in the two modes. In major, VII is a diminished triad whose dissonant pitches, $\hat{7}$ and $\hat{4}$, are poised for a return to the tonic pitches $\hat{1}$ and $\hat{3}$ respectively. It is the least stable of the major mode's diatonic triads. In natural minor, the diatonic VII chord lacks both the leading tone and the characteristic of dissonance. The label "subtonic" corresponds to the labels "submediant" and "subdominant." The label "leading tone" is unacceptable because the pitch that leads to tonic is not present in the chord. In contrast, the II (supertonic) triads in major (a minor triad) and in natural minor (a diminished triad) are used in similar ways by composers, so alternative names are not warranted.

Harmonic Minor

The absence of the leading tone contributes to the solemn, reserved character of the natural minor mode. Many beautiful melodies, such as the opening phrase of *Greensleeves* in Example 10-3, employ the seven diatonic pitches of the mode in wonderful ways.

Example 10-3

Greensleeves

Yet in the context of harmonic progressions, the leading tone's absence is a liability. If, as we have seen, the authentic cadence is the most powerful means by which closure is achieved within a phrase or an entire composition, then a progression from V to I using the diatonic pitches of the natural minor mode falls short. Without the characteristic resolution of the leading tone to tonic, which the major mode invariably invokes, the natural-minor counterpart seems to lack conviction. For this reason, it is common for composers to substitute the V chord of the parallel major key at crucial points such as cadences. Compare the sense of closure in the two excerpts in Example 10-4 by playing them at the keyboard.

Example 10-4

Schumann: *Album for the Young*, The Wild Horseman

A Natural Minor (*not* how Schumann composed it)

With G♯ replacing the G of A Natural Minor (Schumann's version)

modal mixture

harmonic minor scale

It would be appropriate to regard the leading tone's presence in the context of a minor key as a "borrowing" from major—as an instance of ***modal mixture*** (a mixing of pitches from both modes). Yet most musicians use the term ***harmonic minor scale*** for the combination of $\hat{1}$ through $\hat{6}$ of the natural minor scale and the leading tone. Harmonic minor scales in the keys of A and C are shown in Example 10-5. Since these scales contain a pitch that is not diatonic in the context of the natural minor key signature (which is retained), the label $\uparrow\hat{7}$ (read "raised seven") is used instead of $\hat{7}$.

Example 10-5

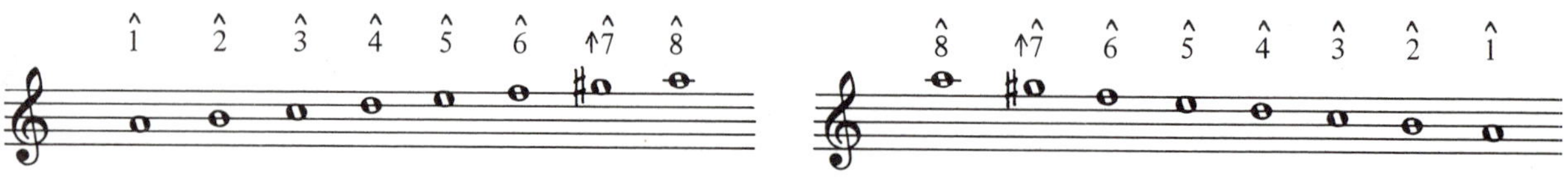

A Harmonic Minor

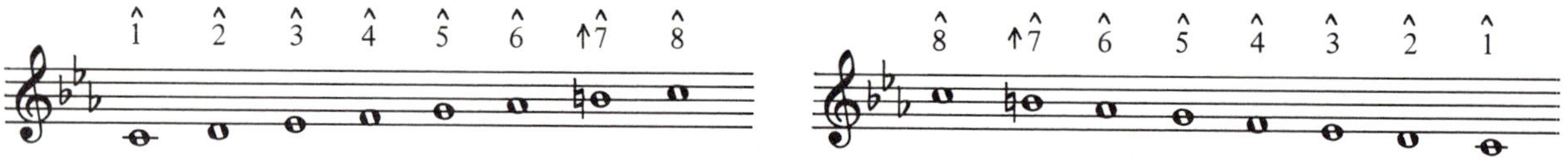

C Harmonic Minor

Most compositions in minor employ both the subtonic pitch class (a whole step below tonic) and the leading tone (a half step below tonic). For example, the III chord almost always contains the subtonic pitch class, while a V chord that precedes I in an authentic cadence almost always contains the leading tone. Thus some interchange between two collections of pitch classes—either natural minor and major, or natural minor and harmonic minor—will occur.

Melodic Minor

The interval formed by the diatonic sixth scale degree ($\hat{6}$) and the leading tone ($\uparrow\hat{7}$) in the harmonic minor scale is an augmented second, a harsh dissonance. The augmented second will rarely occur in a melodic context, such as a stepwise ascent from $\hat{5}$ to $\hat{8}$. In compositions written in the minor mode, the sixth scale degree of major is sometimes borrowed along with the seventh scale degree to avoid the hard-to-sing melodic interval of an augmented second. This collection of pitches forms another variant of natural minor called the ***melodic minor scale***, which differs from natural minor in that both the sixth and seventh scale degrees of major are borrowed during its ascent. The descending pitches of this scale are those of natural minor, because the leading tone is called upon more in ascending to $\hat{8}$ than in descending from $\hat{8}$. However, there are contexts in which the use of $\uparrow\hat{7}$ and $\uparrow\hat{6}$ may be justified during a descent. Melodic minor scales in the keys of A and C are shown in Example 10-6.

melodic minor scale

Example 10-6

A Melodic Minor

C Melodic Minor

Of the four scales commonly used in tonal music—major, natural minor, harmonic minor, and melodic minor—only the melodic minor has differing ascending and descending forms. Example 10-7 displays a comparison of these four scales in the context of the tonic pitch C.

Example 10-7

Major:

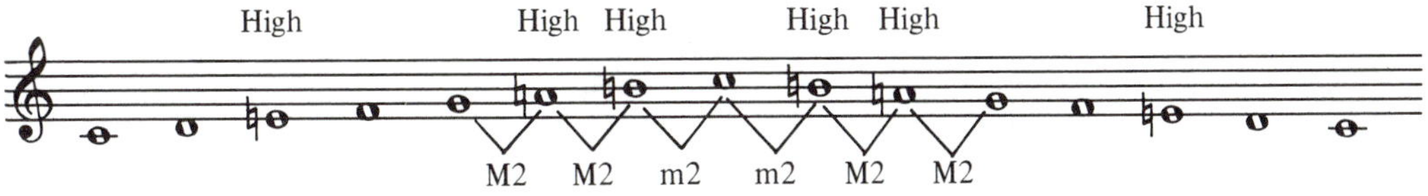

Natural Minor:

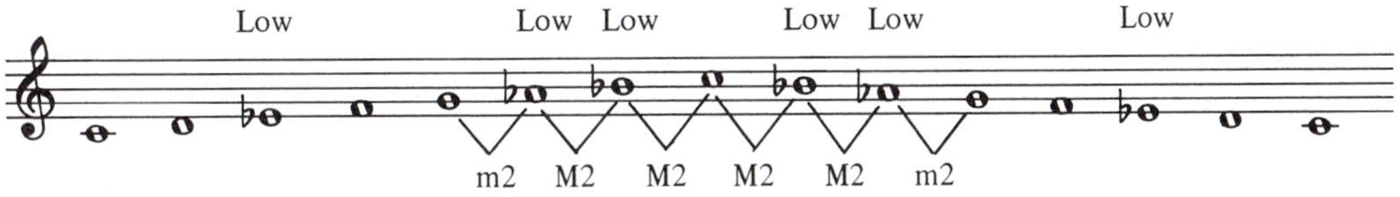

Harmonic Minor:

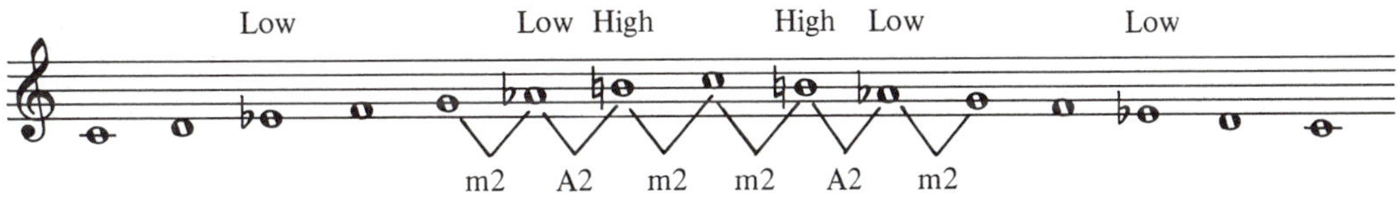

Melodic Minor:

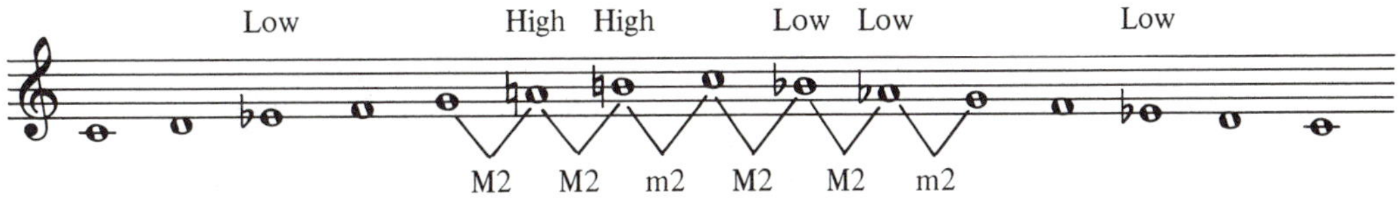

Roman Numerals in the Minor Mode

The alternatives available for the sixth and seventh scale degrees in minor complicate the use of Roman numerals for harmonic analysis. We cannot, for example, use the label VII both for the subtonic and for the leading tone chords. The following general principle will always hold: *Labels that are not modified by accidentals always imply the diatonic pitch classes of the key.* In minor keys, VII represents the subtonic because the natural minor scale contains the seventh scale degree a whole step below tonic. The subtonic pitch class, and not the leading tone, is indicated by the minor key signatures. By a common (though not universal) convention, an accidental to the *left* of a Roman numeral reflects a shift in the *root* of a chord's parent triad, while an accidental to the *right* of a Roman numeral reflects a shift in the *third* of a chord's parent triad, regardless of whether the chord being labeled is in root position or in an inversion.

Example 10-8 should help clarify the preceding discussion. In the key of A minor, the chord notated in Example 10-8a is correctly labeled VII, since its root is the diatonic seventh scale degree. When the leading-tone chord is used instead, as in Example 10-8b, or more commonly in first inversion, as in Example 10-8c, the appropriate label is ♯VII, since a sharp sign is used to raise its *root* from the diatonic seventh scale degree G to G♯ (that is, $\hat{7}$ is replaced by $\uparrow\hat{7}$).

Example 10-8

If instead of ♯VII we use the dominant chord borrowed from major, then the *third* of the chord, not the root, is altered, as in Example 10-9. In this case the Roman numeral should appear as V♯.

Example 10-9

Likewise, if $\uparrow\hat{6}$ replaces $\hat{6}$ in a subdominant chord, the chord should be labeled IV♯, as in the progression shown in Example 10-10.

Example 10-10

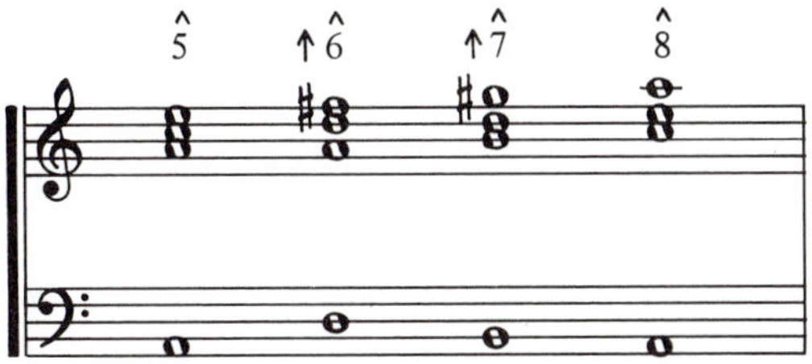

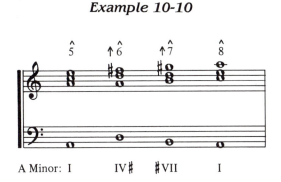

A Minor: I IV♯ ♯VII I

When keys with flat signatures are used, the natural sign, rather than the sharp sign, must often represent the raised half step. Example 10-11 shows a correct analysis.

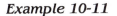

Example 10-11

B♭ Minor: I IV♮ ♮VII I

When keys with sharp signatures are used, the double-sharp symbol must occasionally be employed. Observe the appropriate notation for the melodic minor scale in the key of G♯ in Example 10-12.

Example 10-12

G♯ Melodic Minor

Though it might seem simpler to replace E♯ with F♮ or to replace F𝄪 with G♮ in the ascending scale shown in Example 10-12, those enharmonically equivalent notes would not convey the functions of the ascending sixth and seventh scale degrees. The chords in Example 10-13 would not be understood properly if the enharmonic equivalents F♮ and G♮ were substituted.

Example 10-13

G♯ Minor: IV♯ 𝄪VII V𝄪

If pitches of both the ascending and descending melodic minor scales appear within the same measure, the use of accidentals must be treated with special care. In Example 10-14, the diatonic pitches of the descent from $\hat{8}$ to $\hat{5}$ are notated by applying the accidentals that restore the diatonic scale degrees. Even if the ascent and descent appear in consecutive measures rather than within a single measure, the accidentals that restore the diatonic scale degrees are often provided as a courtesy, to remind the performer to revert to the diatonic pitches.

Example 10-14

A♯ Minor

Figured Bass in the Minor Mode

In figured bass, nondiatonic pitches are indicated using accidentals placed beside the numbers, as in Example 10-15a and b. An accidental may be placed either to the left or to the right of a number. In fact, if the third above the bass is raised, the accidental may appear *instead of* the number rather than *beside* the number. Observe that since figured bass shows only what is *above* the bass, *when the bass itself is the altered pitch, no accidental will appear among the figures.*

Example 10-15

a.

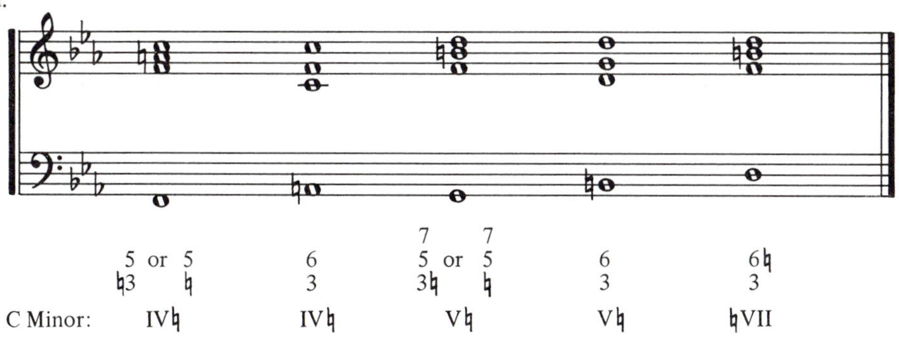

b.

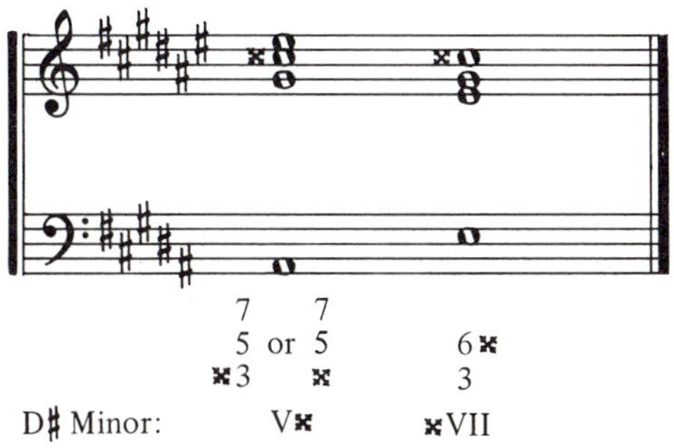

Though different accidentals (♮, ♯, or ×) are used to raise a pitch by a half step depending upon the key, the sharp sign is used when altered chords are discussed without reference to any specific key. Thus ♯VII implies the words "leading tone" or "raised seven" in any discussion in the minor mode, though in specific contexts, when a particular key has been established, the labels ♮VII or ×VII may be required instead.

Pitch exercises for Chapter 10 are on pages 347–354.

RHYTHM

$\frac{2}{2}$, $\frac{3}{2}$, and $\frac{4}{2}$ Meters

All of the meters we have examined to this point contain either two, three, or four beats per measure. The beat has been represented by the quarter note in simple meters and by the dotted quarter note in compound meters. Another group of simple meters employs the half note as the representative of the beat. The $\frac{2}{2}$ meter has two half notes per measure, while $\frac{3}{2}$ and $\frac{4}{2}$ have three and four half notes per measure, respectively. An example of each is shown in Example 10-16.

Example 10-16

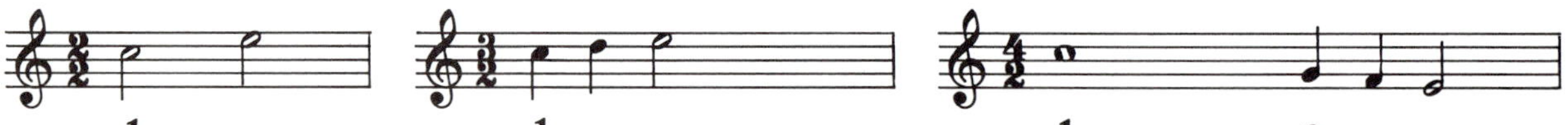

The choice of the half note to represent the beat sometimes implies a faster tempo, though not all composers have regarded it as such. In any event, subdivisions of the beat are easier to notate because fewer beams are required, as Example 10-17 demonstrates. Performances of the two versions shown in Example 10-17a and b will sound identical if equivalent tempos are maintained, for example, 10-17a at ♩ = 60 and 10-17b at 𝅗𝅥 = 60. Appropriate counting syllables are provided.

Example 10-17

a. In $\frac{3}{4}$ (for comparison) — Handel: *Water Music*, Hornpipe

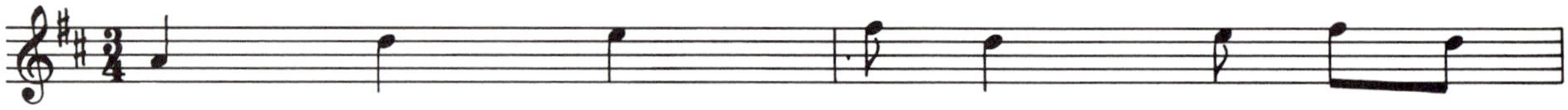

b. In $\frac{3}{2}$ (Handel's version)

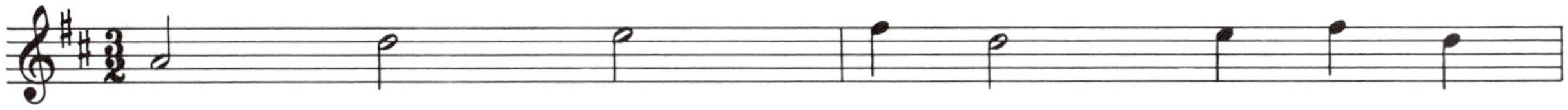

1 ee + ee 2 ee + ee 3 ee + ee 1 ee + ee 2 ee + ee 3 ee + ee

1 ee + ee 2 ee + ee 3 ee + ee 1 ee + ee 2 ee + ee 3 ee + ee 1 ee + ee 2 ee + ee

The $\frac{2}{2}$ meter has a special name, ***alla breve.*** It is often called ***cut time*** in English. As we have seen, the time signature for common time, $\frac{4}{4}$, is sometimes designated with the symbol C. Likewise, alla breve, $\frac{2}{2}$, can be designated with the symbol ₵. Example 10-18 demonstrates its use.

alla breve

cut time

Example 10-18

Bach: "Brandenburg" Concerto No. 4

1 ee + ee 2 ee + ee 1 ee + ee 2 ee + ee 1 ee + ee 2 ee + ee 1 ee + ee 2 ee + ee 1 ee

$\frac{6}{4}$ Meter

Just as simple meters can be notated with the half note rather than the quarter note representing the beat, compound meters can be notated with the dotted half note rather than the dotted quarter note representing the beat. The $\frac{6}{4}$ meter is the most frequently encountered. Three quarter notes (rather than three eighth notes, as in $\frac{6}{8}$) represent the subdivisions of the beat. Like the preceding excerpts, Examples 10-17 and 10-18, that shown in Example 10-19 confirms that by selecting a larger note value to represent the beat, the submetrical rhythmic activity will be less cumbersome to notate. On the other hand, the beams of Example 10-19a guide the eyes in segmenting noteheads into beat groupings.

Example 10-19

a. In $\frac{6}{8}$ (for comparison) Bach: Suite No. 1, Forlane

b. In $\frac{6}{4}$ (Bach's version)

Longer Note and Rest Values

The whole note fills a measure in $\frac{2}{2}$ meter. Longer note values, which may occasionally be encountered in $\frac{3}{2}$ and $\frac{4}{2}$ meters, are notated using the ***dotted whole note*** (Ex. 10-20a) and the ***double whole note*** (Ex. 10-20b). The dotted whole note also fills a measure in $\frac{6}{4}$ meter.

The whole rest is used whenever a full measure of rest is notated in the $\frac{2}{2}$, $\frac{3}{2}$, and $\frac{6}{4}$ meters, as it is in the other meters we have studied. In the $\frac{4}{2}$ meter, however, a ***double whole rest*** (Ex. 10-20c) is used to notate an entire measure of rest. The same width as the whole rest, the double whole rests fills the vertical space between the third and fourth lines on the staff.

dotted whole note

double whole note

double whole rest

Example 10-20

a. b. c.

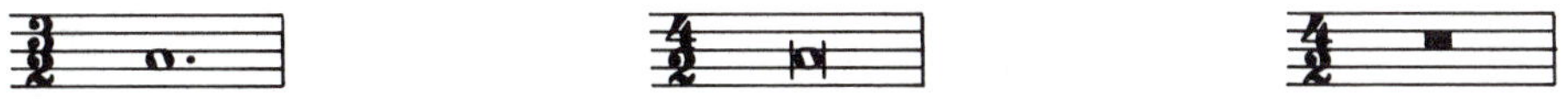

Dotted whole note — Double whole note — Double whole rest

Rhythm exercises for Chapter 10 are on pages 354–356.

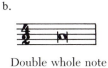

LABORATORY

L10-1.a. Play of the following chord progressions at the keyboard. What type of cadence ends each?

1.

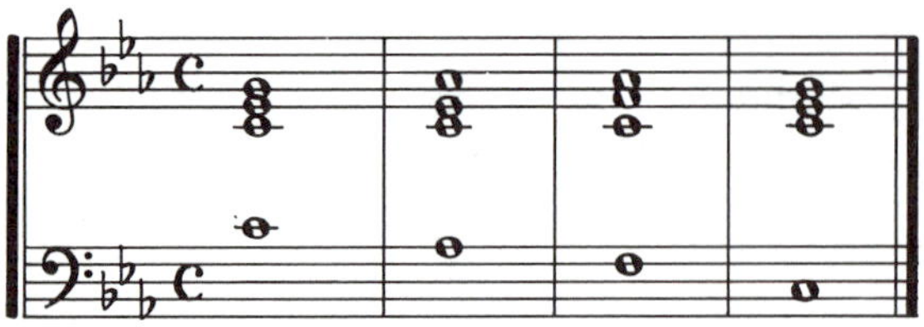

2.

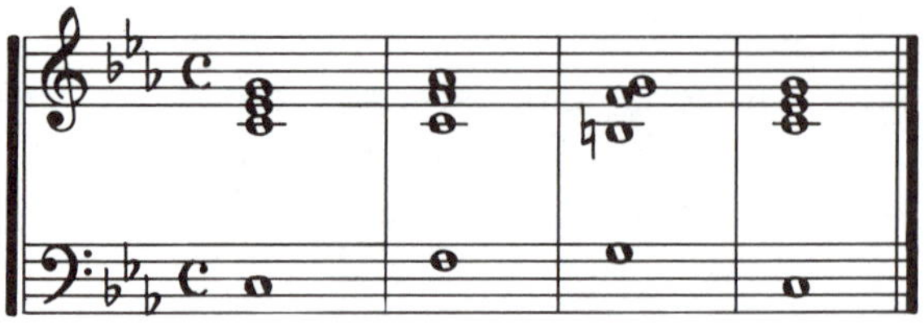

3.

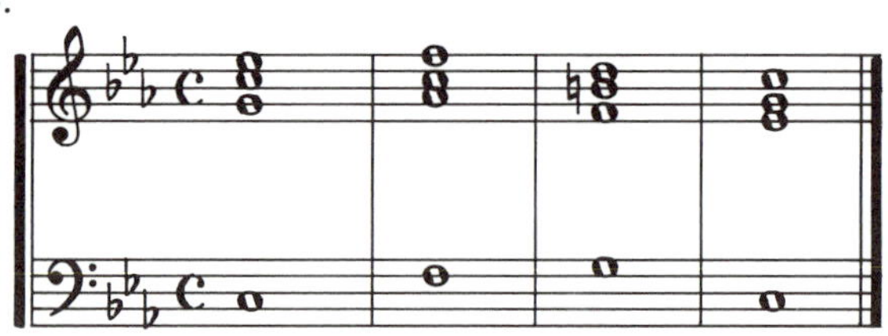

4.

b. Perform each of the following melodies at the keyboard. Recommended fingerings are included.

1.

Bach: Passacaglia

Brahms: Symphony No. 4

2.

3.

Brahms: Symphony No. 4

4. Brahms: *Academic Festival* Overture

Chopin: Nocturne Op. 37, No. 1

5.

Schubert: Winterreise, Op. 89, No. 6

6.

L10-2.a. At the keyboard, perform a chord that corresponds to the given Roman numeral and figured bass. The key signature (minor mode) and bass note are supplied. Play one note with the left hand and three notes with the right hand.

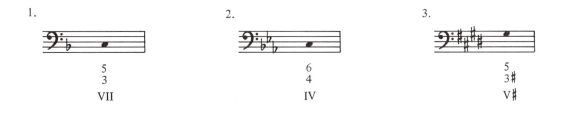

1.

2.

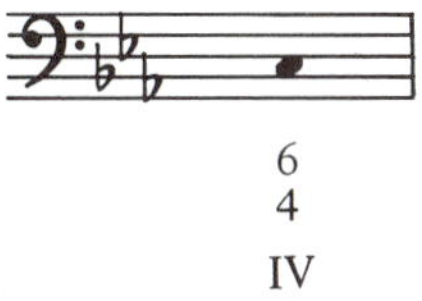

3.

4.

6
3
II

5.

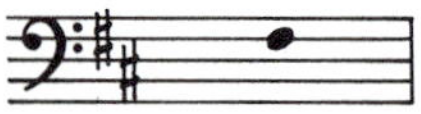

5
3
V

6.

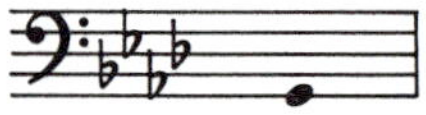

6♮
3
♮VII

7.

5
3
III

8.

6
4
VI

9.

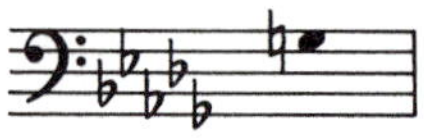

6
3
IV♮

b. At random, select a key from the left column, a Roman numeral from the middle column, and a figured bass from the right column. Then, at the keyboard, perform the chord. Play one note with the left hand and three notes with the right hand. Repeat the exercise until you have developed absolute security with chord construction.

Key	*Roman Numeral*	*Position*
C minor	I	5 3
C♯ minor	II	6 3
D minor	III	6 4
D♯ minor	IV	7 5 3 (with V♯ only)
E minor	IV♯	
F minor	V	
F♯ minor	V♯	
G minor	VI	
G♯ minor	VII	
A minor	♯VII	
B♭ minor		
B minor		

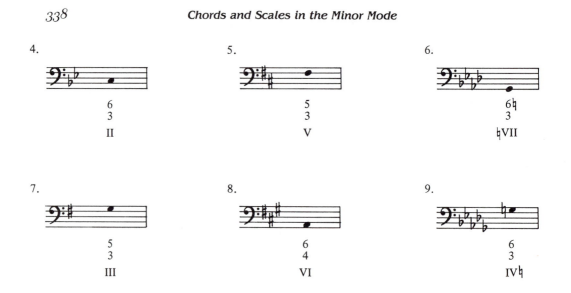

L10-3. Practice the following exercise, changing the reference scale after every two or three attempts.

- Simultaneously sing and play an ascending natural minor scale beginning on a pitch low in your vocal range. Extend up a tenth instead of the customary octave.
- Using both hands, strike scale degrees $\hat{1}$, $\hat{3}$, $\hat{5}$, $\hat{8}$ ($\hat{1}$), and $\hat{10}$ ($\hat{3}$) simultaneously. In this way, the tonal center you have selected is solidly established in your ear.
- Now strike again any one of these five keys and sing that pitch.
- Sing one of the four melodic successions below that corresponds to the pitch performed and then confirm what you have sung by playing the appropriate pitches on the keyboard.

$\hat{1}$	$\hat{3}$	$\hat{5}$	$\hat{8}$	$\hat{10}$
$\hat{1}$–$\hat{3}$	$\hat{3}$–$\hat{1}$	$\hat{5}$–$\hat{1}$	$\hat{8}$–$\hat{1}$	$\hat{10}$–$\hat{1}$
$\hat{1}$–$\hat{5}$	$\hat{3}$–$\hat{5}$	$\hat{5}$–$\hat{3}$	$\hat{8}$–$\hat{3}$	$\hat{10}$–$\hat{3}$
$\hat{1}$–$\hat{8}$	$\hat{3}$–$\hat{8}$	$\hat{5}$–$\hat{8}$	$\hat{8}$–$\hat{5}$	$\hat{10}$–$\hat{5}$
$\hat{1}$–$\hat{10}$	$\hat{3}$–$\hat{10}$	$\hat{5}$–$\hat{10}$	$\hat{8}$–$\hat{10}$	$\hat{10}$–$\hat{8}$

L10-4. Practice the following exercise first in A minor, then in various other minor keys whose scales fall within your vocal range.

- Strike a tonic pitch that appears near the bottom of your vocal range and, starting with that pitch, sing an ascending natural minor or harmonic minor scale, using scale degree numbers.
- Place three fingers over keys that form any triad in the key (II, IV, V♯, ♯VII, etc.), positioning the root higher than the initial tonic pitch. Position the fingers over V♯ or ♯VII only if you have sung the harmonic minor scale. Avoid III in harmonic minor. Strike the root.
- Sing the sounded pitch and, arpeggiating upward, sing the third and fifth of the triad.
- Confirm what you have sung by playing the triadic pitches at the keyboard.

Once the above exercise is going well, add the following steps.

- Strike a tonic pitch that appears in the middle to upper region of your vocal range and, starting with that pitch, sing a descending natural minor or harmonic minor scale, using scale degree numbers.
- Place three fingers over keys that form any triad in the key (♯VII, VI, V♯, etc.), positioning the root lower than the initial tonic pitch. Position the fingers over V♯ or ♯VII only if you have sung the harmonic minor scale. Avoid III in harmonic minor. Strike the root.
- Sing the sounded pitch and, arpeggiating upward, sing the third and fifth of the triad.
- Confirm what you have sung by playing the triadic pitches at the keyboard.

L10-5. Practice the following melodies at the keyboard, simultaneously singing and playing each pitch. Sing the scale-degree number, or the syllable "raised," that corresponds to each pitch, as indicated. If necessary, transpose the entire score up or down one octave.

a. Shenandoah

b. Liszt: Ballade No. 2

c. There Is a Tavern in the Town

L10-6. The following compositions are for voice and keyboard. A student or the instructor could play the keyboard part while other students sing the melody. The keyboard part should be performed as written, but the vocal line may be moved down an octave if necessary.

a. Voice

b. Voice

L10-7. The following compositions are for two voices. Sing the scale-degree number, or the syllable "raised," that corresponds to each pitch, as indicated. If necessary, transpose the entire score up or down one octave.

a. Voice 1

b.

L10-8. Write in the counting syllables below the notated rhythms. Then perform each by clapping the rhythm or playing the pitch C or F at the keyboard, as notated, while pronouncing the counting syllables aloud. Practice until you can perform each exercise at a tempo of about 𝅗𝅥 = 60 or 𝅗𝅥. = 60.

Sample

a.

b.

c.

d.

L10-9. Write in the counting syllables below the notated rhythms. Then perform them by dividing the class into two groups, with each group clapping one part while pronouncing the counting syllables aloud. Alternatively, individual students may perform both parts simultaneously at the keyboard, pronouncing the counting syllables aloud while the index fingers strike the notated pitches.

a.

b.

c.

L10-10. This exercise requires that a student or the instructor serve as the performer at a keyboard.

a. The performer plays a scale, ascending and descending. Indicate whether it is a major scale, a natural minor scale, a harmonic minor scale, or a melodic minor scale.

b. In any minor key, the performer strikes scale degree $\hat{1}$ alone and then strikes scales degrees $\hat{1}$, $\hat{3}$, and $\hat{5}$ simultaneously. The performer then strikes scale degree $\hat{2}$, $\hat{3}$, $\hat{4}$, $\hat{5}$, $\hat{6}$, $\hat{7}$, or $\uparrow\hat{7}$ (either above or below the original $\hat{1}$), followed by a triad built on that scale degree. Indicate the Roman numeral of the triad performed.

Hint: In minor, the I, IV, and V chords are minor, the III, IV♯, V♯, VI, and VII chords are major, and the II and ♯VII chords are diminished.

Audio exercises for Chapter 10 are on pages 357–359.

Name: ______________________
Instructor: ______________________
Date: ______________________

EXERCISES

Pitch Exercises

P10-1. Form minor scales that accommodate both the given notes and the scale types indicated. Show both the ascent and descent of each scale, but do not repeat $\hat{8}$ in the middle. Employ the appropriate key signature.

Sample

Melodic minor

a. Harmonic minor

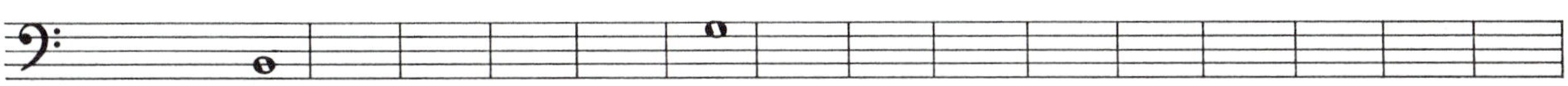

b. Natural minor

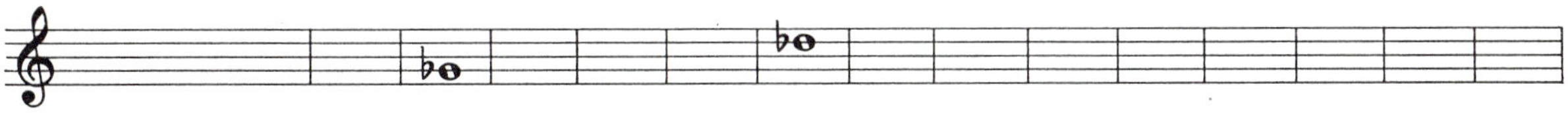

c. Melodic minor

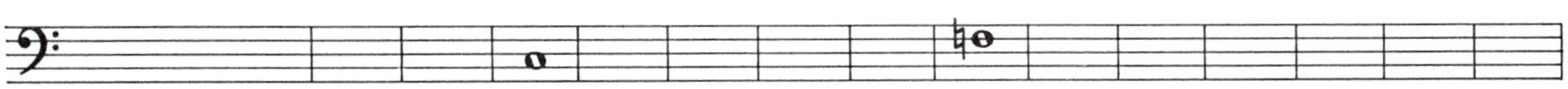

d. Harmonic minor

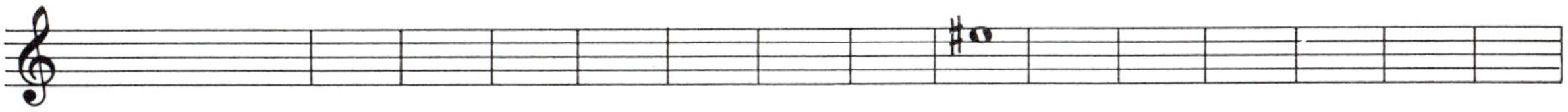

e. Melodic minor

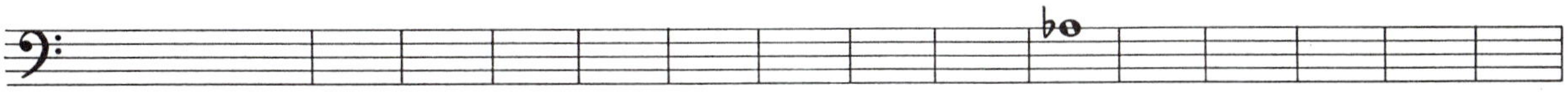

f. Harmonic minor

g. Natural minor $\hat{8}$

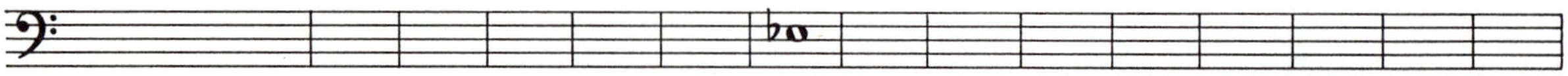

h. Melodic minor $\hat{8}$

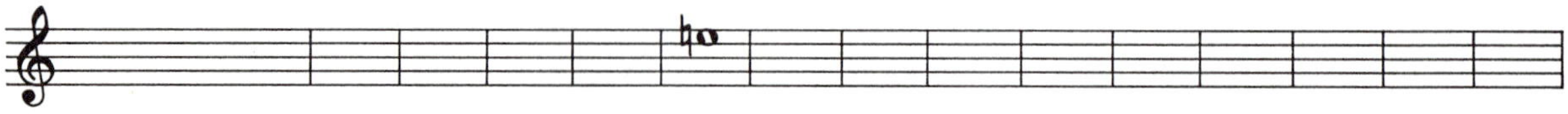

i. Harmonic minor $\hat{8}$

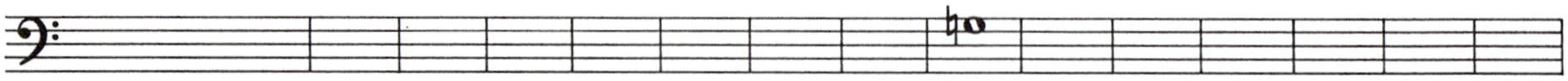

j. Melodic minor $\hat{8}$

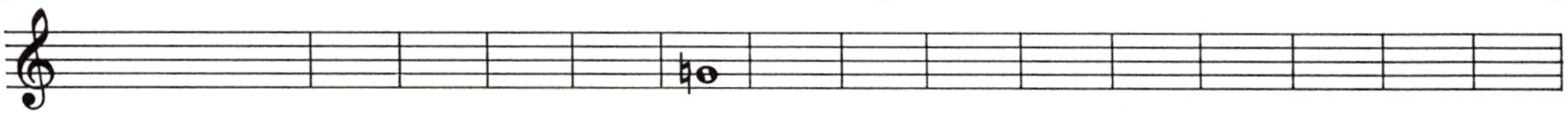

k. Harmonic minor $\hat{8}$

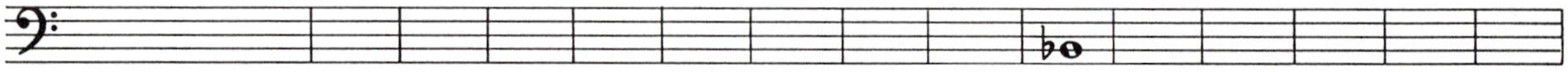

l. Natural minor $\hat{8}$

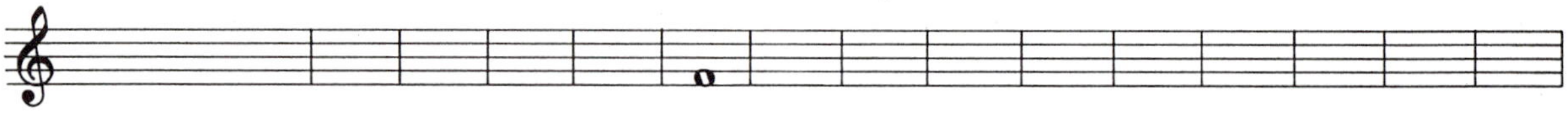

m. Melodic minor $\hat{8}$

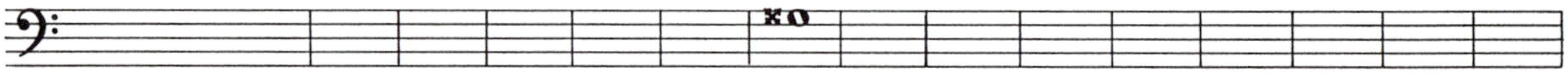

n. Harmonic minor $\hat{8}$

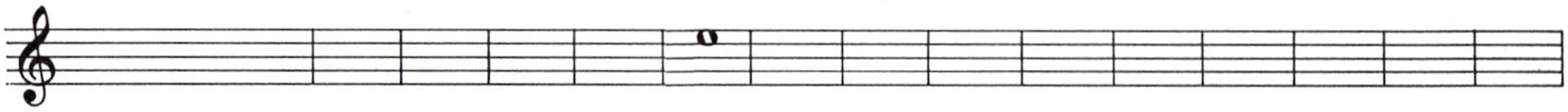

o. Natural minor $\hat{8}$

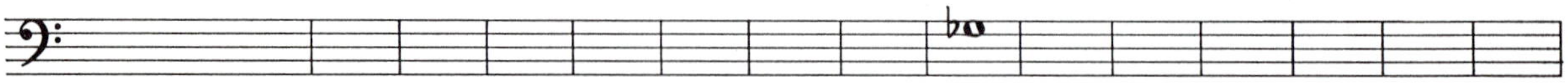

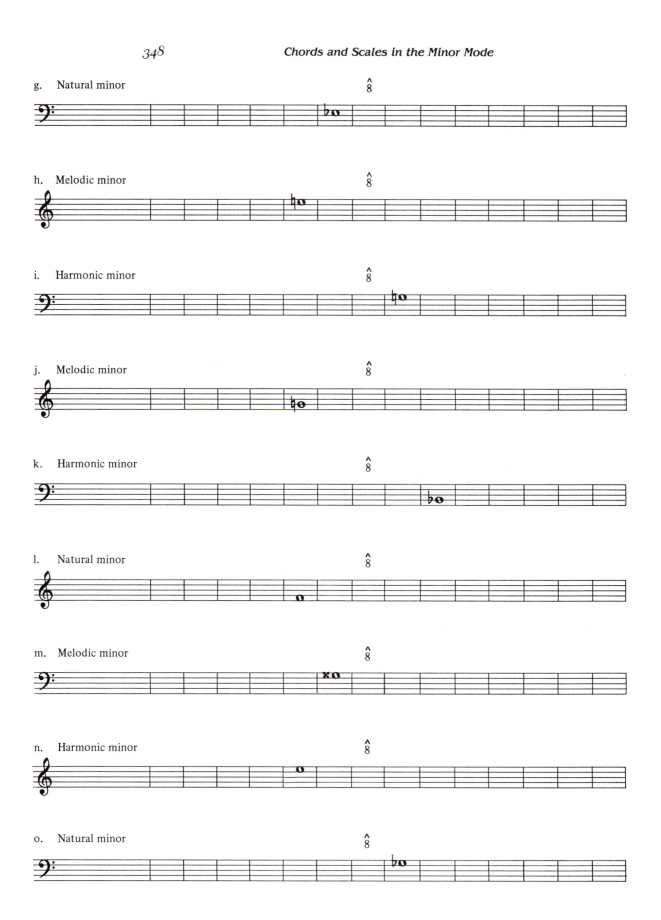

Name: ______________________

Instructor: ______________________

Date: ______________________

P10-2. Form ascending and descending minor scales (melodic, harmonic, or natural) that accommodate the pitches supplied. Indicate which type of minor scale you have used. Employ the appropriate key signature.

Hint: Consult Example 10-7 whenever necessary.

SAMPLE

a.

b.

c.

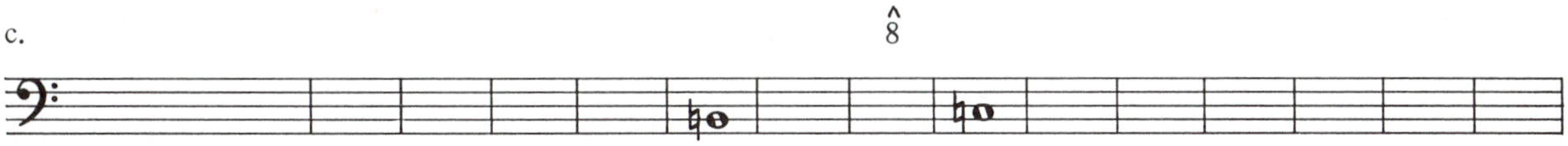

d.

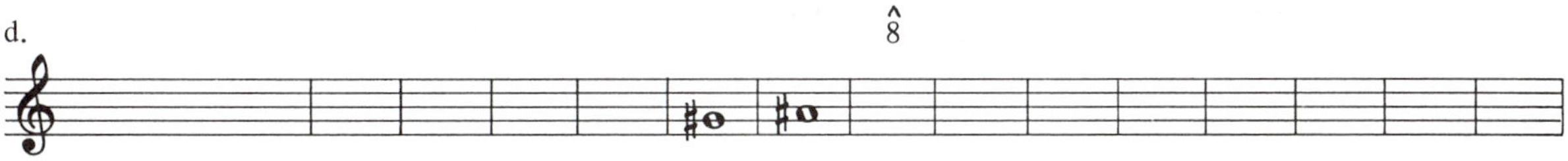

e.

f.

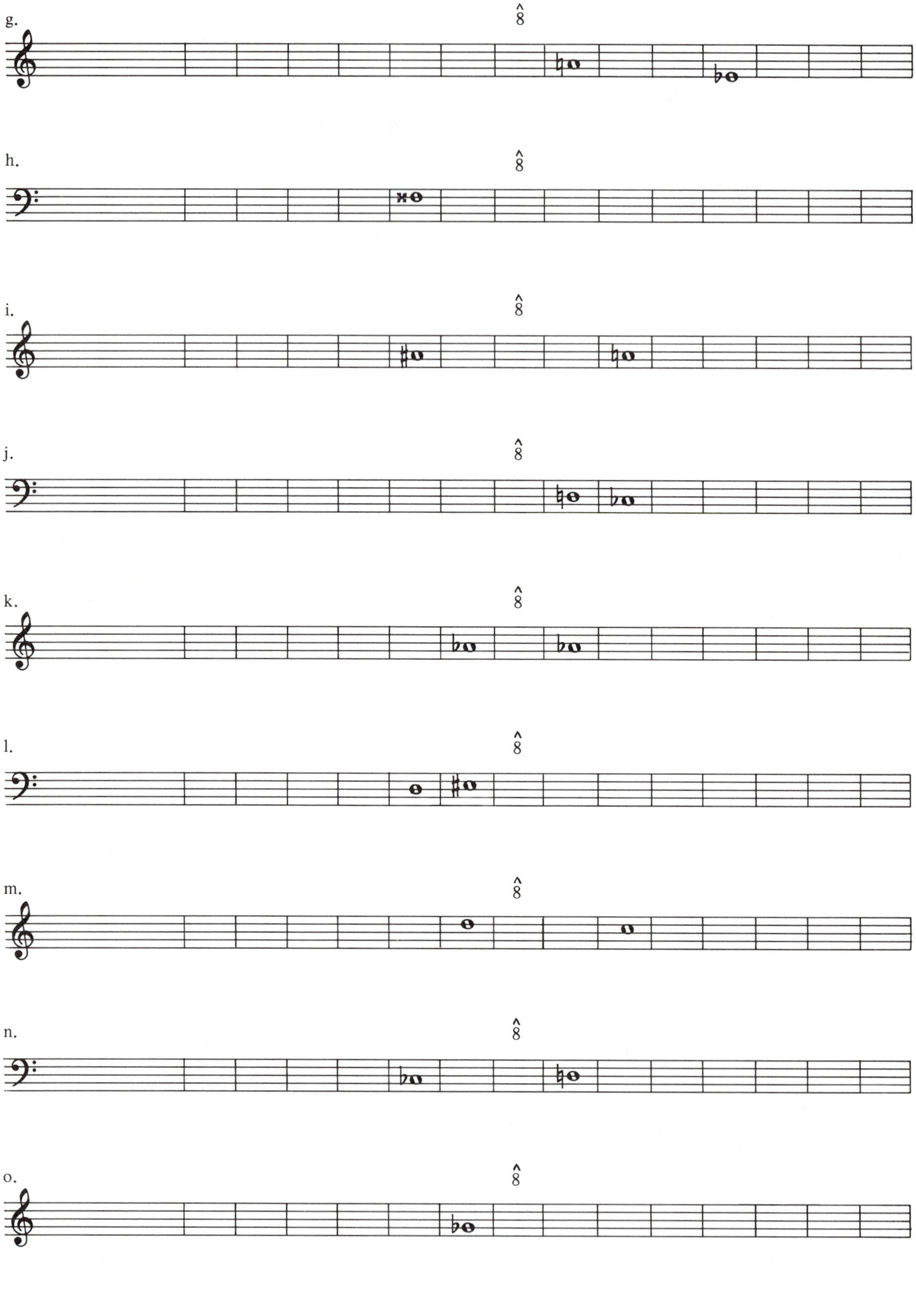
g.
8̂
h.
8̂
i.
8̂
j.
8̂
k.
8̂
l.
8̂
m.
8̂
n.
8̂
o.
8̂

Name: ______________________

Instructor: ______________________

Date: ______________________

P10-3. Determine the minor key in which each example is composed from the key signature. Supply the appropriate figured bass and Roman numeral for each chord.

SAMPLE

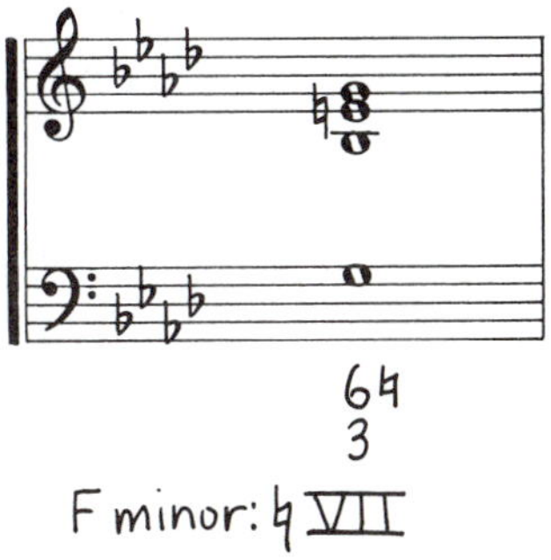

a.

b.

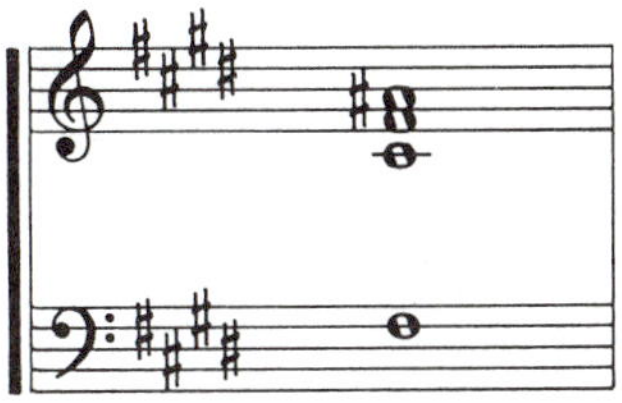

c.

d.

e.

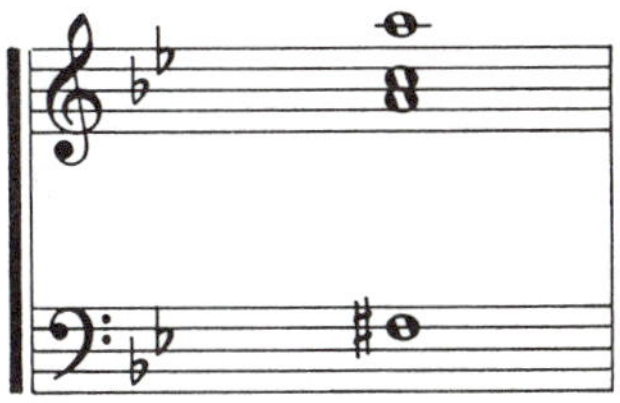

f.

g.

h.

i.

j.

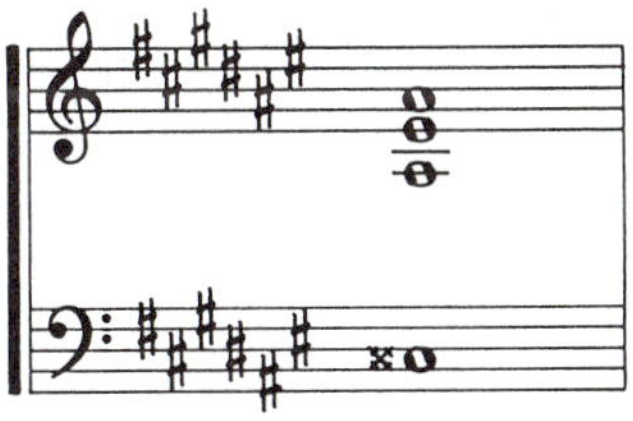

k.

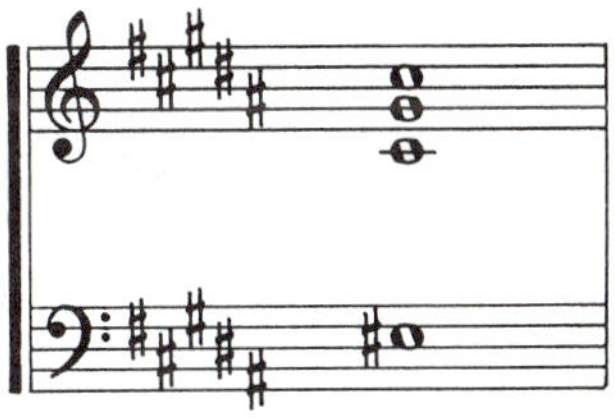

l.

m.

n.

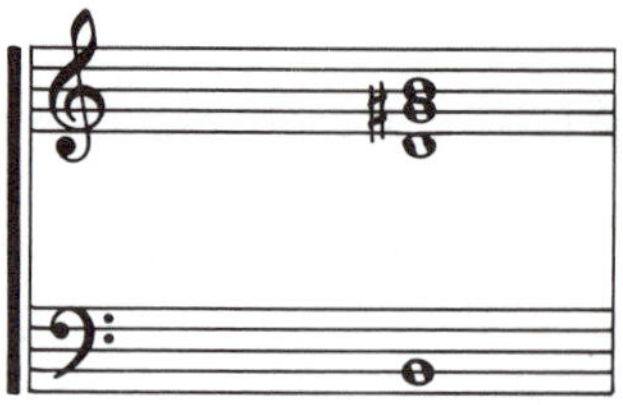

o.

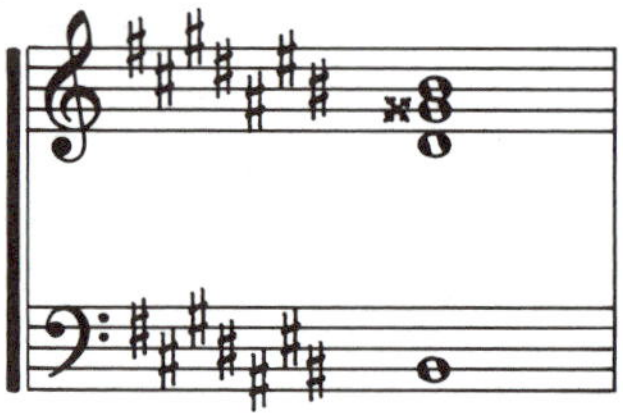

p.

q.

r.

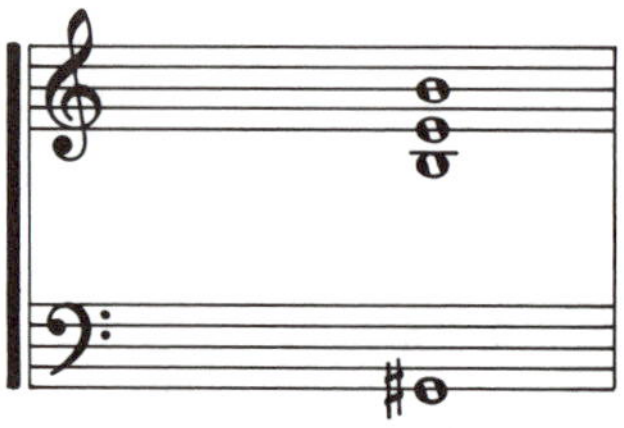

s.

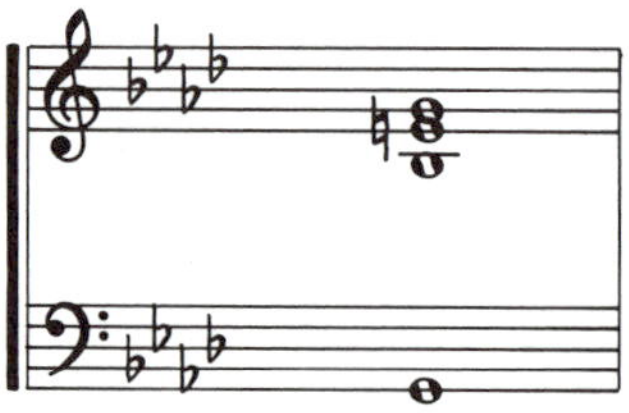

t.

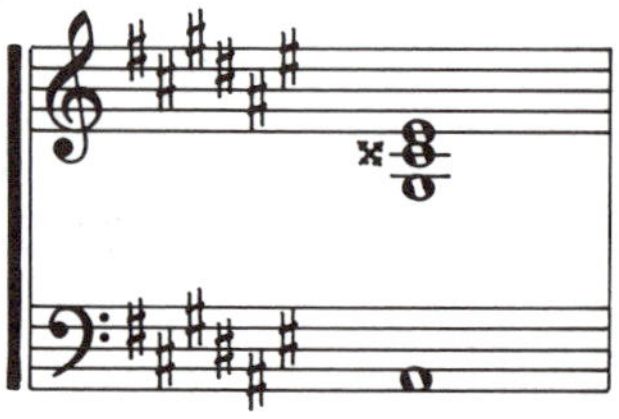

u.

v.

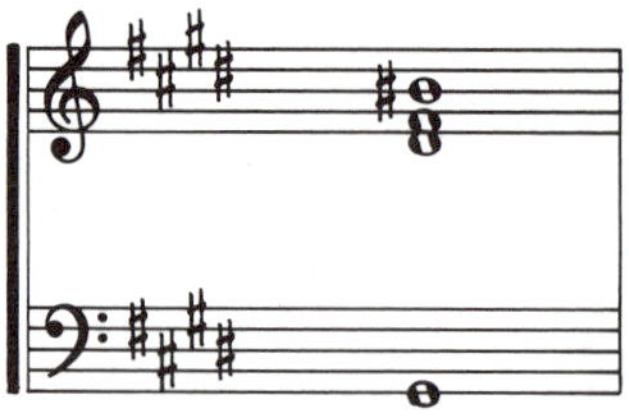

w.

Name: ______________________

Instructor: ______________________

Date: ______________________

P10-4. For each Roman numeral, figured bass, and minor key given, form an appropriate chord in staff notation. Use half notes. Employ the appropriate key signature.

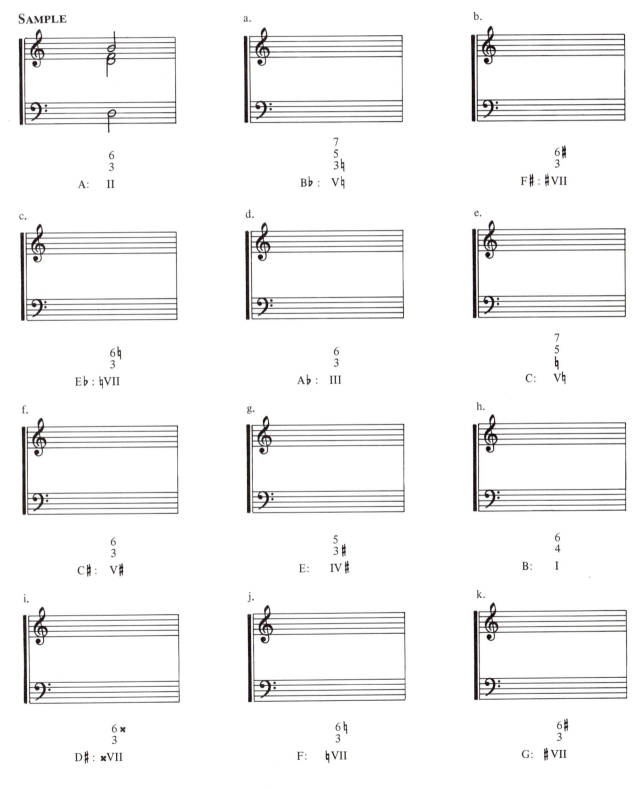

SAMPLE

6
3
A: II

a.

7
5
3♮
B♭: V♮

b.

6♯
3
F♯: ♯VII

c.

6♮
3
E♭: ♮VII

d.

6
3
A♭: III

e.

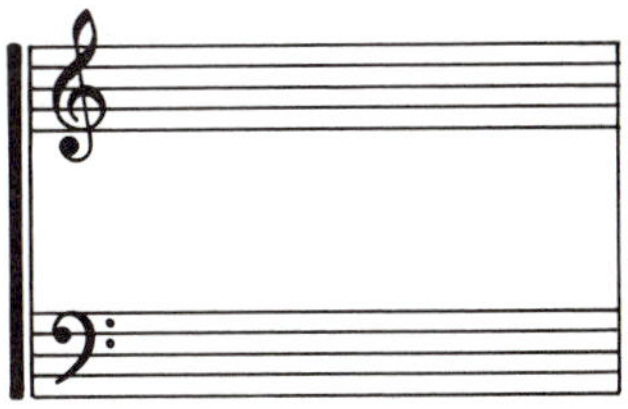

7
5
♮
C: V♮

f.

6
3
C♯: V♯

g.

5
3♯
E: IV♯

h.

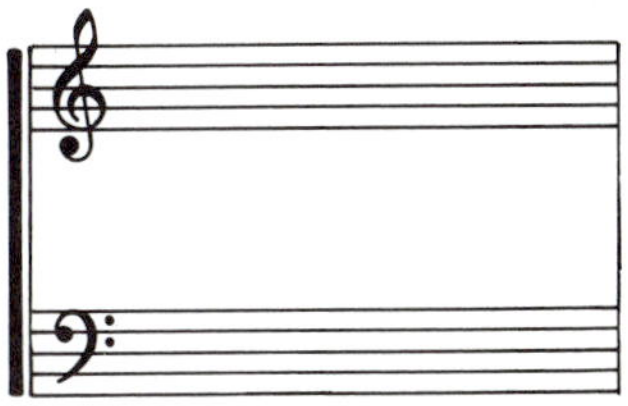

6
4
B: I

i.

6𝄪
3
D♯: 𝄪VII

j.

6♮
3
F: ♮VII

k.

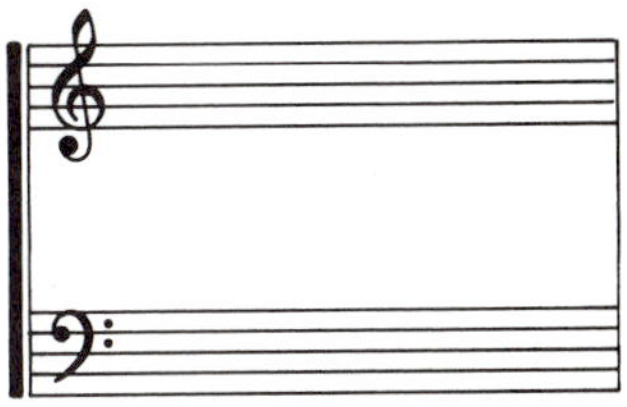

6♯
3
G: ♯VII

l.

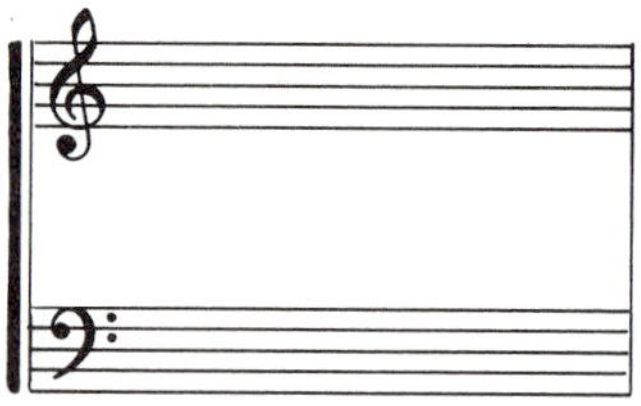

6
3
A♯: VI

m.

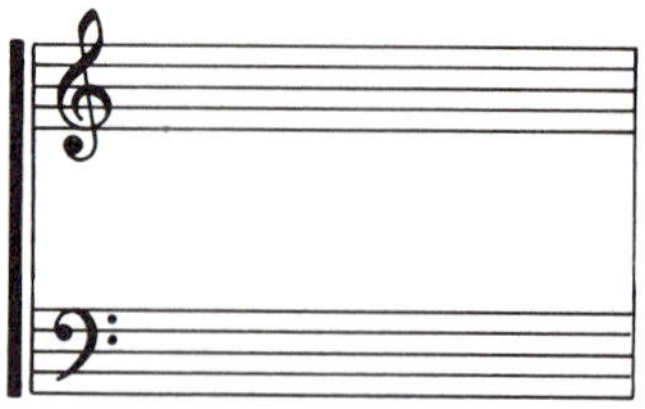

5
3
D: II

n.

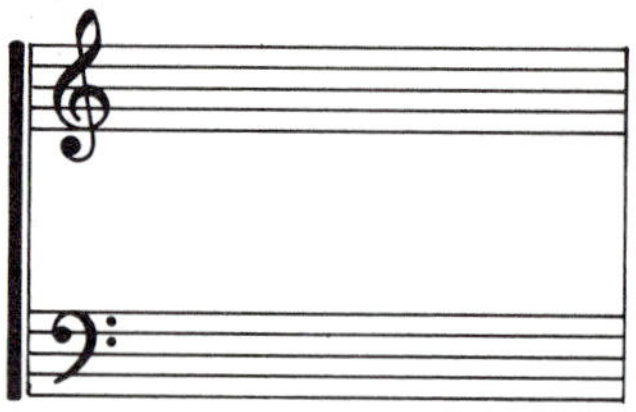

5
3𝄪
G♯: V𝄪

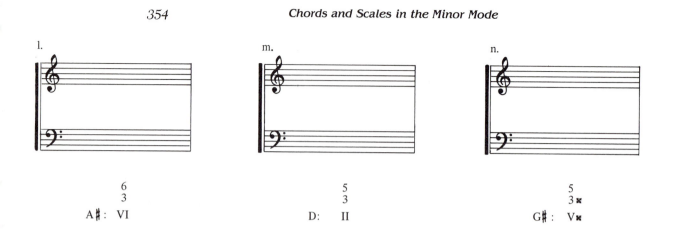

Rhythm Exercises

R10-1. For each of the rhythms in the left column, write an equivalent notation in the right column using the meter indicated.

SAMPLE

Solution

a.

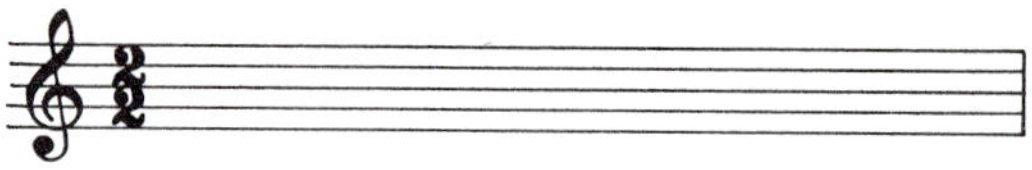

b.

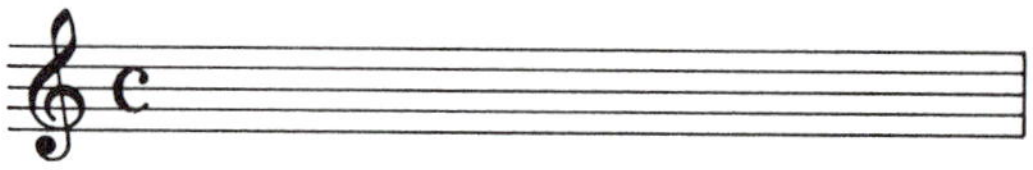

c.

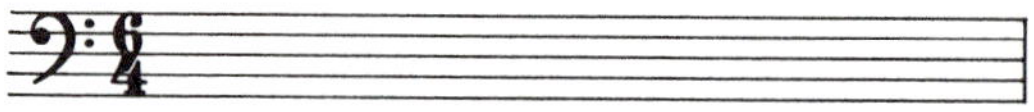

d.

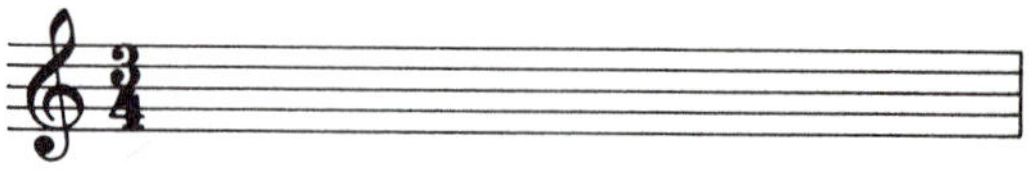

e.

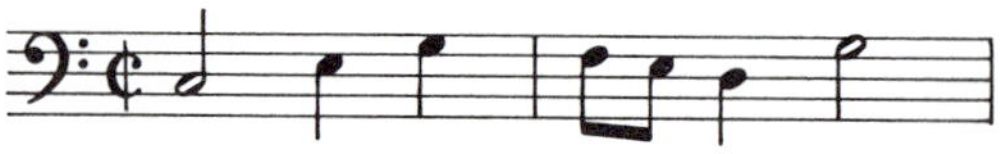

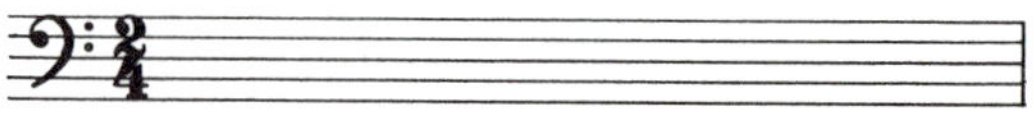

Name: ______________________
Instructor: ______________________
Date: ______________________

f.

g.

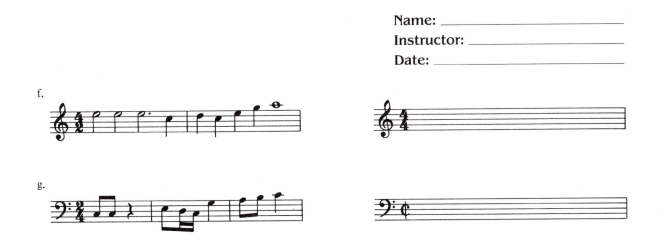

R10-2. Form a melody using the fragments provided. Only one ordering of these fragments results in measures that contain the correct number of beats.

a.

b.

R10-3. Notate the melodies indicated by the positioning of the pitch names in relation to the counting syllables. Use only unisons, seconds, thirds, and fourths as melodic intervals. Do not add rests.

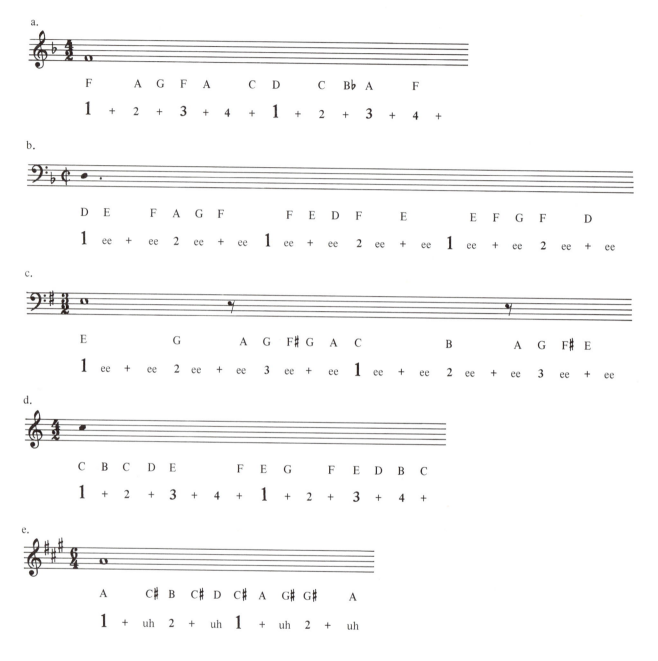

a.

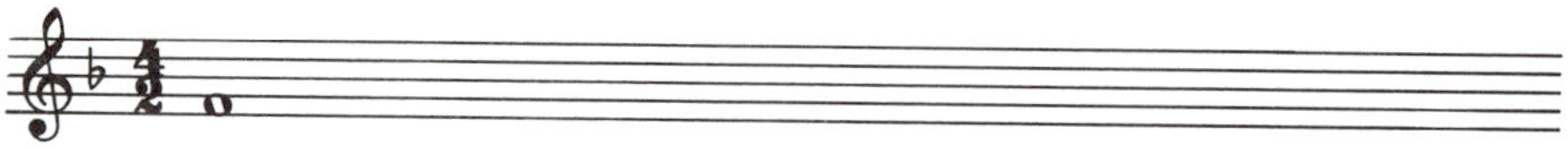

F A G F A C D C B♭ A F

1 + 2 + 3 + 4 + 1 + 2 + 3 + 4 +

b.

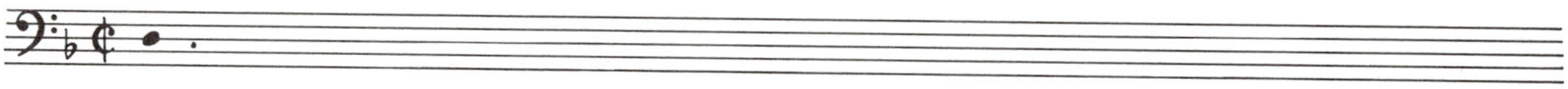

D E F A G F F E D F E E F G F D

1 ee + ee 2 ee + ee 1 ee + ee 2 ee + ee 1 ee + ee 2 ee + ee

c.

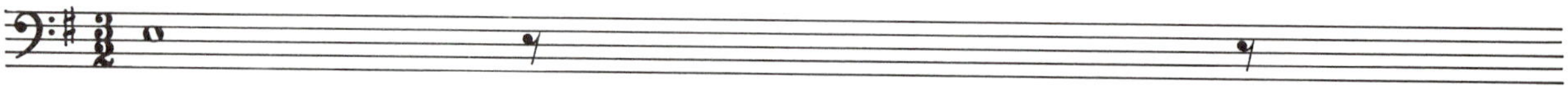

E G A G F♯ G A C B A G F♯ E

1 ee + ee 2 ee + ee 3 ee + ee 1 ee + ee 2 ee + ee 3 ee + ee

d.

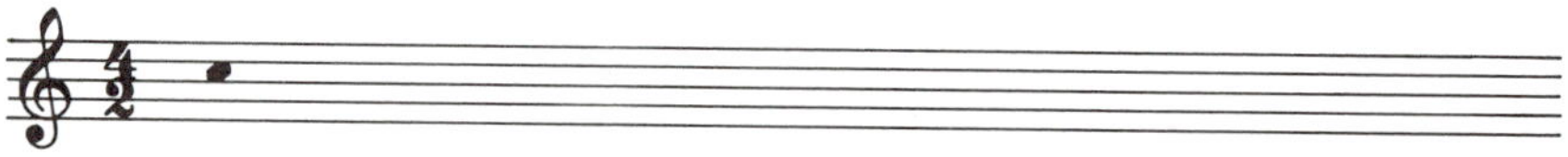

C B C D E F E G F E D B C

1 + 2 + 3 + 4 + 1 + 2 + 3 + 4 +

e.

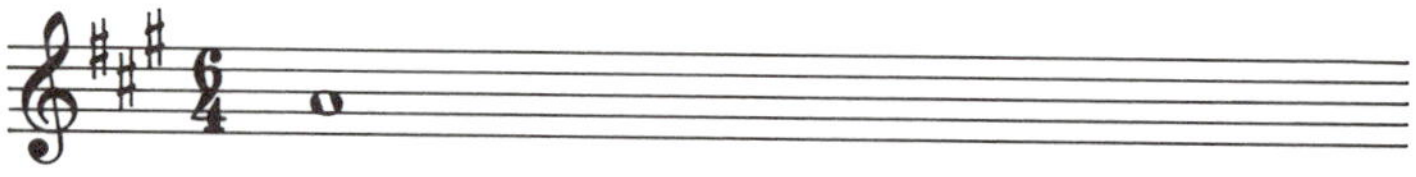

A C♯ B C♯ D C♯ A G♯ G♯ A

1 + uh 2 + uh 1 + uh 2 + uh

Name: ______________________

Instructor: ______________________

Date: ______________________

Audio Exercises

A10-1. A scale will be performed. Indicate whether it is a major scale, a natural minor scale, a harmonic minor scale, or a melodic minor scale.

a.	Major	Natural Minor	Harmonic Minor	Melodic Minor
b.	Major	Natural Minor	Harmonic Minor	Melodic Minor
c.	Major	Natural Minor	Harmonic Minor	Melodic Minor
d.	Major	Natural Minor	Harmonic Minor	Melodic Minor
e.	Major	Natural Minor	Harmonic Minor	Melodic Minor
f.	Major	Natural Minor	Harmonic Minor	Melodic Minor
g.	Major	Natural Minor	Harmonic Minor	Melodic Minor
h.	Major	Natural Minor	Harmonic Minor	Melodic Minor
i.	Major	Natural Minor	Harmonic Minor	Melodic Minor
j.	Major	Natural Minor	Harmonic Minor	Melodic Minor

A10-2. Two triads will be performed in root position, each preceded by a performance of its root alone. If the first triad is interpreted as the tonic (I), what label should be applied to the second triad?

a.	II	III	IV	IV♯	V	V♯	VI	VII	♯VII
b.	II	III	IV	IV♯	V	V♯	VI	VII	♯VII
c.	II	III	IV	IV♯	V	V♯	VI	VII	♯VII
d.	II	III	IV	IV♯	V	V♯	VI	VII	♯VII
e.	II	III	IV	IV♯	V	V♯	VI	VII	♯VII
f.	II	III	IV	IV♯	V	V♯	VI	VII	♯VII
g.	II	III	IV	IV♯	V	V♯	VI	VII	♯VII
h.	II	III	IV	IV♯	V	V♯	VI	VII	♯VII
i.	II	III	IV	IV♯	V	V♯	VI	VII	♯VII
j.	II	III	IV	IV♯	V	V♯	VI	VII	♯VII

A10-3. Six melodies will be performed. The starting pitch for each will be stated before the melody is performed. In each case circle the score that shows the correct pitch notation.

a.

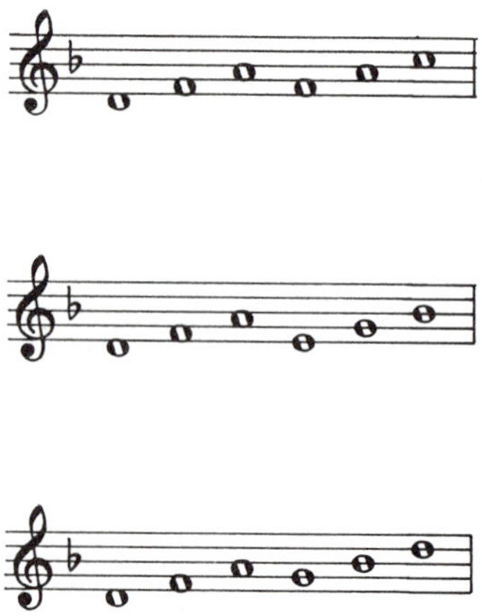

b.

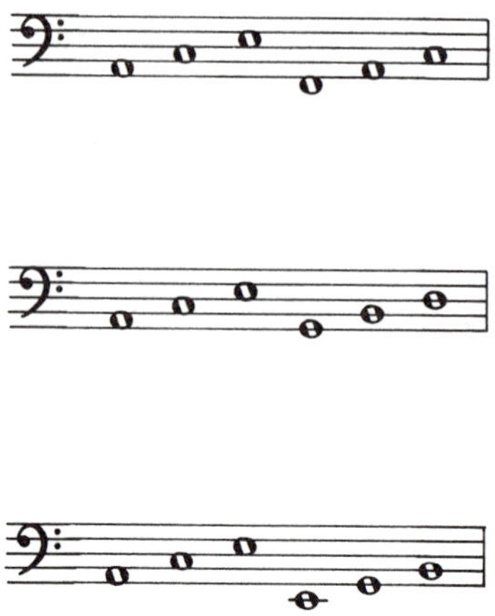

c.

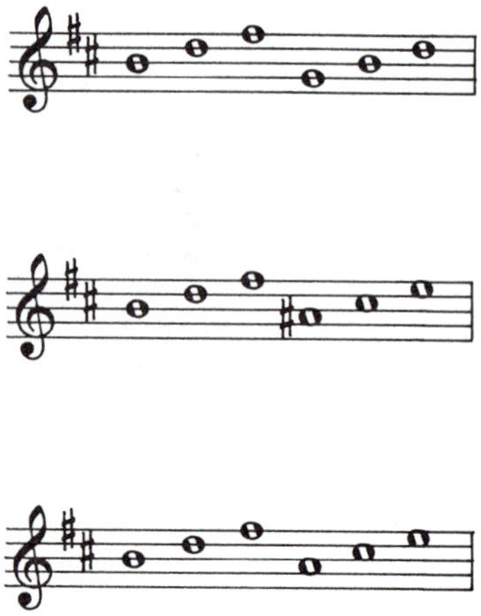

d.

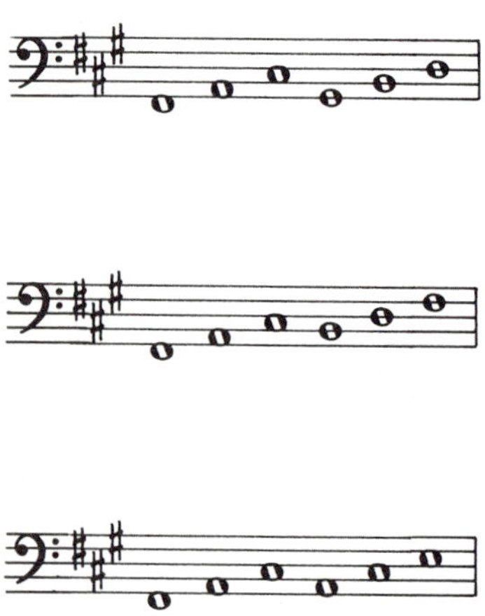

e.

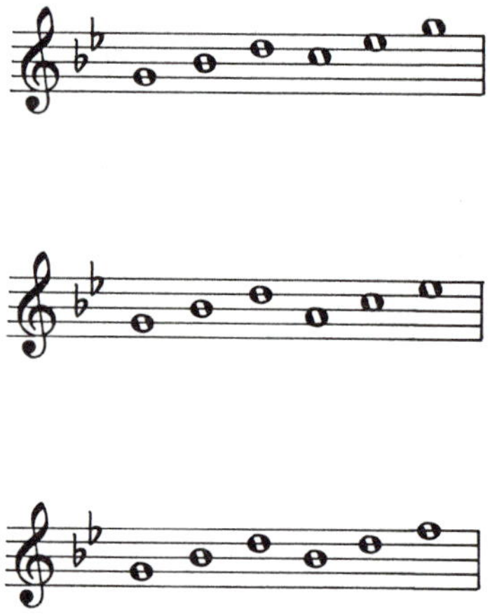

f.

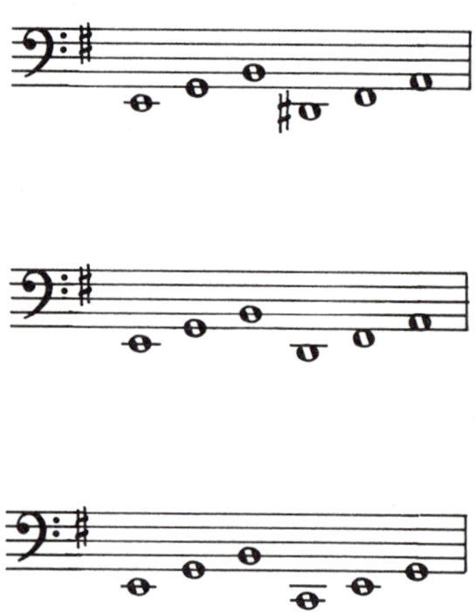

Name: ______________________
Instructor: ______________________
Date: ______________________

A10-4. Four rhythms will be performed. In each case circle the score that shows the correct notation.

a.

b.

c.

d.

Name: ____________________
Instructor: ____________________
Date: ____________________

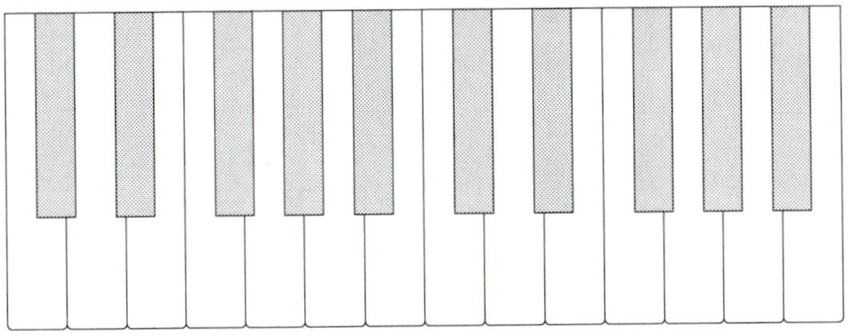

Mastery Test, Chapter 10

_______ 1. Which one of the triads shown functions as the leading tone triad in the key of G♯ minor?

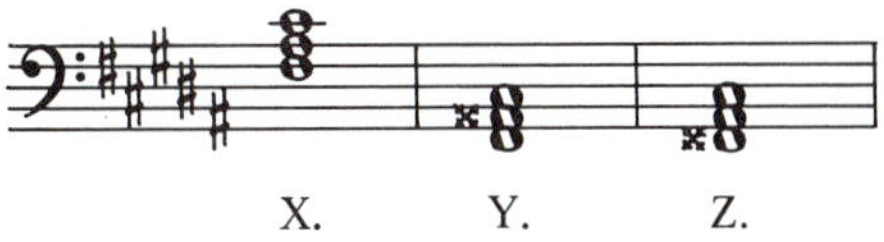

_______ 2. Which one of the triads shown functions as the subtonic triad in the key of B♭ minor?

_______ 3. Which Roman numeral corresponds to a chord of diminished quality in the minor mode?
X. II Y. III Z. VII

For Questions 4 and 5:

_______ 4. What Roman numeral pertains to the chord shown?
X. ♯VII Y. V♯ Z. ♯V

_______ 5. What figured bass pertains to the chord shown?
X. $^{6}_{3}$ Y. $^{6\sharp}_{3}$ Z. $^{6}_{\sharp}$

For Questions 6 and 7:

B minor

_______ 6. What Roman numeral pertains to the chord shown?

X. II Y. VII♯ Z. ♯VII

_______ 7. What figured bass pertains to the chord shown?

X. $^{6}_{3}$ Y. $^{6\sharp}_{3}$ Z. $^{6}_{\sharp}$

For Questions 8 and 9:

A♯ minor

_______ 8. What Roman numeral pertains to the chord shown?

X. ×VI Y. IV× Z. ×IV

_______ 9. What figured bass pertains to the chord shown?

X. $^{6}_{3}$ Y. $^{6\times}_{3}$ Z. $^{6}_{\times}$

_______ 10. In what key does the harmonic minor scale contain in direct succession the pitches B and C×?

X. F♯ minor Y. D♯ minor Z. G♯ minor

_______ 11. In the key of E♭ minor, which set of pitches shown occupies scale degrees $\hat{6}$, $\hat{7}$, and $\hat{8}$ in the ascending melodic minor scale?

X. C♭ D♭ E♭ Y. C♭ D E♭ Z. C D E♭

_______ 12. Which scale descends using different pitches from its ascent?

X. Harmonic minor
Y. Natural minor
Z. Melodic minor

_______ 13. Which time signature is the equivalent of the symbol ₵?

X. $^{2}_{2}$ Y. $^{4}_{2}$ Z. $^{6}_{4}$

_______ 14. What kind of note should be inserted at the arrow to complete the measure?

X. Dotted half note
Y. Quarter note
Z. Dotted quarter note

Name: ______________________

Instructor: ______________________

Date: ______________________

________ 15. What kind of rest should be inserted at the arrow to complete the measure?

X. Eighth rest

Y. Quarter rest

Z. Dotted eighth rest

________ 16. A scale will be performed. Indicate which scale it is.

X. Harmonic minor

Y. Natural minor

Z. Melodic minor

Two triads will be performed in root position, each preceded by a performance of its root alone. If the first triad is interpreted as the tonic (I), what label should be applied to the second triad?

________ 17. X. III Y. IV Z. IV♯

________ 18. X. V Y. V♯ Z. VI

________ 19. A melody that begins with the pitch F will be performed. Which score shows the correct pitch notation?

X.

Y.

Z.

_________ 20. Which score shows the correct notation for the rhythm performed?

X.

Y.

Z.

11

Harmonization: Selecting Chords

Terms and Concepts

harmonize
voice leading

PITCH

The Art of Harmonization

Now that we are acquainted with many of the chords that can be formed in major and minor keys, we can begin to employ them in musical contexts. Chords support melodies. In fact, melodies often imply specific chordal accompaniments —for example, through arpeggiation of the pitches of a specific chord or through emphasis on the leading tone near a cadence point. We must choose from among several ways to ***harmonize,*** or supply chords for, a melody. In the melodies of this and the next two chapters, the three most prominent chords—I, IV, and V—will be used to demonstrate the art of harmonization.

harmonize

The pitches used in building a chord determine what portions of a melody the chord may harmonize. For example, a I chord could be used when $\hat{1}$, $\hat{3}$, or $\hat{5}$ appears in a melody, because those scale degrees form the I chord. Observe, though, that $\hat{5}$ is also found in the V chord (along with $\hat{7}$ and $\hat{2}$). Deciding whether to use I or V when $\hat{5}$ appears in a melody is one of the issues you must consider when harmonizing. The choice is influenced by the melodic context of $\hat{5}$ and by how the chord selected to support $\hat{5}$ interacts with other chords in its vicinity.

The I chord can harmonize $\hat{1}$, $\hat{3}$, and $\hat{5}$; the IV chord can harmonize $\hat{4}$, $\hat{6}$, and $\hat{1}$; and the V chord can harmonize $\hat{5}$, $\hat{7}$, $\hat{2}$, and (when V is in $\substack{7\\5\\3}$ position) $\hat{4}$. We shall use the Roman numeral V whenever the $\substack{5\\3}$ and $\substack{7\\5\\3}$ positions of V are both possible. When only the $\substack{7\\5\\3}$ position is possible, the number 7 will appear to the right side of the Roman numeral, as in V^7. Example 11-1 displays these possibilities.

Example 11-1

The chart in Example 11-2 shows which chords support each scale degree.

Example 11-2

Scale Degree	*Roman Numeral(s)*	*Sample Chord(s) in C Major*
$\hat{1}$	I or IV	 I IV
$\hat{2}$	V	 V
$\hat{3}$	I	 I
$\hat{4}$	IV or V^7	 IV V7
$\hat{5}$	I or V	 I V
$\hat{6}$	IV	 IV
$\hat{7}$	V	 V

A Sample Harmonization

By consulting the harmonization chart in Example 11-2, we can determine the potential chords for a harmonization of "Pop Goes the Weasel." Possible chord choices are shown in Example 11-3.

Example 11-3

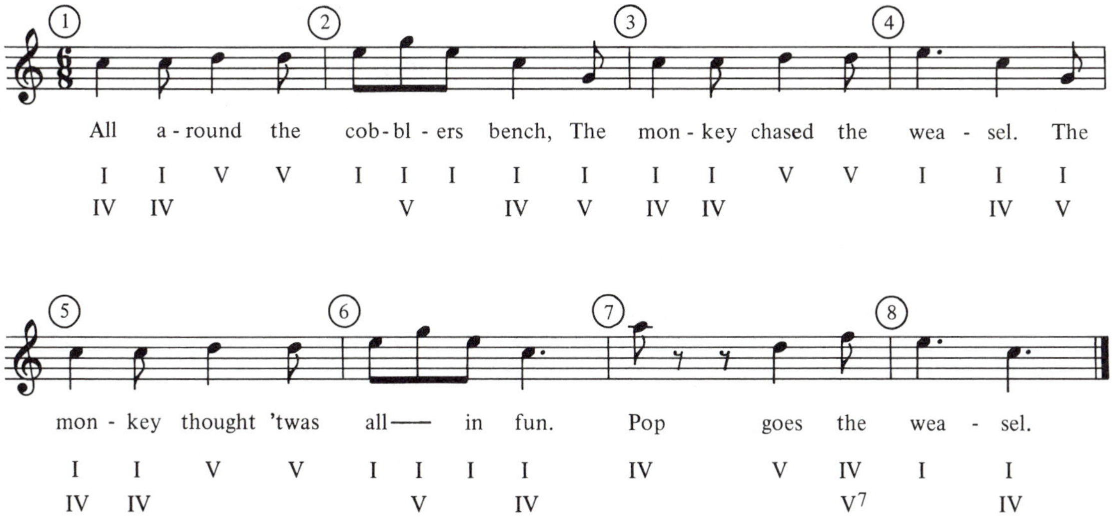

Even though we have restricted ourselves to only three of the seven diatonic chords, over half the notes of the melody could potentially be harmonized in more than one way. Some choices are good, others are not. The following guidelines, illustrated by Examples 11-4 through 11-9, will help us in selecting good alternatives.

1. *Begin and end melodies and phrases with appropriate harmonies.* Almost every composition will begin with a I chord, and every composition will end with a I chord. Individual phrases typically end with an authentic, plagal, or half cadence, resulting in the chord choices I or V at the ends of phrases.

APPLICATION: Measure 1 of "Pop Goes the Weasel" should begin with I rather than with IV. The C in the middle of measure 4 ends the first phrase (the following G is an upbeat to the second phrase), so I, not IV, should be used to form an authentic cadence. Similarly, the final C should be harmonized by I rather than by IV. These choices are illustrated in Example 11-4.

Example 11-4

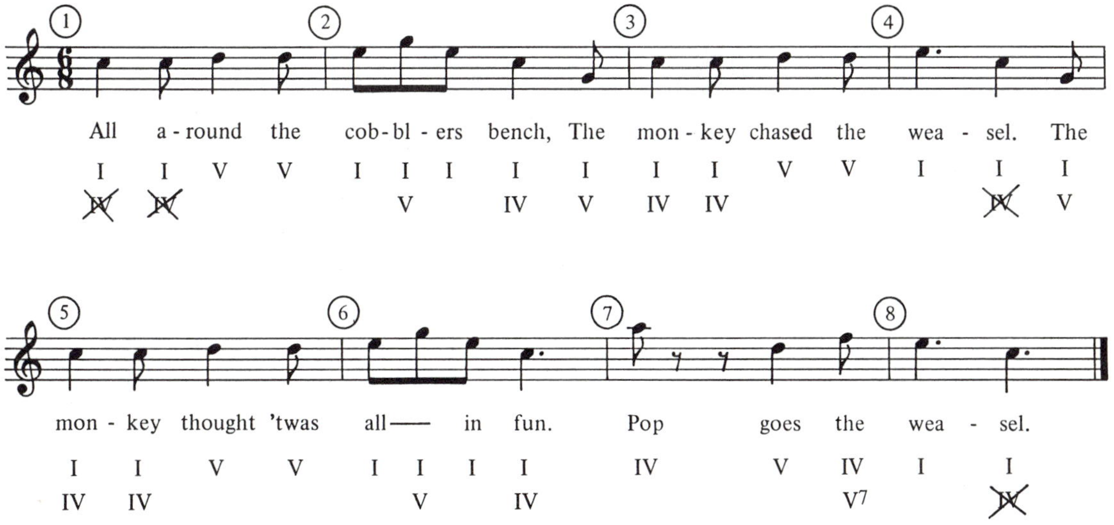

2. *Follow established conventions of chord progression.* The conventions for the progression of the I, IV, and V chords in root position are straightforward. The I chord may serve as a cadence point or lead to IV or V; IV may lead to I or V; and V may serve as a cadence point or lead to I. When V is used at a half cadence, it is generally in $\begin{smallmatrix}5\\3\end{smallmatrix}$ position, rather than $\begin{smallmatrix}7\\5\\3\end{smallmatrix}$ position. When it leads to I, either position is appropriate.

APPLICATION: Because we restrict ourselves to only three chords, and because the only awkward progression among them is from V to IV, chord progression should not be a problem. V does not generally lead to IV because of its strong cadential impulse, resulting from the presence of the leading tone. Though IV contains the leading tone's resolution pitch, $\hat{1}$, it does not contain the resolution pitch for the seventh in the V^7 chord, $\hat{3}$. The I chord is therefore a much more suitable successor to the V chord. (The deceptive cadence, discussed in Chapter 9, requires that IV appear in $\begin{smallmatrix}6\\3\end{smallmatrix}$ position. V–IV$\begin{smallmatrix}6\\3\end{smallmatrix}$ is a suitable progression, but V–IV$\begin{smallmatrix}5\\3\end{smallmatrix}$ is not. Because of its complexity, our discussion of harmonization in Chapters 11 through 13 is limited to chords in $\begin{smallmatrix}5\\3\end{smallmatrix}$ or $\begin{smallmatrix}7\\5\\3\end{smallmatrix}$ position.) The potential progression V–IV in measure 7 is weak and should be avoided, as in Example 11-5.

Example 11-5

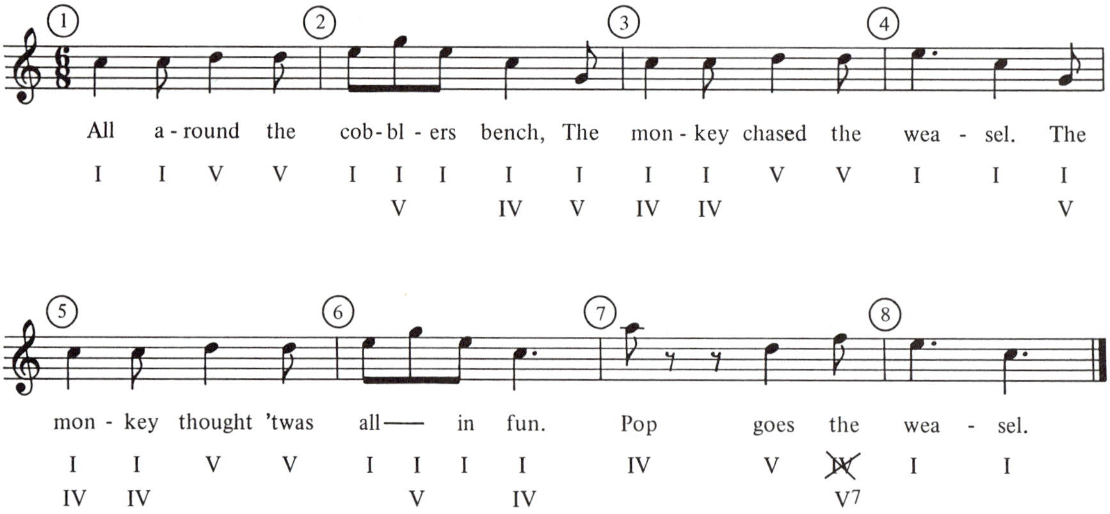

3. *Maintain a consistent rate of chord change.* Typically the number of chords in an accompaniment does not match the number of pitches in a melody. Instead, groups of pitches are harmonized by a single chord. As the melody progresses, this rate of chord change gives a sense of stability or predictability that should rarely be upset unless a special effect is desired. For example, a composer might use more or fewer different chords per measure near a cadence than at other points within a phrase. You should examine the melody for instances of arpeggiation, leading tones, groups of notes that recur, and other features that may warrant special consideration.

APPLICATION: Examining the harmonic choices for "Pop Goes the Weasel," we observe several instances where half a measure *must* be harmonized by a single chord because there are no other choices. Furthermore, no half measure could *not* be harmonized by a single chord. It is therefore desirable to present chords at the rate of two per measure, one for every beat. Consecutive beats might employ the same chord, but within any beat only one chord will sound. The selection of I for the second eighth note in measures 2 and 6 is superior to using V, because I allows for a continuity of chordal statements while V requires that three chords (I–V–I) fit within the span of half a measure. The alternatives for the second halves of measures 2 and 4 are retained, because these measures end with upbeats that begin a new line of text. The preferred harmonic choices are illustrated in Example 11-6.

Example 11-6

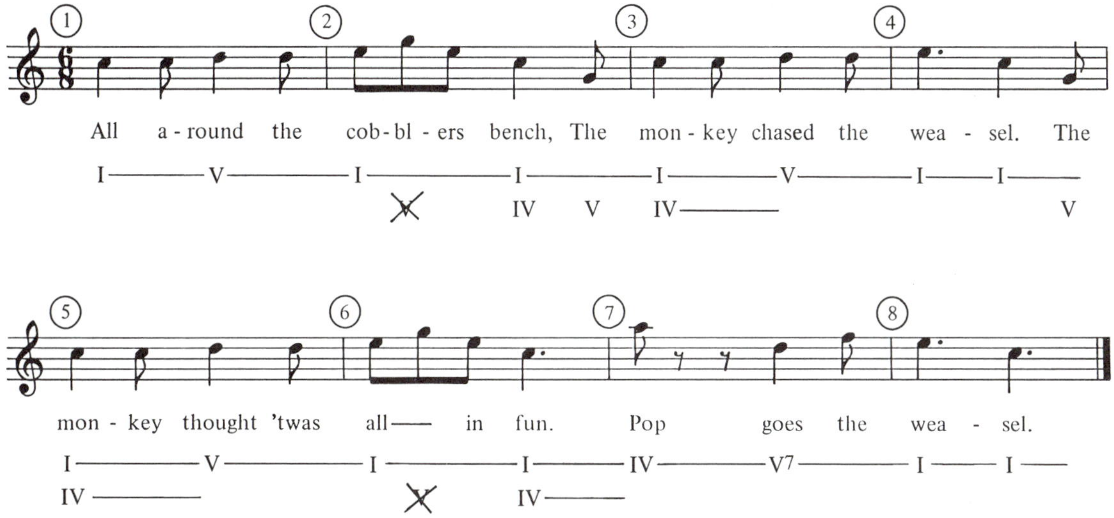

4. Whenever possible, present a new harmony on a strong beat rather than on a weak beat. For harmonic progressions to have the greatest effect, they should coordinate with the meter. Whenever possible, avoid introducing a new harmony in the middle of one measure if that harmony continues over the bar line into the next measure.

APPLICATION: In "Pop Goes the Weasel," the IV chord is a potential choice as the harmonization for the C that ends measure 6. But as we shall use IV again in measure 7, the metrical positioning of IV in measure 6 would be awkward. The situation is especially delicate here because the word "Pop" sounds with the A of measure 7. There should be an element of surprise to accompany that unexpected word of the text. A, the highest pitch in the melody, vividly depicts the weasel's surprise attack on the monkey. By striking the IV chord only with the A, as in Example 11-7, we emphasize the startling effect of this higher note and the unexpected word "Pop." If the IV chord harmonized the preceding half measure as well, then a large part of the surprise would be missing.

Example 11-7

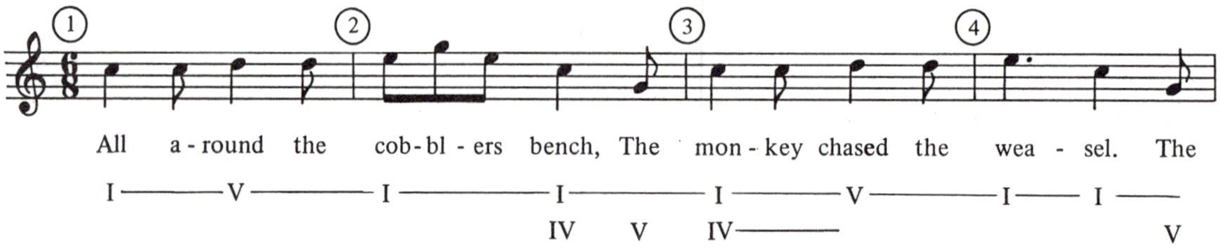

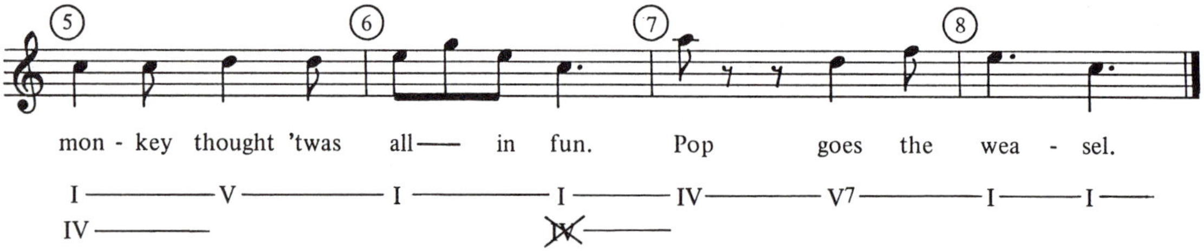

voice leading

5. *Avoid the progression IV–V when the melody proceeds $\hat{1}$–$\hat{2}$ or $\hat{4}$–$\hat{5}$.* ***Voice leading*** is the study of how each of the four "voices," or pitches, of a chord moves in relation to the other three voices. Our restricted selection of chords and the method of chord construction and succession that will be demonstrated in Chapter 12 allow us to avoid, to a large extent, the intricacies of voice leading that are a central concern of more advanced courses in music theory. One issue does, however, demand special attention at this point: the progression from IV to V.

Because the IV and V chords are adjacent to one another, particular problems can arise if the individual voices are not sufficiently independent. It is not desirable for all of the voices to rise up a step when leading from IV to V. Instead, some of the melodic activity must counter this ascent by moving downward. The problem is most acute when the bass is a perfect fifth or perfect octave (simple or compound) from the melody note. These two intervals—the most consonant intervals after the unison—are very stable. Composers have for centuries avoided the direct succession of parallel perfect fifths and octaves. Though there are more advanced techniques of chord construction and voice leading that allow composers to use these harmonies when $\hat{1}$ leads to $\hat{2}$ or when $\hat{4}$ leads to $\hat{5}$ in the melody, at this point these progressions should be avoided. Correct and incorrect harmonizations of $\hat{1}$–$\hat{2}$ and $\hat{4}$–$\hat{5}$ are shown in Example 11-8.

Example 11-8

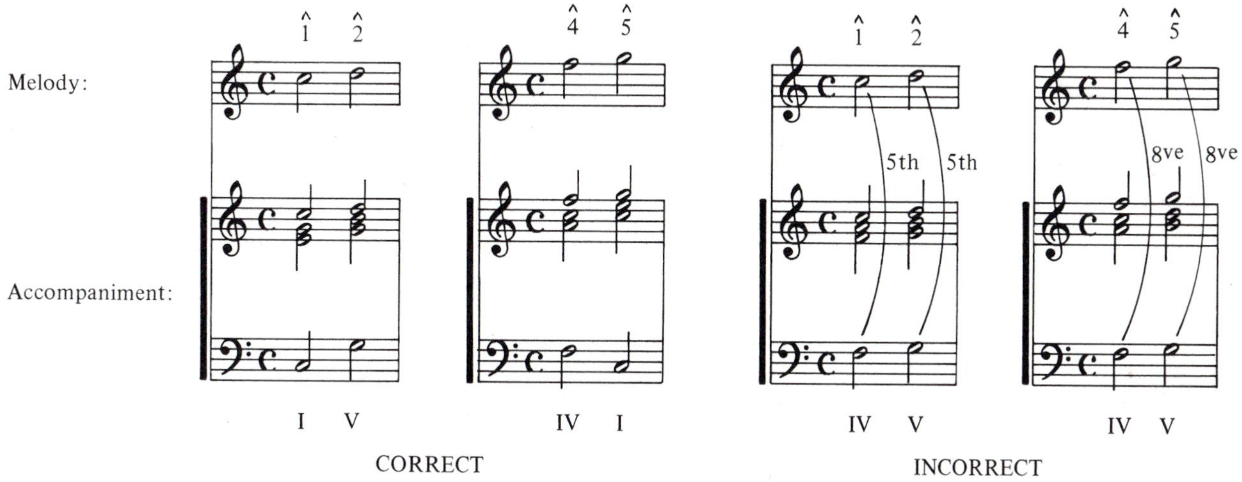

APPLICATION: Measures 3 and 5 of "Pop Goes the Weasel" should begin with I rather than with IV to avoid parallel fifths between the bass of the accompaniment and the melody. Observe also that in this harmonization, the melodic ascent 1̂–2̂–3̂ is treated consistently in measures 1–2, 3–4, and 5–6, as in Example 11-9. As this melody is intended for children, such repetition is appropriate. It also enhances the element of surprise at measure 7, where the precedent of measures 1, 3, and 5 is broken.

Example 11-9

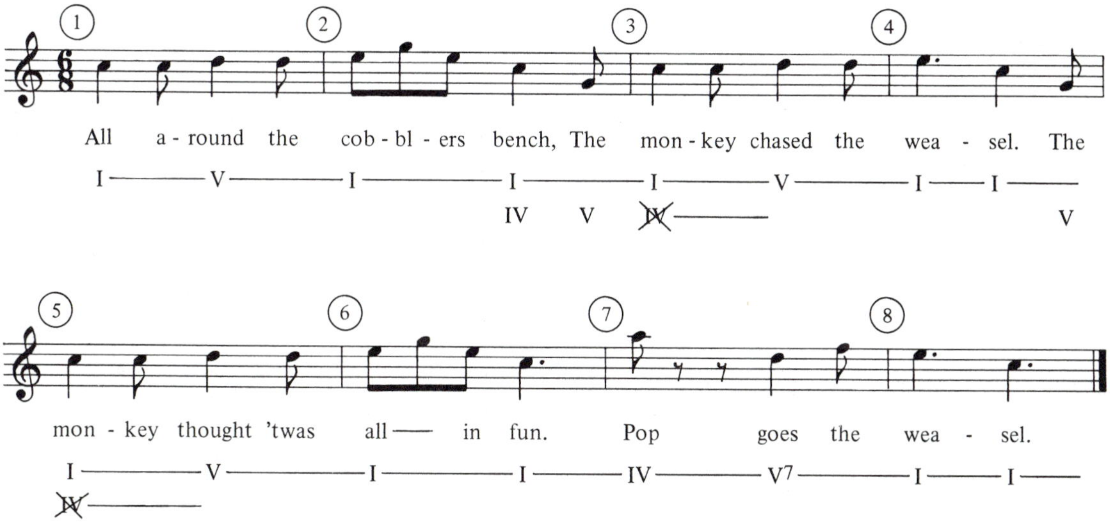

The Roman numerals that remain in Example 11-9 reflect possible harmonizations for "Pop Goes the Weasel." Though few alternatives exist when we limit ourselves to only the I, IV, and V harmonies, observe that in some cases there are two choices. Also remember that where V is indicated, both the $\substack{7\\5\\3}$ and the $\substack{5\\3}$ positions are possible.

Pitch exercises for Chapter 11 are on pages 381–385.

RHYTHM

Variety of Available Meters

Since practices of notating music go back many centuries, and since composers from many countries have contributed to our heritage, we should not expect that uniform standards of notation have always been maintained. For example, much early music was written using clefs that only a small proportion of musicians today can read with fluency. As a result, editors often convert these scores into treble and bass clefs so that users of their editions have easier access to this repertoire.

One might imagine that the time signatures we have studied are adequate for all compositional needs. We can write two, three, or four beats per measure in either simple or compound meter. Yet the earliest examples of notated music do not use our modern time signatures at all. Once these signatures did come into general use in the seventeenth century, composers selected from a wide variety of possibilities. The beat could be represented not only by the quarter note, the dotted quarter note, the half note, and the dotted half note, as do the meters we have used in previous chapters, but also by the eighth note and the dotted eighth note.

The chart in Example 11-10 indicates the meanings of the various time signatures you are likely to encounter when performing tonal music.

Example 11-10

SIMPLE METERS

Unit of the Beat	*Two Beats*	*Three Beats*	*Four Beats*
Eighth note	$\genfrac{}{}{0pt}{}{2}{8}$	$\genfrac{}{}{0pt}{}{3}{8}$	$\genfrac{}{}{0pt}{}{4}{8}$
Quarter note	$\genfrac{}{}{0pt}{}{2}{4}$	$\genfrac{}{}{0pt}{}{3}{4}$, 3	$\genfrac{}{}{0pt}{}{4}{4}$, C
Half note	$\genfrac{}{}{0pt}{}{2}{2}$, ₵, 2	$\genfrac{}{}{0pt}{}{3}{2}$	$\genfrac{}{}{0pt}{}{4}{2}$

COMPOUND METERS

Unit of the Beat	*Two Beats*	*Three Beats*	*Four Beats*
Dotted eighth note	$\genfrac{}{}{0pt}{}{6}{16}$	$\genfrac{}{}{0pt}{}{9}{16}$	$\genfrac{}{}{0pt}{}{12}{16}$
Dotted quarter note	$\genfrac{}{}{0pt}{}{6}{8}$	$\genfrac{}{}{0pt}{}{9}{8}$	$\genfrac{}{}{0pt}{}{12}{8}$
Dotted half note	$\genfrac{}{}{0pt}{}{6}{4}$	$\genfrac{}{}{0pt}{}{9}{4}$	$\genfrac{}{}{0pt}{}{12}{4}$

You will recall that the symbols **C** and **¢** for $\frac{4}{4}$ and $\frac{2}{2}$, respectively, have been introduced in earlier chapters. You may occasionally encounter the symbols **2** (the equivalent of $\frac{2}{2}$) and **3** (the equivalent of $\frac{3}{4}$).

Unusual Meters and Shifting Meters

With an understanding of these meters, you should have little trouble if you encounter novel meters occasionally, or even shifts from one meter to another within the same composition (a practice that has become common in recent music). For example, Tchaikovsky wrote a melody consisting of five beats per measure in the second movement of his Sixth Symphony. Since he selected the quarter note as representative of the beat, his time signature is $\frac{5}{4}$, as shown in Example 11-11.

Example 11-11

Tchaikovsky: Symphony No. 6

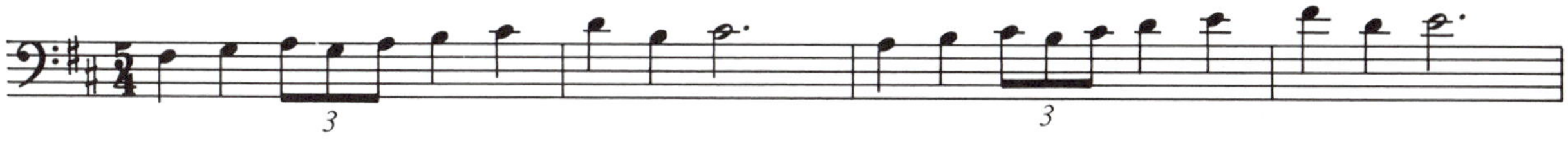

Scriabin's Prelude Op. 11, No. 24, alternates between $\frac{6}{8}$ and $\frac{5}{8}$ meters. A more conventional composer might have indicated these shifts by writing the appropriate time signature at the beginning of every measure where a shift occurs. Scriabin, perhaps because there is a shift with almost every measure, simply wrote both time signatures at the beginning and has left it to the performer to observe whether a given measure contains five or six eighth notes. The first few measures of the right-hand part are shown in Example 11-12. The beaming reveals that he intended for the first and fourth eighth notes in $\frac{5}{8}$ to be stronger than the remaining eighth notes. That is, each measure in $\frac{5}{8}$ meter contains two beats, but the second beat is shorter than the first beat.

Example 11-12

Scriabin: Prelude Op. 11, No. 24

Rhythm exercises for Chapter 11 are on pages 386–388.

LABORATORY

L11-1.a. Perform the following chord progressions at the keyboard. Underneath each chord, write in the appropriate Roman numeral. Though the tempo that you choose might be slow, make sure that it is steady—that every chord is of the same duration. Begin thinking about the next chord during beats two through four of the measure that precedes it.

1.

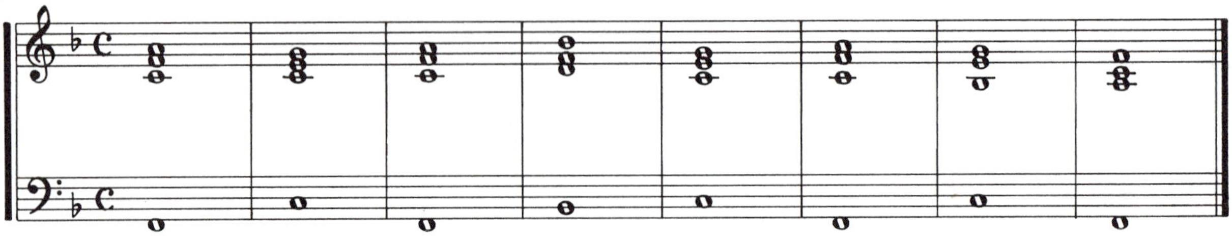

2.

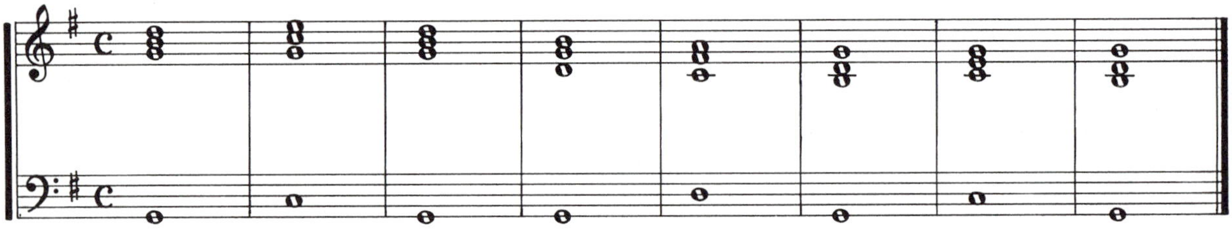

b. Perform each of the following melodies at the keyboard. Recommended fingerings are included.

Bach: Well-Tempered Clavier, Vol. 2, Fugue 11

1.

Bach: French Suite in C Minor, Gigue

2.

Bach: French Suite in E Major, Bourrée

3.

L11-2. Determine which scale degree the given pitch class forms in the key indicated. Choose an appropriate harmony—I, IV, or V—and perform it as a four-note chord, with the given pitch class in the soprano. There may be more than one correct choice.

a. F major: D	**b.** A major: F♯
c. F♯ major: A♯	**d.** B♭ major: B♭
e. G major: D	**f.** E major: G♯
g. D♭ major: C	**h.** G♭ major: D♭
i. E♭ major: F	**j.** D major: C♯
k. B major: E	**l.** A♭ major: B♭

L11-3.a. Practice the following exercise over a period of days or weeks until you have mastered it perfectly.

- Position two fingers on top of keys that are a perfect fourth apart, but do not strike them. Make sure that these keys correspond to pitches within your vocal range.
- Strike the lower key.
- Sing that pitch.
- Sing the pitch a perfect fourth higher.
- Strike the higher key and confirm that it is what you have sung.

b. Once the above exercise is going well, add the following steps.

- Position two fingers on top of keys that are a perfect fourth apart, but do not strike them.
- Strike the upper key.
- Sing that pitch.
- Sing the pitch a perfect fourth lower.
- Strike the lower key and confirm that it is what you have sung.

L11-4. The following melodies are accompanied by a wider variety of harmonies than you will use in your own harmonizations. These accompaniments demonstrate the sorts of chord and inversion choices that would be available to you after further study of music theory. A student or the instructor could play the keyboard part while other students sing the melody. You may wish to sing the melodies one or two octaves lower than notated, though the accompaniment should be performed as written.

Pop Goes the Weasel

a.

b. Twinkle, Twinkle Little Star

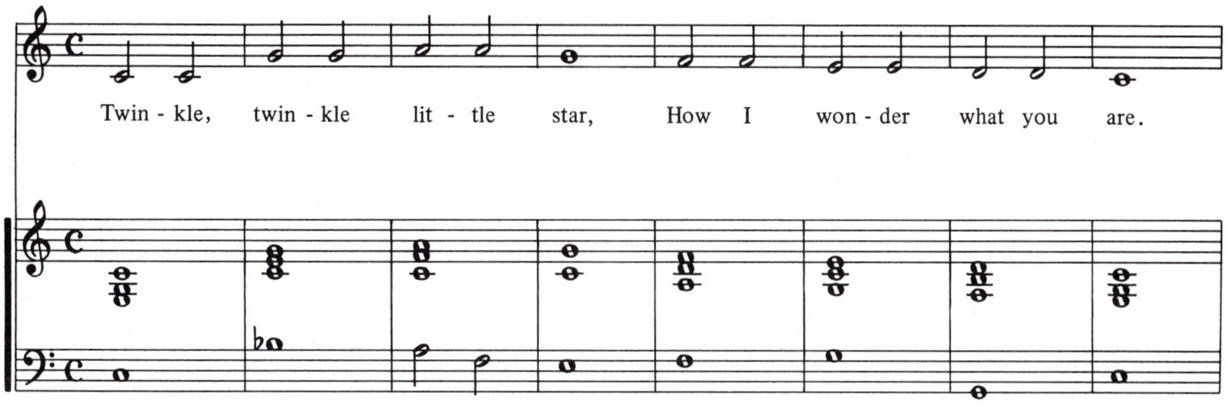
Twin - kle, twin - kle lit - tle star, How I won - der what you are.

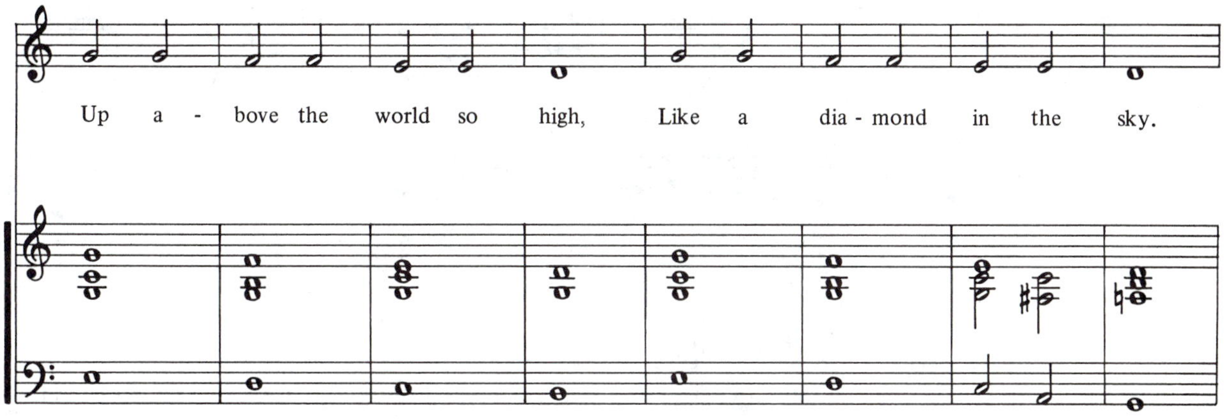
Up a - bove the world so high, Like a dia - mond in the sky.

Twin - kle, twin - kle lit - tle star, How I won - der what you are.

L11-5. The following compositions are for two voices. Sing the scale-degree number, or the syllable "raised," that corresponds to each pitch, as indicated. If necessary, transpose the entire score up or down one octave.

a. Voice 1

b. Voice 1

L11-6. Write in the counting syllables below the notated rhythms. Then perform each by clapping the rhythm or playing the pitch C or F at the keyboard, as notated, while pronouncing the counting syllables aloud.

a.

b.

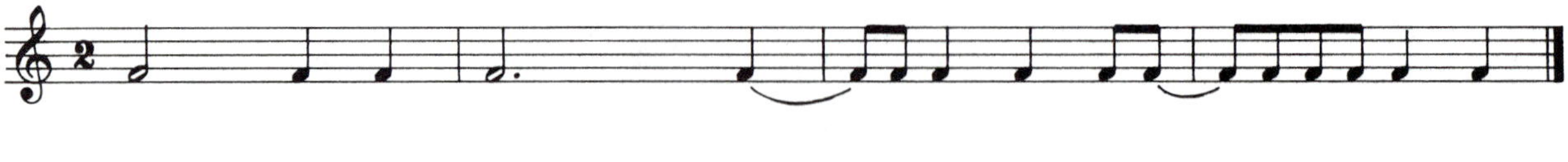

c.

d.

e.

L11-7. Write in the counting syllables below the notated rhythms. Then perform them by dividing the class into two groups, with each group clapping one part while pronouncing the counting syllables aloud. Alternatively, individual students may perform both parts simultaneously at the keyboard, pronouncing the counting syllables aloud while the index fingers strike the notated pitches.

a.

b.

c.

L11-8. This exercise requires that a student or the instructor serve as the performer at a keyboard.

a. The performer plays two pitches in either ascending or descending order, and then plays them together. Indicate whether the interval performed is or is not a perfect fourth.

b. The performer plays an ascending perfect fourth or perfect fifth. Indicate which interval is performed.

c. The performer plays a descending perfect fourth or perfect fifth. Indicate which interval is performed.

d. The performer plays one of the following three chord progressions. Indicate which progression is performed. (When the tonic is minor, substitute V♯ for V.)

I–IV–I
I–V–I
I–IV–V

e. The performer plays the chord progression I–$V^{(7)}$–I, either with or without the 7 in the V chord. Indicate whether the V chord is performed in $\genfrac{}{}{0pt}{}{5}{3}$ or $\begin{smallmatrix}7\\5\\3\end{smallmatrix}$ position.

Audio exercises for Chapter 11 are on pages 389–391.

Name: ______________________

Instructor: ______________________

Date: ______________________

EXERCISES

Pitch Exercises

P11-1. Indicate the scale degree of each pitch in the major key whose key signature appears on the staff. Then list the Roman numerals of the chords that could harmonize it, limiting your choices to I, IV, V (when both $\begin{smallmatrix}5\\3\end{smallmatrix}$ and $\begin{smallmatrix}7\\5\\3\end{smallmatrix}$ positions are possible), and V^7 (when only the $\begin{smallmatrix}7\\5\\3\end{smallmatrix}$ position is possible).

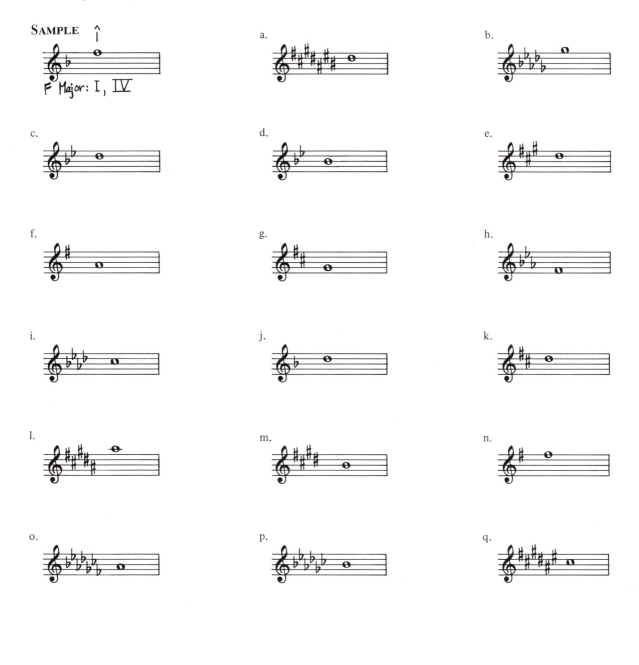

SAMPLE

F Major: I, IV

a.

b.

c.

d.

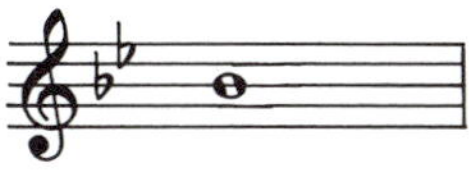

e.

f.

g.

h.

i.

j.

k.

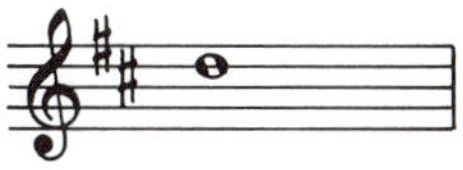

l.

m.

n.

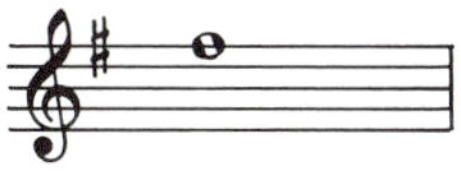

o.

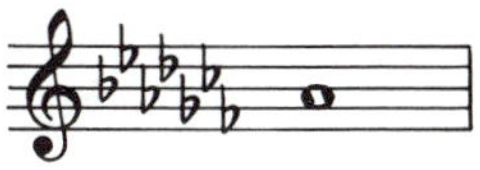

p.

q.

P11-2. For each of the melodic excerpts below, provide Roman numerals (I, IV, V, or V[7]) to indicate a suitable accompaniment. In some cases a single chord may harmonize several melodic notes. Each excerpt is in the major key whose key signature appears on the staff. If you wish, write in the scale-degree number ($\hat{2}$, $\hat{4}$, etc.) above each notehead.

SAMPLE

a.

b.

c.

d.

e.

f.

g.

h.

i.

j.

k.

l.

m.

n.

o.

p.

q.

Name: ______________________________
Instructor: ___________________________
Date: _______________________________

P11-3. Select suitable chords to harmonize the melody "Twinkle, Twinkle Little Star" by following the steps suggested.

a. Indicate all possible chords for each pitch of the melody by placing Roman numerals (using I, IV, V, and V^7) underneath each notehead. If you wish, write in the scale-degree number above each notehead.

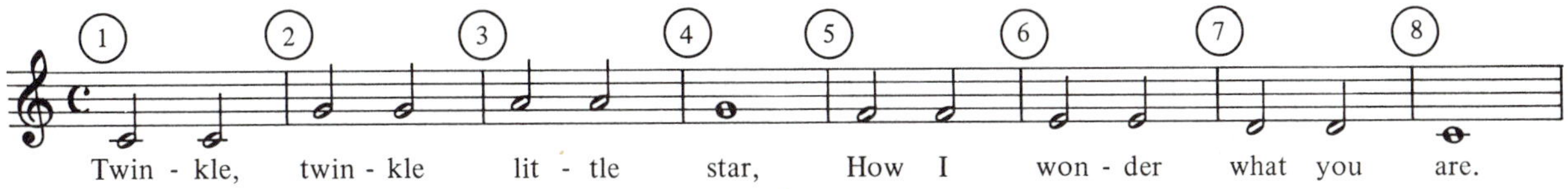

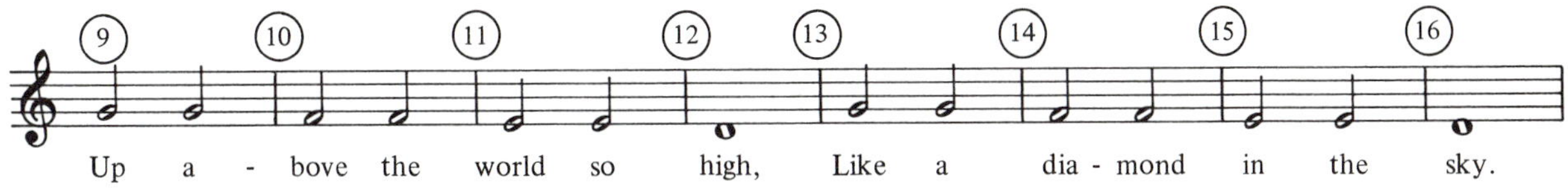

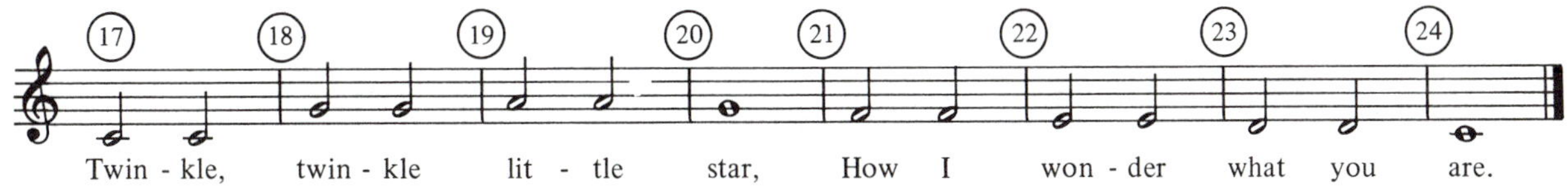

b. In measures 1, 2, 8, 17, 18, and 24 above, cross out the Roman numeral that does not conform to standard procedures regarding how phrases begin and end or to conventions regarding chord progression.

c. The selection of harmonies should now be limited to just one choice in all measures except 4, 5, 9, 10, 13, 14, 20, and 21. Observe that measures 20 and 21 are the same as 4 and 5, and that measures 13 and 14 are the same as 9 and 10. Thus we need work out only the first two pairs, then apply those results to the remaining measures.

For measures 4 and 5, four possible progressions result from the choices available. Fill in the blanks below.

measure 3	measure 4 choice 1	measure 5 choice 1	measure 6

measure 3	measure 4 choice 1	measure 5 choice 2	measure 6

measure 3	measure 4 choice 2	measure 5 choice 1	measure 6

measure 3	measure 4 choice 2	measure 5 choice 2	measure 6

Cross out the choice that contains a faulty chord progression. Try each of the three remaining progressions at the keyboard and decide which one you prefer. Cross out the others.

d. Likewise, for measures 9 and 10, four possible progressions result from the choices available. Consider how measures 9 and 10 function in the context of measures 9 through 12 by filling in the blanks below.

measure 9 choice 1	measure 10 choice 1	measure 11	measure 12

Name: ____________________

Instructor: ____________________

Date: ____________________

________	________	________	________
measure 9 choice 1	measure 10 choice 2	measure 11	measure 12
________	________	________	________
measure 9 choice 2	measure 10 choice 1	measure 11	measure 12
________	________	________	________
measure 9 choice 2	measure 10 choice 2	measure 11	measure 12

Cross out the choice that contains a faulty chord progression. Try each of the three remaining progressions at the keyboard and decide which one you prefer. Cross out the others.

e. Place Roman numerals underneath the noteheads below to indicate your decisions. In Chapter 12 you will learn how to construct and connect the various chords that you have selected.

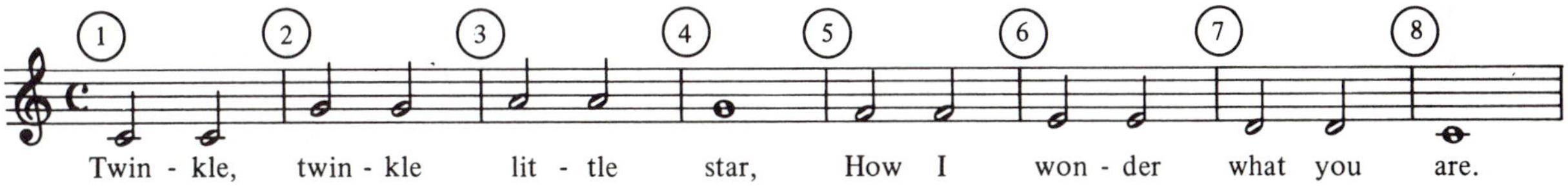

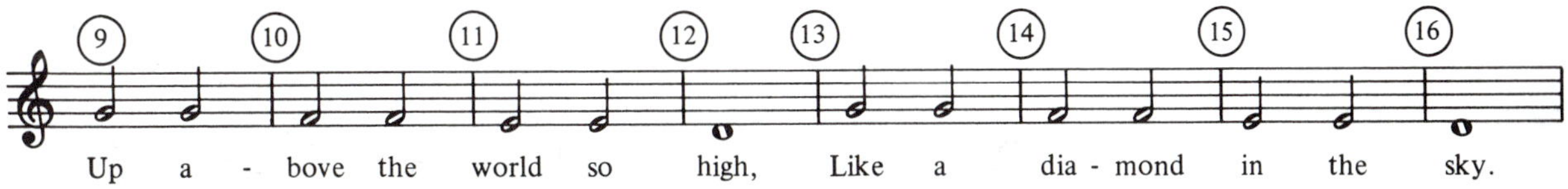

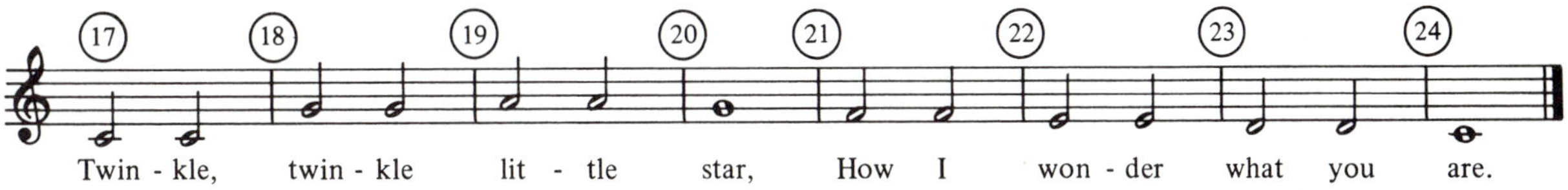

Rhythm Exercises

R11-1. For each of the rhythms in the left column, write an equivalent notation in the middle and right columns using the meters indicated.

SAMPLE

a.

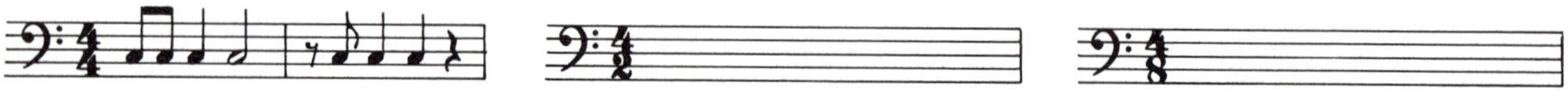

b.

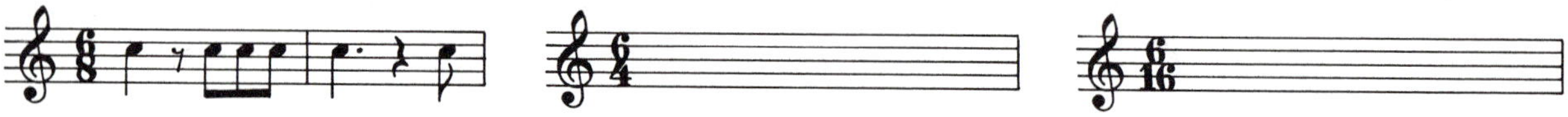

c.

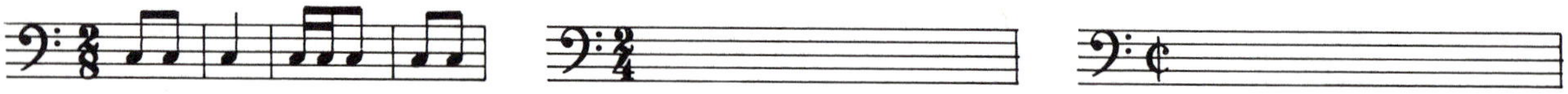

d.

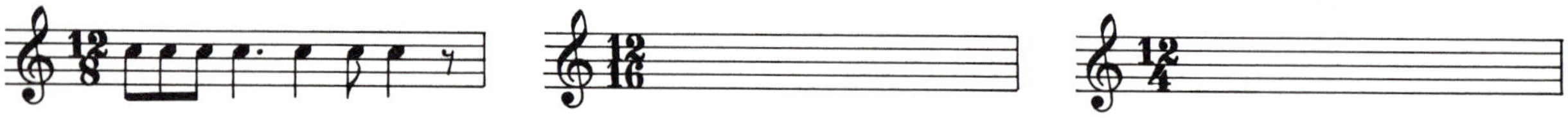

e.

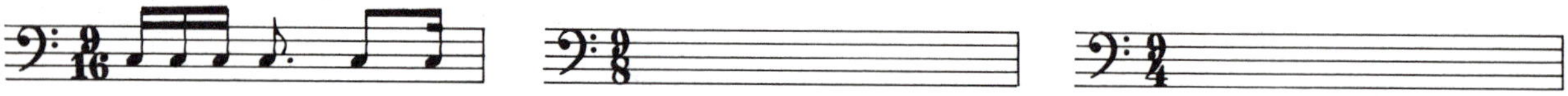

f.

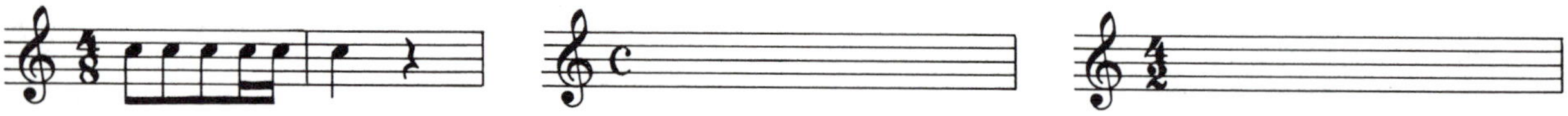

g.

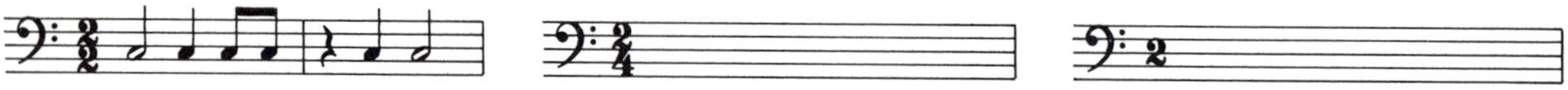

Name: ______________________

Instructor: ______________________

Date: ______________________

h.

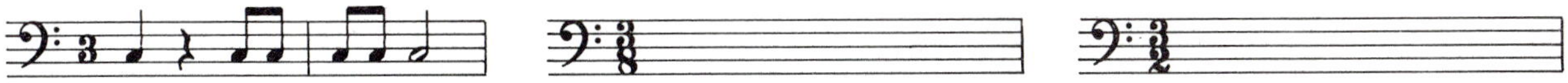

i.

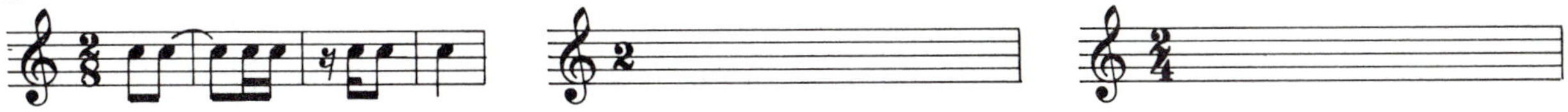

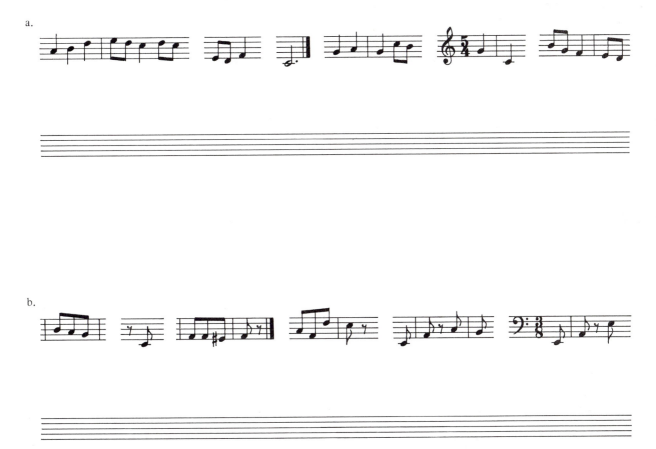

R11-2. Form a melody using the fragments provided. Only one ordering of these fragments results in measures that contain the correct number of beats.

a.

b.

R11-3. Notate the melodies indicated by the positioning of the pitch names in relation to the counting syllables. Use only unisons, seconds, thirds, and fourths as melodic intervals, unless an arrow guides you to use a larger interval. Do not add rests.

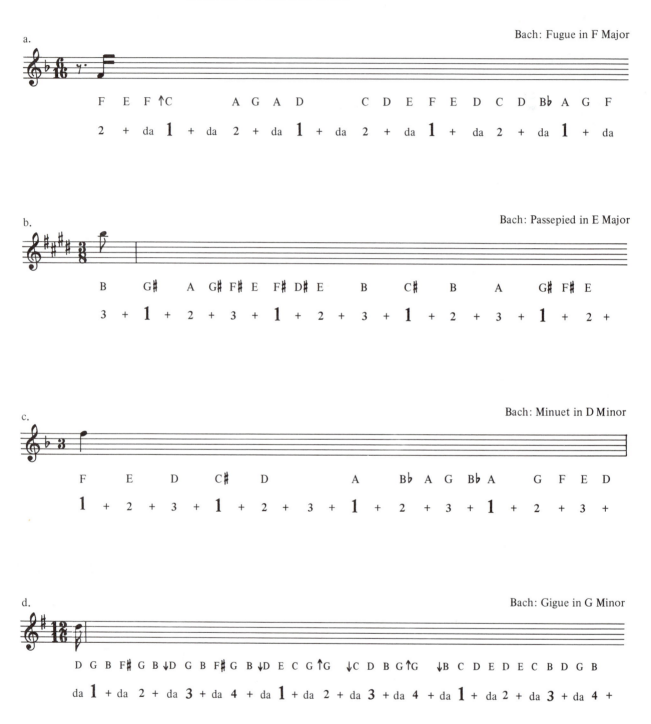

a. Bach: Fugue in F Major

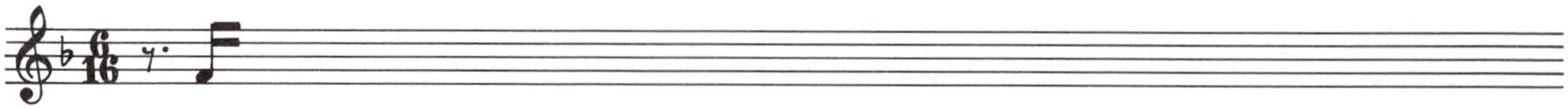

F E F ↑C A G A D C D E F E D C D B♭ A G F

2 + da 1 + da 2 + da 1 + da 2 + da 1 + da 2 + da 1 + da

b. Bach: Passepied in E Major

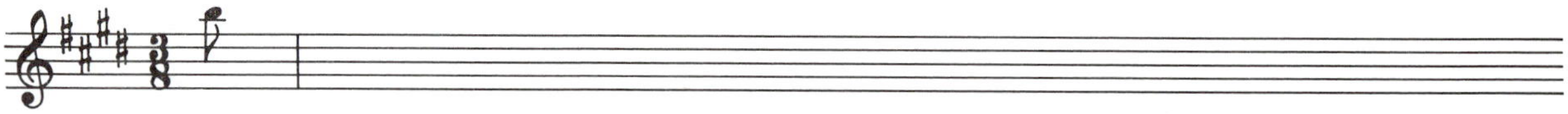

B G♯ A G♯ F♯ E F♯ D♯ E B C♯ B A G♯ F♯ E

3 + 1 + 2 + 3 + 1 + 2 + 3 + 1 + 2 + 3 + 1 + 2 +

c. Bach: Minuet in D Minor

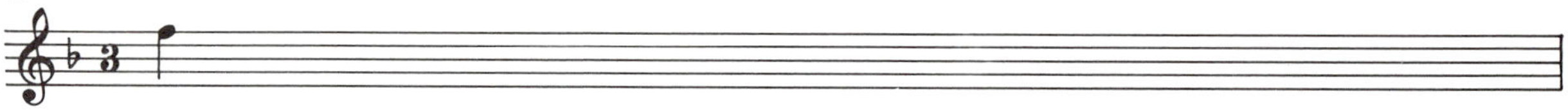

F E D C♯ D A B♭ A G B♭ A G F E D

1 + 2 + 3 + 1 + 2 + 3 + 1 + 2 + 3 + 1 + 2 + 3 +

d. Bach: Gigue in G Minor

D G B F♯ G B ↓D G B F♯ G B ↓D E C G ↑G ↓C D B G ↑G ↓B C D E D E C B D G B

da 1 + da 2 + da 3 + da 4 + da 1 + da 2 + da 3 + da 4 + da 1 + da 2 + da 3 + da 4 +

Name: ______________________

Instructor: ______________________

Date: ______________________

Audio Exercises

A11-1. Ten intervals will be performed, first as two successive pitches, then as two simultaneous pitches. Circle "Yes" if the interval is a perfect fourth, "No" if it is not.

a.	Yes	No	f.	Yes	No
b.	Yes	No	g.	Yes	No
c.	Yes	No	h.	Yes	No
d.	Yes	No	i.	Yes	No
e.	Yes	No	j.	Yes	No

A11-2. A perfect fourth or a perfect fifth will be performed, either ascending or descending. Indicate which of these two intervals is performed.

a.	Perfect Fourth	Perfect Fifth
b.	Perfect Fourth	Perfect Fifth
c.	Perfect Fourth	Perfect Fifth
d.	Perfect Fourth	Perfect Fifth
e.	Perfect Fourth	Perfect Fifth
f.	Perfect Fourth	Perfect Fifth
g.	Perfect Fourth	Perfect Fifth
h.	Perfect Fourth	Perfect Fifth
i.	Perfect Fourth	Perfect Fifth
j.	Perfect Fourth	Perfect Fifth

A11-3. A chord progression will be performed. Indicate which set of Roman numerals corresponds to the harmonies used.

a.	I–IV–I	I–V–I	I–IV–V
b.	I–IV–I	I–V–I	I–IV–V
c.	I–IV–I	I–V–I	I–IV–V
d.	I–IV–I	I–V–I	I–IV–V
e.	I–IV–I	I–V–I	I–IV–V
f.	I–IV–I	I–V–I	I–IV–V
g.	I–IV–I	I–V♯–I	I–IV–V♯
h.	I–IV–I	I–V♯–I	I–IV–V♯
i.	I–IV–I	I–V♯–I	I–IV–V♯
j.	I–IV–I	I–V♯–I	I–IV–V♯
k.	I–IV–I	I–V♯–I	I–IV–V♯
l.	I–IV–I	I–V♯–I	I–IV–V♯

A11-4. The progression I–V$^{(7)}$–I will be performed, either with or without the 7 in the V chord. Indicate whether the V chord was performed in $\begin{smallmatrix}5\\3\end{smallmatrix}$ or $\begin{smallmatrix}7\\5\\3\end{smallmatrix}$ position.

a. $\begin{smallmatrix}5\\3\end{smallmatrix}$ $\begin{smallmatrix}7\\5\\3\end{smallmatrix}$

b. $\begin{smallmatrix}5\\3\end{smallmatrix}$ $\begin{smallmatrix}7\\5\\3\end{smallmatrix}$

c. $\begin{smallmatrix}5\\3\end{smallmatrix}$ $\begin{smallmatrix}7\\5\\3\end{smallmatrix}$

d. $\begin{smallmatrix}5\\3\end{smallmatrix}$ $\begin{smallmatrix}7\\5\\3\end{smallmatrix}$

e. $\begin{smallmatrix}5\\3\end{smallmatrix}$ $\begin{smallmatrix}7\\5\\3\end{smallmatrix}$

f. $\begin{smallmatrix}5\\3\end{smallmatrix}$ $\begin{smallmatrix}7\\5\\3\end{smallmatrix}$

g. $\begin{smallmatrix}5\\3\end{smallmatrix}$ $\begin{smallmatrix}7\\5\\3\end{smallmatrix}$

h. $\begin{smallmatrix}5\\3\end{smallmatrix}$ $\begin{smallmatrix}7\\5\\3\end{smallmatrix}$

i. $\begin{smallmatrix}5\\3\end{smallmatrix}$ $\begin{smallmatrix}7\\5\\3\end{smallmatrix}$

j. $\begin{smallmatrix}5\\3\end{smallmatrix}$ $\begin{smallmatrix}7\\5\\3\end{smallmatrix}$

A11-5. Six chord progressions will be performed. The soprano pitch for the first chord of each progression will be stated before the progression is performed. In each case circle the score that shows the correct pitch notation for the soprano voice.

a.

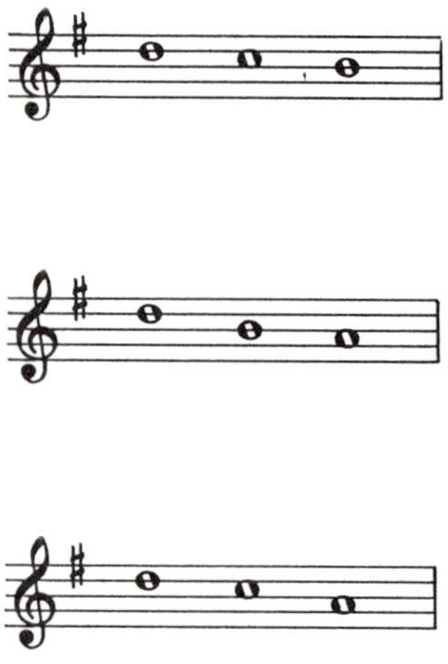

b.

c.

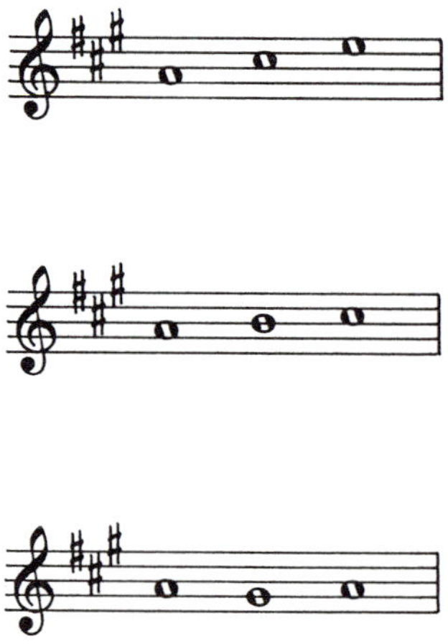

d.

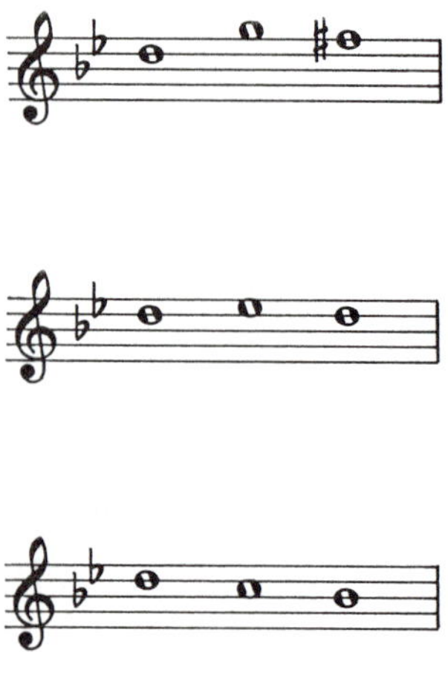

e.

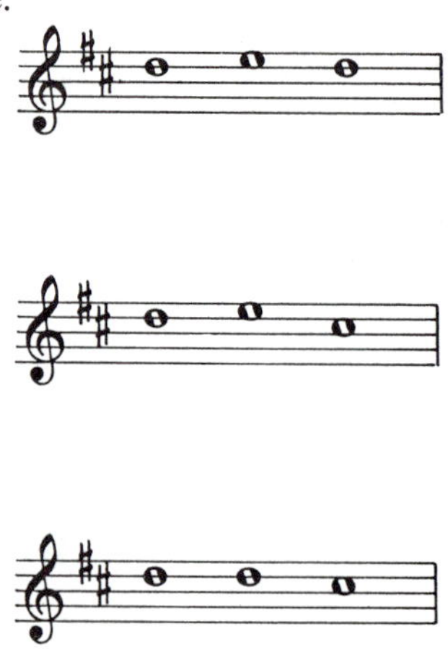

f.

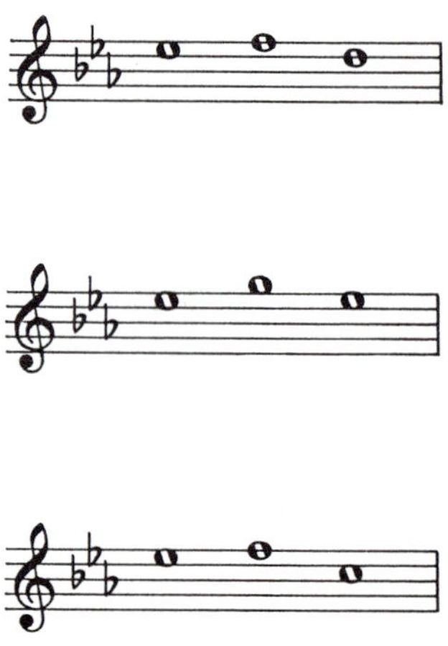

Name: ______________________
Instructor: ______________________
Date: ______________________

A11-6. Four rhythms will be performed. In each case circle the score that shows the correct notation.

a.

b.

c.

d.

Name: ____________________

Instructor: ____________________

Date: ____________________

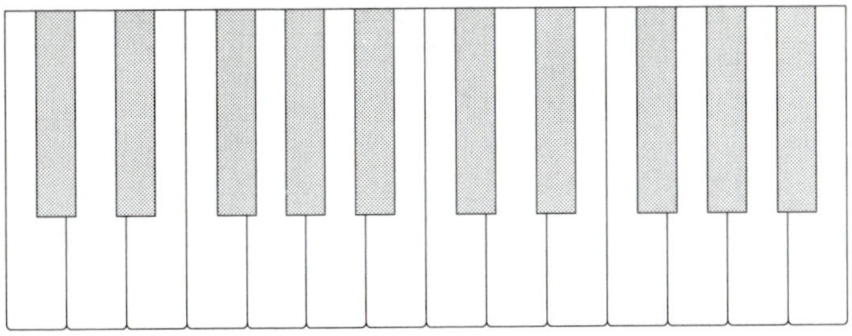

Mastery Test, Chapter 11

________ 1. Which of the chords I and V may harmonize $\hat{5}$?

X. I only Y. V only Z. I and V

________ 2. Which of the chords IV and V may harmonize $\hat{1}$?

X. IV only Y. V only Z. IV and V

________ 3. Which of the chords I, IV, and V is the least likely to end a phrase?

X. I Y. IV Z. V

________ 4. Which of the chord progressions IV–V, I–IV, and V–IV is the least successful?

X. IV–V Y. I–IV Z. V–IV

________ 5. Which of the following chord progressions is best suited to the melody $\hat{4}$–$\hat{5}$ when both chords are in root position?

X. IV–V Y. IV–I Z. I–V

________ 6. Which of the following chord progressions is best suited to the melody $\hat{1}$–$\hat{2}$ when both chords are in root position?

X. IV–V Y. IV–I Z. I–V

For Questions 7–9:

E major

______ 7. If the second and third notes of the melody shown are harmonized by the same chord, which chord would it be?
X. I Y. IV Z. V^7

______ 8. If the second and third notes of the melody shown are harmonized by different chords, which chords would they be?
X. I–V Y. IV–V Z. V^7–I

______ 9. If the fourth note of the melody shown is the last note of a phrase, which chord would best harmonize it?
X. I Y. IV Z. V

For Questions 10–12:

E♭ major

______ 10. Which two chords may harmonize the second note of the melody shown?
X. I and IV Y. IV and V^7 Z. I and V^7

______ 11. Of the two chords that may harmonize the second note of the melody shown, which one requires that the second note be dissonant?
X. I Y. IV Z. V^7

______ 12. If the measures shown appear at the end of a phrase, what type of cadence would likely occur?
X. Authentic Y. Plagal Z. Half

______ 13. Which time signature is equivalent to the symbol **2**?
X. $\frac{2}{2}$ Y. $\frac{2}{4}$ Z. $\frac{2}{8}$

______ 14. What kind of note should be inserted at the arrow to complete the measure?

X. Eighth note
Y. Sixteenth note
Z. Dotted eighth note

______ 15. What kind of rest should be inserted at the arrow to complete the measure?

X. Eighth rest
Y. Quarter rest
Z. Dotted quarter rest

Name: ______________________________

Instructor: ___________________________

Date: _______________________________

A chord progression will be performed. Indicate which set of Roman numerals corresponds to the harmonies used.

________ 16. X. I–IV–I   Y. I–V–I   Z. I–IV–V

________ 17. X. I–IV–I   Y. I–V♯–I   Z. I–IV–V♯

________ 18. The chord progression I–V(7)–I will be performed, either with or without the 7 in the V chord. Indicate whether the V chord was performed in $\begin{smallmatrix}5\\3\end{smallmatrix}$ or $\begin{smallmatrix}7\\5\\3\end{smallmatrix}$ position.

Y. $\begin{smallmatrix}5\\3\end{smallmatrix}$ Z. $\begin{smallmatrix}7\\5\\3\end{smallmatrix}$

________ 19. A chord progression whose soprano begins with the pitch A will be performed. Which score shows the correct pitch notation for the soprano?

X. 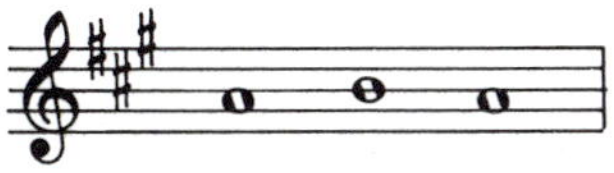

Y. 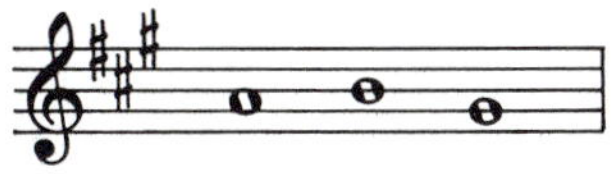

Z. 

________ 20. Which score shows the correct notation for the rhythm performed?

X. 

Y. 

Z. 

12

Harmonization: Writing Accompaniments

Terms and Concepts

thirty-second note	*D. C. al Fine*
thirty-second rest	*Dal Segno al Fine*
first and second endings	*D. S. al Fine*
Da Capo al Fine	*Fine*

PITCH

Constructing Chords for Accompaniments

Having explored how to select a suitable progression of chords to accompany a melody, we now consider how these chords should be written on the staff. Example 12-1 shows all of the versions of the I, IV, and V chords that you might want to employ in the key of C major. This selection can, of course, be transposed to any other major key. These chords are intended for a keyboard accompaniment, with three pitches in the right hand and one pitch in the left hand.

Example 12-1

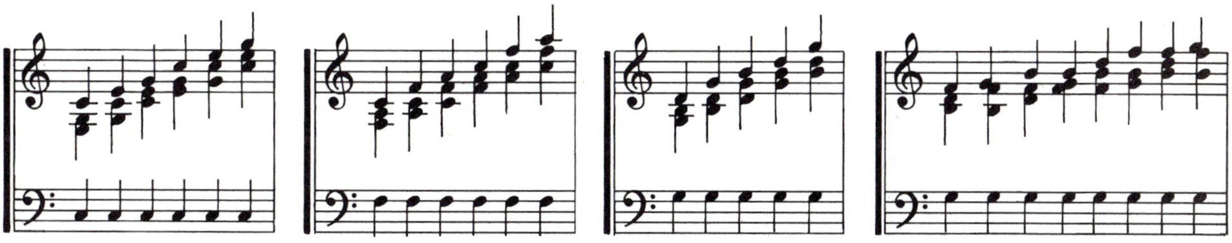

Versions of I · Versions of IV · Versions of V · Versions of V7

After the harmonies for a melody have been selected, an effective accompaniment can be composed by forming successions of these chords. The rules of voice leading are much more complicated than the guidelines below indicate, but by restricting ourselves to the I, IV, and V chords in root position, good accompaniments can result by following them.

Guidelines for Good Voice Leading

1. *The accompaniment may employ pitches as high as the melody pitch or pitches lower than the melody pitch, but should not extend above the melody pitch* (Example 12-2). Our ears hear the top and bottom pitches of a musical texture most distinctly. If the accompaniment extends higher than the melody that it accompanies, confusion could result concerning what the true melody is—the melody itself, or the soprano voice of the accompaniment. It is best for the accompaniment's soprano voice to stay in about the same range as that of the melody that it accompanies. Sometimes the accompaniment's soprano will double, or strike the same pitch as, the melody itself for extended periods. This is a reinforcement of the melody. Whoever sings the melody might appreciate it or even depend upon it. If a melody contains leaps, as in Example 12-2, it is possible that for one or two notes the accompaniment's soprano will be higher than the melody when the melody temporarily leaps down to a lower pitch.

Example 12-2

a. b.

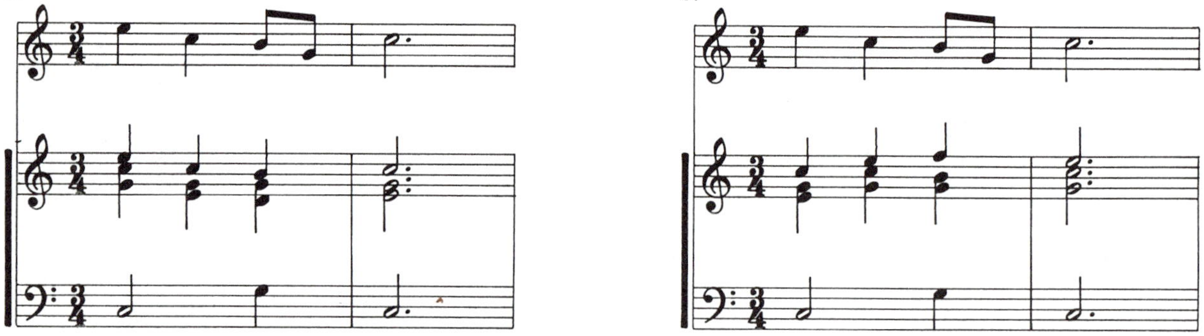

Good use of accompaniment

Poor use of accompaniment

2. *When a harmony persists for more than one beat, a different version of the same chord may be used* (Example 12-3). There will never be problems of voice leading if the pitch classes of the chord are repositioned in the right hand, so long as the left hand continues to play the chord's root. Leaps of thirds and fourths are common in such contexts. You may also proceed from V in $\begin{smallmatrix}5\\3\end{smallmatrix}$ position to V in $\begin{smallmatrix}7\\5\\3\end{smallmatrix}$ position. The opposite—leading from V in $\begin{smallmatrix}7\\5\\3\end{smallmatrix}$ position to V in $\begin{smallmatrix}5\\3\end{smallmatrix}$ position—is much less common, since then the dissonant seventh would be abandoned rather than resolved.

Example 12-3

a.

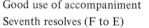

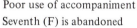

Good use of accompaniment
Seventh resolves (F to E)

b.

Poor use of accompaniment
Seventh (F) is abandoned

3. *Whenever possible, avoid leaps in the accompaniment's soprano voice when moving from one harmony to another* (Example 12-4). Not only will this rule help create a pleasant, smooth accompaniment, it will also help prevent parallel fifths and octaves.

Example 12-4

a.

Good use of accompaniment

b.

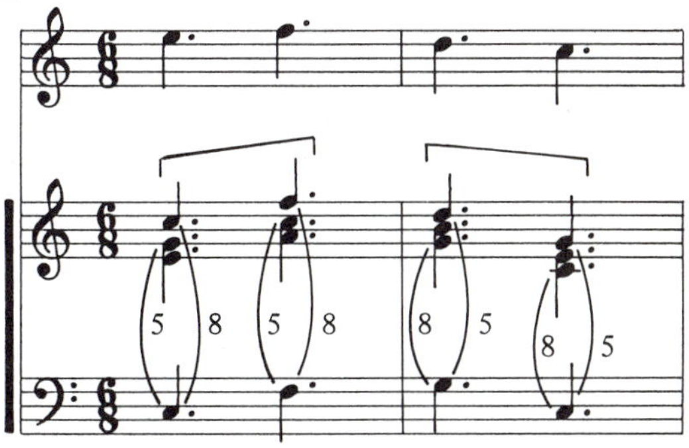

Poor use of accompaniment

4. *In moving from IV to V, either retain the same pitch or use descending motion in each of the accompaniment's three upper voices* (Example 12-5). This rule is essential if parallel fifths and octaves are to be avoided in the accompaniment.

Example 12-5

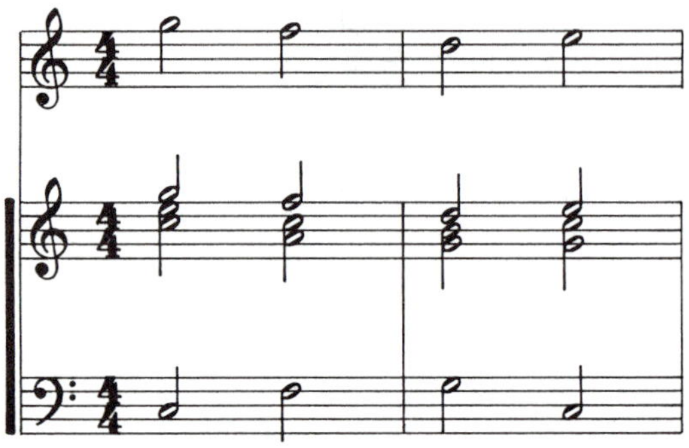

I IV V I

Good use of accompaniment

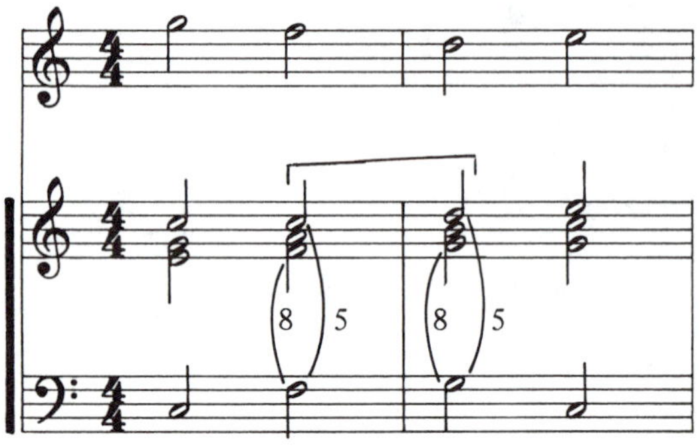

I IV V I

Poor use of accompaniment

5. *When the seventh of a* V^7 *chord appears in the soprano, it should resolve downward by step to* $\hat{3}$ (Example 12-6). Dissonant pitches, especially when in the exposed soprano voice, demand careful attention. In C major, for example, when the F of a V^7 chord is in the soprano, both the E and G of the I chord are stepwise alternatives for the voice leading. E should be selected, as in Example 12-6a, instead of G because of the tendency of the F—a diminished fifth against the leading tone B—to resolve downward. When the seventh of a V^7 chord appears in an inner voice, its tendency to resolve downward is sometimes not fulfilled. You do not need to give special attention to a seventh in an inner voice. The *pitch class* that resolves the seventh will be present in the following I chord, even if sometimes it is positioned an octave away from where you might expect it.

Example 12-6

a.

Good use of accompaniment

b.

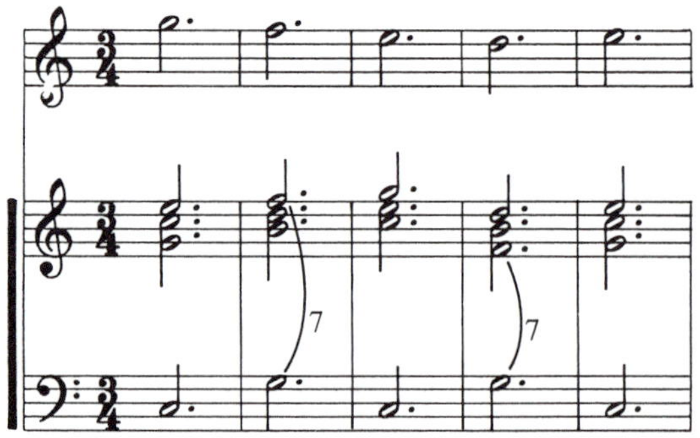

Poor use of accompaniment

A Sample Harmonization

Using the guidelines illustrated in Examples 12-2 through 12-6, Example 12-7 shows a suitable accompaniment for "Pop Goes the Weasel" based on the harmonic choices that were made in Chapter 11.

Example 12-7

Harmonization Enlivened by Rhythm

The chords used to demonstrate harmonization up to this point have all conformed to the models shown in Example 12-1. The clarity of the voice leading that results is very useful in the beginning stages of learning how to harmonize effectively. Once a solid harmonization is achieved, however, it can be enlivened using a variety of techniques that spread the various pitches of the right-hand part over the beat or beats during which a given chord is to be held. In this way, the harmonization attains a sense of rhythmic vitality that may help the accompaniment project a mood appropriate for the melody's text. The examples below demonstrate these procedures.

Example 12-8a shows the first two measures of the harmonization presented in Example 12-7. Since the chord choices and voice leading are correct, we can modify this progression with confidence, in the process making the harmonization more interesting and lively. Example 12-8b shows how the three right-hand pitches may be spread out over the three subdivisions of each beat in compound meter. Such arpeggiations ascend more often than descend. In Example 12-8c the rests in the right hand allow for a clearer projection of the bass, while the three right-hand pitches are divided between the second and third subdivisions of each beat. Finally, Example 12-8d shows an even livelier accompaniment. The increased sound resulting from so many notes being performed might be especially appropriate when a large number of singers is being accompanied.

Example 12-8

a.

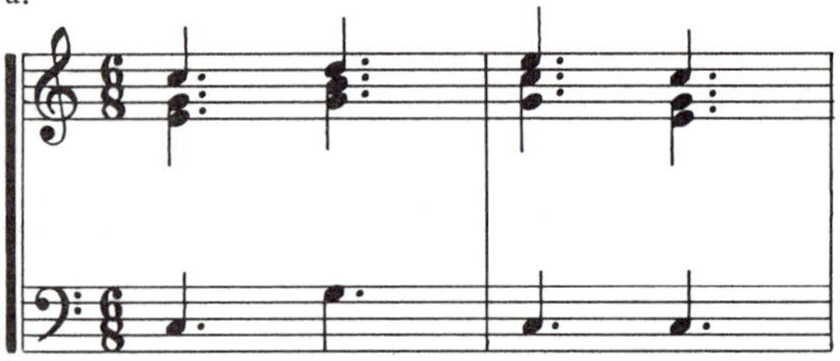

b.

c.

d.

The four versions of a I–IV–V^7–I progression shown in Example 12-9 demonstrate some of the most useful patternings found in simple meters. Example 12-9b is smooth and gentle. Because each chord is held for two beats, four eighth notes can be performed. Since the right-hand part of Example 12-9a contains only three pitches, one of those pitches is repeated in this enlivened version. We saw in Example 12-8c that rests in the right-hand part may coincide with the arrival of new bass pitches. In Example 12-9c bass and right-hand pitches alternate on consecutive beats, while in Example 12-9d the bass is held as the right-hand pitches are arpeggiated beginning on the second half of the first and third beats of each measure.

Example 12-9

The basic chords of Examples 12-8a and 12-9a remain correct and useful in accompaniment. As long as maintaining good voice leading remains challenging, it is not yet time to compose an enlivened accompaniment. But once you have succeeded in creating a correct harmonization using the basic chords of Example 12-1, you should begin to experiment with various alternatives.

Pitch exercises for Chapter 12 are on pages 415–419.

RHYTHM

Thirty-Second Notes and Rests

thirty-second note

thirty-second rest

As we have seen, one flag or beam is used to form an eighth note, whose value is half that of a quarter note. Two flags or beams are used to form a sixteenth note, whose value is half that of an eighth note. Adding a third flag or beam results in a ***thirty-second note.*** Not surprisingly, two thirty-second notes fill the same musical time as one sixteenth note, four thirty-second notes fill the same musical time as one eighth note, and eight thirty-second notes fill a quarter-note beat. Likewise, the ***thirty-second rest*** resembles eighth and sixteenth rests and fills one-eighth of a quarter-note beat. These notational symbols are shown in Example 12-10.

Example 12-10

Thirty-second notes (flags) Thirty-second notes (beams) Thirty-second rest

Double-Dotting

Like flags and beams, augmentation dots can be applied more than once. Adding one augmentation dot increases the time value of a note by one half. Adding a second dot adds an additional one quarter to the note value. For example, a half note with two augmentation dots fills three and one half beats: the time value of the half note is two beats (2), to which half of two (1) and a quarter of two (½) are added to attain the total value of three and one-half beats (3½). Example 12-11 shows the equivalents of several common double-dotted notes.

Example 12-11

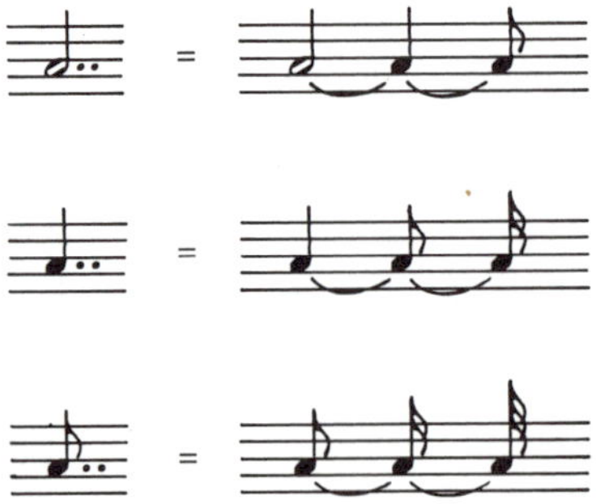

Notes that contain two augmentation dots can never appear alone. Another note or a rest is required to complete the measure or beat, as Example 12-12 demonstrates.

Example 12-12

Space-Saving Conventions

Composers attempt to minimize the effort, paper, and ink that music notation requires. We have already seen how repeat signs can be used when a passage of music is to be played a second time without changes. If changes do occur, they are usually at the end of the material that is repeated, that is, at the cadence. In such cases, it is appropriate to use ***first and second endings,*** alternative ways to proceed at the end of the material that is repeated. Each ending is used once. Brackets are placed above the score to mark first and second endings. Placing "1." and "2." inside the brackets indicates that the material under the first bracket is to be played the first time only, while the material under the second bracket is to be played the second time only. A repeat sign will appear at the right edge of the first ending. When the melody is repeated, the performer will skip the first ending and proceed directly to the second ending.

first & second endings

In Example 12-13, the first ending concludes with $\hat{2}$ in the soprano, a likely spot for a half cadence using the V harmony. In the second ending, the soprano concludes with $\hat{1}$, to be accompanied by a perfect authentic cadence to I. It is common for antecedent and consequent phrases (introduced in Chapter 9) to differ only at their cadences. Observe how the measures are numbered when first and second endings are used.

Example 12-13

Notated:

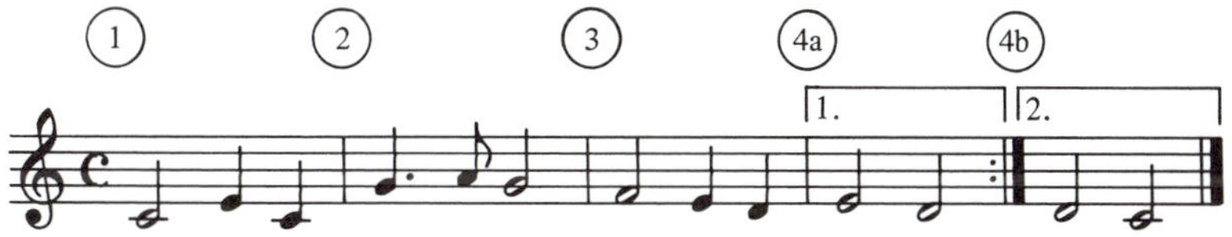

Performed:

Da Capo al Fine

D. C. al Fine

Dal Segno al Fine

D. S. al Fine

Fine

When two performances of the same material are to be separated by some other music, composers will generally use the Italian terms ***Da Capo al Fine,*** sometimes abbreviated ***D. C. al Fine***, or ***Dal Segno al Fine,*** abbreviated ***D. S. al Fine. Da Capo*** means, literally, "from the beginning" and thus instructs the performer to go to the first measure of the composition and to play the music until the word ***Fine*** (Italian for "the end") appears. If the composer wishes for some other earlier point to begin the repetition, the words *Dal Segno* ("from the sign") instruct the performer to return to the point where a sign (𝄋) has been inserted in the score and to proceed *al Fine* ("to the end," the point where the word *Fine* appears). Examples of both are displayed in Example 12-14.

Example 12-14

Notated:

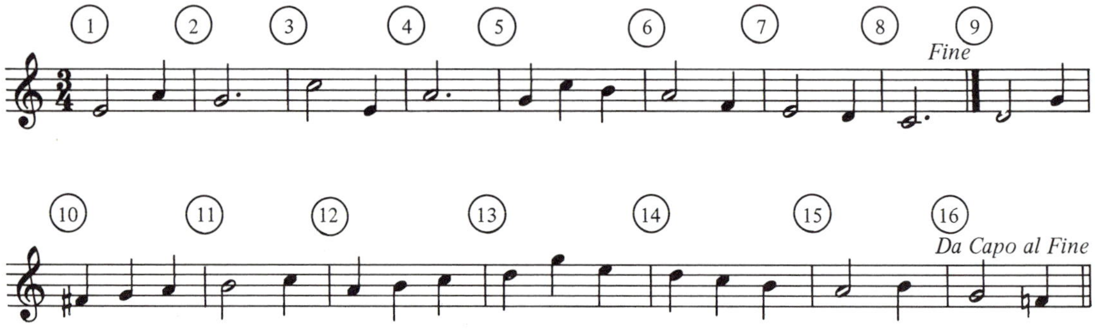

Performed: Measures 1–16; 1–8.

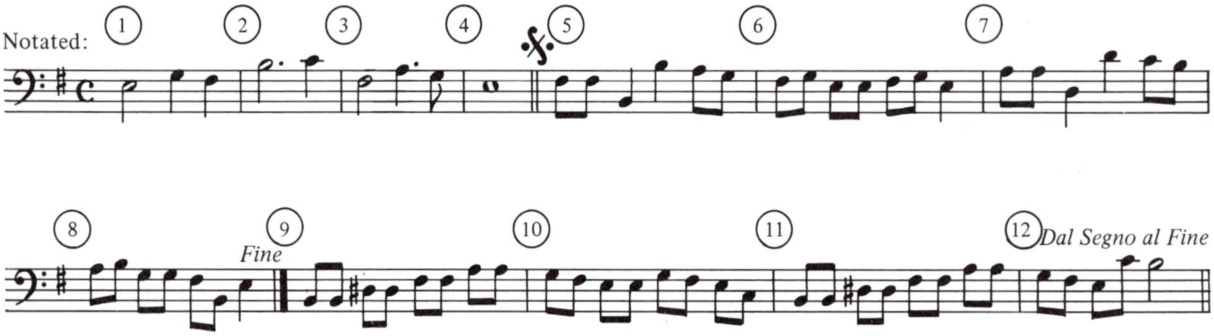

Performed: Measures 1–12; 5–8.

Rhythm exercises for Chapter 12 are on pages 420–423.

LABORATORY

L12-1.a. Perform the following chord progressions at the keyboard. Underneath each chord, write in the appropriate Roman numeral. Though the tempo that you choose might be slow, make sure that it is steady—that every chord is of the same duration. Begin thinking about the next chord during beats two through four of the measure that precedes it.

1.

2.

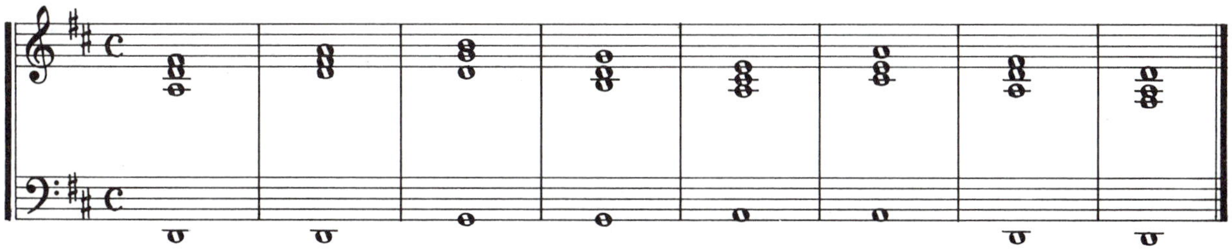

b. Perform the following melodies at the keyboard. Recommended fingerings are included. Slow to moderate tempos should be selected.

Beethoven: Symphony No. 1

1.

Beethoven: Piano Sonata Op. 13

2.

Schubert: Impromptu Op. 90, No. 1

3.

Schubert: Ländler D. 366, No. 14

4.

L12-2. Determine which scale degrees the given pitch classes form in the key indicated. Choose appropriate harmonies—I, IV, or V—and perform them as four-note chords, with the given pitch classes in the soprano. In some cases, alternative solutions are possible.

a. D♭ major: G♭–F	**b.** G♭ major: C♭–B♭
c. F major: C–B♭	**d.** A major: E–F♯
e. E♭ major: E♭–F	**f.** D major: B–A
g. G major: C–D	**h.** E major: F♯–G♯
i. B major: D♯–C♯	**j.** A♭ major: A♭–G
k. F♯ major: G♯–A♯	**l.** B♭ major: A–B♭

L12-3. Sing one of the following intervals, either ascending or descending: minor third, major third, perfect fourth, or perfect fifth. Ask a classmate to identify the interval. Then have the classmate sing one of these intervals, and you identify it.

L12-4. The following melodies are accompanied by a variety of harmonies. A student or the instructor could play the keyboard part while other students sing the melody. You may wish to sing the melodies one or two octaves lower than notated, though the accompaniment should be performed as written.

a.

Pop Goes the Weasel

Twinkle, Twinkle Little Star

b.

Twin - kle, twin - kle lit - tle star, How I won - der what you are.
Up a - bove the world so high, Like a dia - mond in the sky.
Twin - kle, twin - kle lit - tle star, How I won - der what you are.

L12-5. The following compositions are for two voices. Sing the scale-degree number, or the syllable "raised," that corresponds to each pitch, as indicated. If necessary, transpose the entire score up or down one octave.

a. 

b. 

L12-6. Write in the counting syllables below the notated rhythms. Then perform each by clapping the rhythm or playing the pitch C or F at the keyboard, as notated, while pronouncing the counting syllables aloud.

Sample

a.

b.

c.

L12-7. Write in the counting syllables below the notated rhythms. Then perform them by dividing the class into two groups, with each group clapping one part while pronouncing the counting syllables aloud. Alternatively, individual students may perform both parts simultaneously at the keyboard, pronouncing the counting syllables aloud while the index fingers strike the notated pitches.

a.

b.

L12-8. This exercise requires that a student or the instructor serve as the performer at a keyboard.

a. The performer plays two pitches in either ascending or descending order, and then plays them together. Indicate whether the interval performed is a minor third, major third, perfect fourth, or perfect fifth.

b. The performer plays one of the following three chord progressions. Taking turns, students indicate which progression was performed. (When the tonic is minor, substitute V♯ for V.)

I–IV–I–V
I–V–I–V
I–IV–V–I

c. The performer plays the chord progression I–$V^{(7)}$, either with or without the 7 in the V chord. The soprano pitch of the I chord may be $\hat{1}$, $\hat{3}$, or $\hat{5}$, as announced by the performer. Students, taking turns, indicate which scale degree serves as the soprano pitch for the V chord. The choices are $\hat{2}$, $\hat{4}$, $\hat{5}$, and $\hat{7}$.

Audio exercises for Chapter 12 are on pages 424–426.

Name: ______________________
Instructor: ______________________
Date: ______________________

EXERCISES

Pitch Exercises

P12-1. Each accompaniment below contains a flaw. Indicate the error and compose an alternative accompaniment on the system provided. If you wish, use eighth notes, rests, and other variants to enliven your revised accompaniments.

SAMPLE

a.

b.

c.

d.

e.

f.

g.

Name: ______________________

Instructor: ______________________

Date: ______________________

h.

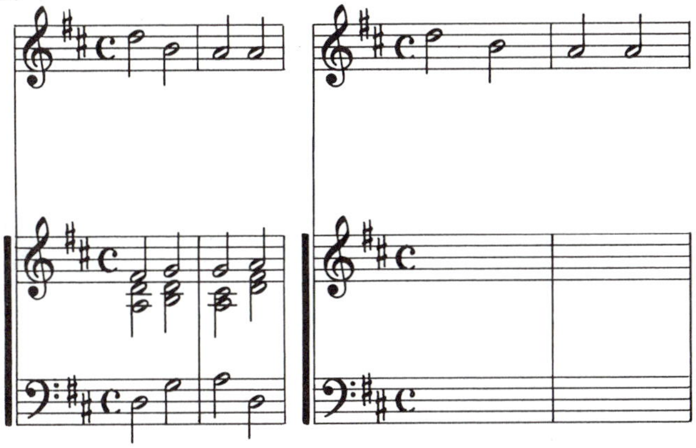

i.

j.

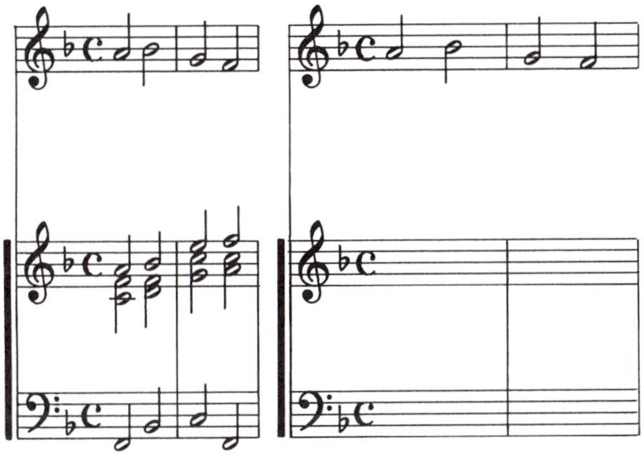

k.

P12-2. Compose an accompaniment for the melody "Twinkle, Twinkle Little Star," using the selection of chords from Chapter 11, Pitch Exercise P11-3e. Pay careful attention to voice leading.

Twinkle, Twinkle Little Star

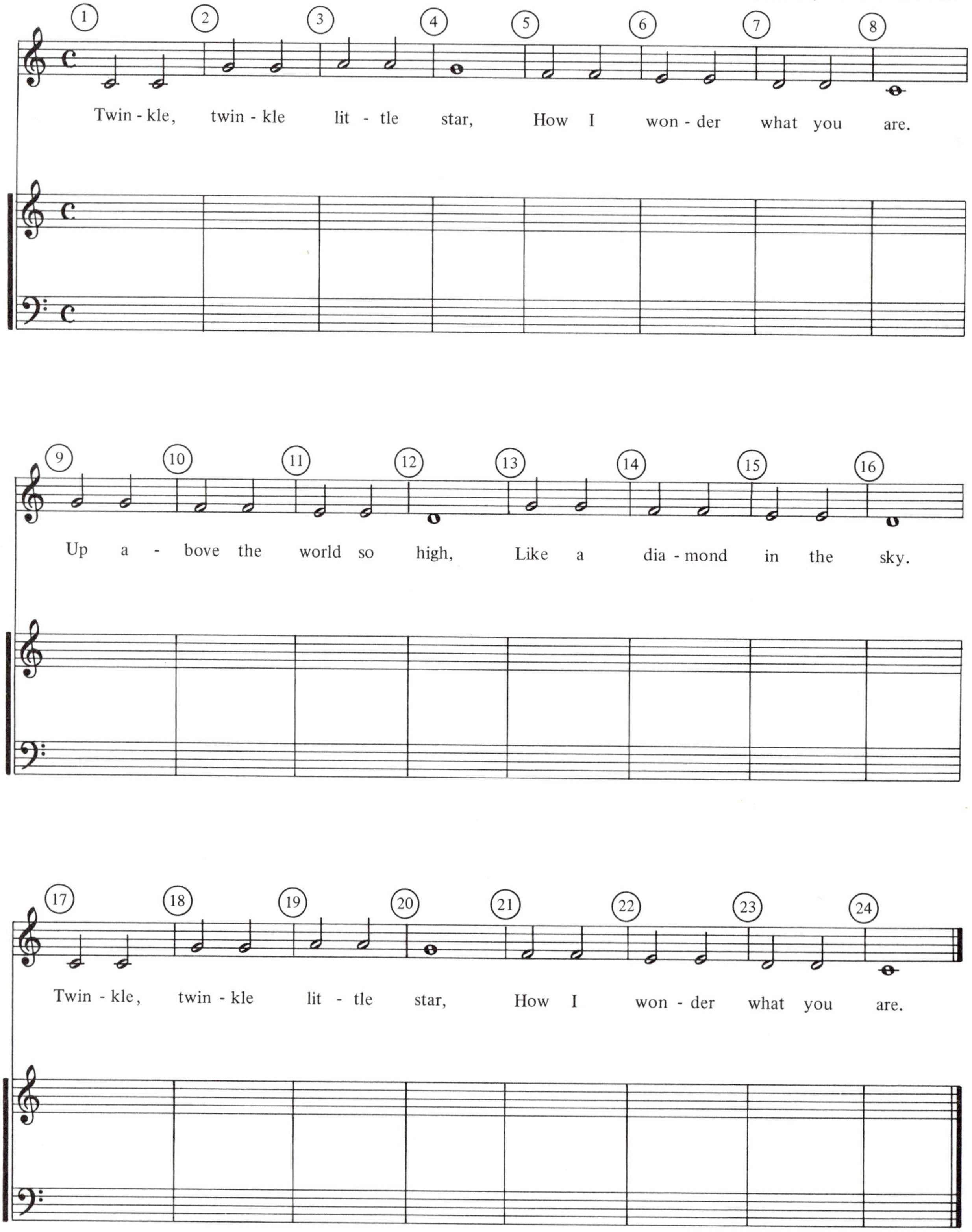

Name: ______________________

Instructor: ______________________

Date: ______________________

P12-3. Compose an accompaniment for the melody "Walking in the Green Grass," first selecting suitable harmonies (I and V in alternation, with one, two, or four chords per measure) and then forming the appropriate chords, paying careful attention to voice leading.

Walking in the Green Grass

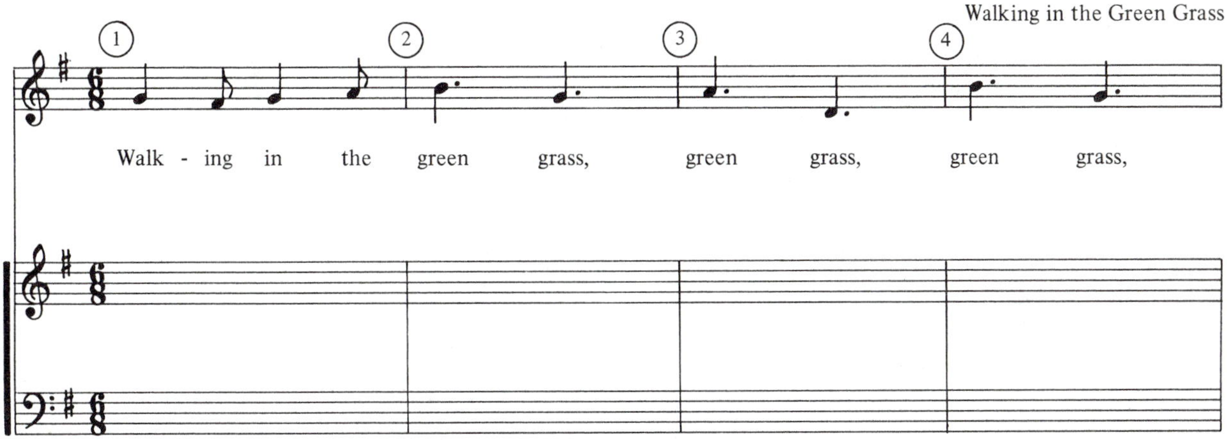

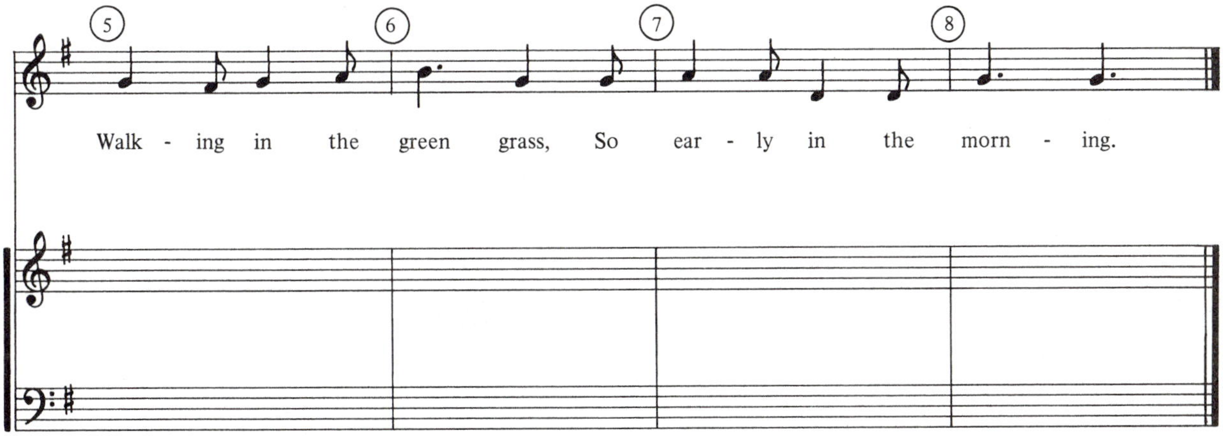

Rhythm Exercises

R12-1. Rewrite each of the melodies below on the staves provided. In place of any abbreviating symbols, write the measures a second time at the appropriate spot using score notation.

a.

b.

Name: ______________________________

Instructor: ___________________________

Date: _______________________________

c.

R12-2. Form a melody using the fragments provided. Only one ordering of these fragments results in measures that contain the correct number of beats.

a.

b.

R12-3. Notate the melodies indicated by the positioning of the pitch names in relation to the counting syllables. The midpoint between syllables is indicated by a dot in some of these exercises. Use only unisons, seconds, thirds, and fourths as melodic intervals, unless an arrow guides you to use a larger interval. Do not add rests.

Beethoven: Sonata Op. 2, No. 2

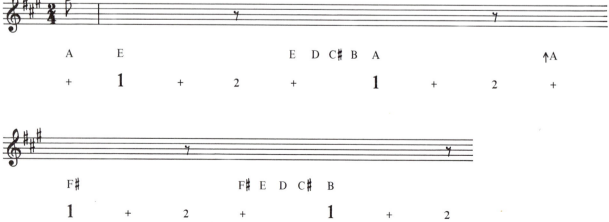

a.

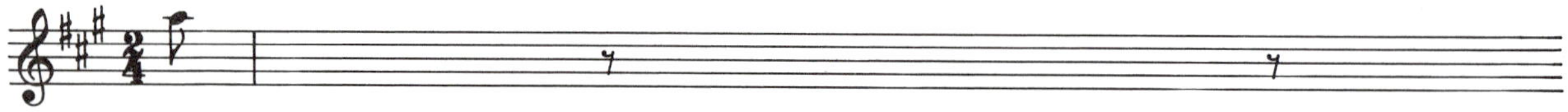

A E E D C♯ B A ↑A

\+ 1 + 2 + 1 + 2 +

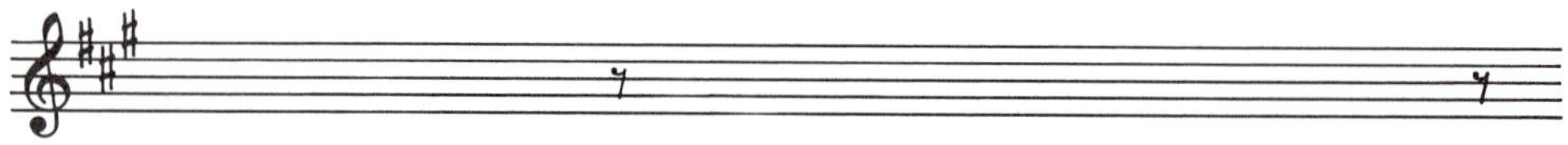

F♯ F♯ E D C♯ B

1 + 2 + 1 + 2

Name: ______________________________

Instructor: __________________________

Date: _______________________________

Beethoven: Sonata Op. 13 (Pathétique)

b.

C C D E♭ E♭ D

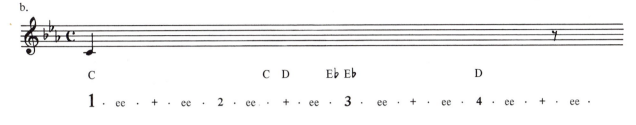

1 · ee · + · ee · 2 · ee · + · ee · 3 · ee · + · ee · 4 · ee · + · ee ·

Brahms: Intermezzo Op. 117, No. 2

c.

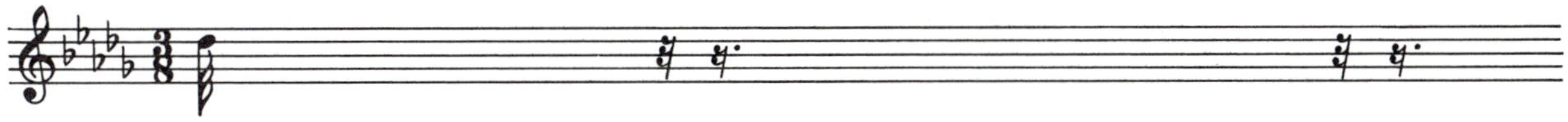

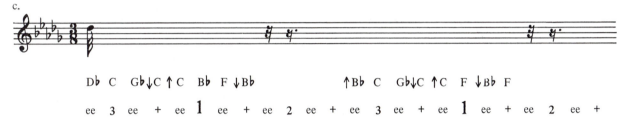

D♭ C G♭↓C ↑C B♭ F ↓B♭ ↑B♭ C G♭↓C ↑C F ↓B♭ F

ee 3 ee + ee 1 ee + ee 2 ee + ee 3 ee + ee 1 ee + ee 2 ee +

Chopin: Nocturne Op. 15, No. 2

d.

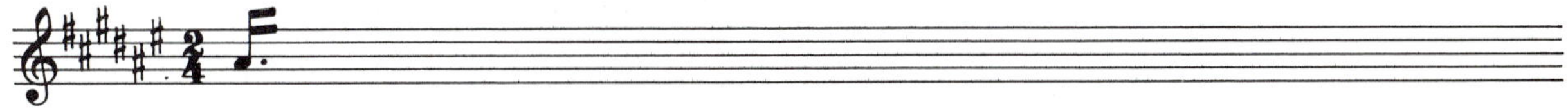

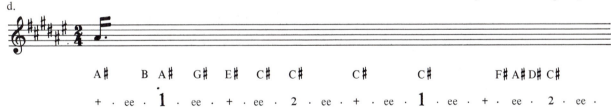

A♯ B A♯ G♯ E♯ C♯ C♯ C♯ C♯ F♯ A♯ D♯ C♯

+ · ee · 1 · ee · + · ee · 2 · ee · + · ee · 1 · ee · + · ee · 2 · ee ·

Audio Exercises

A12-1. A minor third, major third, perfect fourth, or perfect fifth will be performed, either ascending or descending. Indicate which of these intervals is performed.

a.	Minor Third	Major Third	Perfect Fourth	Perfect Fifth
b.	Minor Third	Major Third	Perfect Fourth	Perfect Fifth
c.	Minor Third	Major Third	Perfect Fourth	Perfect Fifth
d.	Minor Third	Major Third	Perfect Fourth	Perfect Fifth
e.	Minor Third	Major Third	Perfect Fourth	Perfect Fifth
f.	Minor Third	Major Third	Perfect Fourth	Perfect Fifth
g.	Minor Third	Major Third	Perfect Fourth	Perfect Fifth
h.	Minor Third	Major Third	Perfect Fourth	Perfect Fifth
i.	Minor Third	Major Third	Perfect Fourth	Perfect Fifth
j.	Minor Third	Major Third	Perfect Fourth	Perfect Fifth

A12-2. A chord progression will be performed. Indicate which set of Roman numerals corresponds to the harmonies used.

a.	I–IV–I–V	I–V–I–V	I–IV–V–I
b.	I–IV–I–V	I–V–I–V	I–IV–V–I
c.	I–IV–I–V	I–V–I–V	I–IV–V–I
d.	I–IV–I–V	I–V–I–V	I–IV–V–I
e.	I–IV–I–V	I–V–I–V	I–IV–V–I
f.	I–IV–I–V	I–V–I–V	I–IV–V–I
g.	I–IV–I–V♯	I–V♯–I–V♯	I–IV–V♯–I
h.	I–IV–I–V♯	I–V♯–I–V♯	I–IV–V♯–I
i.	I–IV–I–V♯	I–V♯–I–V♯	I–IV–V♯–I
j.	I–IV–I–V♯	I–V♯–I–V♯	I–IV–V♯–I
k.	I–IV–I–V♯	I–V♯–I–V♯	I–IV–V♯–I
l.	I–IV–I–V♯	I–V♯–I–V♯	I–IV–V♯–I

A12-3. The chord progression I–V$^{(7)}$ will be performed, either with or without the 7 in the V chord. The soprano pitch of the I chord is given. Indicate which scale degree serves as the soprano pitch for the V chord.

a.	I soprano is $\hat{3}$.	V soprano is:	$\hat{2}$	$\hat{4}$	$\hat{5}$	$\hat{7}$
b.	I soprano is $\hat{5}$.	V soprano is:	$\hat{2}$	$\hat{4}$	$\hat{5}$	$\hat{7}$
c.	I soprano is $\hat{3}$.	V soprano is:	$\hat{2}$	$\hat{4}$	$\hat{5}$	$\hat{7}$
d.	I soprano is $\hat{1}$.	V soprano is:	$\hat{2}$	$\hat{4}$	$\hat{5}$	$\hat{7}$
e.	I soprano is $\hat{5}$.	V soprano is:	$\hat{2}$	$\hat{4}$	$\hat{5}$	$\hat{7}$
f.	I soprano is $\hat{1}$.	V soprano is:	$\hat{2}$	$\hat{4}$	$\hat{5}$	$\hat{7}$
g.	I soprano is $\hat{3}$.	V soprano is:	$\hat{2}$	$\hat{4}$	$\hat{5}$	$\hat{7}$
h.	I soprano is $\hat{3}$.	V soprano is:	$\hat{2}$	$\hat{4}$	$\hat{5}$	$\hat{7}$
i.	I soprano is $\hat{5}$.	V soprano is:	$\hat{2}$	$\hat{4}$	$\hat{5}$	$\hat{7}$
j.	I soprano is $\hat{1}$.	V soprano is:	$\hat{2}$	$\hat{4}$	$\hat{5}$	$\hat{7}$

Name: ______________________________

Instructor: __________________________

Date: _______________________________

A12-4. Six chord progressions will be performed. The bass pitch for the first chord of each progression will be stated before the progression is performed. In each case circle the score that shows the correct pitch notation for the bass voice.

a.

b.

c.

d.

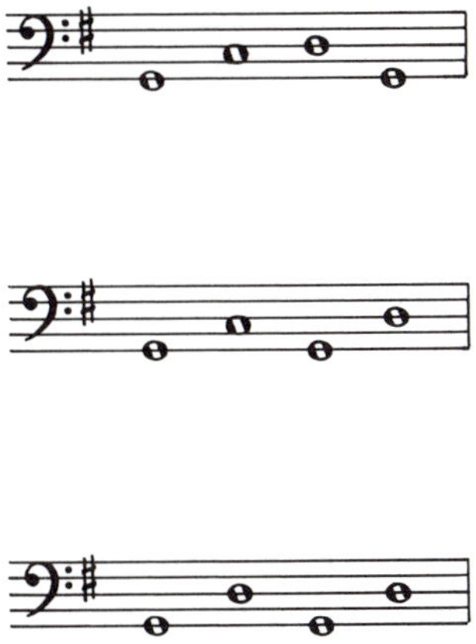

e.

f.

A12-5. Four rhythms will be performed. In each case circle the score that shows the correct notation.

a.

b.

c.

d.

Name: ______________________
Instructor: ______________________
Date: ______________________

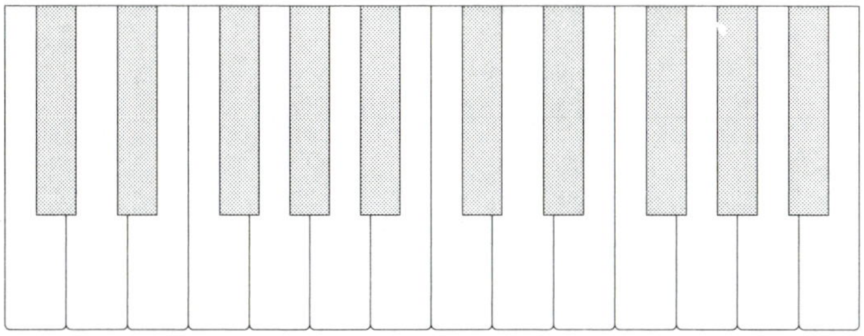

Mastery Test, Chapter 12

The fourteen chords in the following harmonization have been individually numbered. Consult this example to answer questions 1–12.

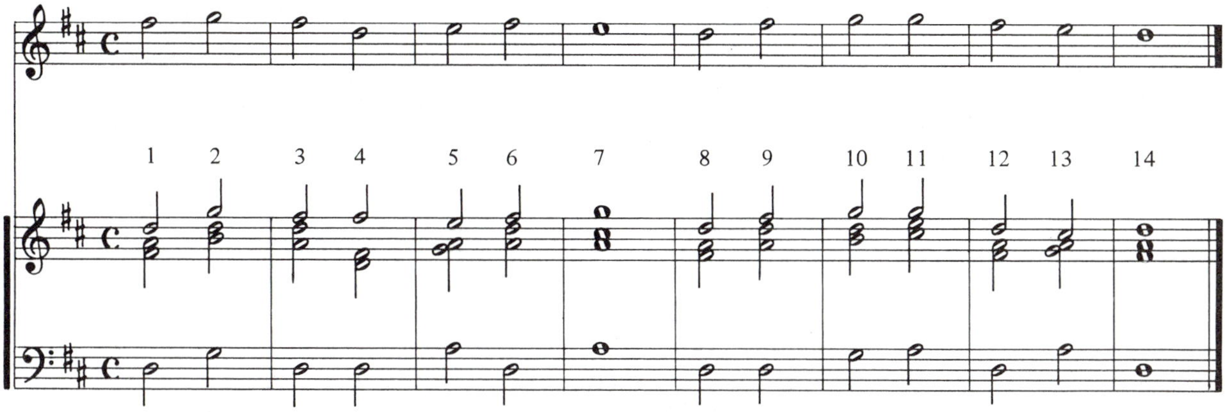

__________ 1. Is Chord 4 correctly constructed?
Y. Yes Z. No

__________ 2. Is Chord 5 correctly constructed?
Y. Yes Z. No

__________ 3. Is Chord 11 correctly constructed?
Y. Yes Z. No

__________ 4. Is Chord 13 correctly constructed?
Y. Yes Z. No

__________ 5. Is the voice leading from Chord 1 to Chord 2 correct?
Y. Yes Z. No

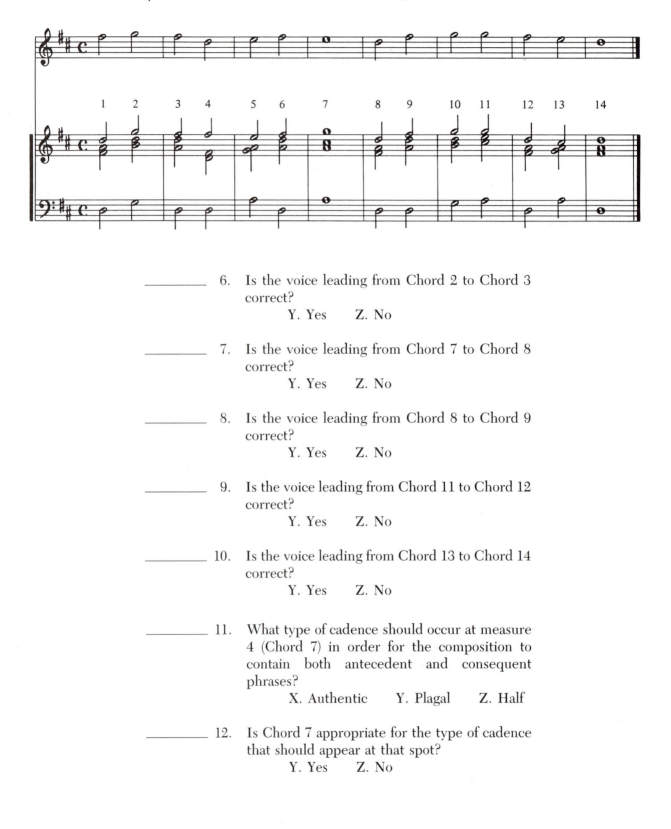

_________ 6. Is the voice leading from Chord 2 to Chord 3 correct?
Y. Yes Z. No

_________ 7. Is the voice leading from Chord 7 to Chord 8 correct?
Y. Yes Z. No

_________ 8. Is the voice leading from Chord 8 to Chord 9 correct?
Y. Yes Z. No

_________ 9. Is the voice leading from Chord 11 to Chord 12 correct?
Y. Yes Z. No

_________ 10. Is the voice leading from Chord 13 to Chord 14 correct?
Y. Yes Z. No

_________ 11. What type of cadence should occur at measure 4 (Chord 7) in order for the composition to contain both antecedent and consequent phrases?
X. Authentic Y. Plagal Z. Half

_________ 12. Is Chord 7 appropriate for the type of cadence that should appear at that spot?
Y. Yes Z. No

Name: ____________________
Instructor: ____________________
Date: ____________________

________ 13. What is the maximum number of thirty-second notes that may appear within one measure in $\frac{3}{4}$ meter?

X. 16 Y. 24 Z. 32

________ 14. What kind of note should be inserted at the arrow to complete the measure?

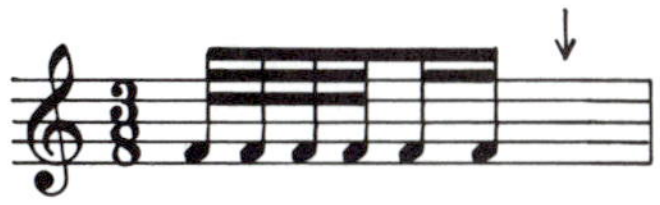

X. Eighth note
Y. Sixteenth note
Z. Thirty-second note

________ 15. What kind of rest should be inserted at the arrow to complete the measure?

X. Eighth rest
Y. Quarter rest
Z. Dotted eighth rest

A chord progression will be performed. Indicate which set of Roman numerals corresponds to the harmonies used.

________ 16. X. I–IV–I–V Y. I–V–I–V Z. I–IV–V–I

________ 17. X. I–IV–I–V♯ Y. I–V♯–I–V♯ Z. I–IV–V♯–I

________ 18. The chord progression I–V^7 will be performed. The soprano pitch of the I chord is $\hat{3}$. Which scale degree serves as the soprano pitch for the V^7 chord?

X. $\hat{4}$ Y. $\hat{5}$ Z. $\hat{7}$

________ 19. A chord progression whose bass begins with the pitch G will be performed. Which score shows the correct pitch notation for the bass?

X. 

Y. 

Z. 

________ 20. Which score shows the correct notation for the rhythm performed?

X. 

Y. 

Z. 

13

Harmonization and Melodic Embellishment

Terms and Concepts

embellishing note
- *passing note*
- *neighboring note*
- *incomplete neighboring note*

hemiola

PITCH

Harmonizing Melodies That Contain Passing Notes

In some melodies, such as "Pop Goes the Weasel" and "Twinkle, Twinkle Little Star," every pitch can be harmonized either as a consonant member of a I, IV, or V chord or as the dissonant seventh of a V^7 chord. Most melodies, however, contain additional pitches that embellish chord notes rather than function as chord notes themselves. These ***embellishing notes*** are often dissonant against the prevailing harmony. They will always be only a whole or half step away from the pitch or pitches that they embellish.

embellishing note

A ***passing note*** connects two harmonic notes in stepwise ascending or descending motion. Since root-position chords generally contain thirds, a passing note will often be used to connect two third-related pitches. Sometimes two passing notes in a row connect fourth-related pitches, as in a melodic ascent $\hat{5}$ $\hat{6}$ $\hat{7}$ $\hat{8}$ harmonized by a I chord.

passing note

The opening measures of "Polly Wolly Doodle" contain upbeat ascents from $\hat{1}$ through $\hat{2}$ to $\hat{3}$. When a $\hat{2}$ lasts for half a measure it might well deserve the harmonic support of V, but here it would be impossible to provide harmonic support for $\hat{2}$ without at the same time overburdening the upbeats with excessive harmonic activity. The two alternatives are shown in Example 13-1.

Example 13-1

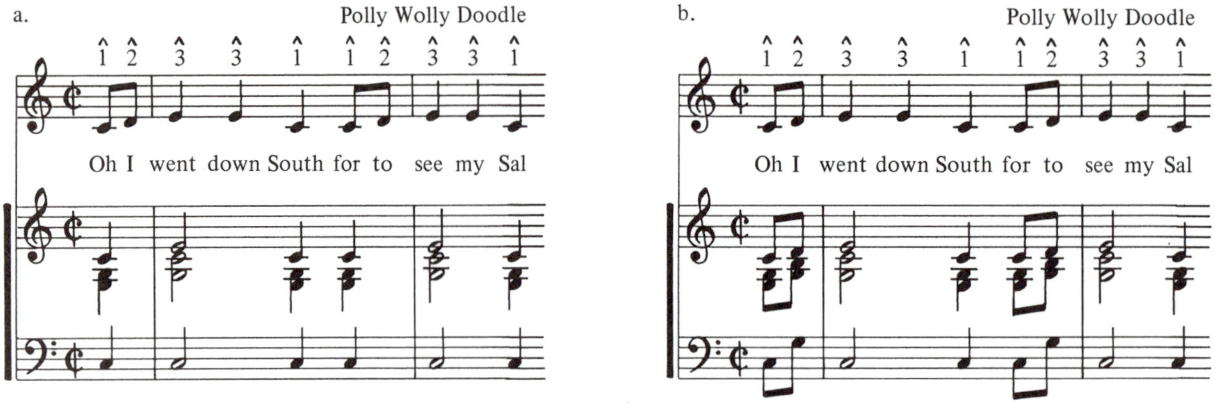

Good accompaniment

Weak accompaniment

Though each D in Example 13-1a forms a dissonant ninth with C, the root of the I harmony, and though playing a ninth in isolation sounds harsh, in this context the dissonance occurs without ill effect.

One might imagine that the dissonant pitches in Example 13-1a are allowed only because they appear in metrically weak positions. That is not the case. The third phrase of "She'll Be Comin' 'Round the Mountain" (Ex. 13-2) contains a passing note on the first beat of the last measure—D against C, E, and G in the accompaniment. It is not important where the dissonance occurs, only that the dissonance leads to consonance in stepwise motion.

Example 13-2

Harmonizing Melodies That Contain Neighboring Notes

neighboring note

The ***neighboring note*** embellishes a single pitch by sounding temporarily in its place. A neighboring note will always be either a half or whole step above or below a pitch that belongs to the harmony; that is, both "upper" and "lower" neighboring notes are possible. The pitch that is embellished appears both before and after the neighboring note.

The first phrase of "Camptown Races" contains an example of an upper neighboring note on the accented first beat of the last measure (Ex. 13-3a), where $\hat{6}$ sounds temporarily in place of $\hat{5}$. Observe in Example 13-3b that even without the neighboring note, an adequate melody would result, but the melody that contains the neighboring note is more interesting and better conveys the lively spirit of the text.

Example 13-3

a. Camptown Races

With neighboring note

b. Camptown Races

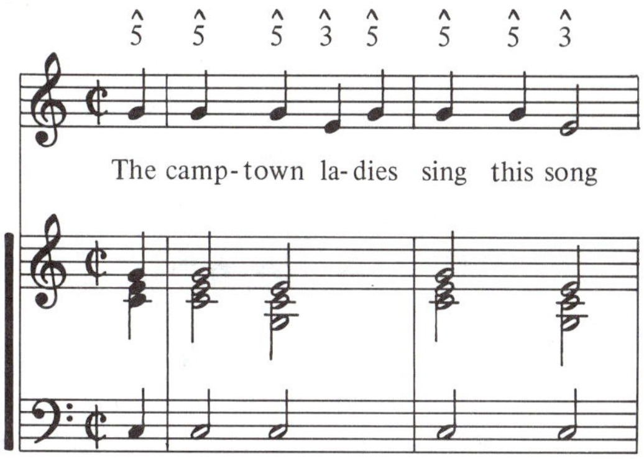

Without neighboring note

incomplete neighboring note

When the pitch that is embellished appears on only one side of the neighboring note (either before or after it), the embellishing pitch is called an ***incomplete neighboring note.*** Though the term might seem to imply that there is something inferior about this type of embellishment, that is not the case. The incomplete neighboring note occurs frequently in melodies that contain leaps, as in the first phrase of "She'll Be Comin' 'Round the Mountain," harmonized in Example 13-4. Because the framework of this melody consists of a series of leaps from one pitch of the tonic harmony to another, a pitch that functions as an incomplete neighbor (either following or preceding $\hat{5}$) can have a good effect. A sketch of the basic melodic contour, where open noteheads represent the pitches that are part of the I harmony and filled-in noteheads represent the embellishing notes, is shown beside the harmonization in Example 13-4.

Example 13-4

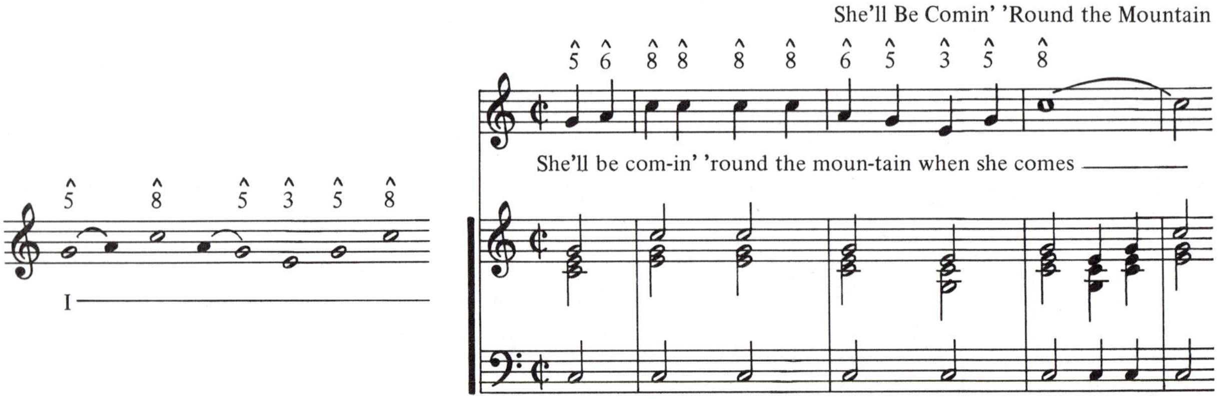

Contour of the phrase

Harmonization

A Sample Harmonization

The task of harmonizing a melody is thus more than merely a series of decisions regarding which of the chords that might support a given scale degree to use. Another central question is *whether* a particular melody pitch should be treated harmonically, or whether its primary function is to embellish another pitch or pitches. In the demonstration harmonization of "She'll Be Comin' 'Round the Mountain," shown in Example 13-5, the harmonic choices available for a given pitch might be rejected so that it may instead serve as a passing or neighboring note. Remember that such decisions are made through listening and experimentation. You should attempt all of your harmonizations at a keyboard, so that your ears help inform your decisions regarding which of several alternatives is the best.

As a first step, the harmonic choices for each pitch of the melody should be written down. In contrast to our procedure in Chapters 11 and 12, we may later choose to reject all the harmonic alternatives for a given pitch, treating it instead as an embellishing note.

Example 13-5

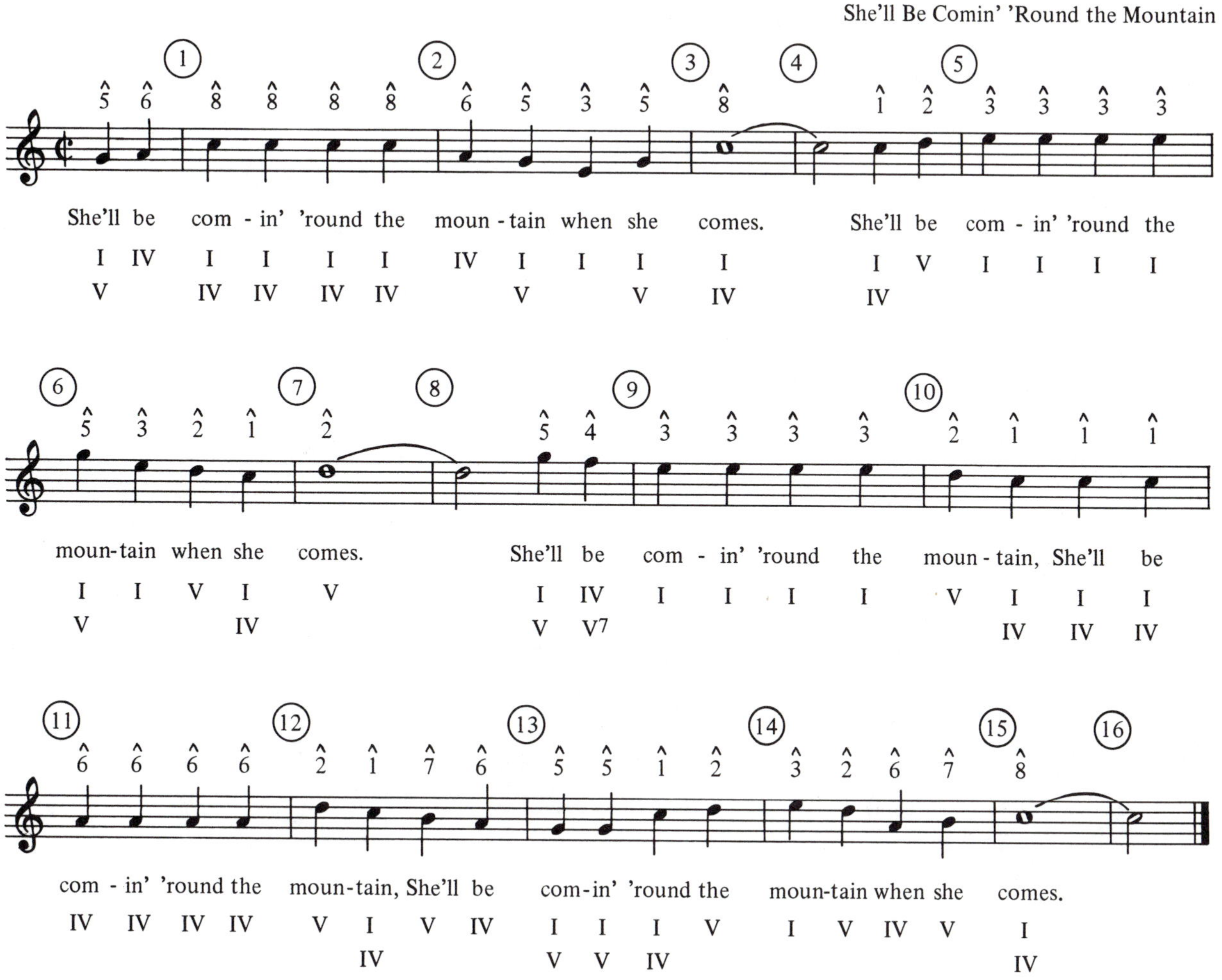

As demonstrated earlier in this chapter, the entire first phrase can be harmonized by I, if $\hat{6}$ is treated as an incomplete neighboring note. In fact, the tonic harmony could continue until the V in measure 7 if we allow $\hat{2}$ (in both measure 4 and measure 6) to serve as a passing note. We have already seen that in measures 9 and 10, the I harmony can be used exclusively, $\hat{2}$ serving again as a passing note. If we wish to maintain the very slow rate of chord change that has prevailed up to this point, then it would be best if measures 11 and 12 were supported by IV, with the first and third notes in measure 12 leading downward to chord notes as an incomplete upper neighboring note and a passing note, respectively. These various decisions are incorporated within the harmonization shown in Example 13-6.

Measures 13 and 14 are the most challenging of the melody. As shown in Example 13-6, the pitches of measure 13 can be supported by the I harmony, while the pitches of measure 14 can be supported by the V harmony. Though this is a faster rate of succession for the harmonies than has occurred in the previous measures, it is appropriate for this cadential spot. What is most unusual is the occurrence of two embellishing notes side by side. The $\hat{2}$ that ends measure 13 appears to be a passing note leading up to $\hat{3}$, which would be a continuation of the I that we have used throughout measure 13. But by introducing V at the beginning of measure 14, this $\hat{3}$ becomes an incomplete upper neighbor of $\hat{2}$. This $\hat{2}$, and not $\hat{3}$, is part of the V harmony. Just as the $\hat{3}$ is a neighbor of $\hat{2}$, so also is the $\hat{6}$ on the next beat a neighbor of $\hat{7}$. In Example 13-6 these various harmonic choices are notated and all embellishing notes are circled.

Example 13-6

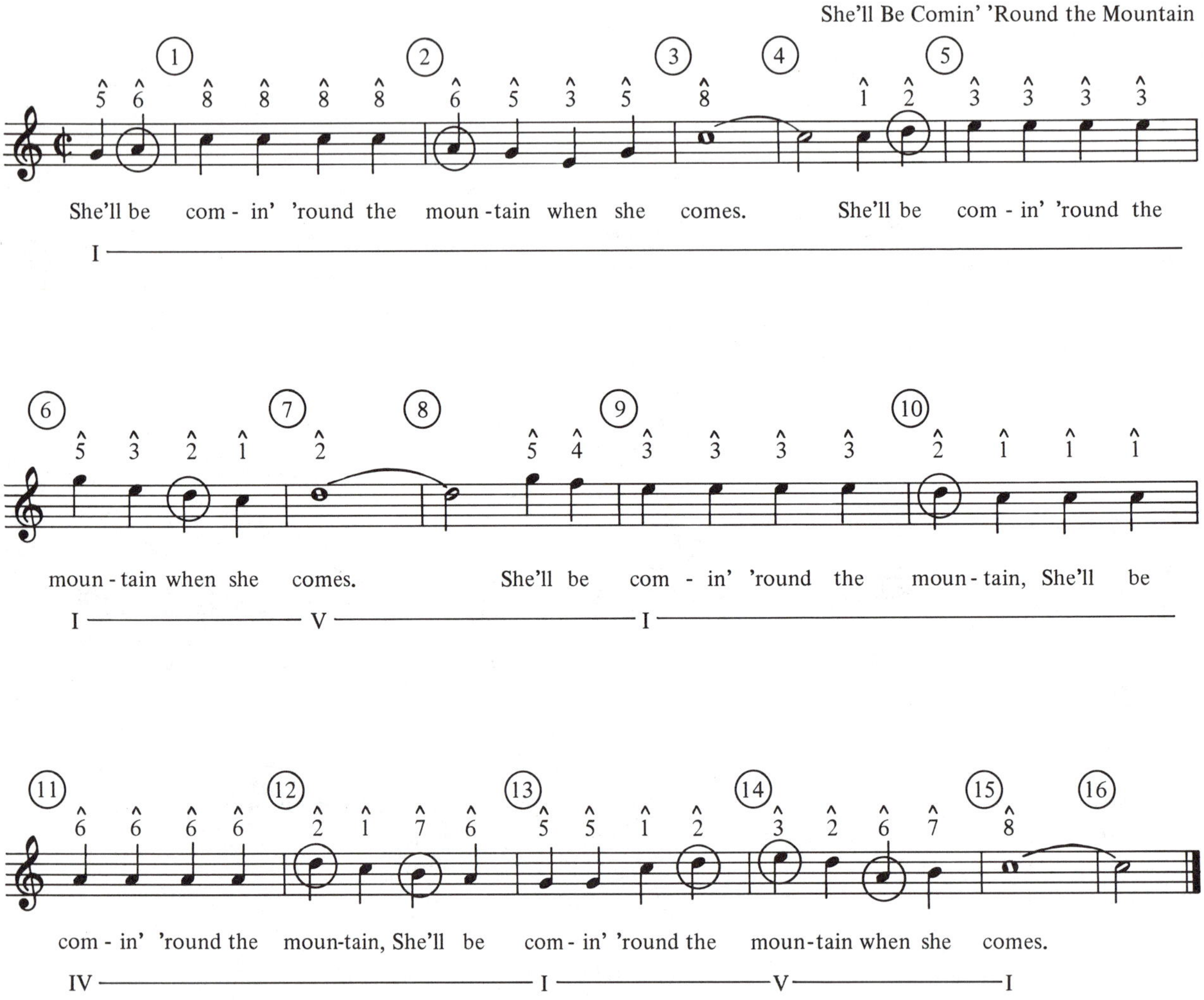

The final step in the process, applying chords in staff notation, is shown in Example 13-7.

Example 13-7

She'll Be Comin' 'Round the Mountain
She'll be com - in' 'round the moun-tain when she comes. She'll be com - in' 'round the
moun - tain when she comes. She'll be com - in' 'round the moun-tain, She'll be
com-in' 'round the moun-tain, She'll be com - in' 'round the moun-tain when she comes.

A Sample Harmonization in the Minor Mode

Melodies in the minor mode are harmonized like those of the major mode. Remember, however, that because alternative pitches are available for $\hat{6}$ and for $\hat{7}$, the IV and V chords might appear with either major or minor quality. If V leads to I within the same phrase, it will likely contain the leading tone unless the melody employs the subtonic pitch. You should examine the melody carefully to locate altered pitches, in particular the altered sixth and seventh scale degrees of the harmonic and melodic minor scales. Similar alterations will likely appear in the accompaniment at those spots. The chart in Example 13-8 shows which chords support each scale degree in the minor mode.

Example 13-8

Scale Degree	*Roman Numerals*	*Sample Chord(s) in C Minor*
$\hat{1}$	I or IV or IV♮	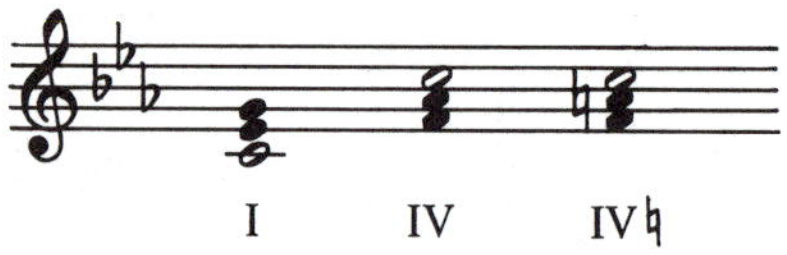
$\hat{2}$	V or V♮	
$\hat{3}$	I	
$\hat{4}$	IV or IV♮ or $V^{7}_{\natural}$	
$\hat{5}$	I or V or V♮	
$\hat{6}$	IV	

Scale Degree	*Roman Numerals*	*Sample Chord(s) in C Minor*
$\uparrow\hat{6}$	IV♮	
$\hat{7}$	V	
$\uparrow\hat{7}$	V♮	

The spirited "Forward March, Grenadiers" in Example 13-9 serves as an example of how a melody in the minor mode might be harmonized. All embellishing notes are circled.

Example 13-9

Forward March, Grenadiers

Pitch exercises for Chapter 13 are on pages 453–458.

RHYTHM

Triplets That Fill Half a Beat or Two Beats

Triplets occur most often when the note value that serves as the beat in a simple meter—for example, the quarter note in $\frac{4}{4}$ meter or the half note in $\frac{4}{2}$ meter—is divided into three parts rather than two. Yet many other triplet formations are possible. For example, the eighth note, which typically divides into two sixteenth notes, may instead divide into triplet sixteenths, with all three notes being performed within the time normally devoted to two sixteenth notes. Or three triplet quarter notes, instead of two, may fill half a measure in $\frac{4}{4}$ meter. Or three triplet half notes, instead of two, may fill half a measure in $\frac{4}{2}$ meter. Example 13-10 demonstrates these possibilities, and includes recommended counting syllables. Observe that when triplets fill two beats, the syllable for the second of those beats will not coincide with the performance of one of the triplet notes, but rather will fall between them as indicated by the arrows in Example 13-10.

Example 13-10

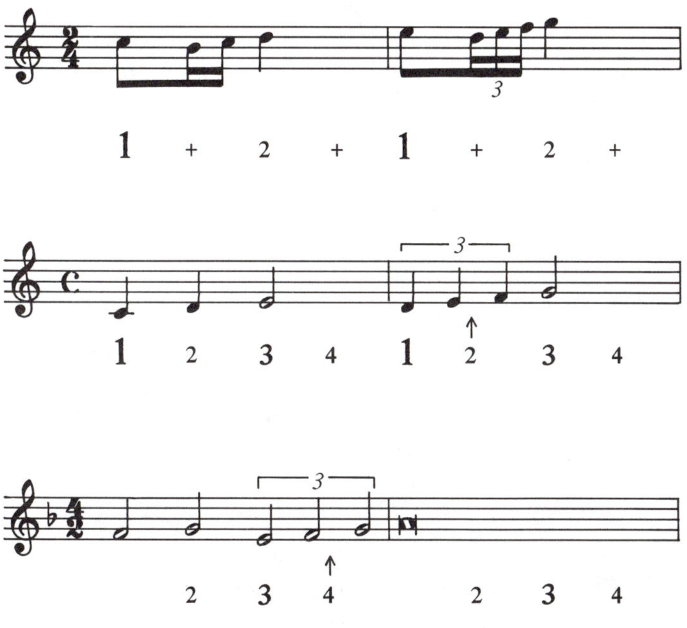

Duple Subdivision in Compound Meters

The triplet divides into thirds a segment of musical time that normally would have two parts. The opposite strategy is to divide the beat in a compound meter into two rather than three parts. In $\frac{6}{8}$, for example, the dotted quarter note usually divides into three eighth notes. If, instead, *two* notes of equal value are desired, they would be notated as eighth notes with the numeral 2 appearing on the stem side, as in Example 13-11a. The two melodies in Example 13-11 would sound identical if Example 13-11a were performed at ♩. = 60 and 13-11b at ♩ = 60. The composer's selection of one meter over the other depends in part upon whether the melody contains more duple or more triple divisions of the beat. Since this melody contains many triple subdivisions and only one duple subdivision, Example 13-11a is the better notated.

Example 13-11

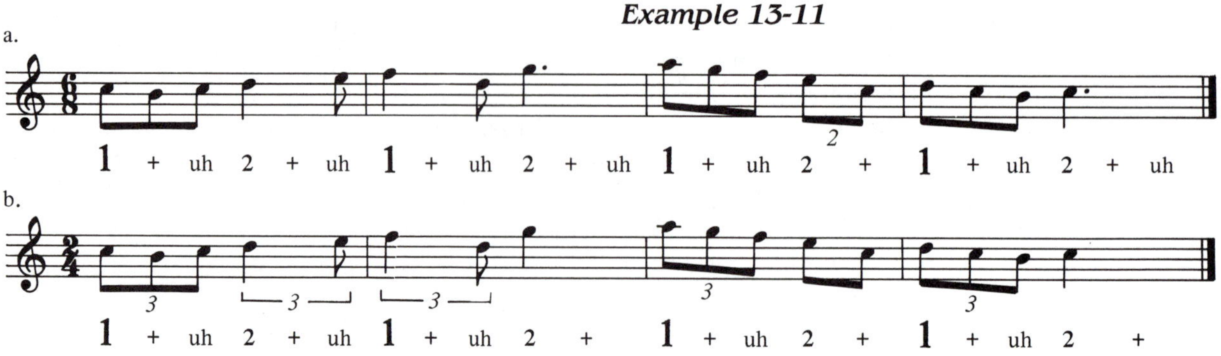

Hemiola

hemiola

The rhythmic patterns described in Examples 13-10 and 13-11 are generally highlighted through the numbers 3 and 2, as shown. Another common departure from conventional metrical patterning, the ***hemiola,*** lacks any special designation—though before the advent of printing, scribes would often use a different color ink when writing hemiolas. A hemiola is a temporary repositioning of strong and weak beats or subdivisions of beats. Two groups of three beats are transformed into three groups of two beats. What might be represented as STRONG-weak-weak STRONG-weak-weak becomes STRONG-weak STRONG-weak STRONG-weak.

The amount of time that each note sounds does not change. Only the perception of individual beats as strong or weak—that is, the accents of beats—changes.

A hemiola can occur whenever a strong-weak-weak relationship is expressed by the meter, either as three beats (as in $\frac{3}{4}$ or $\frac{3}{2}$ meters) or as three subdivisions of the beat (as in $\frac{6}{8}$ or $\frac{6}{4}$ meters). Observe in Example 13-12 how the hemiola in measures 5 and 6 requires the performer to treat as a weak beat what otherwise would be strong (measure 6, beat 1) and to treat as strong what otherwise would be weak (measure 5, beat 3; measure 6, beat 2). The counting syllables reflect the performer's obligation to project *three* measures of two beats each from notes that visually appear to fill only *two* measures.

Example 13-12

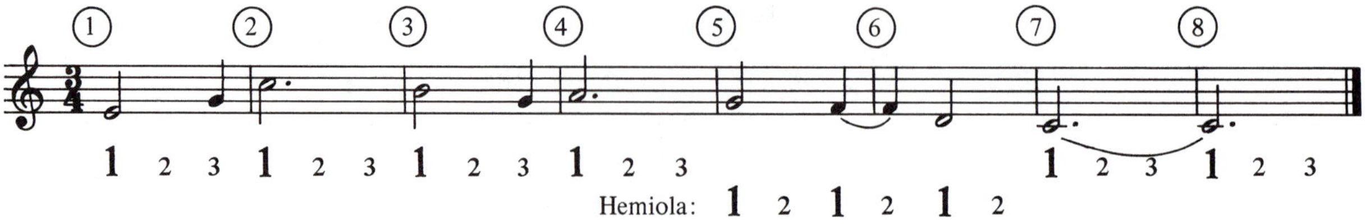

Rhythm exercises for Chapter 13 are on pages 459–461.

LABORATORY

L13-1.a. Perform the following chord progressions at the keyboard. Underneath each chord, write in the appropriate Roman numeral. Though the tempo that you choose might be slow, make sure that it is steady—that every beat is of the same duration.

1.

2.

b. Perform the following melodies at the keyboard. Recommended fingerings are included.

Chopin: Nocturne Op. 32, No. 1

1.

Brahms: Romance Op. 118, No. 5

2.

Debussy: *Suite Bergamasque*, Clair de lune

3.

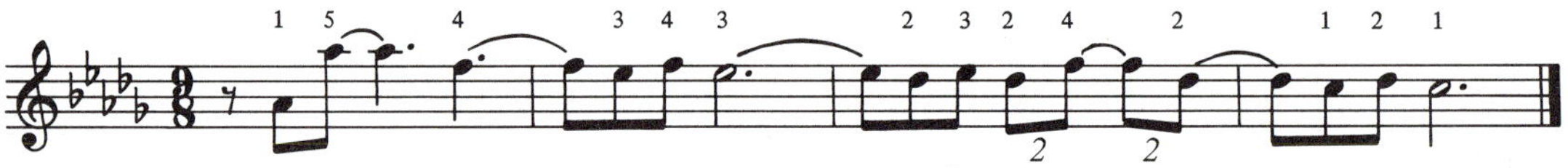

Rimsky-Korsakov: Scheherezade

4.

L13-2. Perform the following progressions at the keyboard. Add an embellishing note at each spot marked by an arrow. Supply suitable inner voices.

a.

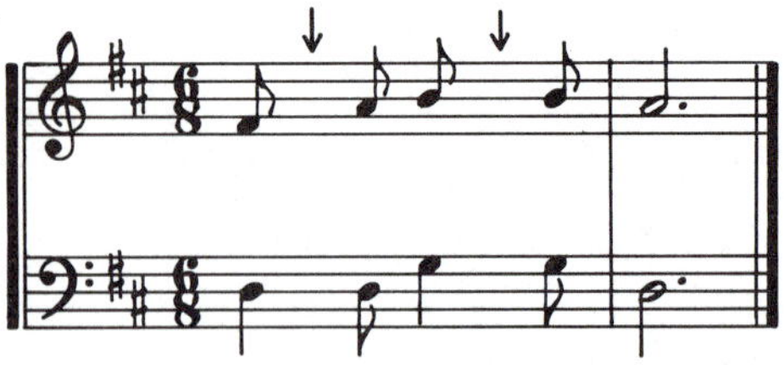

b.

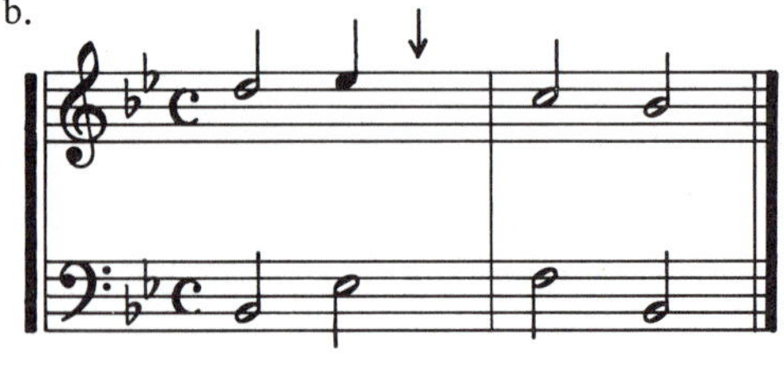

c.

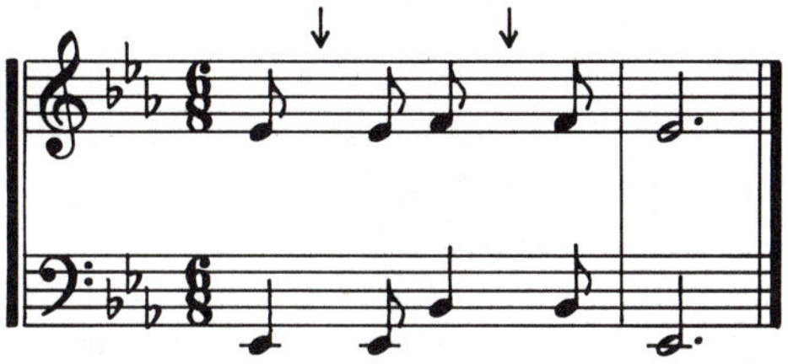

d.

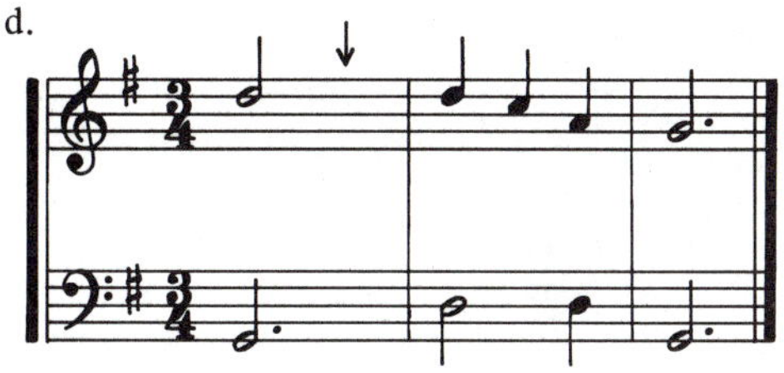

e.

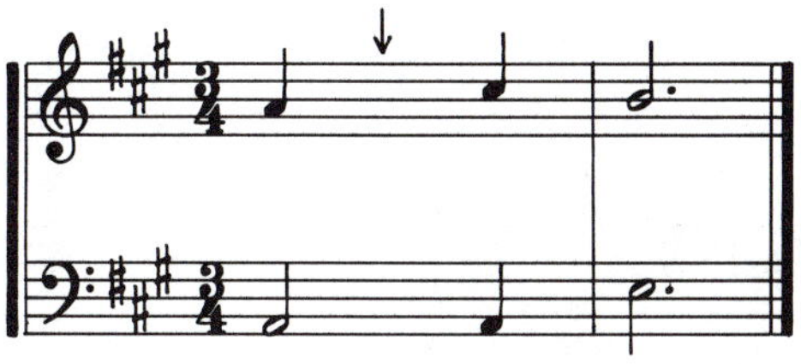

f.

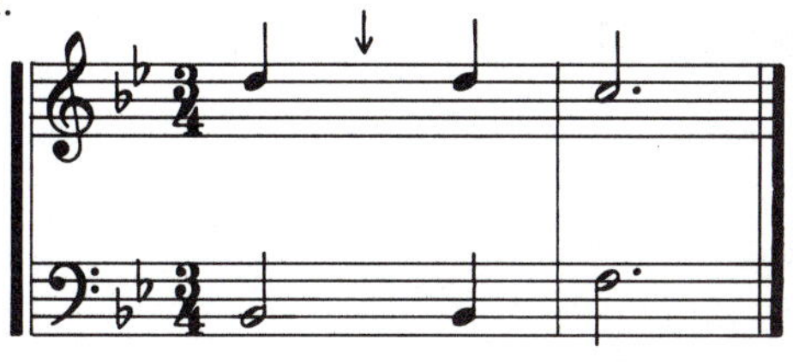

L13-3. Sing the following melodies both starting on C, as notated, and in transpositions to other pitches within your vocal range. Before you sing, play only the starting pitch. Check each performance by playing all three pitches at the keyboard after you have attempted to sing them.

Upper neighbor (minor second)

Upper neighbor (major second)

Lower neighbor (minor second)

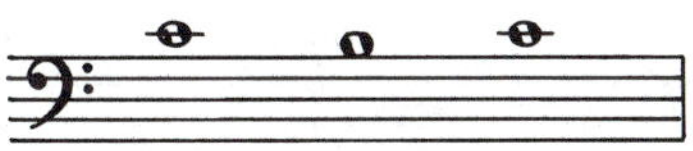

Lower neighbor (major second)

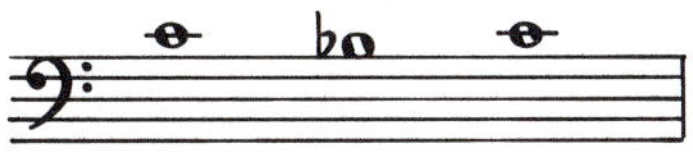

L13-4. The following melodies are accompanied by a variety of harmonies. A student or the instructor could play the keyboard part while other students sing the melody. You may wish to sing the melodies one or two octaves lower than notated, though the accompaniment should be performed as written.

Long, Long Ago

a.

Tell me the tales that to me were so dear, long, long a - go, long, long a - go.
Sing me the songs I de - light - ed to hear, long, long a - go, long a - go.

b.

Clementine

In a cav-ern, in a can-yon Ex-ca - vat - ing for a mine, Dwelt a min-er, for - ty
nin - er And his daugh - ter Clem-en - tine. Oh my dar-ling, oh my dar-ling, Oh my
dar - ling Clem-en - tine, You are lost and gone for - ev - er, Dread-ful sor - ry, Clem-en - tine.

L13-5. The following compositions are for two voices. Sing the scale-degree number, or the syllable "raised," that corresponds to each pitch, as indicated. If necessary, transpose the entire score up or down one octave.

a.

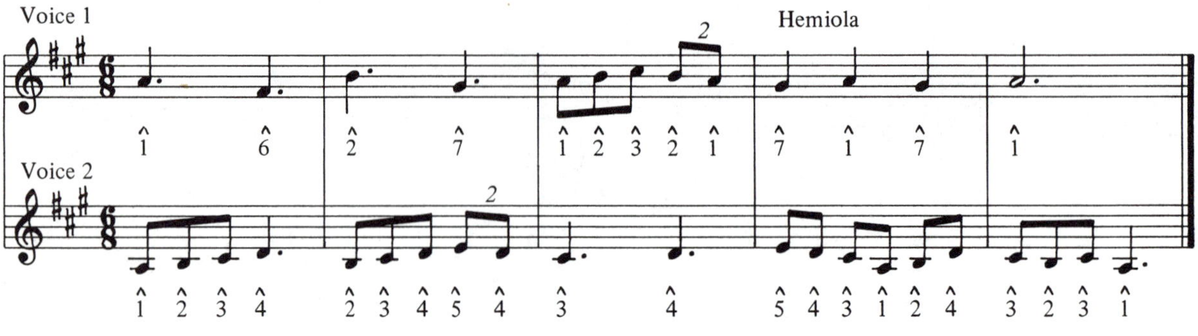

b.

L13-6. Write in the counting syllables below the notated rhythms. Then perform each by clapping the rhythm or playing the pitch C or F at the keyboard, as notated, while pronouncing the counting syllables aloud.

a.

b.

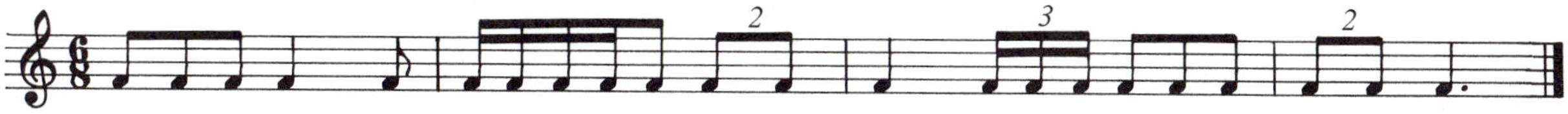

c.

d.

e.

L13-7. Write in the counting syllables below the notated rhythms. Then perform them by dividing the class into two groups, with each group clapping one part while pronouncing the counting syllables aloud. Alternatively, individual students may perform both parts simultaneously at the keyboard, pronouncing the counting syllables aloud while the index fingers strike the notated pitches.

a.

b.

c.

L13-8. This exercise requires that a student or the instructor serve as the performer at a keyboard.

a. The performer plays three pitches, the second of which is a neighbor to the first and third pitches. Indicate whether the neighboring note is a whole or a half step from the pitch that it embellishes.

b. The performer plays one of the following four chord progressions. Indicate which progression is performed. When the tonic is minor, substitute V♯ for V.

I–IV–I–V–I
I–V–I–V–I
I–IV–V–I–V
I–V–I–IV–V

c. The performer plays the chord progression I–$V^{(7)}$–I, either with or without the 7 in the V chord. The soprano pitch of the first I chord may be $\hat{1}$, $\hat{3}$, or $\hat{5}$, as announced by the performer. Indicate which scale degree serves as the soprano pitch for the I chord that ends in progression. The choices are $\hat{1}$, $\hat{3}$, and $\hat{5}$.

Audio exercises for Chapter 13 are on pages 462–464.

Name: ______________________

Instructor: ______________________

Date: ______________________

EXERCISES

Pitch Exercises

P13-1. Use Roman numerals to indicate a suitable accompaniment for each melody below. At least one embellishing note should appear in each melody. Label each embellishing note as a passing note (P), neighboring note (N), or incomplete neighboring note (IN). The first seven melodies (a–g) should be interpreted in the major key whose key signature appears on the staff. The last four (h–k) should be interpreted in the minor key whose key signature appears on the staff. If you wish, write in the scale degree number ($\hat{2}$, $\hat{4}$, etc.) above each notehead.

SAMPLE

a.

b.

c.

d.

e.

f.

g.

h.

i.

j.

k.

P13-2. Provide accompaniments for the following melodies. Sing each melody until you know it well, and experiment with various alternative harmonizations at the keyboard. Circle all notes you choose to treat as embellishment and indicate whether they function as passing notes (P), neighboring notes (N), or incomplete neighboring notes (IN). If you wish, use eighth notes, rests, and other variants to enliven your accompaniments.

a. Long, Long Ago

1 2 3 4 5
Tell me the tales that to me were so dear, long, long a -
6 7 8 9 10
go, long, long a - go. Sing me the songs I de -
11 12 13 14 15 16
light - ed to hear, long, long a - go, long a - go.

Name: ______________________

Instructor: ______________________

Date: ______________________

b. Clementine

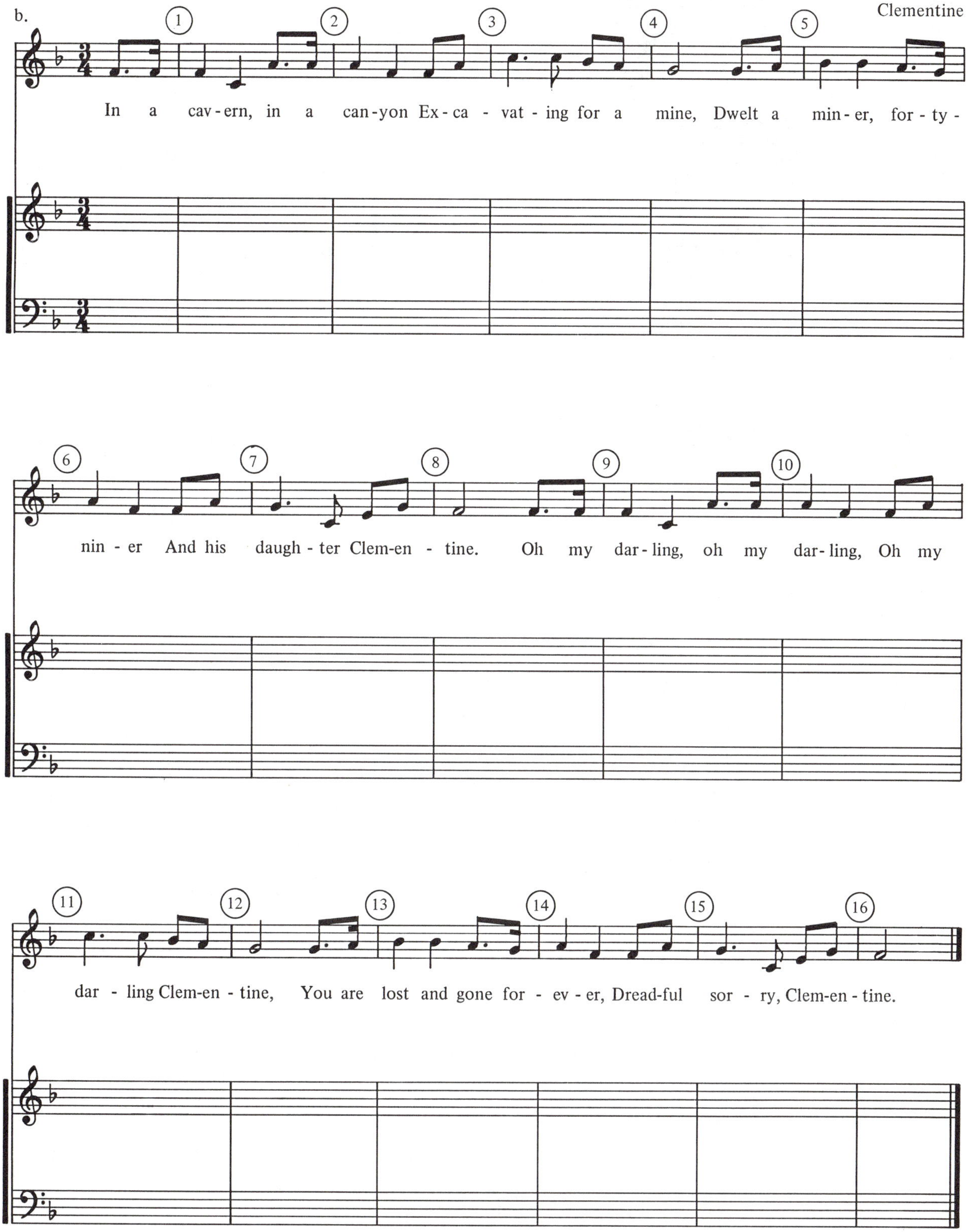

1 2 3 4 5
In a cav-ern, in a can-yon Ex-ca - vat - ing for a mine, Dwelt a min-er, for-ty -
6 7 8 9 10
nin - er And his daugh - ter Clem-en - tine. Oh my dar-ling, oh my dar-ling, Oh my
11 12 13 14 15 16
dar - ling Clem-en - tine, You are lost and gone for - ev - er, Dread-ful sor - ry, Clem-en - tine.

c.

Oh, Susannah

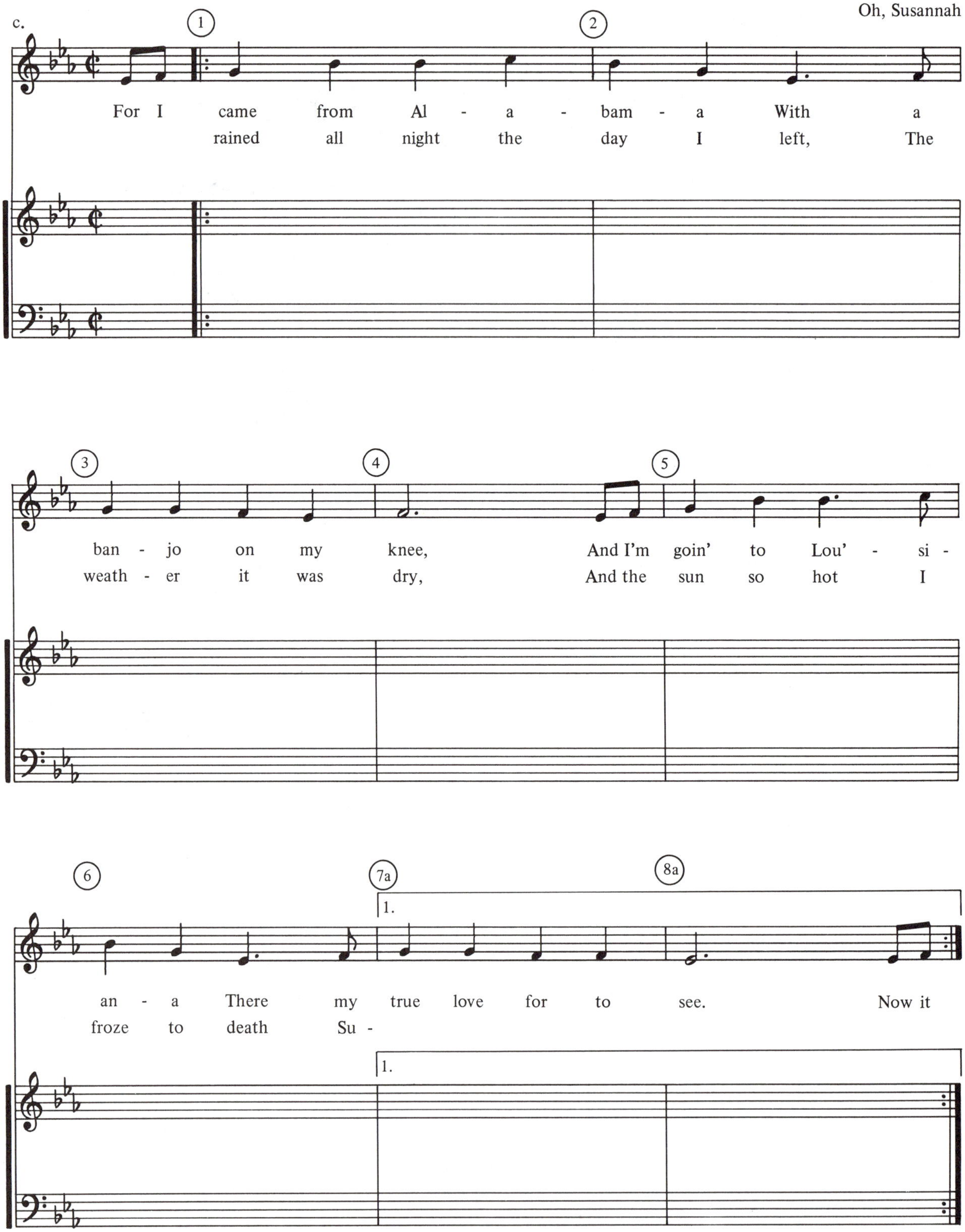
1
2
For I came from Al - a - bam - a With a
rained all night the day I left, The
3
4
5
ban - jo on my knee, And I'm goin' to Lou' - si -
weath - er it was dry, And the sun so hot I
6
7a
8a
1.
an - a There my true love for to see. Now it
froze to death Su -
1.

Name: ____________________
Instructor: ____________________
Date: ____________________

c. (cont'd.)

d. One Lovely Sunday Evening

Name: ______________________________

Instructor: ___________________________

Date: _______________________________

Rhythm Exercises

R13-1. Rewrite each melody in the meter indicated, making use of triplet or duple subdivision notation as appropriate.

SAMPLE

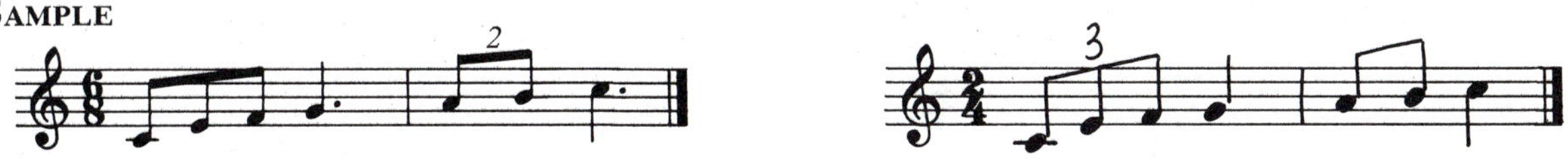

a.

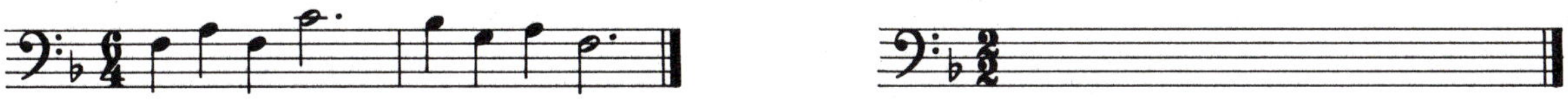

b.

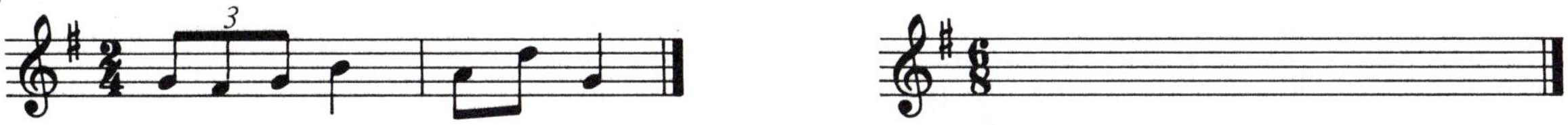

c.

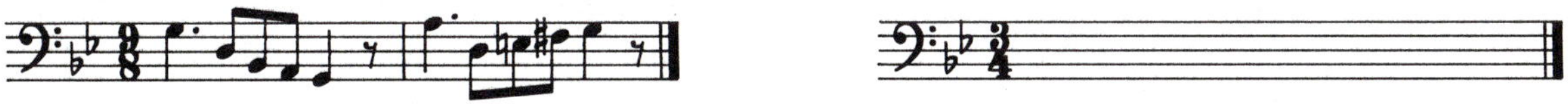

d.

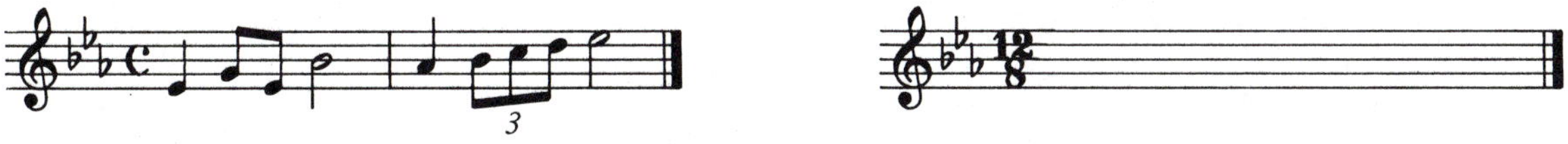

e.

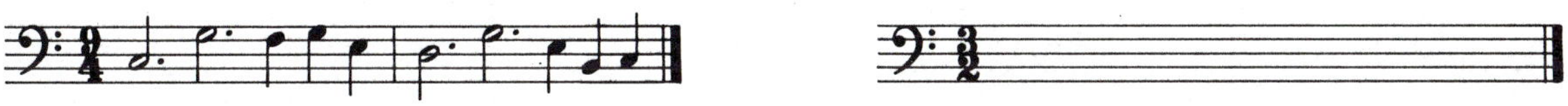

f.

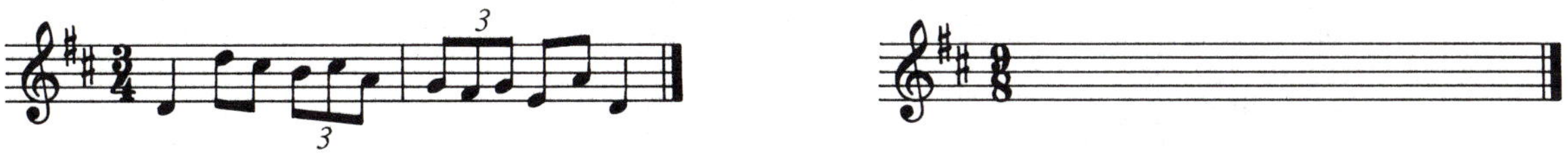

R13-2. Form a melody using the fragments provided. Only one ordering of these fragments results in measures that contain the correct number of beats. Circle any examples of hemiola that you detect.

a.

b.

R13-3. Notate the melodies indicated by the positioning of the pitch names in relation to the counting syllables. The midpoint between syllables is indicated by a dot in Exercise (b). Use only unisons, seconds, thirds, and fourths as melodic intervals, unless an arrow guides you to use a larger interval. Do not add rests. Observe that hemiola occurs in both examples. All bar lines have been supplied.

a.

Schumann: Aufschwung Op. 12

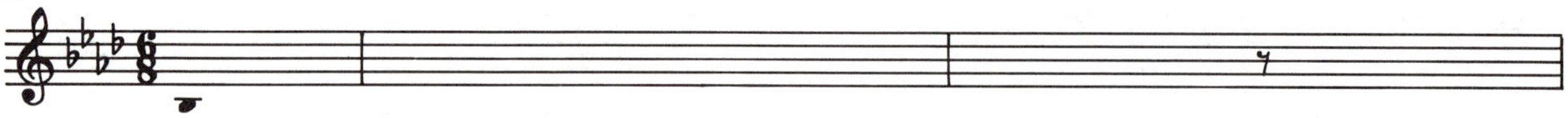

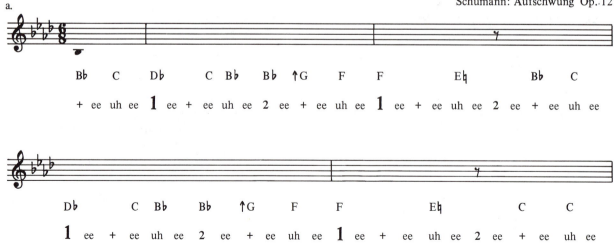

Bb C Db C Bb Bb ↑G F F E♮ Bb C

+ ee uh ee **1** ee + ee uh ee 2 ee + ee uh ee **1** ee + ee uh ee 2 ee + ee uh ee

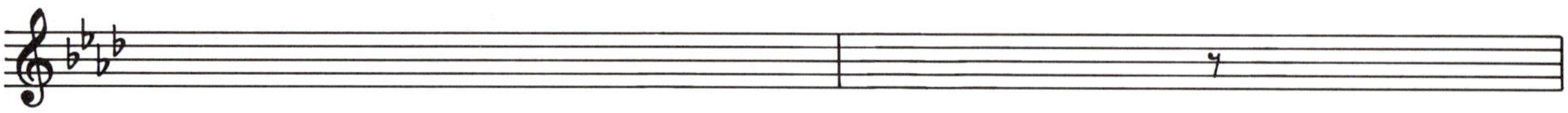

Db C Bb Bb ↑G F F E♮ C C

1 ee + ee uh ee 2 ee + ee uh ee **1** ee + ee uh ee 2 ee + ee uh ee

Name: ____________________

Instructor: ____________________

Date: ____________________

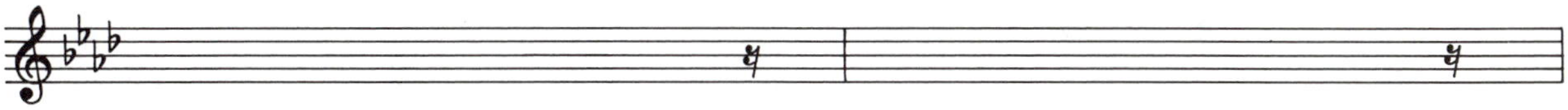

↑C Ab G F Eb Db C Bb

1 ee + ee 2 ee + ee 3 ee + ee 1 ee + ee 2 ee + ee 3 ee + ee

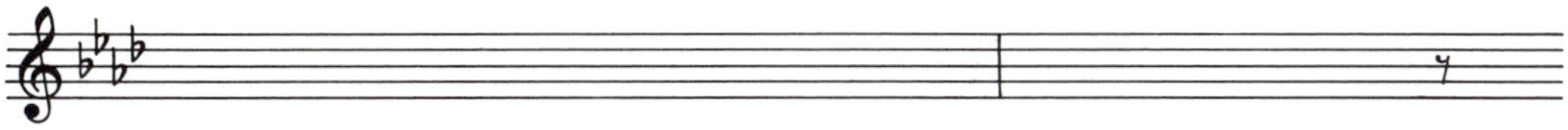

Eb ↓G Ab

1 ee + ee uh ee 2 ee + ee uh ee 1 ee + ee uh ee 2 ee

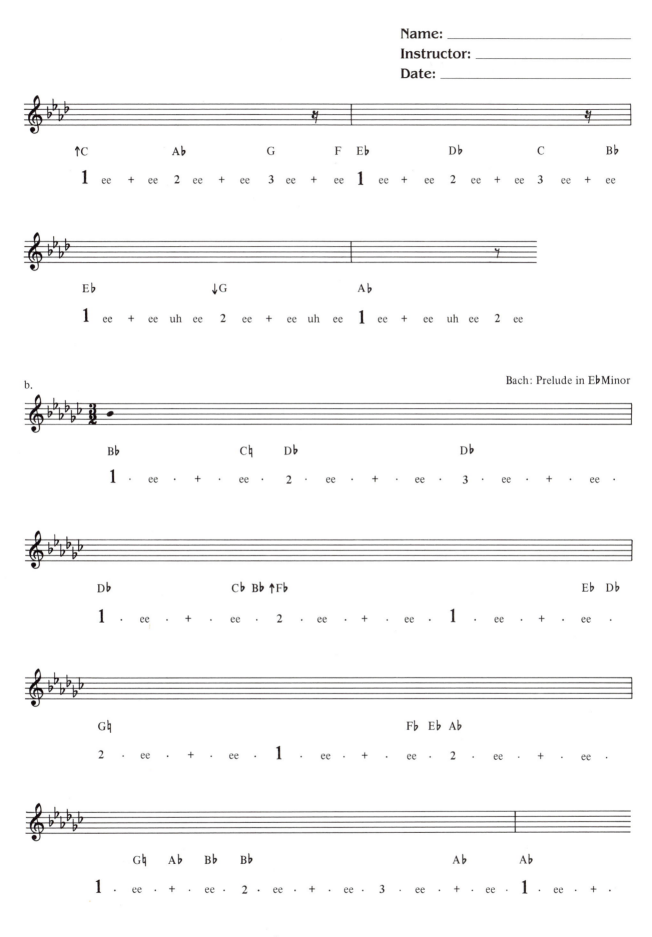

b. Bach: Prelude in Eb Minor

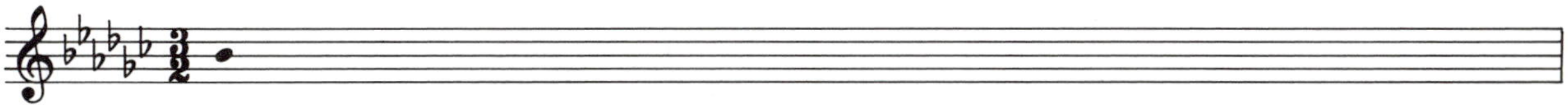

Bb C♮ Db Db

1 · ee · + · ee · 2 · ee · + · ee · 3 · ee · + · ee ·

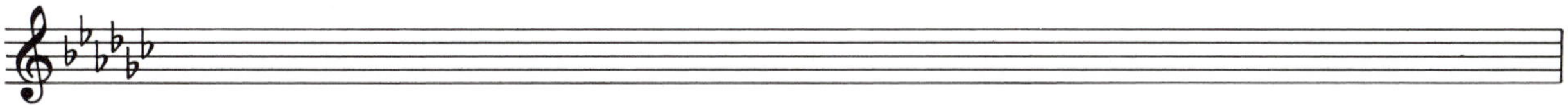

Db Cb Bb ↑Fb Eb Db

1 · ee · + · ee · 2 · ee · + · ee · 1 · ee · + · ee ·

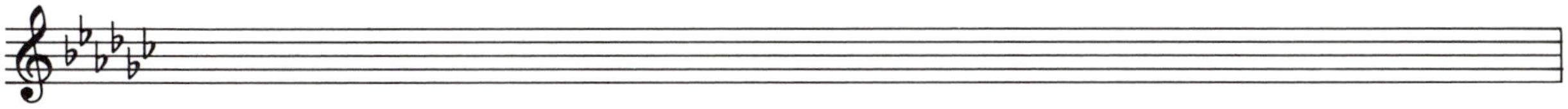

G♮ Fb Eb Ab

2 · ee · + · ee · 1 · ee · + · ee · 2 · ee · + · ee ·

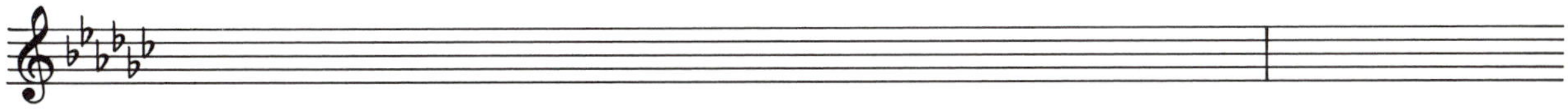

G♮ Ab Bb Bb Ab Ab

1 · ee · + · ee · 2 · ee · + · ee · 3 · ee · + · ee · 1 · ee · + ·

Audio Exercises

A13-1. Three pitches will be performed. Indicate whether the second pitch, which functions as a neighboring note, is a whole or a half step from the first and third pitches.

a. Whole Step Half Step
b. Whole Step Half Step
c. Whole Step Half Step
d. Whole Step Half Step
e. Whole Step Half Step
f. Whole Step Half Step
g. Whole Step Half Step
h. Whole Step Half Step
i. Whole Step Half Step
j. Whole Step Half Step

A13-2. A chord progression will be performed. Indicate which set of Roman numerals corresponds to the harmonies used.

a. I–IV–I–V–I I–V–I–V–I I–IV–V–I–V I–V–I–IV–V
b. I–IV–I–V–I I–V–I–V–I I–IV–V–I–V I–V–I–IV–V
c. I–IV–I–V–I I–V–I–V–I I–IV–V–I–V I–V–I–IV–V
d. I–IV–I–V–I I–V–I–V–I I–IV–V–I–V I–V–I–IV–V
e. I–IV–I–V–I I–V–I–V–I I–IV–V–I–V I–V–I–IV–V
f. I–IV–I–V–I I–V–I–V–I I–IV–V–I–V I–V–I–IV–V
g. I–IV–I–V♯–I I–V♯–I–V♯–I I–IV–V♯–I–V♯ I–V♯–I–IV–V♯
h. I–IV–I–V♯–I I–V♯–I–V♯–I I–IV–V♯–I–V♯ I–V♯–I–IV–V♯
i. I–IV–I–V♯–I I–V♯–I–V♯–I I–IV–V♯–I–V♯ I–V♯–I–IV–V♯
j. I–IV–I–V♯–I I–V♯–I–V♯–I I–IV–V♯–I–V♯ I–V♯–I–IV–V♯
k. I–IV–I–V♯–I I–V♯–I–V♯–I I–IV–V♯–I–V♯ I–V♯–I–IV–V♯
l. I–IV–I–V♯–I I–V♯–I–V♯–I I–IV–V♯–I–V♯ I–V♯–I–IV–V♯

A13-3. The chord progression I–$V^{(7)}$–I will be performed, either with or without the 7 in the V chord. The soprano pitch of the first I chord is given. Indicate which scale degree serves as the soprano pitch for the I chord that ends the progression.

a. First I soprano is $\hat{3}$. Second I soprano is: $\hat{1}$ $\hat{3}$ $\hat{5}$
b. First I soprano is $\hat{5}$. Second I soprano is: $\hat{1}$ $\hat{3}$ $\hat{5}$
c. First I soprano is $\hat{3}$. Second I soprano is: $\hat{1}$ $\hat{3}$ $\hat{5}$
d. First I soprano is $\hat{1}$. Second I soprano is: $\hat{1}$ $\hat{3}$ $\hat{5}$
e. First I soprano is $\hat{1}$. Second I soprano is: $\hat{1}$ $\hat{3}$ $\hat{5}$
f. First I soprano is $\hat{5}$. Second I soprano is: $\hat{1}$ $\hat{3}$ $\hat{5}$
g. First I soprano is $\hat{3}$. Second I soprano is: $\hat{1}$ $\hat{3}$ $\hat{5}$
h. First I soprano is $\hat{1}$. Second I soprano is: $\hat{1}$ $\hat{3}$ $\hat{5}$
i. First I soprano is $\hat{5}$. Second I soprano is: $\hat{1}$ $\hat{3}$ $\hat{5}$
j. First I soprano is $\hat{3}$. Second I soprano is: $\hat{1}$ $\hat{3}$ $\hat{5}$

Name: ______________________________
Instructor: __________________________
Date: _______________________________

A13-4. Six chord progressions will be performed. The soprano pitch for the first chord of each progression will be stated before the progression is performed. In each case circle the score that shows the correct pitch notation for the soprano voice.

a.

b.

c.

d.

e.

f.

A13-5. Four rhythms will be performed. In each case circle the score that shows the correct notation.

a.

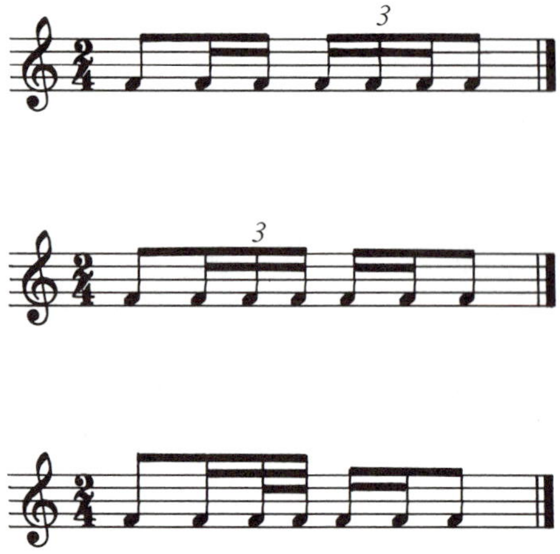

b.

c.

d.

Name: ____________________
Instructor: ____________________
Date: ____________________

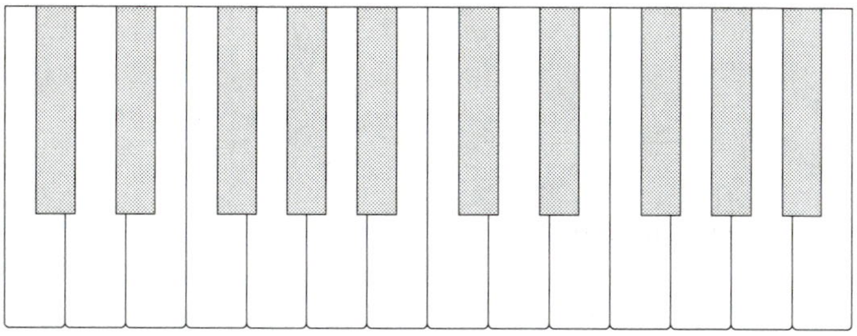

Mastery Test, Chapter 13

Each pitch in the following melody has been individually numbered. Consult this example to answer questions 1–12.

A minor

________ 1. If Pitch 2 is harmonized, what chord could apply to it?
X. I Y. IV Z. V♯

________ 2. If Pitch 2 is treated as an embellishing note, what chord could apply to Pitches 1 through 3?
X. I Y. IV Z. V♯

________ 3. What type of embellishing function could Pitch 2 fulfill?
X. Neighboring note
Y. Passing note
Z. Incomplete neighboring note

________ 4. If Pitch 5 is treated as an embellishing note, what chord could apply to Pitches 4 through 6?
X. I Y. IV Z. V♯

________ 5. If Pitch 4 is treated as an embellishing note, what chord could apply to Pitches 4 and 5?
X. I Y. IV Z. V♯

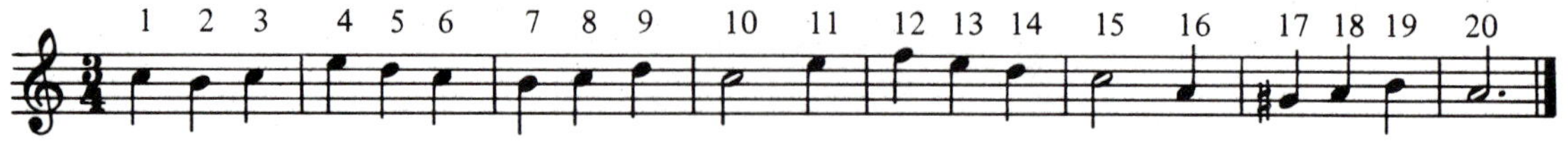

A minor

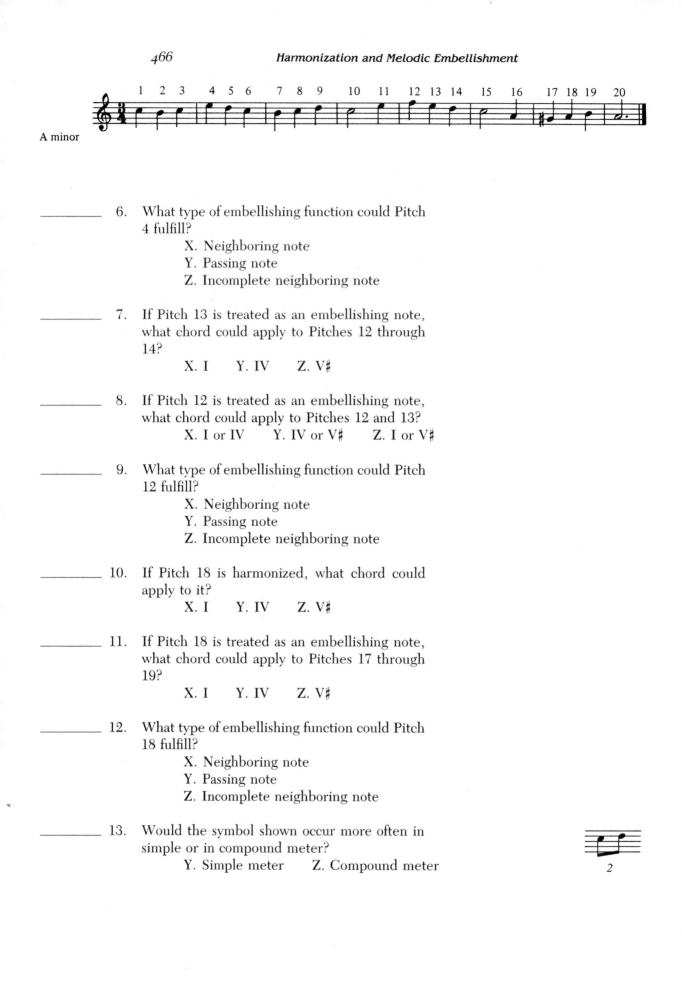

6. What type of embellishing function could Pitch 4 fulfill?
   - X. Neighboring note
   - Y. Passing note
   - Z. Incomplete neighboring note

7. If Pitch 13 is treated as an embellishing note, what chord could apply to Pitches 12 through 14?
   X. I Y. IV Z. V♯

8. If Pitch 12 is treated as an embellishing note, what chord could apply to Pitches 12 and 13?
   X. I or IV Y. IV or V♯ Z. I or V♯

9. What type of embellishing function could Pitch 12 fulfill?
   - X. Neighboring note
   - Y. Passing note
   - Z. Incomplete neighboring note

10. If Pitch 18 is harmonized, what chord could apply to it?
    X. I Y. IV Z. V♯

11. If Pitch 18 is treated as an embellishing note, what chord could apply to Pitches 17 through 19?
    X. I Y. IV Z. V♯

12. What type of embellishing function could Pitch 18 fulfill?
    - X. Neighboring note
    - Y. Passing note
    - Z. Incomplete neighboring note

13. Would the symbol shown occur more often in simple or in compound meter?
    Y. Simple meter Z. Compound meter

Name: ____________________

Instructor: ____________________

Date: ____________________

_________ 14. What kind of note should be inserted at the arrow to complete the measure?

X. Eighth note
Y. Sixteenth note
Z. Dotted sixteenth note

_________ 15. What kind of rest should be inserted at the arrow to complete the measure?

X. Eighth rest
Y. Sixteenth rest
Z. Dotted eighth rest

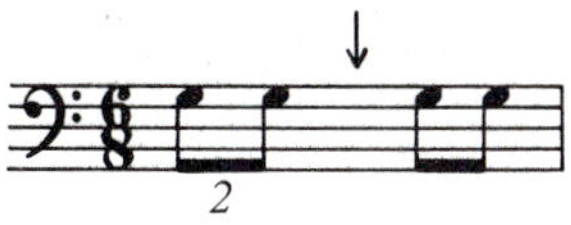

A chord progression will be performed. Indicate which set of Roman numerals corresponds to the harmonies used.

_________ 16.

X. I–IV–I–V–I
Y. I–V–I–V–I
Z. I–IV–V–I–V

_________ 17.

X. I–V♯–I–V♯–I
Y. I–IV–V♯–I–V♯
Z. I–V♯–I–IV–V♯

_________ 18. The chord progression I–V^7–I will be performed. The soprano pitch of the first I chord is $\hat{5}$. Which scale degree serves as the soprano pitch for the second I chord?

X. $\hat{1}$ (or $\hat{8}$)   Y. $\hat{3}$ Z. $\hat{5}$

_________ 19. A chord progression whose soprano begins with the pitch F will be performed. Which score shows the correct pitch notation for the soprano?

X. 

Y. 

Z. 

_________ 20. Which score shows the correct notation for the rhythm performed?

X. 

Y. 

Z. 

GLOSSARY

Accidental Any symbol that modifies the letter name of a pitch or its notehead on the staff; *see* SHARP, FLAT, NATURAL, DOUBLE SHARP, and DOUBLE FLAT. Accidentals applied to individual noteheads retain their effect until the next bar line unless superseded by another accidental.

Acoustics The science of the physical properties of sound.

Alla breve A name applied to the $\frac{2}{2}$ meter, often notated with a symbol (𝄵) in place of the $\frac{2}{2}$ time signature. Also called cut time.

Antecedent and consequent phrases A pair of phrases, the first ending in a half cadence, the second in an authentic cadence. Antecedent and consequent phrases form a period.

Arpeggiation Singing or playing the pitches of a chord successively.

Augmentation dot A single dot placed after a notehead or rest to increase its value by one half. If two augmentation dots are used, the value of the notehead or rest is increased by three-fourths.

Augmented An interval quality applied to all interval sizes. Augmented intervals are a half step larger than major or perfect intervals.

Authentic cadence A complete closure, consisting of the chord succession from a root-position V chord to a root-position I chord. If the tonic pitch class appears in both the soprano and the bass, the cadence is called a perfect authentic cadence. If only in the bass, it is called an imperfect authentic cadence. Also called full cadence.

Bar lines The vertical lines that extend from the first to the fifth line of a staff or the bottom line to the top line of a system to show the divisions between measures.

Bass The lowest note in a chord.

Bass clef A symbol (𝄢) used in notating pitches in the low to middle range on a staff.

Beam A solid horizontal or diagonal line used in forming the eighth, sixteenth, and thirty-second note symbols.

Beats A continuous flow of regular impulses, forming the basis of rhythm. Beats may follow one another at a slow, moderate, or fast rate. Also called pulses.

Bracket A horizontal line placed beyond the stems of noteheads involved in triplets whenever a beam does not connect the stems.

Cadence A succession of chords that invokes a sense of closure at the end of a phrase.

Chord Any combination of three or more simultaneously sounding pitches.

Chromatic *See* DIATONIC.

Circle of fifths An arrangement of the major or minor keys in which adjacent key signatures differ by one sharp or flat, thus corresponding to tonic pitches a perfect fifth apart.

Clef A symbol placed at the left edge of the staff to indicate the pitch that is represented by any notehead drawn on the staff. The most commonly used clefs are the treble clef and the bass clef.

Common time A name applied to the $\frac{4}{4}$ meter, often notated with a symbol (𝄴) in place of the $\frac{4}{4}$ time signature.

Compound interval Any interval larger than an octave.

Compound meter A meter whose beats tend to divide into thirds.

Consequent phrase *See* ANTECEDENT AND CONSEQUENT PHRASES.

Consonant A description of two pitches that sound simultaneously in a stable relationship.

Cut time *See* ALLA BREVE.

Da Capo al Fine An instruction for the performer to return to the beginning of a composition and perform the music that appears until the word *Fine* (end). (Abbreviation: D. C. al Fine.)

Dal Segno al Fine An instruction for the performer to return to a point marked by a sign (𝄋) and perform the music that appears until the word *Fine* (end). (Abbreviation: D. S. al Fine.)

Deceptive cadence A last-moment prevention of closure when an authentic cadence is expected, created through the harmonic progression from V to VI, to IV in $\substack{6\\3}$ position, or to some other substitute for the tonic.

Diatonic (1) A description of the seven pitch classes that form the scale of a given key, in contrast to the five chromatic pitch classes, which are absent from the scale. (2) A diatonic half step is spelled using notes with adjacent letter names (as in C–D♭), while a chromatic half step is spelled using notes with the same letter name (as in C–C♯). The chromatic scale ascends and descends entirely in half steps, as in C, C♯, D, D♯, E, etc.; C, B, B♭, A, A♭, G, etc.

Diminished (1) An interval quality applied to all interval sizes. Diminished intervals are a half step smaller than minor or perfect intervals. (2) A triad quality. The diminished triad has a minor third between its root and third, a minor third between its third and fifth, and a diminished fifth between its root and fifth.

Dissonant A description of two pitches that sound simultaneously in an unstable relationship. Dissonant pitches invoke a tendency toward motion or resolution.

Dominant The pitch class that serves as the fifth scale degree of a key.

Dominant seventh chord A four-note chord built on the fifth scale degree, consisting of the root, third, and fifth of the major triad, plus a minor seventh above the root. Occasionally the fifth is omitted so that the root may be doubled.

Dotted eighth note A symbol (♪.) denoting a pitch lasting three-quarters of a beat in simple meters such as $\substack{2\\4}$, $\substack{3\\4}$, and $\substack{4\\4}$ or half a beat in compound meters such as $\substack{6\\8}$, $\substack{9\\8}$, and $\substack{12\\8}$.

Dotted eighth rest A symbol (𝄾.) denoting a silence lasting three-quarters of a beat in simple meters such as $\substack{2\\4}$, $\substack{3\\4}$, and $\substack{4\\4}$ or half a beat in compound meters such as $\substack{6\\8}$, $\substack{9\\8}$, and $\substack{12\\8}$.

Dotted half note A symbol (𝅗𝅥.) denoting a pitch lasting three beats in simple meters such as $\substack{3\\4}$ and $\substack{4\\4}$ or two beats in compound meters such as $\substack{6\\8}$, $\substack{9\\8}$, and $\substack{12\\8}$.

Dotted quarter note A symbol (♩.) denoting a pitch lasting one and one-half beats in simple meters such as $\substack{2\\4}$, $\substack{3\\4}$, and $\substack{4\\4}$ or one beat in compound meters such as $\substack{6\\8}$, $\substack{9\\8}$, and $\substack{12\\8}$.

Dotted whole note A symbol (𝅝.) denoting a pitch lasting three beats in simple meters such as $\substack{3\\2}$ and $\substack{4\\2}$ and two beats in compound meters such as $\substack{6\\4}$, $\substack{9\\4}$, and $\substack{12\\4}$.

Double bar Two vertical lines, the second of which is thicker than the first, that appear at the end of a composition.

Double flat An accidental (𝄫) that instructs the performer to lower the pitch of the notehead or pitch name to which it is applied by two half steps.

Double sharp An accidental (𝄪) that instructs the performer to raise the pitch of the notehead or pitch name to which it is applied by two half steps.

Double whole note A symbol (𝅜) denoting a pitch lasting one full measure in $\substack{4\\2}$ meter.

Double whole rest A symbol (𝄺) denoting a silence lasting one full measure in $\substack{4\\2}$ meter.

Doubling Reinforcing a pitch class by positioning it in two or more of the four voices of a chord.

Downbeat The first beat of a measure.

Eighth note A symbol (♪ or, when two or more eighth notes appear beside one another, ♫) denoting a pitch lasting one-half of a beat in simple meters such as $\frac{2}{4}$, $\frac{3}{4}$, and $\frac{4}{4}$ or one-third of a beat in compound meters such as $\frac{6}{8}$, $\frac{9}{8}$, and $\frac{12}{8}$. In meters such as $\frac{2}{8}$, $\frac{3}{8}$, and $\frac{4}{8}$, the eighth note represents the beat.

Eighth rest A symbol (𝄾) denoting a silence lasting one-half of a beat in simple meters such as $\frac{2}{4}$, $\frac{3}{4}$, and $\frac{4}{4}$ or one-third of a beat in compound meters such as $\frac{6}{8}$, $\frac{9}{8}$, and $\frac{12}{8}$.

Embellishing note A note that either connects two harmonic notes or temporarily substitutes for a harmonic note. Common embellishing notes include the PASSING NOTE, NEIGHBORING NOTE, and INCOMPLETE NEIGHBORING NOTE.

Enharmonic equivalent A different name that may be applied to a given pitch class, such as B♯ in place of C.

Fifth (1) An interval of size five. *See* INTERVAL SIZE. (2) The highest pitch of a triad.

Figured bass A method of identifying chords by using figures (numbers) such as $\begin{smallmatrix}5\\3\end{smallmatrix}$, $\begin{smallmatrix}6\\3\end{smallmatrix}$, $\begin{smallmatrix}6\\4\end{smallmatrix}$, and $\begin{smallmatrix}7\\5\\3\end{smallmatrix}$ to indicate intervals above the bass.

Fine An Italian term for "the end," use in conjunction with DA CAPO and DAL SEGNO.

First and second endings Alternative ways to proceed at the end of a repeated passage.

First inversion The positioning of the notes of a triad or chord such that the triad's third is the lowest sounding pitch.

Flag A flowing, curved line (⸝) attached to a stem in forming the eighth, sixteenth, and thirty-second note symbols.

Flat An accidental (♭) that instructs the performer to lower the pitch of the notehead or pitch name to which it is applied by one half step.

Fourth An interval of size four. *See* INTERVAL SIZE.

Full cadence *See* AUTHENTIC CADENCE.

Fundamental The lowest component sound in a musical pitch. *See* OVERTONES.

Half cadence A partial closure, created by a harmonic motion to a root-position V chord, preceded most often by I, II, IV, or VI. Also called semicadence.

Half note A symbol (𝅗𝅥) denoting a pitch lasting two beats in simple meters such as $\frac{2}{4}$, $\frac{3}{4}$, and $\frac{4}{4}$ and one beat in simple meters such as $\frac{2}{2}$, $\frac{3}{2}$, and $\frac{4}{2}$.

Half rest A symbol (𝄼) denoting a silence lasting two beats in $\frac{4}{4}$ meter and one beat in simple meters such as $\frac{2}{2}$, $\frac{3}{2}$, and $\frac{4}{2}$.

Half step The distance between adjacent keys on the keyboard, considering both white and black keys.

Harmonic minor scale A variant of the natural minor scale in which the raised seventh scale degree (leading tone) takes the place of the diatonic seventh scale degree (subtonic).

Harmonize To supply appropriate chords for the pitches of a melody.

Harmony The aspect of music involved with chord construction and succession.

Hemiola A temporary rearrangement of beats (or subdivisions of beats) to form three groups of two when two groups of three would otherwise occur within the meter.

Imperfect authentic cadence *See* AUTHENTIC CADENCE.

Imperfect plagal cadence *See* PLAGAL CADENCE.

Incomplete neighboring note. *See* NEIGHBORING NOTE.

Inner voices The notes that sound between the soprano and the bass in a chord.

Interval A relationship between any two pitches, measured both in terms of interval size and interval quality.

Interval size The numerical measure of how close or far apart an interval's two pitches are from one another. For example, an interval written on adjacent lines has size three because three positions (line, space, line) separate the two noteheads.

Interval quality A qualifier, such as major, minor, perfect, augmented, or diminished, to distinguish among various intervals that, though of the same interval size, are not identical in the number of half steps they comprise.

Inversion (1) When applied to a simple interval, the moving of the upper of the two notes down an octave, or the moving of the lower of the two notes up an octave. (2) When applied to a triad or chord, *see* ROOT POSITION, FIRST INVERSION, and SECOND INVERSION.

Key (1) Each of the black or white levers on a piano keyboard. (2) The hierarchy among pitch classes that establishes one pitch class as tonic in conjunction with six subordinate diatonic pitch classes.

Key signature A symbol that designates an automatic application of sharps or flats to noteheads on specific lines and spaces, in order to establish a specific major or minor key. The key signature appears near the left edge of the staff, just after the clef.

Leading tone The pitch class that serves as the seventh scale degree of a key in the major mode.

Ledger line A short horizontal line that serves as a temporary extension of the staff. Also spelled *leger line*.

Lines The five positions corresponding to each of the long horizontal lines on the staff, numbered from the bottom upward.

Major (1) An interval quality applied to seconds, thirds, sixths, sevenths, and their compounds; major intervals are a half step larger than minor intervals and a half step smaller than some augmented intervals. (2) A triad quality; the major triad has a major third between its root and third, a minor third between its third and fifth, and a perfect fifth between its root and fifth. (3) A mode; a major key contains as diatonic pitches a major second, major third, perfect fourth, perfect fifth, major sixth, and major seventh above its tonic pitch. (4) A scale quality; the ascending major scale contains the following steps between adjacent pitches: whole step, whole step, half step, whole step, whole step, whole step, half step.

Measure Each of the groupings of beats in a specific meter, set off in staff notation by bar lines.

Mediant The pitch class that serves as the third scale degree of a key.

Melodic minor scale A variant of the natural minor scale in which the sixth and seventh scale degrees are raised in the ascent and diatonic in the descent.

Meter The segmenting of uniform pulses into groupings and the organization of the pulses within each grouping into strong and weak beats.

Metronome A mechanical device that can be adjusted to tick from forty to over two hundred times per minute, used as an aid in the performance of rhythm.

Middle C A pitch that is notated on the first ledger line below the staff using the treble clef or on the first ledger line above the staff using the bass clef. The key that corresponds to it is found in vertical alignment with your left eye when you are sitting well centered at the keyboard.

Minor (1) An interval quality applied to seconds, thirds, sixths, sevenths, and their compounds; minor intervals are a half step larger than some diminished intervals and a half step smaller than major intervals. (2) A triad quality; the minor triad has a minor third between its root and third, a major third between its third and fifth, and a perfect fifth between its root and fifth. (3) A mode; a minor key contains as diatonic pitches a major second, minor third, perfect fourth, perfect fifth, minor sixth, and minor seventh above its tonic pitch. (4) A scale quality; the ascending natural minor scale contains the following steps between adjacent pitches: whole step, half step, whole step, whole step, half step, whole step, whole step.

Modal mixture A mixing of pitches from the major and natural minor modes.

Modes The two categories (major and minor) in which a key may be established through the interrelationships among diatonic pitch classes.

Natural An accidental (♮) applied to a notehead, canceling any accidental previously applied to that notehead within the measure or indicated by the key signature.

Natural minor A term applied to the minor mode and to its scale to distinguish them from the variants called harmonic minor and melodic minor.

Neighboring note An embellishing note that sounds temporarily in place of a single pitch that appears both before and after it. If the note that is embellished appears on only one side of the neighboring note, the embellishing note is referred to as an incomplete neighboring note.

Note *See* NOTEHEAD.

Notehead A symbol (𝅝 or •) placed through a line or in a space on a staff (or using ledger lines) to represent a specific pitch.

Octave An interval of size eight. *See* INTERVAL SIZE.

Octave transposition *See* TRANSPOSITION.

Overtones The higher pitches that support and enrich the fundamental.

Parallel keys Two keys that share the same tonic pitch but are of different modes and have different key signatures.

Parallel period *See* PERIOD.

Passing note An embellishing note that connects two harmonic notes in stepwise ascending or descending motion.

Perfect An interval quality applied to unisons, fourths, fifths, octaves, and their compounds.

Perfect authentic cadence *See* AUTHENTIC CADENCE.

Perfect plagal cadence *See* PLAGAL CADENCE.

Period Two phrases that form a pair. When the two phrases begin identically, the period is called a parallel period.

Phrase A coherent segment of music shaped by a clearly perceptible beginning and ending, usually two, four, or eight measures in length.

Pickup *See* UPBEAT.

Pitch A specific position within the range of sounds from low to high.

Pitch class A collection of all pitches that have the same letter name, without reference to highness or lowness of range.

Plagal cadence A cadence that attains closure through the harmonic progression from a root-position IV chord to a root-position I chord. If the tonic pitch class appears in both the soprano and the bass, the cadence is called a perfect plagal cadence; if only in the bass, it is called an imperfect plagal cadence.

Pulses *See* BEATS.

Quarter note A symbol (♩) denoting a pitch lasting one beat in simple meters such as $\frac{2}{4}$, $\frac{3}{4}$, and $\frac{4}{4}$ or two-thirds of a beat in compound meters such as $\frac{6}{8}$, $\frac{9}{8}$, and $\frac{12}{8}$.

Quarter rest A symbol (𝄽) denoting a silence lasting one beat in simple meters such as $\frac{2}{4}$, $\frac{3}{4}$, and $\frac{4}{4}$ or two-thirds of a beat in compound meters such as $\frac{6}{8}$, $\frac{9}{8}$, and $\frac{12}{8}$.

Relative keys Two keys, one major, one minor, that use the same collection of diatonic pitches. The distance separating the tonics of these two keys is a minor third. Relative keys share the same key signature.

Repeat sign Either of two symbols (𝄆 and 𝄇) that instruct a performer to repeat the section of a composition they enclose. If only the latter sign is present, the performer is to go back to the beginning of the piece.

Rest A period of silence, notated by various symbols representing specific durations.

Rhythm Patterns of long and short notes whose durations are notated in relation to an underlying pulse.

Roman numerals Analytical symbols that indicate which scale degree functions as a chord's root, in the context of a specific major or natural minor key.

Root The lowest pitch of a triad.

Root position The positioning of a triad or chord such that the root is the lowest sounding pitch.

Scale The arrangement of the seven pitch classes of a key in a linear succession, with the tonic pitch class appearing at both the beginning and end of the succession. A scale may ascend or descend. *See* DIATONIC.

Scale degree An Arabic number topped by a circumflex, such as $\hat{3}$, indicating the numerical position of a pitch within an ascending scale.

Score notation A visual representation of the pitches that are to sound at each moment of a musical work.

Second An interval of size two; the two noteheads of a second appear on an adjacent line and space. *See* INTERVAL SIZE.

Second inversion The positioning of a triad or chord such that the triad's fifth is the lowest sounding pitch.

Semicadence *See* HALF CADENCE.

Seventh An interval of size seven. *See* INTERVAL SIZE.

Sharp An accidental (♯) that instructs the performer to raise the pitch of the notehead or pitch name to which it is applied by one half step.

Simple interval Any interval that falls within the span of an octave.

Simple meter A meter whose beats tend to divide into halves.

Sixteenth note A symbol (𝅘𝅥𝅯 or, when two or more sixteenth notes appear beside one another, ♬) denoting a pitch lasting one-fourth of a beat in simple meters such as $\frac{2}{4}$, $\frac{3}{4}$, and $\frac{4}{4}$ or one-sixth of a beat in compound meters such as $\frac{6}{8}$, $\frac{9}{8}$, and $\frac{12}{8}$.

Sixteenth rest A symbol (𝄿) denoting a silence lasting one-fourth of a beat in simple meters such as $\frac{2}{4}$, $\frac{3}{4}$, and $\frac{4}{4}$ or one-sixth of a beat in compound meters such as $\frac{6}{8}$, $\frac{9}{8}$, and $\frac{12}{8}$.

Sixth An interval of size six. *See* INTERVAL SIZE.

Slur A curved line connecting noteheads that represent different pitches. It implies legato (smooth) connections among pitches in performance or indicates phrasing (the grouping of notes into coherent units).

Soprano The highest note in a chord.

Spaces The four positions corresponding to the spaces between each of the long horizontal lines on the staff, numbered from the bottom upward.

Staff (pl. *staves*) The standard format for score notation, consisting of a set of five evenly spaced horizontal lines.

Stem A vertical line added to one side of a notehead in music notation to form half notes, quarter notes, eighth notes, etc.

Subdominant The pitch class that serves as the fourth scale degree of a key.

Submediant The pitch class that serves as the sixth scale degree of a key.

Subtonic The pitch class that serves as the seventh scale degree of a key in the natural minor mode.

Supertonic The pitch class that serves as the second scale degree of a key.

Syncopation Any temporary contradiction of the prevailing meter.

System A combination of two or more staves.

Tempo The speed at which the beats of the meter follow one another.

Third (1) An interval of size three; the two noteheads of a third appear on adjacent lines or adjacent spaces. *See* INTERVAL SIZE. (2) The middle pitch of a triad.

Thirty-second note A symbol (𝅘𝅥𝅰 or, when two or more thirty-second notes appear beside one another, 𝅘𝅥𝅰𝅘𝅥𝅰) denoting a pitch lasting one-eighth of a beat in simple meters such as 2/4, 3/4, and 4/4 or one-twelfth of a beat in compound meters such as 6/8, 9/8, and 12/8.

Thirty-second rest A symbol (𝄿) denoting a silence lasting one-eighth of a beat in simple meters such as 2/4, 3/4, and 4/4 or one-twelfth of a beat in compound meters such as 6/8, 9/8, and 12/8.

Tie A curved line connecting two noteheads that represent the same pitch, indicating a single pitch whose duration equals the sum of the durations of the notes thus connected.

Time signature A symbol, such as 4/4 or 6/8, that appears near the left edge of the staff to indicate the meter.

Tonal center *See* TONIC.

Tonal music Music in which a specific pitch class serves as tonic.

Tonic The most stable pitch class in a composition. It serves as the first scale degree of a key.

Transposition The operation of moving a melody higher or lower, either with or without a change of key. Octave transposition occurs when the interval of transposition is a simple or compound octave.

Treble clef A symbol (𝄞) used in notating pitches in the middle to high range on a staff.

Triad A combination of three simultaneously sounding pitches notated on three adjacent lines or three adjacent spaces. A triad contains a root, a third, and a fifth. The interval between the root and third is a third, between the root and fifth is a fifth, and between the third and fifth is a third. The most common triad qualities are major, minor, and diminished.

Triplets A group of three notes that divide a rhythmic unit (such as a quarter note) into three equal parts when a duple subdivision would usually occur, as in simple meters.

Tritone A name often used for the augmented fourth.

Unison An interval of size one; the two noteheads of a unison appear on the same line or space. *See* INTERVAL SIZE.

Upbeat A note or notes preceding a downbeat. Also called pickup.

Voice leading The principles by which each of the four voices, or pitches, of a chord move in relation to one another.

Whole note A symbol (𝅝) denoting a pitch lasting four beats in simple meters such as 4/4.

Whole rest A symbol (𝄻) denoting a silence lasting one full measure in all meters except 4/2.

Whole step The combination of two half steps.

INDEX